COMMENTARIES

on

THE PROPHET DANIEL

VOL I

COMMENTARIES

ON THE

BOOK OF THE PROPHET DANIEL

BY JOHN CALVIN

NOW FIRST TRANSLATED FROM THE ORIGINAL LATIN, AND COLLATED
WITH THE FRENCH VERSION, WITH DISSERTATIONS, NEW
TRANSLATION OF THE TEXT, AND COPIOUS INDICES,

BY THOMAS MYERS, M.A.,

VICAR OF SHERIFF-HUTTON, YORKSHIRE

VOLUME FIRST

WIPF & STOCK · Eugene, Oregon

Wipf and Stock Publishers
199 W 8th Ave, Suite 3
Eugene, OR 97401

Commentaries on the Book of the Prophet Daniel, Volume 1
By Calvin, John and Myers, Thomas
Softcover ISBN-13: 979-8-3852-1678-9
Hardcover ISBN-13: 979-8-3852-1679-6
eBook ISBN-13: 979-8-3852-1680-2
Publication date 2/14/2024
Previously published by Baker Book House, 2005

This edition is a scanned facsimile of the original edition published in 2005.

TRANSLATOR'S PREFACE.

The Prophecies of Daniel are among the most remarkable Predictions of the Elder Covenant. They are not confined within either a limited time or a contracted space. They relate to the destinies of mighty Empires, and stretch forward into eras still hidden in the bosom of the future. The period of their delivery was a remarkable one in the history of our race. The Assyrian hero had long ago swept away the Ten Tribes from the land of their fathers, and he in his turn had bowed his head in death, leaving magnificent memorials of his greatness in colossal palaces and gigantic sculptures. The Son of the renowned Sardanapalus, the worshipper of Assarac and Beltis, had already inscribed his name and exploits on those swarthy obelisks and enormous bulls which have lately risen from the grave of centuries. The glory of Nineveh had passed away, to be restored again in these our days by the marvellous excavations at Koyunjik, Khorsabad, and Nimroud. Another capital had arisen on the banks of the Euphrates, destined to surpass the ancient splendour of its ruined predecessor on the banks of the Tigris. The worshipper of the eagle-headed Nisroch—a mighty leader of the Chaldean hordes—had arisen, and gathering his armies from their mountain homes had made the palaces and halls of Nineveh a desert, had marched southwards against the reigning Pharaoh of Egypt—had encountered him at Carchemish—hurried on to the Holy City, and carried away with him to his favourite capital the rebellious people of the Lord. Among them was a captive of no ordinary note. He was at that time a child, yet he lived to see this descendant of the hardy Chasdim grow great in power and fame—to hear the tale of the fall of TYRE, and "the daughter of the ZIDONIANS," and of the triumph over PHARAOH HOPHRA, whom modern researches have discovered in the twenty-sixth dynasty of Egypt's kings. At length the haughty conqueror returns, and dreams mysteriously. This forgotten prisoner becomes the only interpreter of wondrous visions of Empires about to arise and spread over distant centuries. The dreamer is at length gathered to his fathers: yet the interpreter lives on through the reign of the grandson, and explains a mysterious writing on the palace wall, amidst revelry which ends in the city's overthrow. CYRUS and his Persians, DARIUS and his Medes rise rapidly to power, and the Prophet rises with them—till envy throws the aged Seer into a lion's den. But he perishes not till he has seen visions of the future history of mankind. The triumphs of PERSIA and MACEDON are revealed—the division of ALEXANDER's Empire—the wars of his successors—the wide-spread dominion of ROME—the overthrow of the Sacred Sanctuary by TITUS—and THE COMING OF MESSIAH to regenerate and to rule the world when the seventy weeks were accomplished.

The Roll of the Book, containing all these surprising announcements, has naturally excited the attention of the Scholars and Divines of all ages. Among the voluminous Comments of the laborious CALVIN, none will be received by the British public with more heartfelt interest than his LECTURES UPON DANIEL. The various illustrations of DANIEL and THE APOCALYPSE with which the press has always teemed, display the hold which these Divine Oracles have taken of the public mind. Various theories of interpretation have been warmly and even bitterly discussed. The Præterist, and the Futurist, the German Neologian, and the American Divine, have each written boldly and copiously; and the public of Christendom have read with avidity, because they have been taught that these predictions come home to our own times, and to our modern controversies. Abstruse arguments and historical discussions have been rendered popular, through the expectation of seeing either Pope or Turk, or, perhaps, the Saracen in THE WILFUL KING, and THE LITTLE HORN. If Napoleon the First, or Napoleon the Second, if an Emperor of Russia, or a Pacha of Egypt, can be discovered in the King of the South, pushing at the King of the North —then the deep significance of the Prophecy *to us* is at once acknowledged, and the intensity of its brightness descends directly upon *our own* generation. If the "twelve hundred and ninety Days" of the twelfth Chapter be really years, then the blessing of waiting till "The Time of The End" seems to be upon us, since THE FRENCH REVOLUTION, and the waning of the Turkish sway, and the Conquests of Britain in the East, are then foretold in these "words" which have hitherto been "closed up and sealed."

Whether any of these theories be true or false, they have exercised a mighty power over the imaginations of modern Writers on Prophecy, and have so attracted the minds of Theologians to the subject, as to give force to the inquiry, What was CALVIN's view of these stirring scenes? Without anticipating his COMMENTS, it may be replied, that he disposes of the important question in a few lines. "*In numeris non sum Pythagoricus,*" is the expression of both his wisdom and his modesty. In attempting, however, a solution of these great problems in Prophecy, the opinions of THE REFORMERS are most important, and among them all none stands higher as a deep and original thinker than the Author of these Explanatory LECTURES. It is enough for this our Preface to remark, that the bare possibility of the contents of this Book coming home to the daily politics of Europe and the East, adds a charm and a zest to the following pages, which no infirmity in the Commentator can destroy.

In these INTRODUCTORY REMARKS, we shall allude to the present state of opinion respecting the Genuineness and Authenticity of the Book itself, touching upon some of the conjectures advanced since CALVIN's time to the present, and adverting to the scepticism of GERMAN NEOLOGY, and the bold speculations of the amiable ARNOLD. In confutation of all Infidel Objections, we shall next give a general sketch of the History of Assyria and Babylon, as it has been lately disentombed by the labours of MM. Botta and Layard, and rescued from the intricacies of the Cuneiform Inscriptions by Hincks and Rawlinson. By these means, the Nimroud Obelisk in the British Museum—the palatial chambers of Khorsabad and Koyunjik—the Winged Bull of Persepolis —the statue of Cyrus, at Moorghab—and the magnificent sculpture of Darius at Behistun—all become vocal proofs of the truthfulness of Daniel's predictions. A visit to the East India House in London will make us acquainted with the Standard Inscription of Nebuchadnezzar, containing a list of "all the temples built by the king in the different towns and cities of Babylonia, naming the particular gods and goddesses to whom the shrines were dedicated:[1] a journey from Baghdad to the Bir's Nimroud, would shew us *every* ruin to be of the age of Nebuchadnezzar:" the testimony of experience is here decisive. "I have examined the bricks *in situ*," says Major Rawlinson, "belonging, perhaps, to an hundred towns and cities within this area of about 100 miles in length, and thirty or forty in breadth, and I never found any other legend than that of Nebuchadnezzar, the son of Nabopalassar, king of Babylon."[2] These interesting researches into THE TIMES OF Daniel will be followed by some criticism on THE BOOK OF Daniel. Here we might enlarge to an overwhelming extent, but we are necessarily compelled to confine our remarks to Calvin's method of interpreting these marvellous Prophecies. It will next be desirable to point out how succeeding Commentators have differed from our Reformer, while we must leave the reader to form his own opinion of his merits when he has compared his views with those of his successors. We shall present him, however, with sufficient *data* for making this comparison, and by references to some modern Writers of eminence; and by short epitomes of their leading arguments, we hope to render this edition of these celebrated Lectures as instructive and as interesting as the limit of our space will allow.

[1] Major (now Colonel) Rawlinson's Commentary on the Cuneiform Inscriptions of Babylonia and Assyria, p. 78.
[2] P. 76, *Ibid.*

AUTHENTICITY OF THE BOOK OF DANIEL.

THE THIRD CENTURY of Christianity had scarcely commenced, when the Authenticity of this Book was fiercely assailed by the vigorous scepticism of PORPHYRY; and it would be totally unnecessary to allude to so distant an opponent, had not his arguments been reproduced by the later scholars of Germany, and adopted by one of our noble spirits, whom in many things we delight to honour. Although the Jews admitted this Book into their *Hagiographa*, and our Lord referred to its contents when predicting Jerusalem's overthrow, yet these self-sufficient critics of our day have repeated the heathen objection which JEROME so elaborately refuted. If we inquire into the reason for the revival of such obsolete scepticism, we shall find it in the pride of that carnal mind which will not bow down submissively to the miraculous dealings of the Almighty. The Prophecies concerning the times of the Seleucidæ and the Lagidæ are found to be exceedingly precise and minute: hence it is argued, "they are no prophecies at all—they are History dressed in the garb of Prophecy, written by some pseudo-Daniel living during their supposed fulfilment." The Sacred words of Holy Writ become thus branded with imposture: the testimony of the Jews and of our Lord to the integrity of the Sacred Canon is set aside, and the simple trust of the Christian Church both before and since the Reformation is asserted to be a baseless delusion. The judgment and labours of SIR ISAAC NEWTON, the chronological acumen of FABER and HALES, are nothing but "the foolishness of the wise," because BERTHOLDT and BLEEK, DE WETTE and KIRMS, have repeated the cry "*vaticinia post eventum!*" And why this eagerness to degrade this Book to a fabulous compilation of the Maccabæan times? Simply because its reception as the Word of GOD would overthrow the favourite theories of the Rationalists respecting The Old Testament. We cannot undertake to reply to such objections in detail; we can only furnish the reader with a few references to those Writers by whom they have been both propagated and refuted. We shall first indicate and label the poison. The prooemium of ROSENMULLER furnishes us with a succinct abstract of the assertions of EICHHORN in his *Einleit. in das A. T.*,[1] of BERTHOLDT in his *Histor. krit. Einleit*,[2] of BLEEK in his *Theolog. Zeitschr.*,[3] and of GRIESINGER in his *Neue ansicht der auffatze im Buche Daniel.*[4] The antidote to these conjectures is contained in HAVERNICK's article on DANIEL, in KITTO's Cyclopædia of Biblical Literature, and also in his valuable " New Critical Commentary on the Book of Daniel."[5]

Professor HENGSTENBERG[6] of Berlin has ably refuted the Neologian objections of his predecessors: the American reader will find the subject ably treated in the Biblical Repertory of Philadelphia;[7] and the English student may obtain an abstract of the points in dispute from the elaborate " Introduction " of Hartwell HORNE.[8] The various theories of these Neologists imply that the Book was written during the Maccabæan period, by one or more authors who invented the earlier portions by mingling fable with history in inextricable confusion, and by throwing around the history of their own age the garb of prophetic romance! The reception of any such hypothesis would so completely nullify the whole of CALVIN's Exposition, that we feel absolved from the necessity of entering into details. No disciple of this school will even condescend to peruse these LECTURES. It is enough for us to know, that these unworthy successors of the early German Reformers have been met with ability and research by LUDERWALD, STAUDLIN, JAHN, LACK, and STEUDEL. The unbelief of a SEMLER, a MICHAELIS, and a CORRODI, will seem to the follower of CALVIN the offspring of an unsanctified reason which has never been trained in reverential homage to the inspired Word. The keenness of this perverse criticism has attempted to explain away two important facts; first, that EZEKIEL mentions DANIEL as alive in his day, and as a model of piety and wisdom, (ch. xiv. 20, and ch.

---
[1] Pt. iii. § 615, 6—4th edit. [2] P. 1563, &c.
[3] Pt. iii. p. 241, &c. [4] P. 12, &c.
[5] Hamburg, 1838: an excellent treatise, in German.
[6] Die Authentie das Daniel, &c. Berlin, 1831, 8vo.
[7] Vol. iv. N.S., pp. 51, &c. [8] Vol. iv. p. 205, &c. Edit. 8th.

xxviii. 3,[1]) and secondly, that the Canon of the Hebrew Scriptures was finally closed before the times of the Maccabæan warriors. HAVERNICK also treats with the greatest erudition the linguistic character of the Book as a decisive proof of its authenticity. He reminds us that the Hebrew language had ceased to be spoken by the Jews long before the reigns of the Seleucidæ, that the Aramæan was then the vernacular tongue, and yet still there is a difference between the Aramæan of DANIEL and the late Chaldee Paraphrasts of the Old Testament. Oriental scholars have pronounced this testimony to be decisive. Interesting as his illustrations are, the numerous subjects which demand our immediate notice will only admit of our referring the reader to the Professor's "New Critical Commentary on the Book of Daniel."[2]

Happily there exists a strong conservative protection against the injury arising from such speculations. They are perfectly harmless to us when locked up in the obscurity of a foreign language and of a forbidding theology. But it grieves the Christian mind to find a writer worthy of being classed among the boldest of Reformers giving the sanction of his authority to such baseless extravagancies. There are many points of similarity between the characters of ARNOLD and CALVIN. Both were remarkable for an unswerving constancy in upholding all they felt to be right, and in resisting all they knew to be wrong. Both were untiring in their industry, and marvellously successful in impressing the young with the stamp of their own mental vigour. Agreeing in their manful protest against the impostures of priestcraft, they differed widely respecting the Book of Daniel. Our modern interpreter, in a letter to a friend,[3] writes as follows concerning " the latter chapters of Daniel, which, if genuine, would be a clear exception to my canon of interpretation, as there can be no reasonable spiritual meaning made out of

---

[1] *Bleek, De Wette, and Kirms,* suppose some more ancient Daniel to be intended. See Rosen. Proœm., p. 6.
[2] The title is Neue critische untersuchungen uber das Buch Daniel. Hamburg, 1838, pp. 104.
[3] See the Life and Correspondence of the late Dr. Arnold of Rugby, vol. ii. p. 191, edit. 2nd. P. 195, edit. 5th.

The Kings of the North and South. But I have long thought that the greater part of the Book of Daniel is most certainly a very late work, of the time of the Maccabees; and the pretended Prophecy about the Kings of Grecia and Persia, and of the North and South, is mere history, like the poetical prophecies in Virgil and elsewhere. In fact, you can trace distinctly the date when it was written, because the events up to the date are given with historical minuteness, totally unlike the character of real prophecy, and beyond that date all is imaginary." It is not difficult to detect the leading fallacy of this passage in the phrase "my canon of interpretation." This original thinker, with a pertinacity equal to that of CALVIN, had adopted his own method of explaining Prophecy, and determined at all hazards to uphold it. As the writings of this accomplished scholar have been very widely diffused, it will be useful to notice the arguments which he has employed. His "Sermons on Prophecy" contain the dangerous theory, which has been fully and satisfactorily answered by BIRKS in his chapter on "The Historical Reality of Prophecy."[1]

Dr. ARNOLD's statements are as follow: Sacred Prophecy is not an anticipation of History. For History deals with particular nations, times, places, and persons. But Prophecy cannot do this, or it would alter the very conditions of humanity. It deals only with general principles, good and evil, truth and falsehood, God and his enemy. It is the voice of God announcing the issue of the great struggle between good and evil. Prophecy then, on this view, cannot be fulfilled literally in the persons and nations mentioned in its language, it can only be fulfilled in the person of Christ. Thus, every part is said to have a double sense, "one Historical, comprehended by the Prophet and his own generation, in all its poetic features, but never fulfilled answerably to the magnificence of its language, because that was inspired by a higher object: the other Spiritual, the proper form of which

---

[1] Chap. xx. of "The two later Visions of Daniel historically explained." The Editor strongly recommends all the works of Mr. Birks on prophecy; though he differs in opinion on some points of interest, he is deeply impressed by their solid learning and their chastened piety.

neither the Prophet nor his contemporaries knew, but fulfilled adequately in Christ, and his promises to his people as judgment on his enemies." "It is History which deals with the Twelve Tribes of Israel; but the Israel of Prophecy are God's Israel really and truly, who walk with him faithfully, and abide with him to the end." Twice the Prophecies have failed of their fulfilment, first in the circumcised and then in the baptized Church. "The Christian Israel does not answer more worthily to the expectations of Prophecy than Israel after the flesh. Again have the people whom he brought out of Egypt corrupted themselves:" and hence Predictions relating to the happiness of the Church, both before and since the times of the Messiah, have signally and necessarily failed. We cannot undertake the refutation of this general theory, we must refer the reader to the satisfactory arguments of Birks. We can only quote his clear exposition of the manner in which the Visions of Daniel confute these crude speculations:—"Instead of a mere glimpse of the sure triumph of goodness at the last, we have most numerous details of the steps of Providence which lead to that blessed consummation. The seven years' madness of NEBUCHADNEZZAR, and his restoration to the throne; the fate of BELSHAZZAR, and the conquests of the MEDES and PERSIANS; the rise of the Second Empire, the earlier dignity of the Medes, and the later pre-eminence of the Persians over them; the victories of CYRUS westward in Lydia, northward in Armenia, and southward in Babylon; the unrivalled greatness of his Empire, and the exactions on the subject provinces; the three successors of CYRUS, CAMBYSES, SMERDIS, and DARIUS; the accession of XERXES, and the vast armament he led against Greece, are all predicted within the time of the two earlier Empires. In the time of the Third Kingdom a fuller variety of details is given. The mighty exploits of ALEXANDER, his total conquest of Persia, the rapidity of his course, his uncontrolled dominion, his sudden death in the height of his power, the fourfold division of his kingdom, and the extinction of his posterity; the prosperous reign of the first PTOLEMY, and of the great SELEUCUS, with the superior power of the latter before his death; the reign of PHILADELPHUS, and the marriage of BERENICE his daughter with ANTIOCHUS THEUS; the murder of ANTIOCHUS and BERENICE and their infant son by LAODICE; the vengeance taken by EUERGETES, brother of BERENICE, on his accession to the throne; his conquest of Seleucia, the fortress of Syria, and the idol gods which he carried into Egypt; the earlier death of CALLINICUS; the preparations of his sons, SELEUCUS, CERAUNUS, and ANTIOCHUS the Great, for war with Egypt, are all distinctly set before us. Then follows the history of ANTIOCHUS. His sole reign after his brother's death, his eastern conquests and recovery of Seleucia; the strength of the two rival armies, and the Egyptian victory at Raphia; the pride of PTOLEMY PHILOPATER and his partial conquests, with the weakness of his profligate reign; the return of ANTIOCHUS with added strength after an interval of years, and with the riches of the East; his victories in Judea and the capture of Sidon; the overthrow of the Egyptian forces at Panium, the honour shewn by ANTIOCHUS to the Temple, and his care for its completion and beauty; his treaty with Egypt, the marriage of his daughter CLEOPATRA with PTOLEMY PHILOMETOR, and defection from her father's cause; his invasion of the Isles of Greece; his rude repulse by the Roman Consul, and the reproach of tribute which came upon him through his defeat; his return to Antioch and speedy death, are all described in regular order. Then follow the reigns of SELEUCUS and ANTIOCHUS EPIPHANES, given with an equal fulness of prophetic detail, and close the narrative of the Third Empire. Even in the time of the Fourth and last Kingdom, though more remote from the days of the Prophet, the events predicted are not few. We find there, distinctly revealed, the iron strength of the Romans, their gradual subjugation of other powers, their fierce and warlike nature, their cruel and devouring conquests, the stealthy policy of their empire, and its gradual advance in the direction of the East, southward and eastward towards the land of Israel, till it had cast down the noblest Kings, and firmly ingrafted its new dominion on the stock of the Greek Empire. We have next described its oppression of the Jews, the overthrow of their City and Sanctuary by TITUS, the Abomination of Desolation in the Holy Place, and their arrogant pride in standing up against Messiah, the Prince of princes."¹

If the latter portion of these predictions were really written previously to the events, they must be inspired; and if a writer of the Maccabæan period could thus accurately predict the Conquests of Rome in the East, the whole question is decided: there is no reason whatever why the events of the Second and Third Empires should not have been foretold as clearly as those of the Fourth. Thus the very existence of the Book before the Jewish Canon was closed is a fact which proves all that is required. These Visions then become "the voice of Him who sees the end from the beginning, and pronounces in his secret council, even on the destiny of the falling sparrow. They are designed to stoop to the earthly estate of the Church, while they exalt her hopes to the glory that shall be revealed . . . They range through everlasting ages; but they let fall in passing a bright gleam of light that discovers to us the ass's colt, tied at the meeting of their ways, on which the Lord of glory was to ride into Jerusalem. . . . Every step in the long vista of preparation lies before them, from the seven months' reign of SMERDIS and the marriage of BERENICE with ANTIOCHUS, (ch. xi. 2-6,) to the seven months' burial of (corpses) in days to come in the land of Israel, and the marriage supper of the Lamb. . . . They touch, as with an enchanter's wand, the perplexed and tangled skein of human history, and it becomes a woof of curious and costly workmanship, that bespeaks the skill of its Divine Artificer: an outer hanging, embroidered by heavenly wisdom, for that glorious tabernacle in which the God of heaven will reveal himself for ever."²

THE DIVINES OF GERMANY.

Throughout this PREFACE and the subsequent DISSERTATIONS the reader will find frequent reference to THE DIVINES OF GERMANY. Some of these have proposed explanations of our

---

¹ "The two later Visions of Daniel," p. 357. ² Birks, p. 359.

Prophet which appear to the English reader so manifestly erroneous, that he may fancy we have spent too much space in confuting them. But he who would keep pace with the Theological Investigations of the day, may derive improvement from perusing the hypothesis of BERTHOLDT and DE WETTE, and rejoice that they have elicited the able replies of HAVERNICK and HENGSTENBERG. In truth, the reader of DANIEL must put aside for a while the laudable prejudices which he has been taught to cherish from his earliest days, and descend into the arena where the contest is fiercest,—whether our Prophet was contemporary with NEBUCHADNEZZAR or ANTIOCHUS. To many the question itself is startling, and that we may be prepared to meet it, thoroughly furnished with available armory, let us glance over the wide field of Continental Rationalism as far as it concerns the Authenticity of Daniel.

The system under review is a melancholy off-shoot from the teaching of LUTHER and his intrepid followers. They led men away from form, and ceremony, and imposture, to rely upon one BOOK as their Rule of Faith and Duty. They did more—they sifted the chaff from the wheat, and by discarding the APOCRYPHA, placed before the eager attention of mankind the pure word of heaven. LUTHER and CALVIN held very distinct ideas about Revelation and Justification, and enforced very boldly their views of the only Books which were written by the penmanship of the Almighty. Theirs was a work of purification and of reconstruction on the assertion of the existence of a Divine Revelation, of its being contained in the Old and New Testaments, and of these documents being the only Inspired Records of what we are to believe, and how we are to live. In process of time, each Book became the subject of separate study —its history, its criticism, and its preservation were respectively examined with intense eagerness—and a vast amount of information was collected, which was totally unkown to the Early Reformers. It soon became apparent that the Reformed Churches were living under a totally different state of things from that described in the Old Testament. The events, for instance, of this Book of DANIEL all seemed so mingled and so intertwined; the ordinary occurrences of every-day life are so interlaced with marvellous dreams and visions, and the conduct and passions of monarchs seem so singularly controlled by an unseen Mind, that the question occurs, Is all this literally true? Did it all actually come to pass exactly as it is recorded? Or, Is it allegorical, or a historical romance, or only partially inspired by Jehovah, and tinged in its style and diction with the natural exaggeration of Oriental imagery? Such inquiries shew us how the mind seeks to fathom the mysteries of what is offered to its veneration, and have led to the conclusion, that the Sacred Books of the Hebrews are not all pure revelation, but that they contain it amidst much extraneous matter.[1] The writers to whom we refer have ever since the sixteenth century been attempting to define how much of the Hebrew Scriptures is the pure and spiritual Revelation of the Divine Mind to us, and how much is the unavoidable impurity of the channel through which it has been conveyed. With the names of some later critics, the modern Theologian is familiar. GESENIUS, WEGSCHEIDER, and RÖHR, yet retain a powerful influence over the minds of later students, while SCHULTZ at Breslau, GIESELER at Göttingen, ALLMANN at Heidelberg, BRETSCHNEIDER at Gotha, DE WETTE—lately deceased—at Basle, HARE at Jena, and WIENER at Leipsic, are writers who worship irreverently at the shrine of human reason, and either qualify or deny the Inspiration of Revelation.

FALSE SYSTEMS OF SCRIPTURE EXPOSITION.

An important change was necessarily made on the minds of the successors of the Reformers, by the more general spread of Classical Literature, and a far better acquaintance with Hebrew philology. Here, we must allow, that some of the disciples of LUTHER and CALVIN were better furnished for the work of Interpretation than their more Christian-minded masters. ERNESTI, the learned philologer of Leipsic, in 1761 laid down "The Laws of a wise Interpretation," and has ever since been considered as the founder of a scholar-

[1] See Töllner's *Die heilige Eingebund der heiligen Schrift*. Linden, 1771, quoted in *Am. Saintes' Hist. Rat.*, 1849.

like system of Scriptural Exposition. His principles are now universally admitted, viz., that we must make use of history and philology of the views of the period at which each Book was written, and of all those appliances which improved scholarship has provided in the case of the Classical Authors of Greece and Rome. Every attentive reader of German Theology must perceive, that too many of their celebrated Critics have rested in this outward appeal to mere reason and research. SEMLER and TITTMANN, MICHAELIS and HENKE, have pursued this system of accommodation so far, that they have destroyed the very spirit and essence of a Divine Revelation. In the Prophets, and especially in DANIEL, whom SEMLER includes among the doubtful Books, there is a spiritual meaning only to be comprehended by the moral and religious faculties; and except this spirit be elicited, the merely outward form of prophetic diction can effect no religious result. Let RÖHR and PAULUS sneer as they please, at the mysticism and pietism of the Evangelic Reformers, we must still contend, that without a spirituality similar to theirs, all comments are essentially lifeless and profitless to the soul of man. They may display erudition, but they will not aid the spirit which hungers and thirsts after righteousness on its way towards heaven.

Every student who desires to become familiar with these discussions, may consult with advantage the Dissertations of HENGSTENBERG, who has written fully and ably on The Genuineness of our Prophet. He has sketched, historically, the attacks which have been made, and has answered every possible objection. The impurity of the Hebrew, the words supposed to be Greek, the silence of Sirach, the disrespect shewn by the Jews, and the position in the Canon of Scripture, are all ably discussed. The miracles have been called "profuse in number and aimless in purpose;" historical errors have been asserted, and statements called contradictory, or suspicious, or improbable; many ideas and usages have been said to belong to later times. These and similar arguments are used to shew the Book to be the production of the times of ANTIOCHUS EPIPHANES, but they have been fully treated by this orthodox Professor at Berlin. He discusses most ably, and with the most laborious erudition, those marvellous Prophecies of this Sacred Book, which have necessarily provoked a host of assailants. He reminds us that in the earliest ages, PORPHYRY devoted his twelfth book to the assault upon this Prophet, and that we are indebted to JEROME for a knowledge of his objections as well as for their refutation. He asserted that the Book was composed during the reign of ANTIOCHUS EPIPHANES in Greek, "and that DANIEL did not so much predict future events as narrate past ones."[1] Though the imperial commands condemned his works to the flames, yet EUSEBIUS of Cæsarea, METHODIUS of Tyre, and APOLLINARIS of Laodicea, have ably refuted them. In later times, the first scholar-like attack upon the genuineness of various portions was made by J. D. MICHAELIS. COLLINS and SEMLER, SPINOZA and HOBBES, had each condemned the Book after his own manner: but it was left for EICHHORN[2] to lead the host of those later Neologians who have displayed their vanity and their scepticism, by the boastfulness of their learning and the emptiness of their conclusions. HEZEL and CORRODI treat it as the work of an impostor; while BERTHOLDT, GRIESINGER, and GESENIUS, have each their own theory concerning its authorship and contents. Other Critics have followed the footsteps of these into paths most dangerous and delusive.

Having replied to the most subtle objections against the Genuineness of these Prophecies, HENGSTENBERG proceeds to uphold the direct arguments in its favour. He first discusses the testimony of the author himself, and then enters upon its reception into the Canon of the Sacred Writings. He comments at full length on the important passage in JOSEPHUS contra Apion. i. 8, and shews the groundlessness of every assertion which impugns its Canonical value. He next proves that the declaration of our Lord assumes the prophetical authority of the work, and traces its existence in pre-Maccabæan times. The alleged exhibition of these Writings to ALEXANDER THE GREAT and the exposition of their contents to the Grecian Conqueror of the East, form a singular

[1] Jerome's *Prooemium in Dan.*, Op. tom. v. p. 267.
[2] Einleitung in A. T.

episode in the midst of profound criticism. The incorrectness of the Alexandrine Version and its rejection by the Early Church, who substituted that of Theodotion for it, is turned into an argument against the Maccabæan origin of the original; for certainly, a composition of which the author and the translators were nearly contemporary, might be better translated, than one separated by an interval of many ages. Then the peculiar features and complexion of the original language point out the exact period to which the writing is to be assigned. The historical accuracy, the apparent discrepancies, and yet the real agreement with Profane Narratives, all strengthen the assertion, that the writer lived during the times of the Babylonian and Persian Monarchies. Another argument, as strong as any of the former, is deduced from the nature of the symbolism used throughout the Book. The reasonings of HENGSTENBERG have now received additional confirmation from the excavations of LAYARD. The prevalence of animal imagery, rudely grotesque and awkwardly gigantic, is characteristic of Chaldean times, and bespeaks an era previous to the Medo-Persian Sculptures at Persepolis. Summing up his reasonings, the Professor quotes the observation of FENELON: "Lisez DANIEL, dénonçant à Balthasar la vengeance de Dieu toute prête a fondre sur lui, et cherchez dans les plus sublimes originaux de l'antiquité quelque chose qu'on puisse comparer à ces endroits là!"

ENGLISH PHILOSOPHICAL SCHOOL.

The speculations which we have hitherto discussed are not confined within the limits of unreadable GERMAN NEOLOGY: they have been transfused into English Philosophy, and presented in a popular form to the readers of our current literature. In a learned and speculative Work, entitled "The Progress of the Intellect, as exemplified in the Religious Development of the Greeks and Hebrews," the writer [1] has adopted the untenable hypothesis of the German Neologists. In his second section of a chapter on the "Notion of

[1] By Robert William Mackay. 2 vols. 8vo. 1850.

a supernatural Messiah," he writes as follows: "During the severe persecution under ANTIOCHUS EPIPHANES, when the cause of Hebrew faith in its struggle with colossal heathenism seemed desperate, and when, notwithstanding some bright examples of heroism, the majority of the higher class was inclined to submit and to apostatize, an unknown writer adopted the ancient name of DANIEL, in order to revive the almost extinct hopes of his countrymen, and to exemplify the proper bearing of a faithful Hebrew in the presence of a Gentile Tyrant. . . . The object of pseudo-Daniel is to foreshow, under a form adapted to make the deepest impression on his countrymen, by a prophecy, half-allusive, half-apocalyptic, the approaching destruction of heathenism through the advent of Messiah. Immediately after the overthrow of the Four Beasts, emblematic of four successive heathen Empires, the last being the Macedonian with its offset, the Syrian; the 'kingdom' would devolve to the 'Saints of the Most High,' that is, to the Messianic Establishment of Jewish expectation, presided over by a being appearing in the clouds, and distinguished, like the angels, by his human form from the uncouth symbols of the Gentile Monarchies."[1] He treats "Messiah" as a "title which hitherto confined to human anointed authorities, such as kings, priests, or prophets, became henceforth, specifically appropriated to the ideal personage who was to be the Hope, the Expectation, and the Salvation of Israel." He discusses the Seventy Weeks as the fiction of the imaginary DANIEL, and terms the accompanying predictions "adventurous," and as turning out "as fallacious as all that had preceded them." His fourth section on DANIEL'S MESSIAH is, if possible, more wildly conjectural than the two preceding ones. Daniel's idea, says he, of a supernatural leader called "Son of Man," became afterwards "a basis of mystical Christology." Those glowing passages of this Prophet, which fill the Christian mind with awe and delight, are to this theorist "the earthly or Messianic resurrection of pious Hebrews, which was all that was originally contemplated in the prediction." In thus attempting to overthrow the Inspired authority of DANIEL,

---

[1] Vol. ii. § 2, "Time of Messiah's coming," p. 307.

he mingles the Books of Esdras and the Jewish Targum, and is eager to catch at any Jewish fiction as if it were a true interpretation of ancient prophecy. He alludes to puerile Rabbinical fables as really explanatory of the Divine Records, and mingles ZOROASTER and MAIMONIDES, GFRORER and EISENMENGER, as of equal value in determining abstruse points of sound criticism! The sections with which we are concerned evince the greatest research and the crudest opinions all hurried together without the slightest critical skill or philosophical sagacity. With materials gathered together in the richest abundance, he has presented us with results which are alike baseless, futile, and injurious. TOBIT and PAPIAS, the Book of BARUCH and the Book of ENOCH, are all treated as on a level with the writings of MOSES or TACITUS, JUSTIN MARTYR or a German Mystic! The public, too, are in danger of being imposed on by a show of learning and by long Latinized words and phrases, which merely disguise, under classical forms, ideas with which the well-read Divine is already familiar; at the same time, they give such an air of scholarship to these speculations, that the unlearned may be readily deceived by their showy rationalism. The whole work utterly fails in its attempt to explain the rites and symbols of Jewish worship, and to give the slightest explanation of the "theories" and "philosophies" of the Old Testament. The tendency is to reduce it all to mysticism and symbolism, and to any other "theosophy" which leads the mind away from the Christian assurance of one God, one Faith, and one Spirit.

THE RECENT EASTERN DISCOVERIES.

The strongest of all possible arguments against these fallacious theories has lately been derived from Eastern discovery. Fresh importations of sculptured rock are daily arriving in Europe, from the sepulchres of those cities amidst which our Prophet dwelt. The more this new vein is worked, the richer it becomes. Are we to be told by BLEEK that the writer of this Book transferred the events of which he was a spectator to the more ancient times of Assyria and

Babylon ? and that NEBUCHADNEZZAR and BELSHAZZAR were but fabulous characters, of which the original types were ANTIOCHUS and ALEXANDER ?[1] Are EICHHORN and BERTHOLDT to make DANIEL another Homer, or Virgil, or Æschylus? Then let us appeal to the testimony of MM. BOTTA and LAYARD ; let us visit the British Museum, and under the guidance of RAWLINSON and HINCKS, let us peruse, in the arrow-headed characters, the history of the Monarchs of Assyria and Babylon, and observe how exactly those memorials of antiquity illustrate the Visions of our Prophet. The assistance which these excavations afford, for the elucidation of our subject, is too important to be passed over, and we must venture upon such arguments as may properly enter into a General Preface, while they vindicate the historical accuracy of the interpretation which CALVIN has so elaborately set before us in the following LECTURES.

ANCIENT ASSYRIAN REMAINS.

The order of THE VISIONS suggests the propriety of treating, first, THE ANCIENT ASSYRIAN REMAINS ; then those of BABYLON and PERSEPOLIS, with such notices of the EGYPT OF THE PTOLEMIES as the connection of the history may require.

The earliest memorials of ASSYRIA have not been preserved in the records of literature, but by durable engravings on marble and granite. Within the last fifty years the PYRAMIDS OF EGYPT have been compelled to open their lips of stone to speak for God's Word, and the ROSETTA tablet suggested to YOUNG and CHAMPOLLION an alphabet by which they read on sarcophagus and entablature the history of the earliest dynasties of the Nile. What LEPSIUS and BUNSEN have done for Thebes and Memphis, Dendera and Edfou, LAYARD and RAWLINSON are now accomplishing for the long lost NINEVEH, the majestic BABYLON, and the elegant PERSEPOLIS. It has lately been revealed to astonished Europe, that a buried city lies, in all its pristine grandeur, beneath that huge mound which frowns over Mosul on the banks of the Tigris. KHORSABAD and KOYUNJIK, NIMROUD and BEHISTUN,

[1] Rosenmüller Prooem., p. 26.

are now giving up their black obelisks, their colossal bulls, and their eagle-headed warriors, to become "signs and wonders" to our curious generation. In this general sketch we must avoid details, however interesting: we can only allude to the first Assyrian monuments discovered by M. BOTTA, in 1843,[1] as containing a line of Cuneiform Inscriptions amid winged kings and their warlike chariots. They are deposited in the Louvre, and form the most ancient of its esteemed collections. The elegant volumes of LAYARD, and the more tangible proofs of his untiring labours, now deposited in the British Museum, have thrown new light upon the prophetic portion of the Elder Covenant. Two-coned Conquerors, winged Chiefs, carrying either the gazelle or the goat, sacred trees, and their kneeling worshippers—

> The life-like statue and the breathing bust,
> The column rescued from defiling dust—

enable us to guess at the exploits of a long line of kings before the age of Saul or Priam. The name of SARDANAPALUS is now rescued from traditional disgrace, and ennobled in the midst of a hardy race of ancestors and successors. Our progress in interpreting these arrow-headed mysteries, enables us to assign the date 1267 B.C. for the founding of NINEVEH as a settled point in Asiatic chronology. The earliest historical document in the world is that on the north-west palace of NIMROUD, built by ASSAR-ADAN-PAL. He informs us of the existence, and celebrates the exploits of TEMEN-BAR the first, the founder of HALEH, at a time when the Hebrews were just entering the promised land, and the Argives were colonizing the virgin valleys of Hellas! The familiar names of SHALMANESER, SENNACHERIB, and ESARHADDON, are found incised upon the enduring masonry; and it is now possible to ascertain who founded the MESPILA of Xenophon, who constructed the towers in the south-west palace of NIMROUD, and who stamped his annals on the clay cylinders in the British Museum.[2] The NIMROUD obelisk becomes a precious relic, since it enables us to ascertain, for the first time, the events

---

[1] See his letters to M. Mohl in the *Journal Asiatique* for 1843; April 5, June 2, October 31, and also March 22, 1844.

[2] See Major Rawlinson's Commentary on the Cuneiform Inscriptions, p. 57, and his references to the various plates of the British Museum series.

of those nine centuries, during which NINEVEH existed from its rise to its overthrow. We are mainly concerned with the manner in which it confirms the truthfulness of the Prophets of the Hebrews, and with the unanswerable arguments which it supplies against the subtleties of German Neology. The credibility of one Prophet is intimately bound up with that of another. Whatever confirms either ISAIAH or EZEKIEL, throws its reflected light upon DANIEL and HOSEA. The god NISROCH, in whose temple SENNACHERIB was slain, (2 Kings xix. 37, and Isaiah xxxvii. 38,) is repeatedly mentioned on the obelisk as the chief deity of the Assyrians. The " SARGON king of Assyria" (Isaiah xx. 1) is most probably the monarch who founded the city excavated by M. BOTTA; and the occurrence of the name " YEHUDA," in the 33d number of the British Museum series, leads Interpreters to consider the passage as alluding to the conquest of SAMARIA. The very paintings so graphically described by EZEKIEL, (chap. xxiii. 14, 15,) have reappeared upon the walls of these palaces. They are, perhaps, the very identical objects which this Prophet beheld, for he dwelt at no great distance from them on the banks of the Khabur, and wrote the passage about thirteen years after the destruction of the Assyrian Empire. The prophecy bears the date B.C. 593, and " the latest Assyrian sculpture on the site of NINEVEH must be as early as B.C. 634."[1] We would gladly linger over these proofs of the truthfulness of the ancient Prophets; but further details must be inserted in those DISSERTATIONS which accompany the text, and we close this rapid sketch of these Assyrian remains in the touching words of their enterprising Discoverer. " I used,' says Mr. LAYARD, " to contemplate for hours these mysterious emblems, and to muse over their intent and history. What more noble forms could have ushered the people into the temple of their gods? What more sublime images could have been borrowed from nature, by men who sought, unaided by the light of Revealed Religion, to embody their conception of the wisdom, power, and ubiquity of a Supreme Being? They could find no better type of intellect and knowledge, than the head of a man; of

---

[1] See Vaux's Nineveh and Persepolis, p. 263, edit. 2d.

strength, than the body of the lion ; of ubiquity, than the wings of the bird. The winged-human-headed lions were not idle creations, the offspring of mere fancy ; their meaning was written upon them. They had awed and instructed races which had flourished 3000 years ago. Through the portals which they guarded, kings, priests, and warriors had borne sacrifices to their altars, long before the wisdom of the East had penetrated to Greece, and had furnished its mythology with symbols long recognised by the Assyrian votaries. They may have been buried, and their existence may have been unknown, before the foundation of the Eternal City. For twenty-five centuries they had been hidden from the eye of man, and they now stood forth once more in their ancient majesty. But how changed was the scene around them ! The luxury and civilisation of a mighty nation had given place to the wretchedness and ignorance of a few half-barbarous tribes ; the wealth of temples, and the riches of great cities had been succeeded by ruins and shapeless heaps of earth. Above the spacious hall in which they stood, the plough had passed and the corn now waved. Egypt had monuments no less ancient and no less wonderful, but they have stood forth for ages, to testify her early power and renown, while those before me had but now appeared to bear witness in the words of the Prophet, that once ' The Assyrian was a cedar in Lebanon, with fair branches, and with a shadowing shroud of a high stature ; and his top was among the thick boughs. . . . His height was exalted above all the trees of the field, and his boughs were multiplied, and his branches became long, because of the multitude of the waters which he shot forth. All the fowls of heaven made nests in his boughs, and under his branches did all the beasts of the field bring forth their young, and under his shadow dwelt all great nations ;' for now is ' Nineveh a desolation, and dry like a wilderness, and flocks lie down in the midst of her ; all the beasts of the nations, both the cormorant and the bittern lodge in the upper lintels of it ; their voice sings in the windows, and desolation is in the thresholds.' "[1]

[1] Vaux, p. 221.

ANCIENT BABYLONIAN REMAINS.

As we travel onwards in time, and southward in place, our attention is attracted to those Babylonian antiquities which vindicate the correctness of the Comments of CALVIN.

After centuries of extensive empire, NINEVEH yielded to a younger rival. The army of Sennacherib had been annihilated by the angel of the Lord; ESARHADDON, his son, had planted his heathen colonists in the fertile plains of Samaria. NEBUCHADONOSOR had won the battle of Rhagau; PHRAORTES had been slain, and his son, CYAXARES in alliance with NABOPALASSAR, had taken NINEVEH, and destroyed for ever its place in the history of Asia. Palaces of black basalt, bas-reliefs, and hawk-headed heroes, covered with legends of unbounded triumphs, no longer rose at the bidding of the servants of Bar, and the worshippers of Assarac, Beltis, and Rimmon. No more Her obelisks of buried chrysolite proclaimed her far-famed majesty; for her new masters transferred the seat of their empire to the banks of the Euphrates. The renowned son of NABOFALASSAR now commences the era of Babylonian greatness. This enterprising chieftain is no creation of poetic fancy. HERODOTUS and BEROSUS have recorded his exploits, and we have now the testimony of recent discovery to confirm the assertions of Daniel, and to throw fresh light upon his narrative.

"The earliest Babylonian record that we have," says Major RAWLINSON, "is, I think, the inscription engraved on a triumphal tablet at Holwan, near the foot of Mount Zagros; it is chiefly religious, but it seems also to record the victories of a certain king named Temain against the mountaineers. Unfortunately it is in a very mutilated state, and parts of it alone are legible. I discovered this tablet on the occasion of my last visit to Behistun and with the help of a telescope, for there are no possible means of ascending the rock, succeeded in taking a copy of such portions of the writing as are legible. . . . I am not able at present to attempt a classification of the kings of Babylon, such as they are known from the various relics that we possess of them: nor, indeed, can I say with certainty, whether the kings recorded, with the exception of NEBUCHADNEZZAR and his father, may be anterior or posterior to the era of NABONASSAR. The Babylonians certainly borrowed their alphabet from the Assyrians, and it requires no great trouble or ingenuity at the present day to form a comparative table of the characters."[1] " I have examined," says this enterprising traveller, " hundreds of the Hymar bricks, (near Babylon,) and have found them always to bear the name of NEBUCHADNEZZAR." Borsippa was a city in the neighbourhood of Babylon, and there is monumental " evidence of its being the capital of Shinar, as early almost as the earliest Assyrian epoch." Temenbar, the Obelisk king, conquered it in the ninth year of his reign: the bricks upon the spot are exclusively stamped with the name of Nebuchadnezzar, being at this moment tangible proofs of the reality of the words " Is not this the great Babylon that I have built ?" The rebuilding of the city, and the construction and dedication of the great temple is noticed " in the standard inscription of Nebuchadnezzar, of which the India House slab furnishes us with the best and most perfect copy." This valuable monument gives a detail of all the temples which he built throughout the various cities of his extensive provinces, it names the particular deities to whom the shrines were dedicated, and mentions other particulars, which our present ignorance of the language enables us but partially to comprehend. The vast mound of El Kasr contains the remains of a magnificent palace, supposed to be that of NEBUCHADNEZZAR ; but as these recent excavations are more to our present purpose, it is unnecessary to refer at length to this majestic ruin.[2]

PERSIAN AND EGYPTIAN ANTIQUITIES.

Again, in commenting on the ninth chapter, CALVIN has followed the usual method of interpreting it of ALEXANDER and his successors: he naturally assumes them to be real predictions, and believes them to have been accomplished according to the utterance of their Hebrew captive. And

[1] Com. on Cuneif. Inscrip., p. 76.
[2] See a description of the Kasr in Kitto's Bib. Cyc., art. Babylon.

have we no traces of the foot-prints of Alexander now remaining to us? Not long ago, a traveller, amid the barren plains of Persia, lighted unexpectedly on a magnificent ruin —alone, on a deserted plain—its polished marbles, and its chiselled columns all strewed around in wild confusion. This Chehel-Minar, or hall of forty pillars, was built by the Genii, said the Arabs, amid the desert solitudes of Merdusht. The Genii builders have lately been stripped of their disguise of fable, and the long lost Persepolis, destroyed by the mad frolic of Alexander, stands revealed to the world in the Takht-i-Jemshid. The grandeur of these pillared halls, these sculptured staircases, and fretwork fringes of horn-bearing lions, interests the reader of Daniel, through the inscriptions which they bear on their surface. The ingenuity of a Westergaard and a Lassen has been displayed in deciphering them, and has enabled us to discover the original architects. CYRUS and CAMBYSES, DARIUS HYSTASPES and XERXES, each erected his own portion. One portion can be assigned to the Achænenian dynasty, and another to the monarchs of the Sassanian family. These inscriptions also point out where the rulers of Persia formed their sepulchral repose. The tomb of Cyrus at Moorghab, his statue discovered and described by Sir R. K. PORTER, and "the thousand lines" on the sculptured rock of Behistun,[1] throw a clear and brilliant light on the statements of DANIEL, as well as on the narrative of Herodotus. These passing allusions must suffice at present—further discussions must be left for distinct dissertations—while the ninth and tenth chapters of VAUX's Nineveh and Persepolis will supply additional information to all who are inclined to search for it. Enough is introduced, if the reader is impressed with the conviction that DANIEL's Visions and CALVIN's LECTURES are no vague or cunning delusions, no skilful travestying of history, under the garb of either intentional forgery or weak credulity.

As PERSEPOLIS suggests the triumph of the He-goat, and the rising of the four horns towards the four winds of heaven, (chap. viii. 8,) so it leads us forwards towards the subsequent warfare between Asia and Egypt. The mighty

[1] Major Rawlinson in Journ. Royal Geog. Soc., vol. ix.

king stood up, and his kingdom was broken : and the king of the south became strong and mighty, (chap. xi. 3, 4.) An index here points to the valley of the Nile, where there now exists a countless host of monuments, raised by the giants of the very earliest days of our race. On the day when CAMBYSES, flushed with victory, stabbed with his own hand the living Apis, and commanded the bones of the Pharaohs to be beaten with rods, he struck to the heart the genius of the Nile. At that moment, the quarries were teeming with busy sculptors, numerous as swarming bees— massive monoliths were becoming Sphinxes and Memnons, while architraves and propyla, worthy of the TEMPLE OF KARNAK, were emerging from the living rock. They all retired to rest that evening, intending to renew their labour on the morrow, but on the morrow bursts the avenging Persian, and that long train of workers are still for ever. But their unfinished handicraft remains for the astonishment of our later centuries. A perfect statue only awaits one final blow to detach it from its parent rock—there runs the track of the wheels which had come to transport it to either EDFOU or LUXOR ; there may be seen the very marks of the tools which lay by its side all night, and were never used on the next fatal morning.

Henceforth Egyptian art is transferred to the tombs and palaces of the kings of Persia. It is cheering to feel, that as our knowledge of the significance of these treasures advances, they confirm the assertions of Holy Writ. Among the mural sculptures at KARNAK, one of the captives, with a Jewish physiognomy, bears the title which we can now read —YOUDAH MALEK, meaning a king of Judah. THE ROSETTA STONE in our National Museum, which is the basis of modern Egyptology, was sculptured as late as B.C. 195, and contains a decree of PTOLEMY EPIPHANES, to whom DANIEL is supposed to refer. The primæval antiquity of THE ZODIAC on the majestic portico at DENDERA, has now been disproved. "The Greek Inscription on the pronaos refers to TIBERIUS and HADRIAN." The hieroglyphic legends on the oldest portion of its walls belong to the last CLEOPATRA, while the Zodiac was constructed between A.D. 12 and 132. While we willingly allow the connection between Assyria and Egypt as early as the thirteenth century before Christ, and admit the occurrence of its name on the Nimroud obelisk in the British Museum,[1] and on the sculptures of Behistun and Nakhshi-Rustam,[2] yet we contend against that assumption of a false antiquity, which is assumed for the purpose of throwing discredit upon the prophetic portions of our Sacred Oracles. What, then, is the result of our rapid sketch of these remains of the dynasties of former eras ? A complete overthrow of the baseless fabrications of German Neology. Till the arrow-headed character was deciphered, the history of NINEVEH was almost a blank to the world. As Assyria and Babylon now breathe and live in resuscitated glory, so all that DANIEL wrote is confirmed and amplified by the marbles and tombs which have travelled to this Island of the West. Hence this Captive of Judah really lived while the Head of Gold was towering majestically upon the allegorical image. Neither poet nor impostor of the reign of ANTIOCHUS could have fancied or forged characters and events which accord so exactly with the excavations of a LAYARD, or the decipherings of a RAWLINSON. Sceptical infidelity must now hide its head for ever, and speculations of the school of Arnold must shrink into their original insignificance.

POSITIVE EVIDENCE.

The positive evidence of additional facts may also be adduced. This Book was translated by The Seventy many years before the death of ANTIOCHUS, and the translation was well known to JEROME, although it has not come down to our age. Bishop CHANDLER has pointed out fifteen places in which JEROME refers to it;[3] and Bishop HALIFAX has collected many conclusive arguments on these and kindred topics.[4] The words of JOSEPHUS are explicit enough as to the received opinion in his day, " you will find the Book of DANIEL in our Sacred Writings."[5] MAIMONIDES, indeed, has attempted to detract from its high reputation, but has been

[1] Kenrick's Ancient Egypt under the Pharaohs, vol. i. p. 44.
[2] Major Rawlinson's " Commentary," &c. p. 47.
[3] Vindication of the Def., chap. i. § 3.
[4] Warburtonian Lectures. Sermon II. [5] Antiq., Book x. ch. x. 4.

sufficiently refuted by ABARBANEL and the son of JARCHI.[1] The arrangement of the Jews, which places this Book among the Hagiographa, and not among the Prophets, seems also to be intended to depreciate its Canonical value; but while the earlier Talmudists place it with the Psalms and the Proverbs, the later ones range it with Zechariah and Haggai.[2] When Aquila and Theodotion translated their Versions, he was admitted to the Prophetic rank: and although we cannot absolutely determine the point from the MS. of the Septuagint in the Chigian Library at Rome, yet the probability is highly in its favour. ORIGEN places DANIEL among the Prophets and before EZEKIEL, following the example of JOSEPHUS in his first book against Apion.

JEWISH TESTIMONIES.—SINAITIC INSCRIPTIONS.

Instead of following the beaten track of reference to JEWISH COMMENTS and RABBINICAL TRADITIONS, which CALVIN always quoted and refuted, we shall here introduce a collateral branch of singular and valuable evidence. As the surface of the Theological world is much agitated by doubts of historic facts, originating alike with Rationalists and Romanists, it is desirable to fortify our evidence from existing inscriptions of correlative value with those of Nineveh. That far-famed seceder to Rome, Dr. Newman, speaks of some "Scripture Narratives which are quite as difficult to the reason as any miracles recorded in the History of the Saints;" and he then instances that " of the Israelites' flight from Egypt, and entrance into the Promised Land."[3] Anxious as the votary of either Superstition or of Reason may be to suggest doubts as to the recorded facts, THE ROCKS OF SINAI are now vocal with the voices of the moving Tribes! Valley after valley has been found in which these SINAITIC INSCRIPTIONS abound. " Their numbers may be computed by thousands, their extent by miles, and their positions above the valleys being as

[1] Mor. Nevoch. p. ii. ch. 45.
[2] See the Bava-bathra and the Megilla c. ii. Prideaux Connex., p. 1, 65, § 2. Kennicott's Dis. Gen., p. 14, and Disser. Prelim. to Wintle's Translation, p x. &c
[3] See his " *Discourses addressed to Mixed Congregations.*" Edit. 2d.

often measurable by fathoms as by feet."[1] These hitherto unreadable remnants of a former age have now been read, and they become fresh confirmations of the truthfulness of the Mosaic Narrative. It is enough for our present purpose to refer to the conclusive labours of the Rev. CHARLES FORSTER, who has compared the characters used with those of THE ROSETTA STONE, with the Arrow-headed Character, and with the Alphabets of Etruria, Palmyra, and Persepolis; and has been enabled to read what neither BEER could decipher nor POCOCKE explain.[2] By him they are shewn to record the bitterness of the Waters at Marah—the Flight of Pharaoh on horseback—the Miracle of the feathered fowls, the Murmuring at Meribah—and the Uplifting of the hands of Moses at the battle of Rephidim. Thus the "Written Valley," and the "Written Mountain," have rendered their testimony in favour of Revelation. "No difficulties of situation, no ruggedness of material, no remoteness of locality, has been any security against the gravers of the one phalanx of mysterious scribes. The granite rocks of the almost inaccessible Mount Serbal, from its base to its summit, repeat the characters and inscriptions of the Sandstones of the Mokateb." Countless multitudes are supposed to be yet undiscovered. And what people but the Israelites could have engraven them? Professor BEER allows them to be all of the same age—the soil affords no sustenance for hordes of men, and never did provide for the existence of a settled population. This wilderness may be periodically travelled through, but never has been permanently settled by mankind. The very execution of such works requires the use of ladders and platforms, ropes, baskets, and tools, and all the usual instruments of a long established population. But no people could have executed all this unproductive labour without a ready supply of water and food. If, then, a single generation carved and graved these countless Inscriptions, how can we account for the fact, except by the Mosaic narrative? Whence came

[1] Forster's "*One Primæval Language*," p. 33, where Lord Lindsay's letters are quoted.
[2] Details are given at length in the interesting work quoted above. Professor Beer in his "Century of Sinaitic Inscriptions" utterly failed to unravel them. *Leipsic*, 1840.

the bodily aliments, by which so many workmen were enabled to carry out their hazardous employments for so long and continuous a period? Grant that ISRAEL coming out of Egypt performed them, and the difficulty is solved—adopt any other possibility, and the problem becomes perfectly insoluble! We forbear to enter further into this important discussion; it is enough to have awakened this train of thought, in accordance with our previous reasonings.[1]

THE CONTENTS OF THE BOOK OF DANIEL.

The CONTENTS of this Book admits of an easy and natural division. The first part has been called "The Historical," and the second "The Prophetical" portions. Each contains six chapters, and the Comments on each, with the Editor's Dissertations, will respectively occupy a Volume. THE HISTORICAL PORTION contains Predictions; but they were not uttered by DANIEL himself, and seem to spring naturally out of the events of the times. It is not without its difficulties. The learned have differed respecting the existence of a second NEBUCHADNEZZAR, the person and character of CYRUS, and the reign of DARIUS the Mede. Strenuous efforts have been made to shew that one NEBUCHADNEZZAR plundered the Temple, and another was afflicted by madness: that the Koresh of the last verse of the sixth chapter is not CYRUS THE GREAT, but an obscure Satrap of an earlier age. A noble Duke, whose scriptural researches confer higher honour on his name than the coronet he wears, has proposed an elaborate theory for the better explanation of "The Times of DANIEL,"[2] and the hypothesis has met with an equally learned reply by the author of "The Two later Visions of DANIEL."[3] A detail of the arguments on both sides will be found in the DISSERTATIONS previously referred to. The discrepancies between HERODOTUS and XENOPHON, which Archbishop SECKER tried in vain to reconcile, must be again discussed; the criti-

---

[1] Before Professor Beer's attempt to explain them, Montfaucon had drawn the attention of the literary world to their value. See his *Coll. Nov. Patr.*, t. ii. p. 206, where the narrative of Cosmas, the Indian traveller, is found in the original Greek.
[2] The Duke of Manchester.   [3] The Rev. T. R. Birks.

cal value of PTOLEMY's Astronomical Canon ascertained, and many subordinate and collateral events examined. CALVIN makes no pretensions to minute Historical Criticism: he adopts the received opinions of his day, and if he sometimes errs, he does so in ignorance of other sources of knowledge which have since been opened to the world. But his diligence and his judgment have preserved him from errors of any ultimate importance; and it must be always remembered that the Antiquarian Researches of later times have thrown a flood of light upon these distant Eras. Baseless conjecture has, indeed, done much to pervert and mystify the plainest truths; but the materials themselves are of a most varied and intricate character; and the satisfactory adjustment of these historical difficulties requires the highest powers of discrimination, as well as the most comprehensive grasp of all the conflicting evidence by which a doubtful event is embarrassed.

THE SEVENTY WEEKS.

In attempting to appreciate CALVIN's COMMENTS on the Historical Portion of this Book, and of the celebrated period of "THE SEVENTY WEEKS," it will be necessary to advert to some abstruse points of Chronology We would willingly avoid any tedious discussion of dates and figures, but the interest of many important questions now frequently turns upon such arithmetical proofs. A strong assertion of the Chevalier BUNSEN must justify us in the course which we are about to pursue. "All the results," says he, "of Jewish or Christian Research are based upon the Writings of the Old Testament and their Interpretation, and upon the connection between the Chronological data they supply and divine Revelation. There are points therefore, relative to which it is of vital importance, both to the sound thinker and the sound critic, to arrive at a clear understanding before embarking upon his inquiry. . . . The question is, Whether the external History related in the Sacred Books be externally complete, and capable of chronological arrangement?"[1]

[1] Bunsen's Egypt's Place in Universal History, vol. i. p. 162.

The reply should be given "with a deep feeling of the respect due to the general chronological statements of Scripture, which have been considered during so many centuries as forming the groundwork of religious faith, and are even at the present moment intimately connected with the Christian Faith." Let but these principles of the learned Egyptologist guide us in our decisions, and we may hope for the blessing of Heaven in disentangling many of the Historical intricacies which will soon come under our notice.

THE PRÆTERIST, ANTI-PAPAL, AND FUTURIST VIEWS.

In attempting to determine the intrinsic value of these LECTURES, it becomes necessary to compare CALVIN's Prophetic Interpretations with those of the Divines who preceded and have followed him. The scheme proposed for interpreting these VISIONS may be classed generally under this threefold division, viz., the PRÆTERIST, the ANTI-PAPAL, and the FUTURIST VIEWS. The first view is that usually adopted, with some slight modifications, by the Primitive Church and the Earlier Reformers. The second, sometimes called the "Protestant" System, supposes the Papal power to be prominently foretold by both DANIEL and ST. JOHN; while the Third System defers the accomplishment of many of these Prophecies to times yet future. If these three Systems be borne distinctly in mind, it will become easy to understand how the most popular modern explanations differ from those of the earlier period of the Reformation. The Primitive Church has, with few exceptions, agreed in considering The Head of Gold to mean, either the Babylonian Empire or the person of Nebuchadnezzar; the Silver denoting the Medo-Persian; the Brass the Greek; and the Iron the Roman; while the mixture of the Clay denotes the intermingling of Conquered Nations with the power of Heathen Rome. In interpreting the Four Beasts, the Lion denotes the Babylonian Empire; the Eagle Wings relate to Nebuchadnezzar's ambition; the Bear to the Medo-Persians; the Leopard to the Macedonians; and the Fourth Beast to the Romans. The Ten Horns were differently explained; some referring them to Ten individual Kings, and others to Ten Divisions of the Empire; some supposing them to commence with the Roman sway in the East, others not till the Fourth or Fifth Centuries after Christ.

CALVIN differs slightly from the earlier, and most materially from the later Commentators. Supposing the Fourth Beast to typify the Roman Empire, ' The Ten Kings," he says, "were not persons succeeding each other in dominion, but rather the complex Form of the Government instead of a unity under one head." The number " ten " is, he thinks, indefinite, for " many," and the Sway of a Senate instead of a Monarchy is the true fulfilment of the Prophecy. The rise of one King and his oppressing three, refers to the two Cæsars, JULIUS and OCTAVIUS, with LEPIDUS and ANTONY. How unconscious was CALVIN that succeeding Protestant Writers would determine The "Little Horn" to be the POPE, and the Three Kings, the Exarchate of Ravenna, the Kingdom of Lombardy, and the State of Rome. Here the multitude of modern commentators differ most materially from the author of these LECTURES. The " Time, Times, and Half a Time " of this chapter, CALVIN refers to the persecution of the Christian Church under NERO, and similar tyrannical Emperors of Rome, and gives not the slightest countenance to any allusion in these words to a specified number of years. " Time and Times " are with him a long undefined period; and " Half a Time " is added in the spirit of the promise to shorten the time for the Elects' sake. Those modern Writers, who think the Year-Day theory essential to the full exposition of the Visions of DANIEL, will be disappointed by the opinion of our Reformer. He takes no notice of either the 1260 years of the Papacy, or the 1290 years for the reign of Antichrist. Again, there are Writers who deny the Fourth Beast to refer to ROME at all. ROSENMULLER and TODD are instances; and each of these has his own way of interpreting the concluding portion of this chapter. The former asserts it to be fulfilled in the Greek Empire in Asia after ALEXANDER's death, and the latter supposes it to be yet future. According to Dr. TODD and the Futurists, it has yet to be developed. Its fulfilment shall be the precursor of

THE FINAL ANTICHRIST, whom the Lord shall destroy with the brightness of his PERSONAL ADVENT. This Antichrist shall tyrannize in the world for the "Time, Times, and Half a Time," that is, for the definite space of three years and a half, till the Ancient of Days shall proclaim THE FINAL CLOSE OF THE GENTILE DISPENSATION.

The three views, then, of the Interpretation of these Prophecies are thus clearly distinguished. The *Præterist* view treats them as fulfilled in past historical events, taking place under the several Empires of Babylon, Persia, Greece, and Heathen Rome. The modern *Anti-Papal* view treats "The Little Horn" as the Pope, and the days as years; and this stretches the predictions over the Twelve Centuries of European struggle between the Ecclesiastical and the Civil Powers. The *Futurist* is dissatisfied with the Year-Day theory: he cannot agree with the past fulfilment of these glowing images of future blessedness. Hence, instead of either ANTIOCHUS, MAHOMET, NERO, or THE POPE, he sees a future Antichrist in the Eleventh Horn of the seventh chapter, in The Little Horn of the eighth chapter, and in The Wilful King of the eleventh chapter. He rejects entirely the Year-Day explanation, and every assertion which is based upon it; he takes the days literally as days, and supposes them yet unfulfilled. The "Toes" of the image, and the "Horns" of the beasts, are not to him Kingdoms or Successions of Rulers of any kind, but single individual persons. The phrase, THE POPE, as equivalent to a "Horn," is to him a fallacy: as it does not mean one person, like an ALEXANDER or a SELEUCUS; or a single despotic Antichrist—but a long succession of Rulers, one after another.[1] FABER, for example, interprets "the Scriptures of Truth," chap. xi., by extending it throughout all history, till the end of the Gentile Dispensation. Dr. TODD refers it solely to its close, and contends very strongly against the usual explanation of the Fourth verse. ELLIOTT, again, (Horæ Apoc., vol. iii.,) expounds this chapter to the 35th verse with great propriety

[1] A list of the chief "Futurist" writers and of their sentiments will be found in Birks' "First Elements of Sacred Prophecy," where the Year-Day theory is ably advocated, and much useful information condensed.

and clearness, but passes at once from the Ptolemidæ and Seleucidæ to the Pope, as signified by "The Wilful King." The Days then become Years, and the various phases of the Papacy through many centuries are supposed to be predicted here, and fulfilled by the decrees of JUSTINIAN, persecutions of the Waldenses, French Revolutions, and catastrophes and convulsions yet to come. Our American brethren have adopted similar theories. Professor BUSH in his " Hierophant," has inserted an able exposition of the " Little Horn," as unquestionably the Ecclesiastical Power of the " Papacy,"[1] and introduced the GOTHS and CHARLEMAGNE as fulfilling their own portions of this interesting Vision. Professor STUART, however, of Andover, and some of his followers, have returned to the simplicity of the Earlier Expositors.[2]

CALVIN'S PROPHETIC SCHEME.

CALVIN, then, was on the whole, a Præterist. He saw in the history of the world before the times of the Messiah the fulfilment of the Visions of this Book. They extended from NEBUCHADNEZZAR to NERO. " The Saints of the Most High " were to him either the Hebrew or the Christian Church under heathen persecutors. He had a glimpse indeed of the times of the Messiah, and expressed his views in general language ; but he rejected the idea of any series of fulfilments through a succession of either Popes or Sultans. He saw in these four-footed beings, neither MAHOMET, nor JUSTINIAN, nor the Ottoman Empire, nor the Albigensian Martyrs. Heathen Rome, and its Senate, and its early Cæsars were to him what Papal Rome, and its Priesthood, and its Gregories, have been to later Expositors.

Our SECOND VOLUME, which contains THE PROPHETICAL PORTION of the Book, will be illustrated by many *Dissertations*, which will condense the sentiments of later Expositors. Ample scope will then be given to important details. Extracts will be made from the most approved Moderns, and

---

[1] P. 109. New York, 1844.
[2] Hints on the Interpretation of Prophecy, 1842; and Folsom's Daniel. Boston, 1842.

copious references to the best sources of information. It will be sufficient here to insert the reply of Professor BUSH of New York to Professor STUART of Andover, as illustrating the importance of the difference between those who adopt the Year-Day theory and those who do not: " Denying *in toto*, as I do, and disproving, as I think I have done, the truth of your theory in regard to the literal import of *Day*, I can of course see no evidence, and therefore feel no interest in your reasonings respecting the events which you consider as the fulfilment of these splendid Visions. If a *Day* stands for a *Year*, and a *Beast* represents an *Empire*, then we are imperatively remanded to a far different order of occurrences in which to read the realization of the mystic scenery from that which you have indicated. As the Spirit of Prophecy has under his illimitable ken the most distant future as well as the nearest present, I know nothing, in reason or exegesis, that should prevent the affairs of the Christian economy being represented by DANIEL as well as by JOHN. As the Fourth Beast of DANIEL lives and acts through the space of 1260 years, and as the Seven-headed and Ten-horned Beast of JOHN prevails through the same period, and puts forth substantially the same demonstrations, I am driven to the conclusion that they adumbrate precisely the same thing—that they are merely different aspects of the same reality—and this, I have no question, is the *Roman Empire*. This you deny; but I submit that the denial can be sustained only by shewing an adequate reason why the Spirit of God should be debarred from giving such extension to the Visions of the Old Testament Prophets. Until this demand is satisfied, no progress can be made towards convincing the general mind of Christendom of the soundness of your Expositions. The students of Revelation will still reiterate the query, Why the oracles of DANIEL should be so exclusively occupied with the historical fates of ANTIOCHUS EPIPHANES? . . . If I do not err in the auguries of the times, a struggle is yet to ensue on the prophetic field between two conflicting parties, on whose banners shall be respectively inscribed, *Antiochus and Antichrist.*"[1]

[1] Hierophant, May 1843, p. 273. New York.

ŒCOLAMPADIUS, ZUINGLE, AND BULLINGER.

This is precisely the point that these LECTURES will assist in determining, and the following sketches of the opinions of the immediate predecessors and successors of our Reformer, will be useful in guiding the judgment of the reader.

One of the most learned of the Commentators among the Early Reformers was ŒCOLAMPADIUS, the well-known companion of ZUINGLE. BULLINGER published his notes on the Prophets about fifty years before BEZA edited CALVIN'S Lectures. His character for piety and profound erudition stood high among his contemporaries, and his elaborate expositions of the Prophets form a tangible proof of his industry, ingenuity, and Christian proficiency. Some account of the method in which he treats these interesting questions will here be appropriate. He divides the Book into the two natural divisions—the Historical and the Prophetical. His remarks on the former portion contain nothing which demands our notice at present; but his second division contains some valuable comments. He takes the Four Beasts of chapter vii. for the Babylonian, Persian, Grecian, and Roman Empires, dwells on the cruelties of SYLLA and MARIUS, TIBERIUS and NERO; and accuses ABEN-EZRA and the Jews of denying this Fourth Beast to mean Heathen Rome, lest they should be compelled to embrace JESUS as their Messiah. He is not satisfied with JEROME'S opinion, that the Ten Horns mean Ten Kings, who should divide among them the territories of the Roman power. He takes the numbers "ten" and "seven" for complete and perfect numbers, quoting from the parable, "The kingdom of heaven is like *ten* virgins." He quotes and approves of HIPPOLYTUS, who asserts "the Little Horn" to mean the Antichrist, to whom St. PAUL alludes in the Second Epistle to the Thessalonians. APOLLINARIUS and other Ecclesiastical Writers judge rightly in adopting this interpretation, while POLYCHRONIUS is deceived by PORPHYRY in referring it to ANTIOCHUS. But who is this Antichrist? Is he supposed to rule after the destruction of Heathen or of Papal Rome? ŒCOLAMPADIUS furnishes us with many opinions—some supposing MAHOMET, others TRAJAN, and others the PAPAL SEE. He quotes the corresponding passage in the APOCALYPSE, and implies that the successors of MAHOMET and the occupiers of the Chair of ST. PETER are equally intended. By thus introducing the modern history of Europe and of Asia, he leans rather to the second of those divisions into which Commentators on DANIEL have been divided. On this testing question of "the Time, Times, and Half a Time," he assumes it to mean three years and a half: he has no limit of any extension of the time through 1260 years; adding, "there is no reason why we should be religiously bound to that number, or follow puerile and uncertain triflings." He will not allow Antichrist to be only a single person, and thus throws an air of indefiniteness over the whole subject.

Consistently with these principles, he interprets " The Wilful King" of chapter xi. by both MAHOMET and the PAPACY; and explains how this twofold power should be destroyed in the Holy Land. The repetition in the numbers in chapter xii. is treated very concisely. Literal days are said to be intended, and the possibility of ascertaining certainty is doubted. " If any one has detected any certainty in these obscure dates, I do not envy him: the exposition already offered satisfies me; for it is not in our power to know the precise divisions of the time (*articulos temporum*)." Throughout the whole Comment of ŒCOLAMPADIUS, there is a tone of piety, and a proficiency in correct interpretation which we seek for in vain in some disciples of the Early Reformers. He was evidently a spiritually-minded man, and was always preaching Christ in his Comments on the Old Testament. In this respect he equals, and if possible surpasses the more elaborate CALVIN. The extreme spirituality of this eminent Reformer entitles him, in these days, to more notice than he receives. His constant efforts to honour Christ as his Redeemer, and the practical and persevering manner in which he preaches the gospel of his Redeemer, in his *Old* Testament Exposition, should render his writings familiar to every sincere and simple-minded Christian. And we are not surprised when we hear competent judges of the difference between CALVIN and himself prefer the tone of his remarks to that of his more vigorous ally.

GROTIUS.

The Commentary of GROTIUS is also worthy of comparison with that of CALVIN. He is very precise and minute in shewing how the history of the East has borne out the truthfulness of the predictions; and is, perhaps, more accurate in details than his predecessor: he differs, indeed, in a few points of importance, which will be separately noticed, but, on the whole, his remarks are correct and judicious. The Ten Kings of the seventh chapter he considers to be Syrian Monarchs, and enumerates them as Seleuci, Antiochi, and Ptolemæi. POLANUS and JUNIUS, two Commentators who are constantly quoted by POOLE in his Synopsis, treat the passage in a similar way. The king to arise after them is still confined to the Jewish era, and "the Time, Times," &c., are supposed to be literally three years and a half. The 36th verse of chapter xi. GROTIUS interprets of ANTIOCHUS EPIPHANES, and is supported by JUNIUS, POLANUS, MALDONATUS, WILLET, and BROUGHTON. The "Days" of the twelfth chapter are taken literally by all the Commentators quoted by POOLE from CALVIN to MEDE, and all suppose the period intended to be during the reign of the successors of ALEXANDER. MEDE was the well-known reviver of the Year-Day theory. Before his time it was a vague assertion: he first gave it shape, and form, and plausible consistency, and since his day it has been adopted by many intelligent Critics, among whom are Sir ISAAC NEWTON, BISHOP NEWTON, FABER, FRERE, KEITH, and BIRKS.

MALDONATUS.

The Commentary of MALDONATUS, the Jesuit, demands more extended notice, as he lived about the times of our author, and calls him *Patriarcha Hereticorum*, and looks upon the subject from exactly the opposite point of view. His exposition of JEREMIAH, BARUCH, EZEKIEL, and DANIEL, was published at Moguntiæ, (Mentz,) 1611. In his *proœmium* he sketches the life of DANIEL, and defends his Book against PORPHYRY, the Manichæans, and the Anabaptists. He quotes the mention made of DANIEL by EZEKIEL, and lays it down as a rule, that our ignorance of the author of a book does not impeach its Canonical Authority; and in the spirit of his Religious Society, lays special stress upon the judgment and decision of "the Church." He next argues in favour of the Apocryphal Books attributed to this Prophet, and then prefers the authority of his Church to the testimony of JEROME. He defends the canonicity of the stories of Susannah and the Idol Bel, and comments on them in two additional chapters, and places "The Song of the Three Children" between the 23d and 24th verses of chapter iii., translating from Theodotion's version. There is nothing worthy of special notice in his remarks on the first six chapters; but the next six treat of the reigns of Christ and of Antichrist. In accordance with this view, he decides upon the Fourth Beast of the seventh chapter as the Roman Empire, after rejecting the opinion of ABEN-EZRA in favour of the Turks, and that of PORPHYRY, who thought it to be the successors of ALEXANDER. Respecting the "Little Horn," his wrath is stirred up, for "the heretical Lutherans and Calvinists, and other monstrous sects," had dared to pronounce it to be the Roman Pontiff. "But this interpretation even their master, CALVIN, has shewn to be absurd."[1] He combats the notion that by one term all the Roman Pontiffs are intended; and then triumphantly asks, Where are the "Three" whom this single one was to pluck up? He further inquires, Whether all were past in his own day, or all future? He determines that it is all yet to be fulfilled, and thus becomes an adherent to the cause of the Futurists. As neither the Ten Horns nor the Eleventh have yet come into existence, it is natural to conclude the Eleventh to be that Antichrist whom JEROME represents not as a Demon, but a man in whom "a whole Satan shall corporally dwell." He shall reign, he thinks, three years and a half—a distinct and fixed period —objecting to what he calls "figura Calvini," viz., that an

[1] Comment., p. 673, chap. vii. 8.

uncertain period is intended by so clear an expression. The various opinions of his predecessors on the 36th verse of chapter xi. move rather his derision than his wrath. Their notions about CONSTANTINE, and MAHOMET, and the ROMAN PONTIFFS, do not need his serious refutation. Almost all Catholics, he adds, both ancient and modern, refer it to the Antichrist. He also accuses the greater part of "the New Heretics" of stating the Michael of the 12th chapter to be Messiah himself; and treats the "days" of the close of this chapter as partly fulfilled under the Jewish and partly under the Christian dispensations. His inconsistency in this interpretation is more apparent than in the preceding ones; while his work on the whole is worthy of perusal, as he quotes with judgment the opinions of learned Jews and of the earlier Commentators of the Christian Church.

Within the first century after the Reformation, the views of Divines respecting these Prophecies were far more in accordance with the ancient Greek and Latin Fathers than those prevalent in the present day. The student who would know how MELANCTHON, OSIANDER, and BULLINGER treated the subject in reply to BELLARMINE, FERERIUS, and other Romish Divines, may profitably consult WILLET's Hexapla in Danielem, published at Cambridge in 1610, and dedicated to King James I. The arguments of the ancients in reply to "wicked PORPHIRIE" are collected and reviewed, the opinions of various Jewish writers are stated and confuted, and no valuable remark of any preceding Commentator is overlooked. For instance, the Fourth Beast of the seventh chapter is explained according to the Jews, as the Turkish, and to JEROME, of the Roman empire: but he decides it to be the kingdom of Syria, under the sway of Seleucus and his posterity. The "Little Horne" is said to be ANTIOCHUS; and CALVIN's view, connecting it with AUGUSTUS and the following Emperors, is thus treated:—"But though these things may, by way of analogie, be thus applied, yet, historically, as hath been shewed at large, this prophecy was fulfilled before the coming of the Messiah into the world." BULLINGER refers it to the Pope, and others to the Turks; and "These applications, by way of analogie, we mislike not." The "Times" are supposed, by the majority of these writers quoted, to be single years, and the whole period three years and a half. His laborious industry respecting the " Seventy Weeks" is most instructive ; and he deserves the greatest possible credit for the patience with which he has examined all authorities, and the acuteness with which he has discussed the most opposite opinions. He is careful in remarking the various readings of the text, and the different renderings of all preceding versions. The eleventh chapter he treats as all fulfilled in the history of Syria and Palestine before the birth of Christ. He discusses with much ability the question, whether Antichrist is a single person, or a succession of Rulers, as Caliphs or Popes, and presents us with the decisions of the leading Fathers, Romanists, and Reformers on the "notes and markes wherein Antiochus and Antichrist agree." All who would see BELLARMINE fully confuted, and the enormities of this chapter brought home to the several occupants of the See of Rome, will peruse WILLET with eagerness and profit. He will also find CALVIN's Interpretations clearly stated and fairly compared with those of the most celebrated Reformers and their most acute antagonists. The days of the twelfth chapter are taken literally, and no hint is given of any elaborate theory of a dozen centuries, extending through the modern history of Europe. To all who love to trace the progress of opinion, respecting the intercourse between men and angels, " the Auncient of Daies," the Opening of the Books, Michael the Prince, and the application of these Prophecies to the Turks, the Papacy, and the times of a yet future Antichrist, will find in the " Hexapla" a storehouse of valuable material, where he may exercise, with all freedom, the liberty of choice. It proposes and answers 593 questions, and discusses 134 controversies, the greater part of the latter division being directed against the doctrines and practices of the Church of Rome.

JOSEPH MEDE.

A formidable opposition to the principles propounded in these LECTURES is found in the writings of JOSEPH MEDE.

That learned and ingenious author is usually held as the ablest and earliest expositor of the Year-Day theory. It is neither necessary nor possible for us here either to confirm or confute all his hypotheses; we can only refer to his "*Revelatio Antichristi, sive de Numeris Danielis,* MCCXC. MCCCXXXV." (Works, p. 717.) The first part is occupied by refuting BROUGHTON and JUNIUS, who assert those mystic days to have been literally fulfilled during the Wars of ANTIOCHUS. The prediction, he thinks, fulfilled in the twelfth century of our era, when the persecutions of the Papal See, against the Heretics of those days, are said to verify the words of the Prophet. Dr. TODD has thought this treatise worthy of a detailed refutation, and to all who are interested in determining whether Antichrist is a Succession of Rulers or a single person, his learned remarks are worthy of attentive perusal. In pursuance of his own ideas respecting a personal future Antichrist, he is led to dispute the division of ALEXANDER'S empire into four parts, and to quote at full length various authorities, especially VENEMA, who endeavoured to shew the number of divisions to be ten, and that the portion of chap. viii. usually interpreted of the Roman was really fulfilled by the Grecian Empire in the East.[1]

CALVIN then, we find, agrees entirely with VENEMA, and by anticipation confutes the arguments of Dr. TODD. He thinks it surprising, that men versed in Scripture can thus substitute darkness for light. He is supported by MELANCTHON and MICHAELIS, HENGSTENBERG and ROSENMULLER, as well as by THEODORET and most of the Greek Expositors. He treats those more leniently who modestly and considerately suppose the times of ANTIOCHUS to be figurative of those of Antichrist. At this "figura Calvini" MALDONATUS sneers; and yet if we determine that CALVIN'S solution is right, it is the very principle by which the perusal of Holy Scripture becomes profitable to us. "I desire," says he, "to treat the Sacred Oracles reverently; but I require something certain." "If any one wishes to adapt this passage to present use, he

---

[1] See Herm. Venem. Dis. ad Vat. Dan. Emblem., Dis. v. § 3-12, pp. 347-364, 4to. Leovard, 1745, as quoted at length in Todd's Discourses on Antichrist, pp. 505-515.

may refer it to Antichrist," on the principle, " that whatever happened to the Ancient Church, occurred for our instruction." Hence he allows of a double sense, and raises a question which has been ably contended for and against by many subsequent Divines. It is too important to be passed over, and will demand our notice in our Second Volume.

The followers of MEDE have met with a formidable antagonist, and the adherents of CALVIN a staunch supporter in the late Regius Professor of Hebrew in the University of Cambridge. Dr. LEE, in his pamphlet on the Visions of DANIEL and St. JOHN,[1] has stated his reasons for adhering to the Older Interpreters, thus adopting the principle of the Præterists, and entirely discarding the slightest reference to the Pope and the Papacy. His conclusions may be exhibited in a few words. Respecting Nebuchadnezzar's Image, "the feet must of necessity symbolize *Heathen* Rome in its last times."[2] "Papal Rome cannot, therefore, possibly be any prolongation of DANIEL'S Fourth Empire." "These Kings," represented by the *Toes*, "may, therefore, be supposed in a mystical sense to be, as the digits ten, a round number, and signifying a whole series."[3] "The Little Horn" is said to be Heathen Rome—its persecuting Emperors from NERO to CONSTANTINE fulfilling the Prophetic conditions. The phrase "a Time, Times, and a Half," is said to refer to the "latter half (mystically speaking) of the Seventieth Week of our Prophet."[4] "DANIEL'S Week of seven days—equivalent here to EZEKIEL'S period of seven years—is, we find, divided into two parts mystically considered halves, or of three days and a half."[5] . . . "That the Roman Power took away the Daily Sacrifice, and cast down the place of its Sanctuary, it is impossible to doubt. TITUS, during the reign of his father VESPASIAN, desolated Jerusalem by destroying both the City and the Sanctuary." Thus in his general principles of Exposition, this celebrated Hebraist pronounces his verdict in favour of CALVIN and his interpretation.

No notice is taken in these LECTURES of the Deutero-

[1] Seeleys, London, 1851. [2] Sect. i. p. 1. [3] Ibid., p. 2.
[4] P. 16. [5] Introd., p. xliii.

Canonical additions to this Prophet. In the versions of the SEPTUAGINT, and that of THEODOTION, there are some additions to this Book which are not found in the Hebrew Canon. JEROME translated these from the version of THEODOTION, and ably replies to the objection of PORPHYRY, by denying the canonicity of the following treatises viz., The Prayer of Azarias, the Song of The Three Children, the History of Susanna, and The Story of Bel and the Dragon. EUSEBIUS also denies the identity between the Prophet and the Son of Abdias, the priest who ate of the table of the King of Babylon. DE WETTE, in his *Lehrbuch*, has discussed the criticism of these treatises with great ability. As early as the second century, the Septuagint Version of Daniel was superseded by that of Theodotion ; and the former was lost till it was discovered and published at Rome in 1772. The views of DE WETTE, and of " ALBER OF PESTH, who contends against JAHN for the historic truth of these variations," will be found in the Addenda to DANIEL in Kitto's Cyclopædia. The Commentators of the Romish Church feel bound in honour to defend these additional portions. Their best arguments will be found in a praiseworthy attempt of J. G. KERKHERDERE, Historian to his Catholic Majesty Charles III., to explain some difficulties in this Prophet.[1] He considers the number of DANIEL's Treatises to be a dozen. He places the history of his own Youth first, that of Susanna second, the Story of Bel and the Dragon third, and Nebuchadnezzar's Dream fourth ; and then with great precision and clearness, enters upon those historical questions which need both acuteness and research in their treatment.[2] BELLARMINE also dwells on the testimony of the Greek Fathers, but meets with an able opponent in WILLET, the laborious author of the *Hexapla in Danielem*.[3]

It must not be forgotten that portions of this Book, like that of EZRA, are written in Chaldee. From the fourth verse of chap. ii. to the end of chap. vii., the language is Chaldee.

---

[1] See his "Prodromus Danielicus," p. 19. Lovanii, 1711.
[2] See the Appendix where the opinions of various writers are collected—especially pp. 331-336
[3] See the Sixfold Commentarie, p. 10. Edit. 1610.

Rosenmuller assigns as a reason for this, the desire of the author to represent Nebuchadnezzar and the Magi as speaking in the language of their country. However valid this reason may be for the earlier chapters, it is not equally so for the sixth and seventh, since the Medes and Persians probably used the Persian tongue. Abarbenel, in the preface to his *Commentarium*, supposes that Chaldee was no longer in use after the taking of the city; and that Daniel, through ignorance of Persian, returned to the use of Hebrew. C. B. Michaelis, however, demurs to this, and suggests that the use of either tongue was arbitrary, just as modern scholars use either Latin or their own vernacular tongue according to their convenience and taste. The occurrence of this older form of the Aramaic idiom has been seized upon by the opponents of the authenticity of this Book, while its use has been ably explained and vindicated by Hengstenberg.[1]

THE RELIGIOUS, SOCIAL, AND POLITICAL VALUE OF CALVIN'S METHOD OF EXPOSITION.

In concluding our Introductory Remarks it will be useful to offer a few suggestions on the Religious, Social, and Political value of Calvin's Method of Exposition throughout these Lectures. Such suggestions are the more appropriate in these days when views directly adverse to our Reformer's are extensively popular through the ingenious theories of Faber, Elliott, and Cumming. Those who have imbibed their views will pronounce these Volumes profitless and barren. "What can it benefit us," they will ask, "in the present day, to know how many Kings reigned from Cyrus to Xerxes; the changes in the Empire of Alexander; the troops which fought at Raphia; the marriage of Berenice, and the results of the invasion of Greece by Antiochus?"[2] . . . "Why not suffer these antiquated facts

---
[1] *Authentie des Daniel*, p. 310—on the other side, see *Theologische Studien*, 1830, p. 290, *et seq.*; as quoted in Kitto's Biblic. Cyc., Art. Chald. Lang.
[2] Birks, *ibid.* chap. xxi. Though the views of this writer, expressed from chap. xii. to xx. are diametrically opposed to those of Calvin, yet the remarks of chap. xxi. are so *excellent*, that we shall avail ourselves of a few appropriate sentences.

of history to sleep quietly in the dust, and bend our strength to the controversies and practical movements of the present hour?" May we not reply, that he is best able to understand and unfold the religious phases of the age in which he lives, who is most familiar with the events and opinions of all preceding times. No man can permanently impress his own age with the precepts of spiritual wisdom, who knows nothing but what his own eyes have seen, and his own hands have handled. The ever varied messages of the Holy Spirit have always combined historical reality with the deepest spiritual significance. The details of Profane History and its comparison with the Sacred Text will never, by itself, enable us to reap the full harvest of solid improvement from the perusal of these Sacred Oracles. We must dive deeper than the surface. We must look at them in the light of one majestic and solemn truth. They are all "the foreseen counsels and works of the living God; the vast scheme of Providence which he has ordained for his own glory, and steps in the fulfilment of his everlasting counsel."

We are fully aware, that many will pronounce these Volumes deficient in spiritual life, and in Protestant zeal. But the Christian who dares not dogmatize beyond the direct teachings of the Spirit of God, will apply them indirectly to the events of the present era, on the intelligible principles of SACRED ANALOGY. They thus become a portion of that Divine Lesson which fulfilled Prophecy is ever reading to the Church of God. They display His ceaseless dominion over the wills of Sovereigns and over the destinies of Nations. When abstract truths are felt to be powerless in breaking the spell of worldliness, and in piercing within the charmed circle of social strife and political party, these embodied proofs of an ever-watchful Deity may awe men into submission to his sovereign will. The hollow maxims of earthly policy will never be superseded till men reverence the GOD OF DANIEL, and, like the heavenly Elders, cast all their crowns of intellect and renown before His throne. From the days of NEBUCHADNEZZAR and of CYRUS, we see in every change the foot-prints of a guiding Deity. "The reigns of CAMBYSES, SMERDIS, and DARIUS; the armament of XERXES, with its countless myriads ; the marches, and counter-marches, and conflicts, the subtle plots and shifting alliances of contending kings, long before they occurred, were noted down in ' the Scriptures of Truth'—the Secret Volume of the Divine counsels. All of them, before they rose into birth, were revealed by the Son of God to his holy Prophets ; and they remain till the end of time an imperishable monument of His Providence and foreknowledge. All was foreseen by His wisdom and ordained by his Sovereign power. The passing generations of mankind, while they see this blue arch of Providence above them, and around them, sure and steadfast, age after age, like Him who has ordained it, must feel a deep and quiet reverence take possession of their soul." The minuteness of detail in the visions concerning ALEXANDER and PTOLEMY SOTER, and the repulse of ANTIOCHUS, convey the same instructive lesson. " Every royal marriage, like that of BERENICE or CLEOPATRA, with all its secret issues of peace or war, of discord or union ; the levying of every army, the capture of every fortress, the length of every reign, the issue of every battle, the lies of deceitful ambition, the treachery of councillors, the complex web of policy, woven out of ten thousand human wiles, and each of them again the product of ten thousand various influences of good and evil, all are pourtrayed with unerring accuracy in ' the Scriptures of Truth.' " .... " The pride of ANTIOCHUS the Great, his successful ambition and military triumphs, his schemes of politic affinity, nay, even his prudent regard for the house of God, cannot avert the sentence written against him, for his fraud and violence in the Word of Truth. In the height of seeming power, his own reproach is turned against him, and he tumbles and falls, and is not found."

If, then, we conclude with CALVIN, that the persecution of the Little Horn and the idolatries of the Wilful King are past, on what principle are we to derive instruction from their perusal ? By the inductions of a Divine analogy, by the assertion that "*all which has passed is in some sense typical of all that is to come.*" " The Saints of the Most High" are always the special objects of Jehovah's regard ; they ever meet with an oppressor as fierce as ANTIOCHUS, and as hateful as " the Man of Sin ;" but still, whatever their sufferings under a GUISE or an ALVA, they shall ultimately " take the Kingdom," and possess it for ever. Strongholds of Mahuzzim there always will be, under either the successors of MEDICI or the descendants of MAHOMET. The evidence of GIBBON, which has been used so freely by many modern theorists, is equally valuable on the hypothesis, that similar relations between the Church and the world occur over and over again in the course of successive ages. A parallel may often be drawn by an ingenious mind between the persecutions of Heathen and of Papal Rome, and the temptation is always great to refer the fulfilment of Prophecy exclusively to that system of things with which we are immediately and personally concerned. Military ambition, subtle policy, the arts of Statesmen, the voice of excited multitudes, the passions of every hour, the delusions of every age—all must pass in silent review under the eye of heaven. They are repeated with every successive generation under an infinite variety of outward form, but with a perfect identity in spirit and in feeling. It may be safely asserted, that every social and political change from the times of NEBUCHADNEZZAR to those of CONSTANTINE, have had their historic parallel from the days of CHARLEMAGNE to those of NAPOLEON. Hence, Predictions which originally related to the Empires of the East, may be naturally transferred to the transactions of Western Christendom. At the same time, there never may have been the slightest intention in the mind of the writer to apply them in this double sense. We cannot venture to discuss all the arguments either for or against the double sense of Prophecy. CALVIN, at least, opposed it strongly, and whenever he swerved from the literal version, he substituted the principle of accommodation, according to the educated taste of an experienced Expounder of Holy Writ. It will, perhaps, be our truest wisdom to listen to the judicious advice of Bishop HORSLEY :—" Every single text of prophecy is to be considered as a portion of an entire system, and to be understood in that sense which may best connect it with the whole. The sense of Prophecy, in general, is to be sought in the events which have actually taken place. . . . To qualify the Christian to make a judicious application of these rules, no skill is requisite in verbal criticism—no proficiency in the subtleties of the logician's art—no acquisition of recondite learning. That degree of understanding with which serious minds are ordinarily blessed—those general views of the schemes of Providence, and that general acquaintance with the Prophetic language which no Christian can be wanting in . . . these qualifications will enable the pious, though unlearned Christian, to succeed in the application of the Apostle's rules." (2 Pet. i. 20, 21.)[1] While this sentiment is cheering to the humble-minded believer, another principle laid down by the same author must never be omitted. The meaning of a prediction "never can be discovered without a general knowledge of the principal events to which it alludes." Let CALVIN, then, be judged by this simple test—and before we venture to condemn him, let us be equally patient, and equally careful to gather all the information within our reach.

CONTEMPORARY EVENTS IN FRANCE.

The period when our Reformer addressed these LECTURES TO ALL THE PIOUS WORSHIPPERS OF GOD IN FRANCE, is now worthy of our attention. CALVIN writes from GENEVA at the close of the month of August A.D. 1561, immediately preceding that Colloquy at POISSY, to which reference was made in the preface to EZEKIEL.[2] His Letter depicts so faithfully the state of persecution in which the Christians of France were placed, and compares it so efficiently with the condition of DANIEL and the pious worshippers of God under NEBUCHADNEZZAR, that the more we know of the times in which CALVIN wrote, the more complete the parallel appears. An animated sketch of this eventful era has lately been published by the Queen's Professor of Modern History in the University of Cambridge; and as the views of the Editor accord with those of the Professor "On the Reformation and the Wars of Religion" in France, we shall abridge and condense his narrative, as the best suited to our purpose.

[1] See his four Sermons on this passage. [2] Calvin on Ezekiel, vol. i. p. xxix.

THE GENERAL SYNOD OF PROTESTANTS AT PARIS.

When CALVIN addressed his followers in France, as desirous of the firm establishment of Christ's kingdom in their native land, he was at his College in Geneva ; but his labours and his Writings were all-powerful in influence with the Reformed in France. Their numbers were large throughout the cities and villages of the Empire   LEFEVRE and FAREL were as father and son in ceaseless efforts to make known to these Gentiles " the unsearchable riches of Christ." Their evangelical preaching was signally blessed. BRICONNET, the Bishop of Meaux, aided them in translating the Evangelists and in heralding the word of God, and so rapidly and widely had their gospel been received, that " a Heretic of Meaux" became the popular title for an opponent of the Papacy. Notwithstanding the hideous spectacle and the odious MASSACRE of the 29th of January 1535, when Francis I. celebrated the Fête of Paris by the Martyrdom of the Saints of God, the Reformers were so numerous throughout the realm, that a serious conflict was approaching between themselves and their foes.   On the 25th of May 1559, a GENERAL SYNOD OF ALL PROTESTANT CONGREGATIONS was solemnly convened and held at Paris—the ecclesiastical system of their Patriarch at Geneva was adopted, and his "*Institution Chrétienne*" became the source and basis of their Confession of Faith. Paris was but the energizing centre of an organized Church throughout the Sixteen Provinces of the Realm, while Synods, and Consistories, and Conferences formed a kind of Spiritual Republic, spreading like network over the land. But the hand and the eye of the Persecutor was upon them. Rome had its despotic tyrants both in Court and Camp. In the very midst of the Parliament at Paris, a confessor of the true faith appeared—but his courage was extinguished by his condemnation. DUBOURG, a magistrate of eminent learning and illustrious family, in the presence of the King, in his place in Parliament, invoked a National Council for the Reform of Religion, and denounced the persecution of Heretics as a crime against Him whose holy name they were accustomed to adore with their dying breath.

He expiated his audacity by his death, and before the grave had been opened for him it had closed upon the Royal Tyrant, HENRY II., who bequeathed his crown to a second FRANCIS in his sixteenth year. And who knows not the crafty, treacherous, and intriguing wickedness of the Queen-mother, CATHERINE OF MEDICI? Who knows not the ambitious worldliness of the two sons of CLAUDE OF LORRAINE—Francis, the DUKE OF GUISE—the savage butcher of the HUGUENOTS of Champagne, and Charles, the CARDINAL LORRAINE, the subtle agent of Rome's most hateful policy? These artful brothers worked their way to supreme influence in the national councils. Having married their niece, MARY QUEEN OF SCOTS, to their youthful Sovereign, they employed their vast influence for the wholesale martyrdom of the defenceless flock of Christ. In every Parliament of the kingdom they established Chambers for trying and burning all persons charged with heresy, which obtained the unenviable notoriety of "*chambres ardentes.*" "But deep," says the eloquent Lecturer, "called unto deep." The alarmed and exasperated HUGUENOTS, confident in their strength and deriving courage from despair, rose in many parts of France to repel, or at least to punish their antagonists. In the midst of the anarchy of the times, a voice was raised in calm and earnest remonstrance, urging toleration and peace. In August 1560, the renowned Chancellor L'HÔPITAL appeared before the King and an assembly of notables at Fontainebleau. He presents a Petition from the whole Reformed Church of the realm, and requests the royal permission for the free performance of public worship. "Your Petition," says the King, "is without a signature!" "True, sire," replies COLIGNY, "but if you will allow us to meet for the purpose, I will obtain 50,000 signatures in one day in Normandy alone!" His zeal might occasion a slight exaggeration—but the phrase presents us with data for conjecturing the number of "the pious" whom our Reformer addressed about a year afterwards. As soon as opportunity was given for listening to the glad tidings of salvation, large accessions were made to the hosts of the believers. FAREL, though advanced in years, preached the truth to large and enthusiastic assemblages. In the neighbourhood of Paris, the followers of BEZA were numerous, and his admirers reckoned them at 40,000. L'HÔPITAL presented to the Queen-mother a list of 2150 Reformed Congregations, each under the ministry of a separate pastor, and he reckoned the number of the HUGUENOTS as one-third of that of the Romanists!

EDICT OF POISSY.

At the very moment when CALVIN was penning in his study the Letter which is prefixed to these LECTURES ON DANIEL, the Edict of July 1561 was issued. It bears the impress of the restored influence of the House of LORRAINE, which ever proved an implacable foe to the Gospel of Christ as preached by THE CALVINISTS. That Edict forbad their public assemblies, and yet tolerated their private and social worship. It protected them from injury on account of their opinions, and provided for a National Council which should, if possible, settle differences which were in their nature irreconcilable. This important enactment was issued in the Assembly at Poissy, held a few weeks after the date of the Letter which follows this Preface, and which has been alluded to in the Preface to EZEKIEL. CALVIN was absent, because the French Court refused to give those securities for his safety which the Republic of Geneva required. But he was ably represented by BEZA, and a dozen ministers, and twenty-two lay deputies of the Churches. The dramatic taste of the French mind was gratified by the scene, for the tournaments of belted knights had now given way to those of theological disputants. In the Refectory of the great Convent the boy King was seated on a temporary throne. The members of his family, the officers and ladies of his Court, were stationed on one side, six Cardinals, with an array of mitred Bishops, were assembled on the other. The rustic garb of BEZA and his associates, as they were introduced to their Sovereign by the Chancellor, contrasted strongly with the gorgeous apparel and the showy splendour of the Court and its attendants. The political CARDINAL OF LOR-

RAINE and the subtle General of the Jesuits, IAGO LASQUEZ, conducted the dispute against BEZA. The Doctors of the Sorbonne watched the sport with official keenness, while CATHERINE listened to the debate with secret contempt, having long ago determined to root out every Heretic as soon as she could throw the mantle of policy over her cruelty.

PARALLEL BETWEEN THE PROTESTANTS IN FRANCE AND THE JEWS IN BABYLON.

The matured Christian is now enabled to see at a glance, that such Conferences are, of necessity, worthless as to any progress of vital religion in the soul. The narrative, however, may enable the reader to enter a little into the state of the Christians in France when CALVIN indited his Prefatory Letter, and may justify the comparison which he makes between their lot, under the tyranny of such merciless rulers, and that of DANIEL under the sway of the imperious NEBUCHADNEZZAR, and at the tender mercy of his colleagues under DARIUS. The parallel is as complete as it could possibly be between the temporal position of the pious in FRANCE, and that of the devout Jews in BABYLON—and the graphic description of the Royal Professor of Modern History fully justifies the pastoral anxiety of the austere Theologian of Geneva.

ARRANGEMENT OF THE PRESENT WORK.

The CONTENTS of these Volumes are as follow:—

The FIRST VOLUME contains a translation of CALVIN's elaborate Address to All the Faithful in France; and also of his PREFACE to his LECTURES. Their translation is continued to the end of the Sixth Chapter, which closes the Historical portion of the Book. DISSERTATIONS explanatory of the subject-matter of the Commentary close the Volume, containing various historical, critical, and exegetical remarks, illustrating the Sacred Text as expounded by our Reformer. The chief of them are as follow, viz.:

CHAP. I. The Date of JEHOIAKIM'S Reign.
NEBUCHADNEZZAR—one King or two?
His Ancestors and Successors.
The CHALDEANS.
The Three Children.
CORESH—was he Cyrus the Great?

CHAP. II. The Dream.
The Image.
The Stone cut without hands.

CHAP. III. The Statue at DURA.
The Magistrates.
The Musical Instruments.
The SON OF GOD.

CHAP. IV. The Watcher.
The Madness.
The Edict of Praise.

CHAP. V. BELSHAZZAR and the feast.
The Queen.
The Handwriting.
The MEDES AND PERSIANS.
DARIUS the Mede.
The Capture of BABYLON.

CHAP. VI. The Three Presidents.
The King's Decease.
The Prolongation of DANIEL'S Life.

The SECOND VOLUME proceeds with the Translation of the remaining Chapters, which are the peculiarly Prophetic portion of the Book; and the interest which every sound Exposition of these Prophecies has always excited throughout the Theological world, will render the following ADDENDA acceptable to the reader.

I. DISSERTATIONS EXPLANATORY OF THE LAST SIX CHAPTERS OF DANIEL, fully elucidating all important questions.

II. A CONNECTED TRANSLATION OF CALVIN'S VERSION, illustrated by the peculiar words and phrases of his Commentary.

III. A SUMMARY OF THE HISTORICAL AND PROPHETIC POR-
TIONS OF THE BOOK, according to CALVIN'S view of
their contents.
IV. A NOTICE OF SOME ANCIENT CODEXES AND VERSIONS.
V. A LIST OF THE MOST VALUABLE ANCIENT AND MODERN
BRITISH AND FOREIGN EXPOSITIONS OF DANIEL,
with concise Epitomes of the contents of the most
important.
VI. AN INDEX OF THE SCRIPTURAL PASSAGES QUOTED IN THE
LECTURES.
VII. A COPIOUS INDEX OF THE CHIEF WORDS AND SUBJECTS
treated in these Volumes.

Before concluding these Prefatory Observations, THE
EDITOR would briefly refer to the fundamental rules of THE
CALVIN TRANSLATION SOCIETY, which very wisely exclude
all expressions of private opinion. He hopes that no remarks in this PREFACE will be deemed inconsistent with so
judicious a regulation. The clear illustration and the comprehensive defence of our Venerable Reformer seem to demand the candid statement of some views which are adverse
to the popular current; but this necessity need not induce
him to step beyond the limits of his province. It has
been his desire conscientiously to vindicate his Author's
Interpretations wherever he is able to do so, and as fearlessly to point out wherever CALVIN is allowed to be in
error; but in both cases, the EDITOR has scrupulously
avoided taking any one-sided view of a great argument.
He has attempted to exercise the utmost impartiality in
quoting from a great variety of Standard Works which contain the most opposite conclusions; and yet, in accordance
with the first principles of these Translations, he has at the
same time carefully abstained from pressing any sentiments
of his own on the attention of the intelligent reader.

T. M.

SHERIFF-HUTTON VICARAGE,
May 1852.

THE PRINTER WISHES HEALTH FROM THE LORD TO THE PIOUS READER.

HAIL to thee, Christian Reader!—I present to thee the LECTURES of the most illustrious JOHN CALVIN, in which he has interpreted THE PROPHECIES OF DANIEL, with his usual diligence and clearness, and with that singular fidelity which shines throughout all his Expositions of Sacred Scripture. The manner in which they have been edited by those two brethren, JOHN BUDÆUS and CHARLES JOINVILLE, it would be superfluous to dwell upon, since that has been clearly made manifest in the way in which the TWELVE MINOR PROPHETS were brought out two years ago by JOHN CRISPIN. For, in treating these Lectures, they have followed entirely the same course as they did in the former ones. Lest, perhaps, you should be surprised at the addition of the Hebrew context to the Latin version, I will explain the matter in a few words. Some studious and learned men very much wished to have the Hebrew text in the former Lectures which I mentioned, for the following reason chiefly, among others. It is exceedingly agreeable to Hebrew scholars to have that very fountain placed before their eyes from which this most faithful Interpreter drew the genuine sense of the Prophet. It is by no means unpleasing to those less skilled in the language, to see Daniel speaking not only in a foreign, but in his native tongue, and to understand how anything is originally expressed. Hence we have thought it right not to pass over the original words of the holy man. In addition to this, the same learned Interpreter, CALVIN, is accustomed first to read each verse in Hebrew, and then to turn it into Latin. It was desirable to introduce this short preface, that you may understand his whole method of teaching. Besides, every one will judge better by his own perusal, what copious and abundant fruit all may derive from these Lectures. Farewell, and if you profit at all, ascribe the praise to GOD alone, who deserves it, and always pray much for CALVIN, his most faithful servant.[1]

GENEVA, *August* 27*th,* 1561, A.D.

[1] This is the address of Bartholomew Vincent in his edition, A.D. 1571, which has the Hebrew and Latin texts printed together. It has been repeated in the edition at Geneva, 1591, with the omission of the clause "*ante biennium a Joanne Crispino;*" since, like the former, it contains the Hebrew and Chaldee text opposite the Latin, with a running Hebrew title.
In the collected edition of Calvin's works, Amsterdam, vol. v., a Dedication to that Volume occurs, dated 10mo Cal. Aug. 1563, which, although preceding Daniel, has no reference to his Prophecies, and is consequently omitted in this our work. It concerns the disputes of that period respecting the Lord's Supper, and certain heretical perversions of the truth then current.
The Address of the Printer to the Reader prefixed to the same volume, refers to Jeremiah, Lamentations, Twelve Minor Prophets, and Daniel generally; but as it contains nothing suitable to our purpose, it is of course omitted.

DEDICATORY EPISTLE.

JOHN CALVIN

TO ALL THE PIOUS WORSHIPPERS OF GOD WHO DESIRE THE KINGDOM OF CHRIST TO BE RIGHTLY CONSTITUTED IN FRANCE.

HEALTH.

ALTHOUGH I have been absent these six-and-twenty years, with little regret, from that native land which I own in common with yourselves, and whose agreeable climate attracts many foreigners from the most distant quarters of the world; yet it would be in no degree pleasing or desirable to me to dwell in a region from which the Truth of God, pure Religion, and the doctrine of eternal salvation are banished, and the very kingdom of Christ laid prostrate! Hence, I have no desire to return to it; yet it would be neither in accordance with human nor Divine obligation to forget the people from which I am sprung, and to put away all regard for their welfare. I think I have given some strong proofs, how seriously and ardently I desire to benefit my fellow-countrymen, to whom perhaps my absence has been useful, in enabling them to reap the greater profit from my studies. And the contemplation of this advantage has not only deprived my banishment of its sting, but has rendered it even pleasant and joyful.

Since, therefore, throughout the whole of this period I have publicly endeavoured to benefit THE INHABITANTS OF FRANCE, and have never ceased privately to rouse the torpid, to stimulate the sluggish, to animate the trembling, and to encourage the doubtful and the wavering to perseverance, I must now strive to the utmost that my duty towards them may not fail at a period so urgent and so pressing. A most excellent opportunity has been providentially afforded to me; for in publishing the LECTURES which contain my INTERPRETATION OF THE PROPHECIES OF DANIEL, I have the very best occasion of shewing you, beloved brethren, in this mirror, how God proves the faith of his people in these days by various trials; and how with wonderful wisdom he has taken care to strengthen their minds by ancient examples, that they should never be weakened by the concussion of the severest storms and tempests; or at least, if they should totter at all, that they should never finally fall away. For although the servants of God are required to run in a course impeded by many obstacles, yet whoever diligently reads this Book will find in it whatever is needed by a voluntary and active runner to guide him from the starting-post to the goal; while good and strenuous wrestlers will experimentally acknowledge that they have been sufficiently prepared for the contest.

First of all, a very mournful and yet profitable history will be recorded for us, in the exile of DANIEL and his companions while the kingdom and priesthood were still standing, as if God, through ignominy and shame, would devote the choicest flower of his elect people to extreme calamity. For what, at first sight, is more unbecoming, than that youths endued with almost angelic virtues should be the slaves and captives of a proud conqueror, when the most wicked and abandoned despisers of God remained at home in perfect safety? Was this the reward of a pious and innocent life, that, while the impious were sweetly flattering themselves through their escape from punishment, the saints should pay the penalty which they had deserved? Here, then, we observe, as in a living picture, that when God spares and even indulges the wicked for a time, he proves his servants like gold and silver; so that we ought not to consider it a grievance to be thrown into the furnace of trial, while profane men enjoy the calmness of repose.

Secondly, we have here an example of most manly prudence and of singular consistency, united with a magnanimity truly heroic. When pious youths of a tender age are tempted by the enticements of a Court, they not only overcome the temptations presented to them by their temperance, but perceive themselves cunningly enticed to depart by degrees from the sincere worship of God; and then, when they have extricated themselves from the snares of the devil, they boldly and freely despise all poison-stained honour, at the imminent risk of instant death. A more cruel and formidable contest will follow when the companions of DANIEL, as a memorable example of incredible constancy, are never turned aside by atrocious threats to pollute themselves by adoring the Image, and are at length prepared to vindicate the pure worship of God, not only with their blood, but in defiance of a horrible torture set before their eyes. Thus the goodness of God shines forth at the close of this tragedy, and tends in no slight degree to arm us with invincible confidence.

A similar contest and victory of DANIEL himself will be added ; when he preferred to be cast among savage lions, to desisting from the open profession of his faith three times a-day ; lest by perfidious dissembling he should prostitute the Sacred Name of God to the jests of the impious. Thus he was wonderfully drawn out of the pit which was all but his grave, and triumphed over Satan and his faction. Here philosophers do not come before us skilfully disputing about the virtues peacefully in the shade ; but the indefatigable constancy of holy men in the pursuit of piety, invites us with a loud voice to imitate them. Therefore, unless we are altogether unteachable, we ought to learn from these masters, if Satan lays the snares of flattery for us, to be prudent and cautious that we are not entangled in them ; and if he attacks us violently, to oppose all his assaults by a fearless contempt of death and of all evils. Should any one object, that the examples of either kind of deliverance which we have mentioned are rare, I confess indeed that God does not always stretch forth his hand from heaven in the same way to preserve his people ; but it ought to satisfy us that he has promised that he will be a faithful guardian of our life, as often as we are harassed by any trouble. We cannot be exposed to the power of the impious without his restraining their furious and turbulent plots against us, according to his pleasure. And we must not look at the results alone ; but observe how courageously holy men devoted themselves to death for the vindication of God's glory ; and although they were snatched away from it, yet their willing alacrity in offering themselves as victims is in no degree less deserving of praise.

It is also worth while to consider how variously the Prophet was tossed about and agitated during the Seventy years which he spent in exile. No King treated him so humanely as NEBUCHADNEZZAR, and yet he found him act like a wild beast. The cruelty of others was greater, until after the sudden death of BELSHAZZAR and the taking of the City, he was delivered up to its new masters, THE MEDES AND PERSIANS. Their hostile irruption struck terror into the minds of all, and there is no doubt that the Prophet partook of the general feeling. Although he was kindly received by DARIUS, so that his slavery was rendered tolerable, yet the envy of the nobles and their wicked conspiracy against him subjected him to the greatest dangers. But he was more anxious for the common safety of the Church than for his own personal security. He evidently suffered the greatest grief, and was distracted with the utmost anxiety, when the position of affairs discovered no limit to so severe and miserable an oppression of the people. He acquiesced indeed, in the Prophecy of JEREMIAH; still it was a proof of his incomparable forbearance that his hope, so long suspended, did not languish; nay, that when tossed hither and thither amidst tempestuous waves, it was not entirely drowned.

I come now to THE PROPHECIES themselves. The former part were uttered against THE BABYLONIANS; partly, because God wished to adorn his servants with sure testimonies, which might compel that most proud and victorious Nation to revere him; and partly, because His Name ought to be held in reverence with the profane. Thus he would exercise the prophetic gift among his own people more freely, through being endued with authority. After his name had become celebrated among THE CHALDEANS, God entrusted him with Prophecies of greater moment, which were peculiar to his elect people. Moreover, God so accommodated them to the use of his Ancient people, and they so soothed their sorrows by suitable remedies, and sustained their vacillating minds till THE ADVENT OF CHRIST—that they have no less value in our time; for whatever was predicted concerning the changing and vanishing splendour of these Monarchies, and the perpetual existence of Christ's Kingdom, is *in these days* no less useful to be known than formerly. For God shews how all earthly power which is not founded on Christ must fall; and he threatens speedy destruction to all Kingdoms which obscure Christ's glory by extending themselves too much. And those Kings whose sway is most extended shall feel by sorrowful experience how horrible a judgment will fall upon them, unless they willingly submit themselves to the sway of Christ! And what is less tolerable than to deprive Him of his right by whose protection their dignity remains safe? And we see how few of their number admit THE SON OF GOD; nay, how they turn every stone and try every possible scheme to prevent his entrance into their territories! Many of their Councillors studiously use their utmost endeavours and influence to close every avenue against him. For while they put forward the name of Christianity, and boast themselves to be the best defenders of the Catholic Faith, their frivolous vanity is easily refuted, if men hold the true and genuine definition of the Kingdom of Christ. For his throne or sceptre is nothing else but the doctrine of the Gospel. Nor does his Majesty shine elsewhere, nor his Empire otherwise exist, than when all, from the highest to the lowest, hear His voice with the calm docility of sheep, and follow wherever he calls them. These Kings not only completely reject this doctrine, which contains the substance of True Religion, and the lawful Worship of God, in which the eternal salvation of men and their true happiness consists; but they drive it far away from them by threats and terrors, by the sword and flame, nor do they omit any violence in their efforts to exterminate it. How great, how prodigious this blindness, when they cannot bear that those whom the only-begotten Son of God invites mercifully to himself should embrace him! But many in their own pride, forsooth, think themselves reduced to the common level, if they lower their ensigns of royalty to the Supreme King: others are unwilling to bridle their lusts, and since hypocrisy seizes on all their senses, they seek darkness, and dread to be dragged into light. No plague is worse than this fear, like Herod's! as if he who offers a celestial empire to the least and most despised of the people, would snatch away the kingdoms of the earth from its monarchs. In addition to this, when each regards the opinion of others, this mutual league retains them all bound in a distinctive bond under the yoke of impiety. For if they would seriously apply their minds to inquire what is true and right; nay, if they would only open their eyes, they could not fail to discover it.

Since it has often been found, by experience, that when Christ goes forth with his Gospel serious commotions arise, thus Kings have a plausible pretext for rejecting the heavenly doctrine by consulting for the public safety. I confess, indeed, that all change which occasions disturbance ought to be esteemed odious; but the injustice to God is great, unless this also is attributed to his *power*, that whatever tumults arise he allays them, and thus the kingdom of his Son is established! Although the heavens should mingle with the earth, the worship of God is so precious, that not even the least diminution of it can be compensated at any price. But those who pretend that the Gospel is the source of disturbances, accuse it falsely and unjustly. (Hag. ii. 7.) It is indeed true, that God thunders therein with the vehemence of His voice, which shakes heaven and earth; but while the Prophet gains attention to its preaching by this testimony, such concussion is to be wished for and expected. And, surely, if God's glory did not shine forth in its own degree, until all flesh was humbled, it would be necessary that man's pride should be humbled by the bold and strong hand of

God; since that pride raises itself against him, and never yields of its own accord. But if the earth trembled at the promulgation of the Law, (Exod. xix. 18,) it is not surprising that the force and efficacy of the Gospel should appear more resplendent. Wherefore, it becomes us to embrace that consoling doctrine which raises the dead from the grave, and opens heaven, and implants unaccustomed vigour in those whom the earth is unworthy to sustain, as if all the elements were subservient to our salvation.

But, lo! storms and tempests now flow from another fountain! Because the Rulers and Governors of the world do not willingly submit to the yoke of Christ, now even the rude multitude reject what is salutary before they even taste it. Some delight themselves in filth, like pigs, and others excited by fury rejoice in slaughter. The devil instigates by especial fury those whom he has enslaved to himself to tumults of all sorts. Hence the clash of trumpets; hence conflicts and battles. Meanwhile, THE ROMAN PRIEST—a Heliogabalus—with his red and sanguinary cohorts and horned beasts,[1] rages with a hasty rush against Christ, and fetches from every side his allies from the filth of his foul Clergy,[2] all of whom sup the food on which they subsist from the same pot, though it be not equally dainty. Many hungry fellows also run up to offer their assistance. Most of the Judges are accustomed to gratify their appetites at these sumptuous banquets, and to fight for the kitchen and the kettle! and besides this, the haunts of the Monks,[3] and the dens of the Sorbonne,[4] send forth their gluttons who add fuel to the flame. I omit the clandestine arts and wicked conspiracies of which my best witnesses are these notorious enemies to piety! I mention no one by name: it is enough to point with the finger to those who are too well known to you. In this confused assault of wild beasts, it is not surprising if those who depend only on the complicated events of things hesitate through perplexity, while they unjustly and unfairly throw the blame of their distrust upon the Sacred Gospel of Christ. Let us suppose that all the infernal regions with their furies should offer us battle, will God sit at ease in heaven, and desert and betray his own cause? and when he has entered into the conflict, will either the crafty, cunning, or the impetuous rush of men deprive Him of his victory?

THE POPE, they say, will draw with him a large faction—it is the just reward of unbelief to tremble at the sound of a falling leaf!

---

[1] The Cardinals and Bishops. [2] The Romish priesthood.
[3] The monasteries. [4] The Sorbonne was a Popish seminary

(Lev. xxvi. 36.) Why, O ye counsellors, have ye so little foresight? Christ will take care that no novelty shall disturb you. In a short time ye will feel how far more satisfactory it is to have God propitious, to despise terrors as of no moment, and to rest in His protection, than to harass Him by open warfare, through fear of the wrath of the evil and the hypocritical. In truth, after all these discussions, the superstition which has hitherto reigned is with the defenders of the Pope, nothing else but well-placed evil,[1] and they think it cannot be removed, because the attempt would occasion irreparable damage. But those who regard the glory of God, and are endued with sincere piety, ought to have far higher objects in view, and so to submit themselves to the will of God as to approve of all the events of his providence. If he had not promised us anything, there might be just cause for fear and constant vacillation; but since he has so often declared, that his help shall never be wanting in upholding the kingdom of his Christ, the reliance on this promise is the one sole basis of right action.

Hence it is your duty, dearest brethren, as far as lies in your power, and your calling demands it, to use your hearty endeavours, that true religion may recover its perfect state. It is not necessary for me to relate how strenuously I have hitherto endeavoured to cut off all occasion for tumult; yea, I call you all with the angels to witness before the Supreme Judge of all men, that it is no fault of mine if the kingdom of Christ does not progress quietly without any injury. And I think it is owing to my carefulness that private persons have not transgressed beyond their bounds. Now, although God by his wonderful skill has carried forward the restoration of his Church further than I had dared to hope for, yet it is well to remember what Christ taught his disciples, namely, that they should possess their souls in patience. (Luke xxi. 19.)

This is one object of the Vision which DANIEL has explained. The Stone by which those kingdoms were destroyed, which had made war on God, was not formed by the hand of man: and although it was rude and unpolished, yet it increased to a great mountain. I thought that ye required reminding of this, that ye may remain calm amidst the threatening thunders, while the empty clouds vanish away through being dispersed by heavenly agency.

---

[1] Latine, "*malum bene positum:*" the French translation takes the phrase as a proverb—"*comme dit le proverb, un mal qui est bien en repos.*" Anglice, "well-poised."

It does not escape me, while I pass by the numberless fires of thirty years, that ye have endured very great indignities during the last six months. How often in many places an irruption was made against you by a ferocious populace, and how often ye were attacked at one time by stones, and at another by swords! How your enemies plotted against you, and repressed your peaceful assemblies by sudden and unlooked for violence! How some were slain in their dwellings, and others by the wayside, while the bodies of your dead were dragged about as a laughing-stock, your women ravished, and many of your party wounded, and even the pregnant female with her offspring pierced through, and their homes ransacked and made desolate. But, although more atrocious things should be yet at hand, that ye may be approved as Christ's disciples, and be wisely instructed in his school, you must use every effort, that no madness of the impious who act thus intemperately, should deprive you of that moderation by which alone they have thus far been conquered and broken down. And if the length of your affliction should cause you weariness, bear in mind that celebrated prophecy in which the Church's condition is depicted to the life. God therein shews his Prophet what contests and anxieties, troubles and difficulties, awaited the Jews from the close of their exile, and from their joyful return to their country, until the advent of Christ.

The similarity of the times adapts these predictions to ourselves, and fits them for our own use. DANIEL congratulated the wretched Church which had so long been submerged in a deluge of evils, when he collected from the computation of the years, that the day of deliverance predicted by Jeremiah was at hand. (Jer. xxv. 12, and xxix. 10.) But he receives for an answer, that the lot of the people from the time of their permission to return would be more bitter, so that they would scarcely breathe again under a continual series of oppressive evils. With the bitterest grief, and with many sorrows, the people had dragged on in hope for seventy years, but now God increases the period sevenfold, and inwardly inflicts a deadly wound on their heart. He not only pronounces that the people, after their return home, should collect their strength and build their city and temple, and then suffer new anxieties, but he predicts fresh troubles amidst the very commencement of their joy, whilst they had scarcely tasted the sweetness of grace. Then with regard to the calamities which shortly followed, the multiform catalogue here presented affrights us even who have only heard of them: then how bitter and how distressing were they to that rude nation! To see the temple profaned by the audacity of a sacrilegious tyrant, its sacred rites shamefully mingled with foul pollutions, all the books of the law cast into the fire, and the whole of the ceremonies abolished,—how horrible the spectacle! Since all who professed to persist boldly and constantly in the worship of God were seized and subjected to the same burning, how could the tender and weak behold this without the greatest consternation! Yet this was the tyrant's plan, that the cruelty might excite the less earnest to deny their faith. Under the Maccabees, some relaxation seems to have taken place, but yet such as is soon deformed by the most cruel slaughters, and was never without its share of lamentation and wo. For since the enemy far excelled them in forces and in every equipment for war, nothing was left for those who had taken up arms for the defence of the Church but to hide themselves in the dens of wild beasts, or to wander through the woods in the greatest distress, and in utter destitution. Another source of temptation was added, since impious and abandoned men, in the boasting of a fallacious zeal, as DANIEL says, joined the party of Judas and his brethren, by which artifice of Satan infamy became attached to the band which Judas had collected, as if it had been a band of robbers. (Chap. xi. 34.)

But nothing was a source of greater sorrow to the righteous, than to find the priests themselves betraying the temple and worship of God, by wicked compacts according to the prompting of their interested ambition. For not only was that sacred dignity both bought and sold, but it was purchased by mutual murders and parricides. Hence it happened, that men of all ranks grew more and more profane, and corruptions multiplied everywhere with impunity, although circumcision and the sacrifices still remained in use, so that the expectation of the kingdom of God, when Christ appeared, was a strange and unheard of marvel. Very few, indeed, are entitled to even this praise. If then, in that unworthy deformity of the Church, if in the midst of its many dispersions and its dreadful terrors, of the devastation of the lands, the destruction of the dwellings, and the consequent dangers to life itself, this prophecy of DANIEL sustained the spirit of the pious, when the religious ceremonies were involved in obscure shadows, and doctrine was almost extinct, when the priests were most degenerate, and all sacred ordinances abolished,—how ashamed should we be of our cowardice, if the clearness of the Gospel, in which God shews to us his paternal face, does not raise us above all obstacles, and prop us up with unwearied constancy?

There is no doubt that the servants of God accommodated to

their own times the predictions of this Prophet concerning the exile at Babylon, and thus lightened the pressure of present calamities. Thus, also, we ought to have our eyes fixed on the miseries of the Fathers, that we may not object to be joined with the body of that Church to which it was said, " O, thou little flock, borne down by the tempest and deprived of comfort, behold, I take thee up." (Isaiah liv. 11.) And, again, after she has complained that her back had been torn by the ungodly, like a field cut up by the course of the furrows, yet she boasts immediately afterwards, that their cords were cut away by a just God, so that they did not prevail against her. (Psalm cxxix. 1-4.) The Prophet, then, not only animates us to hope and patience, by the example of those times, but adds an exhortation dictated by the Spirit, which extends to the whole reign of Christ, and is applicable to us. Wherefore it is no hardship to us to be comprehended in the number of those whom he announces shall be proved and purified by fire, since the inestimable happiness and glory which springs from this process more than compensates for all its crosses and distresses. And although these things are insipid to the majority, lest their sloth and stupidity should render us too sluggish, we should fix deeply in our hearts the denunciation of the Prophets, namely, that the ungodly will act impiously, since they understand nothing; while the sons of God will be endued with wisdom to hold on the course of their divine calling. It is worth while, then, to perceive the origin of that gross blindness which is commonly observed, so that the heavenly doctrine may make us wise. Hence, it too often happens that the multitude revile Christ and his Gospel; they indulge themselves without either care, or fear, or any perception of their dangers, and they are not aroused by God's wrath to an ardent and serious desire for that redemption which alone snatches us from the abyss of eternal destruction. In the meantime they are caught or rather fascinated by luxuries, pleasures, and other enticements, and pay no regard to the prospect of a happy eternity. Although there are many sects who contemptuously despise the teaching of the Gospel, some are remarkable for pride, others for imbecility, some for want of sobriety of mind, and others for a sleepy torpidity, yet we shall find that contempt flows from profane security, since no one descends into himself to shake off his own miseries, by finding a remedy for them. Yet, when God's curse rests upon us, and his just vengeance urges us, it is the height of madness to cast aside all anxiety, and to please ourselves as if we need fear nothing. Yet it is a very common fault for those who are guilty of a thousand sins, and deserve a thousand eternal deaths, to discharge with levity a few frivolous ceremonies towards God, and then give themselves up to sloth and lethargy. Moreover, Paul denounces the savour of the Gospel (1 Cor. ii. 16) to be deadly towards all whose minds are fascinated by Satan ; so that to taste of its life-giving savour, it is necessary for us to stand at God's tribunal, and there also to cite our own consciences when wounded with serious terror.

Thus, we esteem, according to its proper worth and value, that reconciliation which Christ procured for us by his precious blood. Thus, the angel, that he might acquire reverence and respect for Christ's authority, brings a message concerning eternal justice which he sealed by the sacrifice of his death, and expresses the mode and plan by which iniquity was abolished and expiated. Thus, while the world revels in its lusts, let the knowledge of the condemnation which we have deserved inspire us with fear, and humble us before God : and while the profane involve themselves in the whirl of earthly gratifications, let us eagerly embrace this incomparable treasure, in which solid blessedness is laid up. Let our enemies jeer as they please, every man ought to take care to have God propitious to him, and it is clear that the very foundation of the faith is overthrown by those who think he is to be doubtfully invoked. Let them deride our faith with as much petulance as they please, but let us be sure of this, that no one obtains this privilege except by God's good gift, for men can only call God " Father" by relying on the advocacy of Christ, through a free and peaceful confidence. But the pursuit of piety will never flourish in us as it ought, until we learn to raise our minds upwards, since they are too inclined to grovel upon earth, and we should exercise them in continual meditation upon the heavenly life. And in this respect, the surprising vanity of the human race manifests itself, since though all speak eloquently, like philosophers, on the shortness of life, yet no one aspires to that perpetual existence. So that when Paul commends the faith and charity of the Colossians, he very truly says, that they were animated by a hope laid up in the heavens. (Col. i. 5.) And when discussing elsewhere the results of the grace which is open to us in Christ, he says—we must be so built up therein, that all impiety and worldly desires must be mortified, and we must live soberly, justly, and piously in this world, and wait for the blessed hope, and glorious advent of the great God and our Saviour Jesus Christ. (Tit. ii. 12, 13.)

Let, then, this expectation free us from all hinderances, and draw us towards itself, and though the world is steeped in more than epicurean pollution, lest the contagion should reach us, we ought to strive the more earnestly until we arrive at the goal. Although it is truly a matter of grief, that so great a multitude should wilfully perish, and rush devotedly on their own destruction, yet their foolish fury need not disturb us; for another admonition of DANIEL should succour us, namely, that certain salvation is laid up for all who have been found written in the book. But although our election is hidden in God's secret counsel, which is the prime cause of our salvation, yet, since the adoption of all who are inserted into the body of Christ, by faith in the gospel, is by no means doubtful, be ye content with this testimony, and persevere in the course which ye have happily begun. But if ye must contend still longer, (and I announce, that contests more severe than ye contemplate yet remain for you,) by whatsoever attack the madness of the impious bursts forth, as if it stirred up the regions below, remember that your course has been defined by a heavenly Master of the contest, whose laws ye must obey the more cheerfully, since he will supply you with strength unto the end.

Since, then, it is not lawful for me to desert the station to which God has appointed me, I have DEDICATED to you this my labour, as a pledge of my desire to help you, until at the completion of my pilgrimage our heavenly Father, of his immeasurable pity, shall gather me together with you, to his eternal inheritance.

May the LORD govern you by His Spirit, may He defend my most beloved brethren by His own protection, against all the plots of their enemies, and sustain them by his invisible power.

JOHN CALVIN.

GENEVA, *August* 19, 1561.

THE PRAYER

WHICH JOHN CALVIN WAS ACCUSTOMED TO USE AT THE COMMENCEMENT OF HIS LECTURES.

GRANT unto us, O LORD, to be occupied in the mysteries of thy Heavenly wisdom, with true progress in piety, to thy glory and our own edification.—AMEN.

⁎ This prayer is not inserted in the Geneva edition of 1617, but is found in that of 1571. The FRENCH TRANSLATION renders it as follows:—
" May the Lord grant us grace so to treat the secrets of His celestial wisdom, that we may truly profit in the fear of His holy name, to His glory and to our edification. Amen."

COMMENTARIES

ON

THE PROPHET DANIEL.

JOHN CALVIN'S PREFACE
TO HIS LECTURES ON DANIEL.

Lecture First.

THE BOOK OF THE PROPHET DANIEL follows these Remarks, and its utility will be better understood as we proceed; since it cannot be conveniently explained all at once. I will, however, just present the Reader with a foretaste to prepare his mind, and render him attentive. But before I do so, I must make a brief SUMMARY OF THE BOOK. We may divide the Book into two parts, and this partition will materially help us. For DANIEL relates how he acquired influence over the unbelieving. It was necessary for him to be elevated to the prophetic office in some singular and unusual manner. The condition of the Jews, as is well known, was so confused, that it was difficult for any one to determine whether any Prophet existed. At first JEREMIAH was alive, and after him EZEKIEL. After their return, the Jews had their own Prophets: but Jeremiah and Ezekiel had almost fulfilled their office, when DANIEL succeeded them. Others too, as we have already seen, as HAGGAI, MALACHI, and ZECHARIAH, were created Prophets for the purpose of exhorting the people, and hence their duties were partially restricted. But DANIEL would scarcely have been considered a Prophet, had not God, as we have said, appointed him in a remarkable way. We shall perceive at the close of the sixth chapter, that he was divinely endued with remarkable signs, so that the Jews might surely ascertain that he had the gift of prophecy, unless they were basely ungrateful to God. His name was known and respected by the inhabitants of Babylon. If the Jews had despised what even the profane Gentiles admired, was not this purposely to suffocate and trample on the grace of God? DANIEL, then, had sure and striking marks by which he could be recognised as God's Prophet, and his calling be rendered unquestionable.

A Second Part is afterwards added, in which God predicts by his agency the events which were to occur to his elect people. The Visions, then, from the seventh chapter to the end of the Book, relate peculiarly to the Church of God. There God predicts what should happen hereafter. And that admonition is the more necessary, since the trial was severe, when the Jews had to bear an exile of seventy years; but after their return to their country, instead of seventy years, God protracted their full deliverance till seventy weeks of years. So the delay was increased sevenfold. Their spirits might be broken a thousand times, or even utterly fail; for the Prophets speak so magnificently about their redemption, that the Jews expected their state to be especially happy and prosperous, as soon as they were snatched from the Babylonish Captivity. But since they were oppressed with so many afflictions, and that, too, not for a short period, but for more than four hundred years, their redemption might seem illusory since they were but seventy years in exile. There is no doubt, then, that Satan seduced the minds of many to revolt, as if God were mocking them by bringing them out of Chaldea back again to their own country. For these reasons God shews his servant in a Vision what numerous and severe afflictions awaited his elect people. Besides, DANIEL so prophesies that he describes almost historically events previously hidden. And this was necessary, since in such turbulent convulsions the people would never have tasted that these had been divinely revealed to DANIEL, unless the heavenly testimony had been proved by the event. This holy man ought so to speak and to prophesy concerning futurity, as if he were relating what had already happened. But we shall see all these things in their own order.

I return, then, to what I commenced with, that we may see in few words how useful this Book is to the Church of Christ. First of all, the matter itself shews how DANIEL did not speak from his own discretion, but whatever he uttered was dictated by the Holy Spirit: for whence could he conceive the things which we shall afterwards behold, if he were only endued with human prudence? for instance, that other Monarchies should arise to blot out that Babylonian Empire which then had the greatest authority in all the world? Then, again, how could he divine concerning Alexander the Great and his Successors? for long before Alexander was born, DANIEL predicted what he should accomplish. Then he shews that his kingdom should not last, since it is directly divided into four horns. Other events also clearly demonstrate that he spoke by the dictation of the Holy Spirit. But our confidence in this is strengthened by other narratives, where he represents the various miseries to which the Church should be subject between two most cruel enemies, the kings of Syria and Egypt. He first recites their treaties, and then their hostile incursions on both sides, and afterwards so many changes, as if he pointed at the things themselves with his finger; and he so follows through their whole progress, that God appears to speak by his mouth. This then, is a great step, and we shall not repent of taking it, when we acknowledge DANIEL to have been only the organ of the Holy Spirit, and never to have brought anything forward by his own private inclination. The authority, too, which he obtained, and which inspired the Jews with perfect confidence in his teaching, extends to us also. Shameful, indeed, and base would be our ingratitude, if we did not embrace him as God's Prophet, whom the Chaldeans were compelled to honour—a people whom we know to have been superstitious and full of pride. These two nations, the Egyptians and Chaldeans, placed themselves before all others; for the Chaldeans thought wisdom's only dwelling-place was with themselves: hence they would never have been inclined to receive DANIEL, unless the reality had compelled them, and the confession of his being a true prophet of God had been extorted from them.

Since DANIEL's authority is thus established, we must now say a few words about the subjects which he treats. Respecting THE INTERPRETATION OF THE DREAMS, the first of those of Nebuchadnezzar embraces a matter of great importance, as we shall see, namely, how all the splendour and power of the world vanish away, Christ's kingdom alone remaining stable, and that nothing else is self-enduring. In the Second Dream of Nebuchadnezzar, DANIEL's admirable constancy is displayed. Very invidious, indeed, was the office of throwing down the mightiest Monarch of the whole world as he did : "Thou exceptest thyself from the number of men, and art worshipped like a god ; thou shalt hereafter become a beast!" No man of these days would dare thus to address Monarchs ; nay, who dares to admonish them even mildly, if they have sinned at all ? When, therefore, DANIEL intrepidly predicted to King Nebuchadnezzar the disgrace which awaited him, he thus gave a rare and memorable proof of his constancy. And in this way, again, his calling was sealed, since this fortitude sprang from God's Spirit.

But the Second Part is peculiarly worthy of notice, since we there perceive how God cares for his Church. God's providence is, indeed, extended to the whole world. For if a sparrow does not fall to the ground without his permission, he, doubtless, is mindful of the human race ! (Matt. x., and Luke xii.) Nothing, therefore, happens to us by chance, but God in this Book affords us light, while we know his Church to be so governed by him, as to be the object of his peculiar care. If matters ever were so disturbed in the world, that one could suppose God to be asleep in heaven, and to be forgetful of the human race, surely such were the changes of those times, nay, so multiform, so extensive, and so various were they, that even the most daring must be confounded, since there was no end to the wars. Egypt prevailed at one time, while at another there were commotions in Syria. Seeing, then, all things turned up-side down, what judgment could be passed, except that God neglected the world, and the Jews were miserably deceived in their hope? They thought that as God had been their deliverer, so would he have been the perpetual guardian of their safety. Although all nations were then subject in common to various slaughters, yet if the Syrians were victorious over the Egyptians, they abused their power against the Jews, and Jerusalem lay exposed as their prey, and the reward of their victory: if, again, the opposite side were the conquerors, they revenged the injury, or sought compensation against the Jews. Thus on every side those miserable people were fleeced, and their condition was much worse after their return to their country, than if they had always been exiles or strangers in other regions. When, therefore, they were admonished concerning the future, this was the best prop on which they could repose. But the use of the same doctrine is at this day applicable to us. We perceive, as in a glass or picture, how God was anxious about his Church, even when he seemed to cast away all regard for it: hence when the Jews were exposed to the injuries of their enemies, it was but the accomplishment of his designs.

From the Second Part we recognise their wonderful preservation, and that too, by a greater and more surprising exercise of God's power, than if they had lived in peace, and no one had molested them. We learn this from the seventh to the ninth chapters. Now, when DANIEL numbers the years till THE ADVENT of CHRIST, how clear and distinct is the testimony which we may oppose against Satan, and all the taunts of the impious! and how certain it is that the Book of DANIEL was familiarly used by men before this event. But when he enumerates THE SEVENTY WEEKS, and says, that Christ should then come, all profane men may come, and boast, and swell with increased swaggering, yet they shall fall down convicted, since Christ is that true Redeemer whom God had promised from the beginning of the world. For He was unwilling to make him known without the most certain demonstration, such as all the mathematicians can never equal. First of all, it is worthy of observation, that DANIEL afterwards discoursed on the various calamities of the Church, and prophesied the time at which God pleased to shew his only-begotten Son to the world. His dissertation on the office of Christ is one of the principal supports of our faith. For he not only describes his Advent, but announces the abolition of the shadows of the Law, since the Messiah would bring with him its complete fulfilment. And when he predicts the Death of Christ, he shews for what purpose he should undergo death, namely, to abolish Sin by his sacrifice, and to bring in Eternal Righteousness. Lastly, this also must be noticed,—as he had instructed the people to bear their cross, so also he warns them that the Church's state would not be tranquil even when the Messiah came. The sons of God should be militant until the end, and not hope for any fruit of their victory until the dead should rise again, and Christ himself should collect us into his own Celestial Kingdom. Now, we comprehend in few words, or rather only taste how useful and fruitful this Book is to us.

I now come to the words themselves: I wished, as I said, just to catch a foretaste of a few things, and the reading of the Book will shew us better what advantage we may derive from each of its chapters.

CHAPTER FIRST.

1. In the third year of the reign of Jehoiakim king of Judah came Nebuchadnezzar king of Babylon unto Jerusalem, and besieged it.
2. And the Lord gave Jehoiakim king of Judah into his hand, with part of the vessels of the house of God, which he carried into the land of Shinar, to the house of his god; and he brought the vessels into the treasure-house of his God.

1. Anno tertio regni Jehoiakim regis Jehudah venit Nebuchadnezzar rex Jerosolyma Babylonis, et obsedit eam.
2. Et tradidit Deus in manum regis Jehoiakim Regem Jehuda, et partem vasorum domus Dei, et traduxit ea[1] in terram Sinear in domum dei sui[2] quod vasa posuerit in domo thesauri dei sui.

These are not two different things, but the Prophet ex-

[1] Or *eos*. Either may be read; for the Hebrews do not use the neuter gender; yet I had rather use the neuter gender, on account of what follows. —*Calvin*.
[2] This would not suit either the king or the captives: hence the Prophet seems to speak of "vessels;" and a repetition of the same sentence afterwards follows.—*Calvin*.

plains and confirms the same sentiments by a change of phrase, and says that the vessels which Nebuchadnezzar had brought into the land of Sinaar were laid up in the house of the treasury. The Hebrews, as we know, generally use the word "house" for any place, as they call the temple God's "house." Of the land of Sinaar, it must be remarked, that it was a plain adjacent to Babylon; and the famous temple of Belus, to which the Prophet very probably refers, was erected there.

Here Daniel marks the time in which he was led into captivity together with his companions, namely, in the third year of Jehoiakim. A difficult question arises here, since Nebuchadnezzar began to reign in the fourth year of Jehoiakim. How then could he have besieged Jerusalem in the third year, and then led away the people captives according to his pleasure? Some interpreters solve this difficulty by what appears to me a frivolous conjecture, that the four years ought to refer to the beginning of his reign, and so the time may be brought within the third year. But in the second chapter we shall see Daniel brought before the king in the second year of his reign. They explain this difficulty also by another solution. They say —the years are not reckoned from the beginning of the reign, and,—this was the second year from the Conquest of the Jews and the taking of Jerusalem; but this is too harsh and forced. The most probable conjecture seems to me, that the Prophet is speaking of the first King Nebuchadnezzar, or at least uses the reign of the second, while his father was yet alive. We know there were two kings of the same name, father and son; and as the son did many noble and illustrious actions, he acquired the surname of Great. Whatever, therefore, we shall afterwards meet with concerning Nebuchadnezzar, cannot be understood except of the second, who is the son. But Josephus says the son was sent by his father against the Egyptians and the Jews: and this was the cause of the war, since the Egyptians often urged the Jews to a change of affairs, and enticed them to throw off the yoke. Nebuchadnezzar the younger was carrying on the war in Egypt at the death of his father, and

speedily returned home, lest any one should supersede him.
When, however, he found all things as he wished, Josephus
thinks he put off that expedition, and went to Jerusalem.
There is nothing strange, nay, it is very customary to call
him King who shares the command with his father. Thus,
therefore, I interpret it : In the third year of the reign of
Jehoiakim, Nebuchadnezzar came, under the command and
direction of his father, or if any one prefers it, the father
himself came. For there is nothing out of place, whether
we refer it to the father or to the son. *Nebuchadnezzar*, then,
king of Babylon, came to Jerusalem, that is, by the hand
of his son besieged Jerusalem. But if a different explanation is preferred, since he was there himself and carried on
the war in person, that view may be taken : still, the events
happened in the third year of Jehoiakim's reign. Interpreters make many mistakes in this matter. Josephus, indeed,
says this was done in the eighth year, but he had never
read the Book of Daniel.[1] He was an unlearned man,
and by no means familiar with the Scriptures ; nay, I think
he had never read three verses of Daniel. It was a
dreadful judgment of God for a priest to be so ignorant a
man as Josephus. But in another passage on which I
have commented, he seems to have followed Metasthenes and
others whom he cites, when speaking of the destruction of
that monarchy. And this seems to suit well enough, since
in the third year of the reign of Jehoiakim the city was once
taken, and some of the nobles of the royal race were led
away in triumph, among whom were Daniel and his companions. When Jehoiakim afterwards rebelled, his treatment was far more severe, as Jeremiah had predicted. But
while Jehoiakim possessed the kingdom by permission of
King Nebuchadnezzar, Daniel was already a captive, so that
Jeremiah's prediction was fulfilled—the condition of the
figs prematurely ripe was improved ; for those who were

---

[1] Calvin's expression is *tam brutus homo* in Latin, and *si stupide et
brutal* in French ; but he is evidently too severe on so valuable an annal-
ist, who, in so many passages, confirms and elucidates the scriptural narrative. Besides, Calvin seems to have overlooked the passage in his Antiq.,
lib. xi. cap. 8, § 5, where this Book is mentioned, and its contents alluded
to at length.

led into exile last thought themselves better off than the rest. But the Prophet deprives them of their vain boast, and shews the former captives to have been better treated than the remnant of the people who as yet remained safe at home. (Jer. xxiv. 2, 8.) I assume, then, that Daniel was among the first fruits of the captivity; and this is an instance of God's judgments being so incomprehensible by us. For had there been any integrity in the whole people, surely Daniel was a remarkable example of it: for EZEKIEL includes him among the three just men by whom most probably God would be appeased. (Chap. xiv. 14.) Such, then, was the excellence of Daniel's virtues, that he was like a celestial angel among mortals; and yet he was led into exile, and lived as the slave of the king of Babylon. Others, again, who had provoked God's wrath in so many ways, remained quiet in their nests: the Lord did not deprive them of their country and of that inheritance which was a sign and pledge of their adoption.[1]

Should any wish here to determine why DANIEL was among the first to be led into captivity, will he not betray his folly? Hence, let us learn to admire God's judgments, which surpass all our perceptions; and let us also remember the words of Christ, "If these things are done in the green tree, what will be done in the dry?" (Luke xxiii. 31.) As I have already said, there was an angelic holiness in Daniel, although so ignominiously exiled and brought up among the king's eunuchs. When this happened to so holy a man, who from his childhood was entirely devoted to piety, how great is God's indulgence in sparing us? What have we deserved? Which of us will dare to compare himself with Daniel? Nay, we are unworthy, according to the ancient proverb, to loosen the tie of his shoes. Without the slightest doubt Daniel, through the circumstances of the time,

---

[1] Much light has been thrown upon the chronology of these times since the age of Calvin: later Commentators have dated from the third year of Jehoiakim's restoration to his kingdom after his rebellion. See 2 Kings xxiv. 2, 3. The subject is discussed with clearness by Bleek in his Theolog. Zeitschrift. Pt. iii p. 280, &c.; and R. Sal. Jarchi on this passage may be consulted, p. 735, edit. Gothæ, 1713. See DISSERTATION I. at the end of this Volume.

wished to manifest the singular and extraordinary gift of God, since this trial did not oppress his mind and could not turn him aside from the right course of piety. When, therefore, Daniel saw himself put forward as an example of integrity, he did not desist from the pure worship of God. As to his assertion that Jehoiakim was delivered into the hand of King Nebuchadnezzar by God's command, this form of speech takes away any stumblingblock which might occur to the minds of the pious. Had Nebuchadnezzar been altogether superior, God himself might seem to have ceased to exist, and so his glory would have been depressed. But Daniel clearly asserts that King Nebuchadnezzar did not possess Jerusalem, and was not the conqueror of the nation by his own valour, or counsel, or fortune, or good luck, but because God wished to humble his people. Therefore, Daniel here sets before us the providence and judgments of God, that we may not think Jerusalem to have been taken in violation of God's promise to Abraham and his posterity. He also speaks by name of the vessels of the temple. Now, this might seem altogether out of place, and would shock the minds of the faithful. For what does it mean? That God's temple was spoiled by a wicked and impious man. Had not God borne witness that his rest was there? This shall be my rest for ever: here will I dwell because I have chosen it. (Ps. cxxxii. 14.) If any place in the world were impregnable, here truly honour ought to remain entire and untainted in the temple of God. When, therefore, it was robbed and its sacred vessels profaned, and when an impious king had also transferred to the temple of his own god what had been dedicated to the living God, would not, as I have said, such a trial as this cast down the minds of the holy? No one was surely so stout-hearted whom that unexpected trial would not oppress. Where is God, if he does not defend his own temple? Although he does not dwell in this world, and is not enclosed in walls of either wood or stone, yet he chose this dwelling-place for himself, (Ps. lxxx. 1, and xcix. 1, and Isa. xxxvii. 16,) and often by means of his Prophets asserted his seat to be between the Cherubim. What then is the meaning of this? As I have already said, Daniel recalls us to the judgment of God, and by a single word assures us that we ought not to be surprised at God inflicting such severe punishments upon impious and wicked apostates. For under the name of God, there is a silent antithesis; as the Lord did not deliver Jehoiakim into the hand of the Babylonians without just reason: *God*, therefore, exposed him as a prey that he might punish him for the revolt of his impious people. It now follows:—

3. And the king spake unto Ashpenaz, the master of his eunuchs, that he should bring *certain* of the children of Israel, and of the king's seed and of the princes.

3. Et mandavit[1] Rex Aspenazo[2] principi eunuchorum, ut eduzeret e filiis Israel et ex semine regio, et ex principibus.[3]

Here Daniel pursues his narrative, and shews the manner in which he was led away together with his companions. The king had demanded young men to be brought, not from the ordinary multitude, but from the principal nobility, who stood before him, that is, ministered to him. Hence, we ascertain why Daniel and his companions were chosen, because they were noble young men and of the royal seed, or at least of parents who surpassed others in rank. The king did this purposely to shew himself a conqueror; he may also have taken this plan designedly, to retain hostages in his power; for he hoped, as we shall see, that those who were nourished in his palace would be degenerate and hostile to the Jews, and he thought their assistance would prove useful to himself. He also hoped, since they were born of a noble stock, that the Jews would be the more peaceable, and thus avoid all danger to those wretched exiles who were relations of the kings and the nobles. With regard to the words, he calls this *Aspenaz* the prince of eunuchs, under which name he means the boys who were nourished in the king's palace to become a seminary of nobles; for it is scarcely possible that this Aspenaz was set over other leaders. But we gather from this place, that the boys

[1] Or, declared.—*Calvin*.
[2] Or, said to Aspenaz, as those who retain the Hebrew phrase translate it.— *Calvin*.
[3] Or, elders.—*Calvin*.

whom the king held in honour and regard were under his custody. The Hebrews call eunuchs סריסים, *serisim*, a name which belongs to certain prefects; for Potiphar is called by this name though he had a wife. So this name is everywhere used in Scripture for the satraps of a king; (Gen. xxxvii. 36; xl. 2, 7;) but since satraps also were chosen from noble boys, they were probably called eunuchs, though they were not made so, yet Josephus ignorantly declares these Jewish children to have been made eunuchs. But when eunuchs existed among the luxuries of Oriental kings, as I have already said, those youths were commonly called by this name whom the king brought up as a kind of school of nobles, whom he might afterwards place over various provinces.

The king, therefore, commanded some of the children of Israel of the royal seed and of the nobles to be brought to him. So the sentence ought to be resolved; he did not command any of the common people to be brought to him, but some of the royal race, the more plainly to shew himself their conqueror by doing all things according to his will. He means those "elders" who yet were in chief authority under the king of Judah. And Daniel also was of that tribe, as we shall afterwards see. The word פרתמים, *pharth-mim*, "princes," is thought to be derived from *Perah*, which is the Euphrates, and the interpreters understand prefects, to whom the provinces on the banks of the Euphrates were committed; but this does not suit the present passage where Jews are treated of. We now see the general signification of this name, and that all the elders ought to be comprehended under it.[1]—*The rest to-morrow.*

---

[1] This word has caused great difference of opinion among commentators. Theodotion does not attempt to explain it. Symmachus takes it for the Parthians. Jerome interprets it by *tyranni*, and Saadias by their offspring. Aben-Ezra considers it a foreign word; and R. Salom. Jarchi calls it Persian, and translates it "leaders" Hottinger and Aug. Pfeiffer both treat it as Persian, but derive it from different roots. "Nobles" or "elders" seems its best English equivalent.

PRAYER.

Grant, Almighty God, since thou settest before us so clear a mirror of thy wonderful providence and of thy judgments on thine ancient people, that we may also be surely persuaded of our being under thy hand and protection :—Grant, that relying on thee, we may hope for thy guardianship, whatever may happen, since thou never losest sight of our safety, so that we may invoke thee with a secure and tranquil mind. May we so fearlessly wait for all dangers amidst all the changes of this world, that we may stand upon the foundation of thy word which never can fail; and leaning on thy promises may we repose on Christ, to whom thou hast committed us, and whom thou hast made the shepherd of all thy flock. Grant that he may be so careful of us as to lead us through this course of warfare, however troublesome and turbulent it may prove, until we arrive at that heavenly rest which he has purchased for us by his own blood.—Amen.

Lecture Second.

4. Children in whom *was* no blemish, but well-favoured, and skilful in all wisdom, and cunning in knowledge, and understanding science, and such as *had* ability in them to stand in the king's palace, and whom they might teach the learning and the tongue of the Chaldeans.

4. Pueros, quibus nulla esset macula[1] et pulchros aspectu,[2] et intelligentes in omni prudentia,[3] et intelligentes scientiam, et diserte exprimentes cognitionem, et in quibus vigor, ut starent in palatio regis, et ad docendum ipsos literaturam et linguam Chaldæorum.

In yesterday's Lecture we saw how the prefect or master of the eunuchs was commanded to bring up some noble youths, the offspring of the king and the elders; and Daniel now describes their qualities, according to Nebuchadnezzar's order. They were *youths*, not so young as seven or eight years, but growing up, *in whom there was no spot;* that is, in whom there was no defect or unsoundness of body. They were also of *beautiful aspect*, meaning of ingenuous and open countenance: he adds also, *skilled in all prudence, and understanding knowledge;* and then, *expressing their thoughts.* I think those interpreters right who take this participle

---
[1] For I omit the Hebraism which has already been explained.—*Calvin.*
[2] Or countenance.—*Calvin.*   [3] That is, skilled in all wisdom.—*Calvin.*

actively, otherwise the repetition would be cold and valueless. Their eloquence seems to me pointed out here; because there are some who inwardly understand subjects presented to them, but cannot express to others what they retain in their minds; for all have not the same dexterity in expressing exactly what they think. Daniel, therefore, notices both qualifications here—the acquisition of knowledge, and the power of communicating it.

And in whom was vigour: for כֹּהַ, *cach*, usually signifies fortitude, as in Isaiah. (Chap. xl. 9.) Those who fear God shall change their fortitude, or renew their vigour. Then in Psalm xxii., (ver. 15,) "my strength or vigour has failed." He adds, the fortitude or vigour of intelligence, knowledge, and eloquence; or a healthy habit of body, which is the same thing.[1] *That they might stand in the king's palace, and be taught literature,* (I cannot translate the particle סֵפֶר, *sepher*, otherwise: verbally it is a "letter," but it means learning or discipline,) *and the language of the Chaldees.* We now see how the king regarded not only their rank, when he ordered the most excellent of the royal and noble children to be brought to him; but he exercised his choice that those who were to be his servants should be clever; they were of high birth, as the phrase is; so they ought to prevail in eloquence and give hopeful promise of general excellence in both body and mind. Without doubt he wished them to be held in great estimation, that he might win over other Jews also. Thus, if they afterwards obtained authority, should circumstances allow of it, they might become rulers in Judea, bearing sway over their own people, and yet remain attached to the Babylonian empire. This was the king's design; it affords no reason why we should praise his liberality, since it is sufficiently apparent that he consulted nothing but his own advantage.

Meanwhile, we observe, that learning and the liberal arts were not then so despised as they are in this age, and

---

[1] It can scarcely be correct to confound bodily with mental endowments. *Wintle* explains the three clauses very appositely, referring the first to "excellent natural abilities," the second to "the greatest improvement from cultivation," and the last to "the communication of our perceptions in the happiest manner to others."

in those immediately preceding it. So strongly has barbarism prevailed in the world, that it is almost disgraceful for nobles to be reckoned among the men of education and of letters! The chief boast of the nobility was to be destitute of scholarship—nay, they gloried in the assertion, that they were " no scholars," in the language of the day ; and if any of their rank were versed in literature, they acquired their attainments for no other purpose than to be made bishops and abbots: still, as I have said, they generally despised all literature. We perceive the age in which Daniel lived was not so barbarous, for the king wished to have these boys whom he caused to be so instructed, among his own princes, as we have said, to promote his own advantage ; still we must remark upon the habit of that age. As to his requiring so much knowledge and skill, it may seem out of place, and more than their tender age admitted, that they should be so accomplished in prudence, knowledge, and experience. But we know that kings require nothing in moderation : when they order anything to be prepared, they often ascend beyond the clouds. So Nebuchadnezzar speaks here ; and Daniel, who relates his commands, does so in a royal manner. Since the king commanded all the most accomplished to be brought before him, if they really manifested any remarkable qualities, we need not be surprised at their knowledge, skill, and prudence. The king simply wished those boys and youths to be brought to him who were ingenious and dexterous, and adapted to learn with rapidity ; and then those who were naturally eloquent and of a healthy constitution of body. For it follows directly, *that they might learn* or be taught *the literature and language of the Chaldees.* We perceive that King Nebuchadnezzar did not demand teachers, but boys of high birth, and good talents, and of promising abilities ; he wished them to be liberally instructed in the doctrine of the Chaldees : he was unwilling to have youths of merely polished and cultivated minds without natural abilities. His desire to have them acquainted with the language of Chaldea arose from his wish to separate them by degrees from their own nation, to induce them to forget their Jewish birth, and to acquire the Chaldean manners, since language is a singular bond of communication. Respecting their learning, we may ask, whether Daniel and his companions were permitted to learn arts full of imposition, which we know to be the nature of the Chaldean learning. For they professed to know every one's fate, as in these days there are many impostors in the world, who are called fortunetellers. They abused an honourable name when they called themselves mathematicians, as if there were no scientific learning separate from those arts and diabolic illusions. And as to the use of the word, the Cæsars, in their laws, unite Chaldeans and mathematicians, treating them as synonymous. But the explanation is easy,—the Chaldeans not only pursued that astrology which is called "Judicial," but were also skilled in the true and genuine knowledge of the stars. The ancients say, that the course of the stars was observed by the Chaldeans, as there was no region of the world so full of them, and none possessed so extensive an horizon on all sides. As the Chaldeans enjoyed this advantage of having the heavens so fully exposed to the contemplation of man, this may have led to their study, and have conduced to the more earnest pursuit of astrology. But as the minds of men are inclined to vain and foolish curiosity, they were not content with legitimate science, but fell into foolish and perverse imaginations. For what fortune-tellers predict of any one's destiny is merely foolish fanaticism. Daniel, therefore, might have learned these arts; that is, astrology and other liberal sciences, just as Moses is said to have been instructed in all the sciences of Egypt. We know how the Egyptians were infected with similar corruptions; but it is said both of Moses and of our Prophet, that they were imbued with a knowledge of the stars and of the other liberal sciences. Although it is uncertain whether the king commanded them to proceed far in these studies, yet we must hold that Daniel abstained, as we shall see directly, from the royal food and drink, and was not drawn aside nor involved in these Satanic impostures. Whatever the king's commandment was, I suppose Daniel to have been content with the pure and genuine knowledge of natural things. As far as the king is concerned, as we have already said, he consulted simply his own interests; wishing Daniel and his companions to pass over into a foreign tribe, and to be drawn away from their own people, as if they had been natives of Chaldea. It now follows:—

5. And the king appointed them a daily provision of the king's meat, and of the wine which he drank: so nourishing them three years, that at the end thereof they might stand before the king.

5. Et constituit illis rex demensum diei in die suo[1] ex frusto[2] cibi regis, et ex vino potus ejus. Et ut educarentur annis tribus: et a fine illorum[3] starent coram rege.

In this verse, Daniel shews that the king had ordered some youths to be brought to him from Judea, and to be so nourished as to be intoxicated with delicacies, and thus rendered forgetful of their own nation. For we know that wherever there is any cunning in the world, it reigns especially in kings' palaces! So Nebuchadnezzar, when he perceived he was dealing with an obstinate people, (and we know the Jews to have been of a hard and unsubdued spirit,) wished to acquire servants spontaneously obedient, and thus endeavoured to soften them with luxuries. This was the reason why he provided for them *an allotment of his own meat and drink;* as at present it is the greatest honour at princes' tables to be served with a *bon-bouche,* as they say. Nebuchadnezzar wished this Daniel and his companions, though but captives and exiles, to be brought up not only splendidly but royally, as if of the royal race. Through his right of conquest he had drawn them away violently from their country, as we said yesterday. Hence he does not act thus from any feeling of liberality, and his feeding those miserable exiles from his own table should not be esteemed a virtuous action; but, as we have said, he cleverly reconciles the minds of the boys to be reckoned Chaldeans rather than Jews, and thus to deny their own race. This, then, was the king's intention; but we shall see how God governed

[1] דבר, *deber*, " the matter," for each day.—*Calvin.* " The allotment for each day."—*Wintle.* It means "daily bread," as in our Lord's Prayer, and occurs often in Exodus.

[2] Verbally, it here signifies a portion.—*Calvin.*

[3] Some translate it " a part," meaning " some part of them," but there is no doubt that the Prophet means a space of time, as we shall soon see. —*Calvin.*

Daniel and his companions by His Spirit, and how they became aware of these snares of the devil, and abstained from the royal diet, lest they should become polluted by it. This point will hereafter be treated in its place—we are now only commenting on the craftiness of the king. He commanded a daily portion of diet to be distributed to them, not that the spirit of parsimony dictated this daily portion, but the king wished their food should be exactly the same as his own and that of the chiefs.

He adds, *that they should be educated for three years;* meaning, until they were thoroughly skilled in both the language and knowledge of the Chaldeans. Three years were sufficient for both these objects, since he had selected youths of sufficient talent to learn with ease both languages and sciences. As they were endued with such capacity, it is not surprising that the space of three years had been prescribed by the king. At length, he says, *at the end of them,* meaning of the three years. We have shewn how this ought not to be referred to the boys, as if the king afterwards selected some of them, for we shall see in its own place that a distinct time was fixed beforehand; hence no long refutation is needed. It is certain, then, that the Prophet speaks of the close of the three years. It had been said just before, *that they might stand in the palace;* but this ought also to be understood of the time of which mention has been made. They did not stand before the king immediately, but were reserved for this purpose. Since the king commanded them to be brought up for the purpose of using their services afterwards. Daniel twice repeats — they were splendidly educated—seeing the king wished them to become his servants at table and in other duties.

6. Now among these were, of the children of Judah, Daniel, Hananiah, Mishael, and Azariah;
7. Unto whom the prince of the eunuchs gave names : for he gave unto Daniel *the name* of Belteshazzar ; and to Hananiah, of Shadrach ; and to Mishael, of Meshach ; and to Azariah, of Abednego.

6. Et fuit in illis ex filiis Jehudah Daniel, Hananiah, Misael, et Azariah.
7. Et imposuit illis princeps eunuchorum[1] nomina : imposuit inquam, Danieli Balthsazar, et Hananiæ Sadrak, et Misael Mesack, et Azariæ Abednego.

[1] That is, the master of the eunuchs.—*Calvin.*

The Prophet now comes to what properly belongs to his purpose. He did not propose to write a full narrative, but he touched shortly on what was necessary, to inform us how God prepared him for the subsequent discharge of the prophetic office. After he had stated their selection from the royal and noble seed, as excelling in talent, dexterity, and eloquence, as well as in vigour of body, he now adds, that he and his companions were among them. He leaves out the rest, because he had nothing to record of them worthy of mention; and, as I have said, the narrative hitherto is only subsidiary. The Prophet's object, then, must be noticed, since he was exiled, and educated royally and sumptuously in the palace of King Nebuchadnezzar, that he might afterwards be one of the prefects, and his companions be elevated to the same rank. He does not say that he was of the royal house, but only of the tribe of Judah; but he was probably born of a noble rather than of a plebeian family, since kings more commonly selected their prefects from their own relations than from others. Moreover, since the kingdom of Israel was cut off, perhaps through a feeling of modesty, Daniel did not record his family, nor openly assert his origin from a noble and celebrated stock. He was content with a single word,— he and his companions were of the tribe of Judah, and brought up among the children of the nobility. He says —*their names were changed;* so that by all means the king might blot out of their hearts the remembrance of their own race, and they might forget their own origin. As far as interpretations are concerned, I think I have said enough to satisfy you, as I am not willingly curious in names where there is any obscurity, and especially in these Chaldee words. As to the Hebrew names, we know Daniel's name to mean the judge, or judgment of God. Therefore, whether by the secret instinct of God, his parents had imposed this name, or whether by common custom, Daniel was called by this name, as God's judge. So also of the rest; for Hananiah has a fixed meaning, namely, one who has obtained mercy from God; so Misael means required or demanded by God; and so Azariah, the help of God, or one whom God helps. But all these things have already been better explained to you, so I have only just touched on these points, as the change has no adequate reason for it. It is enough for us that the names were changed to abolish the remembrance of the kingdom of Judah from their hearts. Some Hebrews also assert these to have been the names of wise men. Whether it was so or not, it was the king's plan to draw away those boys that they should have nothing in common with the elect people, but degenerate to the manners of the Chaldeans. Daniel could not help the prince or master of the eunuchs changing his name, for it was not in his power to hinder it; the same must be said of his companions. But they had enough to retain the remembrance of their race, which Satan, by this artifice, wished utterly to blot out. And yet this was a great trial, because they suffered from their badge of slavery. Since their names were changed, either the king or his prefect Aspenaz wished to force them under the yoke, as if he would put before their eyes the judgment of their own slavery as often as they heard their names. We see, then, the intention of the change of name, namely, to cause these miserable exiles to feel themselves in captivity, and cut off from the race of Israel; and by this mark or symbol they were reduced to slavery, to the king of Babylon and his palace. This was, indeed, a hard trial, but it mattered not to the servants of God to be contemptuously treated before men, so long as they were not infected with any corruption; hence we conclude them to have been divinely governed, as they stood pure and spotless. For Daniel afterwards says—

| 8. But Daniel purposed in his heart that he would not defile himself with the portion of the king's meat, nor with the wine which he drank: therefore he requested of the prince of the eunuchs that he might not defile himself. | 8. Et posuit Daniel super cor suum,[1] ne pollueretur in portione cibi regis, et in vino potuum ejus: et quæsivit a magistro[2] Eunuchorum, ne pollueretur. |

Here Daniel shews his endurance of what he could neither cast off nor escape; but meanwhile he took care that he did

[1] Or in his heart: that is, determined or decreed with himself.—*Calvin.*
[2] That is, asked the master.—*Calvin.*

not depart from the fear of God, nor become a stranger to his race, but he always retains the remembrance of his origin, and remains a pure, and unspotted, and sincere worshipper of God. He says, therefore,—*he determined in his heart not to pollute himself with the king's food and drink, and that he asked the prefect,* under whose charge he was, that he should not be driven to this necessity. It may be asked here, what there was of such importance in the diet to cause Daniel to avoid it? This seems to be a kind of superstition, or at least Daniel may have been too morose in rejecting the king's diet. We know that to the pure all things are pure, and this rule applies to all ages. We read nothing of this kind concerning Joseph, and very likely Daniel used all food promiscuously, since he was treated by the king with great honour. This, then, was not perpetual with Daniel; for he might seem an inconsiderate zealot, or this might be ascribed, as we have said, to too much moroseness. If Daniel only for a time rejected the royal food, it was a mark of levity and inconsistency afterwards to allow himself that liberty from which he had for the time abstained. But if he did this with judgment and reason, why did he not persist in his purpose? I answer, —Daniel abstained at first from the luxuries of the court to escape being tampered with. It was lawful for him and his companions to feed on any kind of diet, but he perceived the king's intention. We know how far enticements prevail to deceive us; especially when we are treated daintily; and experience shews us how difficult it is to be moderate when all is affluence around us, for luxury follows immediately on plenty. Such conduct is, indeed, too common, and the virtue of abstinence is rarely exercised when there is an abundance of provisions.

But this is not the whole reason which weighed with Daniel. Sobriety and abstinence are not simply praised here, since many twist this passage to the praise of fasting, and say Daniel's chief virtue consisted in preferring pulse to the delicacies of a palace. For Daniel not only wished to guard himself against the delicacies of the table, since he perceived a positive danger of being eaten up by such enticements; hence he simply determined in his heart not to taste the diet of the court, desiring by his very food perpetually to recall the remembrance of his country. He wished so to live in Chaldea, as to consider himself an exile and a captive, sprung from the sacred family of Abraham. We see, then, the intention of Daniel. He desired to refrain from too great an abundance and delicacy of diet, simply to escape those snares of Satan, by which he saw himself surrounded. He was, doubtless, conscious of his own infirmity, and this also is to be reckoned to his praise, since through distrust of himself he desired to escape from all allurements and temptations. As far as concerned the king's intention, this was really a snare of the devil, as I have said: Daniel rejected it, and there is no doubt that God enlightened his mind by his Spirit as soon as he prayed to him. Hence, he was unwilling to cast himself into the snares of the devil, while he voluntarily abstained from the royal diet. This is the full meaning of the passage.

It may also be asked, Why does Daniel claim this praise as his own, which was shared equally with his companions? for he was not the only one who rejected the royal diet. It is necessary to take notice, how from his childhood he was governed by the Spirit of God, that the confidence and influence of his teaching might be the greater; hence he speaks peculiarly of himself, not for the sake of boasting, but to obtain confidence in his teaching, and to shew himself to have been for a long period formed and polished by God for the prophetic office. We must also remember that he was the adviser of his companions; for this course might never have come into their minds, and they might have been corrupted, unless they had been admonished by Daniel. God, therefore, wished Daniel to be a leader and master to his companions, to induce them to adopt the same abstinence. Hence also we gather, that as each of us is endued more fruitfully with the grace of the Spirit, so should we feel bound to instruct others. It will not be sufficient for any one to restrain himself and thus to discharge his own duty, under the teaching of God's Spirit, unless he also extend his hand to others, and endeavour to unite in an alliance of piety, and of the fear and worship of God. Such an example is here proposed to us in Daniel, who not only rejected the delicacies of the palace, by which he might be intoxicated and even poisoned; but he also advised and persuaded his companions to adopt the same course. This is the reason why he calls tasting the king's food pollution or abomination, though, as I have said, there was nothing abominable in it of itself. Daniel was at liberty to eat and drink at the royal table, but the abomination arose from the consequences. Before the time of these four persons living in Chaldea, they doubtless partook of ordinary food after the usual manner, and were permitted to eat whatever was offered to them. They did not ask for pulse when at an inn, or on their journey; but they began to desire it when the king wished to infect them with his delicacies, and to induce them if possible to prefer that condition to returning to their own friends. When they perceived the object of his snares, then it became both a pollution and abomination to feed on those dainties, and to eat at the king's table. Thus we may ascertain the reason why Daniel thought himself polluted if he fared sumptuously and partook of the royal diet; he was conscious, as we have already observed, of his own infirmities, and wished to take timely precautions, lest he should be enticed by such snares, and fall away from piety and the worship of God, and degenerate into the manners of the Chaldeans, as if he were one of their nation, and of their native princes. I must leave the rest till to-morrow.

PRAYER.

Grant, Almighty God, as long as our pilgrimage in this world continues, that we may feed on such diet for the necessities of the flesh as may never corrupt us; and may we never be led aside from sobriety, but may we learn to use our abundance by preferring abstinence in the midst of plenty: Grant also, that we may patiently endure want and famine, and eat and drink with such liberty as always to set before us the glory of thy Name. Lastly, may our very frugality lead us to aspire after that fulness by which we shall be completely refreshed, when the glory of thy countenance shall appear to us in heaven, through Jesus Christ our Lord.—Amen.

Lecture Third.

9. Now God had brought Daniel into favour and tender love with the prince of the eunuchs.

9. Dederat autem Deus Danielem[1] in clementiam et miserationes coram prefecto eunuchorum.

DANIEL, yesterday, related what he had asked from the master to whose care he had been committed: he now inserts this sentence, to shew this demand to be quite unobjectionable, since the prefect of the eunuchs treated him kindly. The crime would have been fatal had Daniel been brought into the king's presence. Although very probably he did not use the word "pollution," and openly and directly call the royal diet a "defilement," yet it may be easily conjectured from these words which he now records, that he asked the prefect to be permitted to eat pulse, because he did not think himself permitted to partake of the royal diet. We yesterday gave the reason; but the king of Babylon would immediately have been angry, had he known this. What! he would say, I honour those captives, when I might abuse them as slaves; nay, I nourish them delicately like my own children, and yet they reject my food, as if I were polluted. This, therefore, is the reason why Daniel here relates his being in favour with that prefect. For, as we shall see in the next verse, the prefect simply denied his request. Where was then any favour shewn? But though he was not willing to acquiesce in the prayers of Daniel, he shewed a singular kindness in not taking him before the king, since courtiers are ready for any accusation for the sake of obtaining favour. Then, very probably, the prefect would know that this had been granted to Daniel by his servant. If then there was any connivance on the part of the prefect, this is the favour and pity of which Daniel now speaks. His intention, then, is by no means doubtful, since he did not hesitate to adopt a different course of life, in order to remain pure and spotless, and uncontaminated with the delicacies of the palace of Babylon. He expresses how he escaped the danger, because the prefect treated

[1] Had put Daniel.—*Calvin.*

him kindly, when he might have instantly caused his death. But we must notice the form of speech here used;—*God placed him in favour and pity before that prefect.* He might have used the usual phrase, merely saying he was favourably treated; but, as he found a barbarian so humane and merciful, he ascribes this benefit to God. This phrase, as we have expounded it, is customary with the Hebrews; as when it is said, (Ps. cvi. 46,) God gave the Jews favour in the sight of the heathen who had led them captive; meaning, he took care that their conquerors should not rage so cruelly against them as they had done at first. For we know how the Jews were often treated harshly, roughly, and contemptuously. Since this inhumanity was here mitigated, the Prophet attributes it to God, who prepared mercies for his people. The result is this,—Daniel obtained favour with the prefect, since God bent the heart of a man, otherwise unsoftened, to clemency and humanity. His object in this narrative is to urge us to greater earnestness in duty, if we have to undergo any difficulties when God calls us.

It often happens that we cannot discharge everything which God requires and exacts without imminent danger to our lives. Sloth and softness naturally creep over us, and induce us to reject the cross. Daniel, therefore, gives us courage to obey God and his commands, and here states his favour with the prefect, since God granted his servant favour while faithfully performing his duty. Hence let us learn to cast our care upon God when worldly terror oppresses us, or when men forbid us with threats to obey God's commands Here let us acknowledge the power of God's hand to turn the hearts of those who rage against us, and to free us from all danger. This, then, is the reason why Daniel says the prefect was kind to him. Meanwhile, we gather the general doctrine from this passage, that men's hearts are divinely governed, while it shews us how God softens their iron hardness, and turns the wolf into the lamb. For when he brought his people out of Egypt, he gave them favour with the Egyptians, so that they carried with them their most precious vessels. It is clear enough that the Egyptians were hostile towards the Israelites. Why then did they so freely offer them the most valuable of their household goods? Only because the Lord inspired their hearts with new affections. So, again, the Lord can exasperate our friends, and cause them afterwards to rise up in hostility against us. Let us perceive, then, that on both sides the will is in God's power, either to bend the hearts of men to humanity, or to harden those which were naturally tender. It is true, indeed, that every one has a peculiar disposition from his birth: some are ferocious, warlike, and sanguinary; others are mild, humane, and tractable. This variety springs from God's secret ordination; but God not only forms every one's disposition at his birth, but every day and every moment, if it seems good to him, changes every one's affections. He also blinds men's minds, and rouses them again from their stupor. For we sometimes see the rudest men endued with much acuteness, and shew a singular contrivance in action, and others who excel in foresight, are at fault when they have need of judgment and discretion. We must consider the minds and hearts of men to be so governed by God's secret instinct, that he changes their affections just as he pleases. Hence there is no reason why we should so greatly fear our enemies, although they vomit forth their rage with open mouth, and are overflowing with cruelty; for they can be turned aside by the Lord. And thus let us learn from the example of Daniel to go on fearlessly in our course, and not to turn aside, even if the whole world should oppose us; since God can easily and readily remove all impediments: and we shall find those who were formerly most cruel, become humane when the Lord wishes to spare us. We now understand the sense of the words of this verse, as well as the Prophet's intention. It follows:

10. And the prince of the eunuchs said unto Daniel, I fear my Lord the king, who hath appointed your meat and your drink: for why should he see your faces worse liking than the

10. Et dixit præfectus eunuchorum Danieli, Timeo ego Dominum meum regem qui, constituit[1] cibum vestrum, et potus vestros: quare videbit facies vestras tristes,[2] præ

[1] For מנה, *minneh*, which is "to relate," means to "ordain," "appoint." — *Calvin*.

[2] Or emaciated, or austere, or sullen: for, it is derived from the word זעף, *zegneph*, which signifies "to be angry," and hence, by a change of object, faces are called emaciated, austere, or sullen. — *Calvin*.

children which *are* of your sort? then shall ye make *me* endanger my head to the king.

pueris, qui sunt vobis similes,¹ et obnoxium² reddetis caput meum regi.

Daniel suffers a repulse from the prefect; and truly, as I have lately remarked, his humanity is not praised through his listening to Daniel's wish and prayer; but through his burying in silence whatever might have brought him into difficulties. And his friendship appears in this; for although he denies his request, yet he does so mildly and civilly, as if he had said he would willingly grant it unless he had feared the king's anger. This, therefore, is the meaning,—the prefect, though he did not dare to comply with Daniel's request, yet treated both him and his companions kindly by not endangering their lives. He says,—*he was afraid of the king who had ordered the food.* He is not to be blamed as if he feared man more than the living God, for he could not have any knowledge of God. Although he may have been persuaded that Daniel made his request in the earnest pursuit of piety, yet he did not think himself authorized to comply; for he thought the Jews had their peculiar method of worship, but meanwhile he clung entirely to the religion of Babylon. Just as many profane persons now think us quite right in casting away superstitions, but yet they slumber in this error,—it is lawful for themselves to live in the ancient manner, since they were so brought up and instructed by their forefathers. Hence they use rites which they allow to be disapproved by us. So also this prefect might feel rightly concerning Daniel and his associates; at the same time he was not so touched by them as to desire to learn the difference between the two religions. Therefore he simply excuses himself, as not being at liberty to grant Daniel's request, since this would endanger his own head with the king. It now follows:—

11. Then said Daniel to Melzar, whom the prince of the eunuchs had

11. Et dixit Daniel ad Meltsar, quem constituerat præfectus eu-

[1] Others translate "equals," "those who are like you:" this may be the sense, because they are now like you, but will afterwards become fat and stout while you are lean. This change will endanger me.—*Calvin.*

[2] For בוֹכ, *chob*, in Hebrew is "debtor:" whence this word is derived, signifying to "render subject."—*Calvin.*

set over Daniel, Hananiah, Mishael, and Azariah,	nuchorum super Danielem, Hananiah, Misael, et Azariah,
12. Prove thy servants, I beseech thee, ten days; and let them give us pulse to eat, and water to drink.	12. Proba[1] servos tuos diebus decem, et apponantur nobis de leguminibus,[2] et comedemus,[3] et aquæ, quas bibamus.
13. Then let our countenances be looked upon before thee, and the countenance of the children that eat of the portion of the king's meat; and as thou seest, deal with thy servants.	13. Et inspiciantur coram facie tua vultus nostri, et vultus puerorum, qui vescuntur portione[4] cibi regis: et quemadmodum videris fac cum servis tuis.

Since Daniel understood from the answer of the prefect that he could not obtain his wish, he now addresses his servant. For the prefect had many servants under him, according to the custom of important stewardships. Most probably the steward's duty was similar to that of the Chief Steward of the Household,[5] as it exists at this time in France. Daniel and his companions were under the care of one of these servants; Daniel descends to this remedy and obtains his wish, though, as we shall see, not without some artifice. And here Daniel's singular constancy is observable, who after trying the matter once in vain, did not cease to pursue the same object. It is a clear and serious proof of our faith, when we are not fatigued when anything adverse occurs, and never consider the way closed against us. Then if we do not retrace our steps, but try all ways, we truly shew the root of piety fixed in our hearts. It might have seemed excusable in Daniel, after he had met with his first repulse; for who would not have said he had discharged his duty, and that an obstacle had prevailed over him! But since he did not prevail with the chief prefect, he goes to his servant. Thus voluntarily to incur risk was the result of no common prudence. For this servant could not make the same objection, as we have just heard the prefect did. Without doubt he had heard of Daniel's request, and of his repulse and denial; hence Daniel is beforehand with him, and shews how the servant may comply without the slightest danger; as if he had said,—We, indeed, did not obtain our wish from

[1] Or try.—*Calvin.*
[3] Which we may eat.—*Calvin.*
[5] Du grand Escuyer.—*Fr. Trans.*

[2] Simply pulse.—*Calvin.*
[4] A piece, as we said.—*Calvin.*

the prefect because he was afraid of his life, but I have now thought of a new scheme by which you may both gratify us and yet not become chargeable with any crime, as the whole matter will be unknown. *Try thy servants, therefore, for ten days, and prove them ; let nothing but pulse be given us to eat and water to drink.* If after that time our faces are fresh and plump, no suspicion will attach to thee, and no one will be persuaded that we are not treated delicately according to the king's commandment. Since, then, this proof will be sufficiently safe for thee, and cautious enough for us both, there is no reason why you should reject our prayers. Besides, without the slightest doubt, when Daniel brought this forward, he was directed by God's Spirit to this act of prudence, and was also impelled to make this request. By the singular gift of the Holy Spirit Daniel invented this method of bending the mind of the servant under whose care he was placed. We must hold, then, that this was not spoken rashly or of his own will, but by the instinct of the Holy Spirit. It would not have been duty but rashness, if Daniel had been the author of this plan, and had not been assured by the Lord of its prosperous issue. Without doubt he had some secret revelation on the subject ; and if the servant allowed him and his associates to feed on pulse, it was a happy answer to his prayers. Hence, I say, he would not have spoken thus, except under the guidance and command of the Spirit. And this is worthy of notice, since we often permit ourselves to do many things which turn out badly, because we are carried away by the mere feelings of the flesh, and do not consider what is pleasing to God. It is not surprising, then, when men indulge in various expectations, if they feel themselves deceived at last, since every one occasionally imposes upon himself by foolish hopes, and thus frustrates his designs. Indeed, it is not our province to promise ourselves any success. Hence let us notice how Daniel had not undertaken or approached the present business with any foolish zeal ; and did not speak without due consideration, but was assured of the event by the Spirit of God.

But he says, *let pulse be put before us to eat, and water to drink*. We see, then, that the four youths did not abstain from the royal food for fear of pollution; for there was no law to prevent any one drinking wine, except the Nazarites, (Numb. vi. 2,) and they might eat of any kind of flesh, of which there was abundance at the royal table. Whence then sprang this scrupulousness? because, as we said yesterday, Daniel was unwilling to accustom himself to the delicacies of the palace, which would cause him to become degenerate. He wished, therefore, to nourish his body not only frugally, but abstemiously, and not to indulge in these tastes; for although he was raised to the highest honours, he was always the same as if still among the most wretched captives. There is no occasion for seeking other reasons for this abstinence of Daniel's. For he might have fed on ordinary bread and other less delicate food; but he was content with pulse, and was continually lamenting and nourishing in his mind the remembrance of his country, of which he would have been directly forgetful if he had been plunged into those luxuries of the palace. It follows:

14. So he consented to them in this matter, and proved them ten days.	14. Et audivit eos in hoc verbo, et probavit eos decem diebus.
15. And at the end of ten days their countenances appeared fairer and fatter in flesh than all the children which did eat the portion of the king's meat.	15. Et a fine decem dierum visus est vultus eorum pulcher,[1] et *ipsi* pinguiores carne præ omnibus pueris,[2] qui comedebant portiones cibi regii.

Now this surprising event took place,—Daniel contracted neither leanness nor debility from that mean food, but his face was as shining as if he had continued to feed most delicately; hence we gather as I have already said, that he was divinely impelled to persist firmly in his own design, and not to pollute himself with the royal diet. God, therefore, testified by the result that he had advised Daniel and his companions in this their prayer and proposal. It is clear enough that there is no necessary virtue in bread to nourish us; for we are nourished by God's secret blessing, as Moses says, Man lives not by bread alone, (Deut. viii 3,) implying that the bread itself does not impart

---

[1] Or plump.—*Calvin*.   [2] Namely, the rest.—*Calvin*.

strength to men, for the bread has no life in it; how then can it afford us life? As bread possesses no virtue by itself, we are nourished by the word of God; and because God has determined that our life shall be sustained by nourishment, he has breathed its virtue into the bread—but, meanwhile, we ought to consider our life sustained neither by bread nor any other food, but by the secret blessing of God. For Moses does not speak here of either doctrine or spiritual life, but says our bodily life is cherished by God's favour, who has endued bread and other food with their peculiar properties. This, at least, is certain,—whatever food we feed on, we are nourished and sustained by God's gratuitous power. But the example which Daniel here mentions was singular. Hence God, as I have said, shews, by the event, how Daniel could not remain pure and spotless with his companions, otherwise than by being content with pulse and water. We must observe, for our improvement, in the first place,—we should be very careful not to become slaves of the palate, and thus be drawn off from our duty and from obedience and the fear of God, when we ought to live sparingly and be free from all luxuries. We see at this day how many feel it a very great cross if they cannot indulge at the tables of the rich, which are filled with abundance and variety of food. Others are so hardened in the enjoyment of luxuries, that they cannot be content with moderation; hence they are always wallowing in their own filth, being quite unable to renounce the delights of the palate. But Daniel sufficiently shews us, when God not only reduces us to want, but when, if necessary, all indulgences must be spontaneously rejected. Daniel indeed, as we saw yesterday, does not attach any virtue to abstinence from one kind of food or another; and all we have hitherto learnt has no other object than to teach him to guard against imminent danger, to avoid passing over to the morals of a strange nation, and so to conduct himself at Babylon as not to forget himself as a son of Abraham. But still it was necessary to renounce the luxuries of the court. Although delicate viands were provided, he rejected them of his own accord; since, as we have seen, it would be deadly pollution, not in itself but in its consequences. Thus Moses, when he fled from Egypt, passed into a new life far different from his former one; for he had lived luxuriously and honourably in the king's palace, as if he had been the king's grandson. But he lived sparingly in the Desert afterwards, and obtained his support by very toilsome labour. He preferred, says the Apostle, the cross of Christ to the riches of Egypt. (Heb. xi. 26.) How so? Because he could not be esteemed an Egyptian and retain the favour which had been promised to the sons of Abraham. It was a kind of self-denial always to remain in the king's palace.

We may take this test as a true proof of our frugality and temperance, if we are able to satisfy the appetite when God compels us to endure poverty and want; nay, if we can spurn the delicacies which are at hand but tend to our destruction. For it would be very frivolous to subsist entirely on pulse and water; as greater intemperance sometimes displays itself in pulse than in the best and most dainty dishes. If any one in weak health desires pulse and other such food which is injurious, he will surely be condemned for intemperance. But if he feeds on nourishing diet, as they say, and thus sustains himself, frugality will have its praise. If any one through desire of water, and being too voracious, rejects wine, this as we well know would not be praiseworthy. Hence we ought not to subsist on this kind of food to discover the greatness of Daniel's virtue. But we ought always to direct our minds to the object of his design, namely, what he wished and what was in his power—so to live under the sway of the king of Babylon, that his whole condition should be distinct from that of the nation at large, and never to forget himself as an Israelite—and unless there had been this great difference, Daniel would have been unable to sharpen himself and to shake off his torpor, or to rouse himself from it. Daniel necessarily kept before his mind some manifest and remarkable difference which separated him from the Chaldeans; he desired pulse and water, through the injurious effects of good living.

Lastly, this passage teaches us, although we should meet with nothing but the roots and leaves of trees, and even if the earth herself should deny us the least blade of grass, yet God by his blessing can make us healthy and active no less than those who abound in every comfort. God's liberality, however, is never to be despised when he nourishes us with bread and wine and other diet ; for Paul enumerates, among things worthy of praise, his knowing how to bear both abundance and penury. (Phil. iv. 12.) When, therefore, God bountifully offers us both meat and drink, we may soberly and frugally drink wine and eat savoury food ; but when he takes away from us bread and water, so that we suffer from famine, we shall find his blessing sufficient for us instead of all nutriment. For we see that Daniel and his companions were ruddy and plump, and even remarkably robust by feeding on nothing but pulse. How could this occur, unless the Lord, who nourished his people in the Desert on manna alone, when other diet was deficient, even at this day turns our food into manna, which would otherwise be injurious to us. (Exod. xvi. 4.) For if any one asks the medical profession, whether pulse and other leguminous plants are wholesome ? they will tell us they are very injurious, since they know them to be so. But at the same time, when we have no choice of viands and cannot obtain what would conduce most to our health, if we are content with herbs and roots, the Lord, as I have said, can nourish us no less than if he put before us a table well supplied with every dainty. Temperance does not exist in the food itself, but in the palate—since we are equally intemperate if pleasure entices us to gratify the appetite on inferior food—so, again, we may remain perfectly temperate though feeding on the best diet. We must form the same opinion of the properties of various viands, which do not support us by their own inherent qualities, but by God's blessing, as he sees fit. We sometimes see the children of the rich very emaciated, although they may receive the greatest attention. We see also the children of the country people most beautiful in form, ruddy in countenance, and healthy in condition ; and yet they feed on any kind of food, and sometimes upon what is injurious. But although they are deprived of tasty sauces, yet God gives them his blessing, and their unripe fruit, pork, lard, and even herbs, which seem most unwholesome, become more nourishing than if the people abounded in every delicacy. This, therefore, must be remarked in the words of Daniel. It follows:

16. Thus Melzar took away the portion of their meat, and the wine that they should drink, and gave them pulse.	16. Et factum est, ut Melsar tolleret sibi portionem cibi illorum et vinum potionum eorum,[1] et daret illis legumina.

After Melsar saw it possible to gratify Daniel and his companions without danger and promote his own profit, he was humane and easily dealt with, and had no need of long disputation. For an intervening obstacle often deters us from the pursuit of gain, and we forbear to seek what we very much crave when it requires oppressive labour; but when our profit is at hand, and we are freed from all danger, then every one naturally pursues it. We see, then, what Daniel means in this verse, namely, when Melsar saw the usefulness of this plan, and the possibility of his gaining by the diet assigned by the king to the four youths, then he gave them pulse. But we must notice also Daniel's intention. He wishes to shew that we ought not to ascribe it to the kindness of man, that he and his companions could preserve themselves pure and unspotted. Why so? Because he never could have obtained anything from this man Melsar, until he perceived it could be granted safely. Since, therefore, Melsar consulted his own advantage and his private interest, and wished to escape all risks and hazards, we easily gather that the benefit is not to be ascribed entirely to him. Daniel and his companions obtained their wish, but God's providence rendered this man tractable, and governed the whole event. Meanwhile, God openly shews how all the praise was due to himself, purposely to exercise the gratitude of Daniel and his associates.

[1] That is wine, which the king had appointed them to drink.—*Calvin.*

PRAYER.

Grant, Almighty God, since we are now encompassed by so many enemies, and the devil does not cease to harass us with fresh snares, so that the whole world is hostile to us, that we may perceive even the devil himself to be restrained by thy bridle. Grant, also, that all the impious may be subjected to thee, that thou mayest lead them whithersoever thou wishest. Do thou direct their hearts, and may we be experimentally taught how safe and secure we are under the protection of thy hand. And may we proceed, according to thy promise, in the course of our calling, until at length we arrive at that blessed rest which is laid up for us in heaven, by Christ our Lord.—Amen.

Lecture Fourth.

17. As for these four children, God gave them knowledge and skill in all learning and wisdom: and Daniel had understanding in all visions and dreams.

17. Et pueris illis quatuor, dedit, *inquam*, illis Deus cognitionem et scientiam in omni literatura et sapientia: et Daniel intellexit in omni visione et somniis.

THE Prophet here shews what we have already touched upon, how his authority was acquired for exercising the prophetic office with greater advantage. He ought to be distinguished by fixed marks, that the Jews first, and foreigners afterwards, might acknowledge him to be endued with the prophetic spirit. But a portion of this favour was shared with his three companions; yet he excelled them all, because God fitted him specially for his office. Here the end is to be noticed, because it would be incorrect to say that their reward was bestowed by God, because they lived both frugally and heavenly, and spontaneously abstained from the delicacies of the palace; for God had quite a different intention. For he wished, as I have already said, to extol Daniel, to enable him to shew with advantage that Israel's God is the only God; and as he wished his companions to excel hereafter in political government, he presented them also with some portion of his Spirit. But it is worth while to set Daniel before our eyes; because, as I have said, before God appointed him his Prophet, he wished to adorn him with his own *insignia,* to procure confidence in his teaching. He says, therefore, *to those four boys,* or youths, *knowledge and science were given in all literature and wisdom.* Daniel was endued with a very singular gift—he was to be an interpreter of dreams, and an explainer of visions. Since Daniel here speaks of literature, without doubt he simply means the liberal arts, and does not comprehend the magical arts which flourished then and afterwards in Chaldea. We know that nothing was sincere among unbelievers; and, on the other hand, I have previously admonished you, that Daniel was not imbued with the superstitions in those days highly esteemed in that nation. Through discontent with genuine science, they corrupted the study of the stars; but Daniel and his associates were so brought up among the Chaldeans, that they were not tinctured with those mixtures and corruptions which ought always to be separated from true science. It would be absurd, then, to attribute to God the approval of magical arts, which it is well known were severely prohibited and condemned by the law itself. (Deut. xviii. 10.) Although God abominates those magical superstitions as the works of the devil, this does not prevent Daniel and his companions from being divinely adorned with this gift, and being very well versed in all the literature of the Chaldees. Hence this ought to be restricted to true and natural science. As it respects Daniel, he says, he *understood even visions and dreams:* and we know how by these two methods the Prophets were instructed in the will of God. (Num. xii. 6.) For while God there blames Aaron and Miriam, he affirms this to be his usual method; as often as he wishes to manifest his designs to the Prophets, he addresses them by visions and dreams. But Moses is treated out of the common order of men, because he is addressed face to face, and mouth to mouth. God, therefore, whenever he wished to make use of his Prophets, by either visions or dreams, made known to them what he wished to be proclaimed to the people. When, therefore, it is here said,—*Daniel understood dreams and visions,* it has the sense of being endued with the prophetic spirit. While his companions were superior masters and teachers in all kinds of literature, he alone was a Prophet of God.

We now understand the object of this distinction, when an acquaintance with visions and dreams was ascribed peculiarly to Daniel. And here our previous assertion is fully confirmed, namely, that Daniel was adorned with the fullest proofs of his mission, to enable him afterwards to undertake the prophetic office with greater confidence, and acquire greater attention to his teaching. God could, indeed, prepare him in a single moment, and by striking terror and reverence into the minds of all, induce them to embrace his teaching; but he wished to raise his servant by degrees, and to bring him forth at the fitting time, and not too suddenly: so that all might know by marks impressed for many years how to distinguish him from the common order of men. It afterwards follows:

18. Now, at the end of the days that the king had said he should bring them in, then the prince of the eunuchs brought them in before Nebuchadnezzar.
19. And the king communed with them; and among them all was found none like Daniel, Hananiah, Mishael, and Azariah: therefore stood they before the king.
20. And in all matters of wisdom *and* understanding, that the king enquired of them, he found them ten times better than all the magicians *and* astrologers that *were* in all his realm.

18. Et a fine dierum, quibus edixerat Rex ut producerentur, introduxit eos princeps[1] eunuchorum coram Nebuchadnezzar.
19. Et loquutus est cum illis rex: et non inventus est ex omnibus sicut Daniel, Hananiah, Misael, et Azariah, et steterunt coram rege.
20. Et in omni verbo, sapientia et intelligentia, quod sciscitatus est ab eis rex, invenit eos decuplo supra omnes genethliacos et astrologos[2] qui erant in toto regno ejus.

Now, Daniel relates how he and his companions were brought forward at a fixed time, since three years was appointed by the king for their instruction in all the science of the Chaldees: and on that account the prefect of the eunuchs produces them. He shews how he and his companions were approved by the king, and were preferred to all the rest. By these words he confirms my remark, that the Lord through a long interval had adorned them with much favour, by rendering them conspicuous throughout the royal

[1] Or, prefect.—*Calvin.*
[2] That is, superior to all the soothsayers and astrologers.—*Calvin.*

palace, while the king himself acknowledged something uncommon in them. He, as well as the courtiers, ought all to entertain such an opinion concerning these four youths, as should express his sincere reverence for them. Then God wished to illustrate his own glory, since without doubt the king was compelled to wonder how they could surpass all the Chaldeans. This monarch had spared no expense on his own people, and had not neglected to instruct them; but when he saw foreigners and captives so superior, a spirit of rivalry would naturally spring up within him. But, as I have already said, God wished to extol himself in the person of his servants, so that the king might be compelled to acknowledge something divine in these young men. Whence, then, was this superiority? for the Chaldeans boasted of their wisdom from their birth, and esteemed other nations as barbarians. The Jews, they would argue, are eminent beyond all others; verily the God whom they worship distributes at his will talent and perception, since no one is naturally gifted unless he receives this grace from heaven. God, therefore, must necessarily be glorified, because Daniel and his comrades very far surpassed the Chaldeans. Thus God usually causes his enemies to gaze with wonder on his power, even when they most completely shun the light. For what did King Nebuchadnezzar propose, but to extinguish the very remembrance of God? For he wished to have about him Jews of noble family, who should oppose the very religion in which they were born. But God frustrated this plan of the tyrant's, and took care to make his own name more illustrious. It now follows:

21. And Daniel continued *even* unto the first year of king Cyrus.

21. Et fuit Daniel usque ad annum primum Cyri regis.

Expositors are puzzled with this verse, because, as we shall afterwards see, the Vision occurred to Daniel in the third year of Cyrus's reign. Some explain the word היה, *haiah*, by to be "broken;" but this is by no means in accordance with the history. Their opinion is right who say that Daniel continued to the first year of the reign of Cyrus in the discharge of the prophetic office, although expositors do not openly say so; but I state openly what they say obscurely. For since he afterwards set out into Media, they say this change is denoted here. But we may understand the words better in the sense of Daniel's flourishing among the Chaldeans and Assyrians, and being acknowledged as a celebrated Prophet; because he is known to have interpreted King Belshazzar's vision, on the very night on which he was slain. The word here is simple and complete —*he was*—but it depends on the succeeding ones, since he always obtained the confidence and authority of a Prophet with the kings of Babylon. This, then, is the true sense.[1]

CHAPTER SECOND.

In this second chapter we are informed how God brought Daniel into a theatre, to exhibit that prophetic office to which he had been destined. God had already engraven, as we have said, distinct marks by which Daniel might be acknowledged as a Prophet, but he wished really to prove the effect of the grace which he had conferred upon Daniel. First of all, a simple history is narrated, then Daniel proceeds to the interpretation of a dream. This is the heading of the chapter.

1. And in the second year of the reign of Nebuchadnezzar, Nebuchadnezzar dreamed dreams, wherewith his spirit was troubled, and his sleep brake from him.

1. Anno autem secundo regni Nebuchadnezzar somniavit Nebuchadnezzar somnia: et contritus fuit spiritus ejus, et somnus ejus interruptus est ei.[2]

Daniel here says,—King Nebuchadnezzar dreamt in the second year of his reign. This seems contrary to the opinion expressed in the first chapter. For if Nebuchadnezzar besieged Jerusalem in the first year of his reign, how could Daniel be already reckoned among the wise men and astrologers, while he was as yet but a disciple? Thus it is easily gathered from the context that he and his companions were already brought forward to minister before the king. At the first glance these things are not in accordance, because in the first year of Nebuchadnezzar's reign Daniel and his companions were delivered into training; and

[1] See the DISSERTATIONS at the end of this Volume.
[2] As they translate, or "departed from him,' or was upon him.—*Calvin.*

in the second he was in danger of death through being in the number of the Magi. Some, as we have mentioned elsewhere, count the second year from the capture and destruction of the city, for they say Nebuchadnezzar was called king from the time at which he obtained the monarchy in peace. Before he had cut off the City and Temple with the Nation, his Monarchy could not be treated as united; hence they refer this to the capture of the city, as I have said. But I rather incline to another conjecture as more probable —that of his reigning with his father, and I have shewn that when he besieged Jerusalem in the time of Jehoiachim, he was sent by his father; he next returned to Chaldea from the Egyptian expedition, through his wish to repress revolts, if any one should dare to rebel. In this, therefore, there is nothing out of place. Nebuchadnezzar reigned before the death of his father, because he had already been united with him in the supreme power; then he reigned alone, and the present narrative happened in the second year of his reign. In this explanation there is nothing forced, and as the history agrees with it, I adopt it as the best.

He says—*he dreamt dreams*, and yet only one Dream is narrated; but since many things were involved in this dream, the use of the plural number is not surprising. It is now added, *his spirit was contrite*, to shew us how uncommon the dream really was. For Nebuchadnezzar did not then begin to dream, and was not formerly so frightened every night as to send for all the Magi. Hence, in this dream there was something extraordinary, which Daniel wished to express in these words. The clause at the end of the verse which they usually translate *his sleep was interrupted*, does not seem to have this sense; another explanation which our brother D. Antonius gave you[1] suits it better; namely,—his sleep was upon him, meaning he began to sleep again. The genuine and simple sense of the words seems to me—*his spirit was confused*, that is, very great terror had seized on his mind. He knew, indeed, the dream to be sent from heaven; next, being astonished, he slept

[1] This clause "which our brother D. Antonius gave you," is omitted in the French editions of 1562 and 1569.

again, and became like a dead man, and when he considered the interpretation of the dream, he became stupified and returned to sleep and forgot the vision, as we shall afterwards see. It follows—

2. Then the king commanded to call the magicians, and the astrologers, and the sorcerers, and the Chaldeans, for to shew the king his dreams. So they came and stood before the king.	2. Et edixit rex ut vocarentur[1] astrologi, et conjectores, et divini, et Chaldei, annuntiarent regi somnia sua:[2] et venerunt et steterunt in conspectu regis.

This verse more clearly proves what I have already said—that the dream caused the king to feel God to be its author. Though this was not his first dream, yet the terror which God impressed on his mind, compelled him to summon all the Magi, since he could not rest even by returning to sleep. He felt as it were a sting in his mind, since God did not suffer him to rest, but wished him to be troubled until he received an interpretation of the dream. Even profane writers very correctly consider dreams connected with divine agency. They express various opinions, because they could not know anything with perfect certainty; yet the persuasion was fixed in their minds relative to some divine agency in dreams. It would be foolish and puerile to extend this to all dreams; as we see some persons never passing by a single one without a conjecture, and thus making themselves ridiculous. We know dreams to arise from different causes; as, for instance, from our daily thoughts. If I have meditated on anything during the daytime, something occurs to me at night in a dream; because the mind is not completely buried in slumber, but retains some seed of intelligence, although it be suffocated. Experience also sufficiently teaches us how our daily thoughts recur during sleep, and hence the various affections of the mind and body produce many dreams. If any one retires to bed in sorrow from either the death of a friend, or any loss, or through suffering any injury or adversity, his dreams will partake of the previous preparation of his mind. The body itself causes dreams, as we see in the case of those

---

[1] I hardly know by what equivalent expressions to render these Hebrew words. I will speak, therefore, of the thing itself.—*Calvin.*
[2] That is, to expound his dreams to the king.—*Calvin.*

who suffer from fever; when thirst prevails they imagine fountains, burnings, and similar fancies. We perceive also how intemperance disturbs men in their sleep; for drunken men start and dream in their sleep, as if in a state of phrensy. As there are many natural causes for dreams, it would be quite out of character to be seeking for divine agency or fixed reason in them all; and on the other hand, it is sufficiently evident that some dreams are under divine regulation. I omit events which have been related in ancient histories; but surely the dream of Calphurnia, the wife of Julius Cæsar, could not be fictitious; because, before he was slain it was commonly reported, " Cæsar has been killed," just as she dreamt it. The same may be said of the physician of Augustus, who had ordered him to leave his tent the day of the battle of Pharsalia, and yet there was no reason why the physician should order him to be carried out of the tent on a litter, unless he had dreamt it to be necessary. What was the nature of that necessity? why, such as could not be conjectured by human skill, for the camp of Augustus was taken at that very moment. I doubt not there are many fabulous accounts, but here I may choose what I shall believe, and I do not yet touch on dreams which are mentioned in God's word, for I am merely speaking of what profane men were compelled to think on this subject. Although Aristotle freely rejected all sense of divination, through being prejudiced in the matter, and desiring to reduce the nature of Deity within the scope of human ingenuity, and to comprehend all things by his acuteness; yet he expresses this confession, that all dreams do not happen rashly, but that μαντική, that is " divination," is the source of some of them. He disputes, indeed, whether they belong to the intellectual or sensitive portion of the mind, and concludes they belong to the latter, as far as it is imaginative. Afterwards, when inquiring whether they are causes or anything of that kind, he is disposed to view them only as symptoms or accidents fortuitously contingent. Meanwhile, he will not admit dreams to be sent from heaven; and adds as his reason, that many stupid men dream, and manifest the same reason in them as the wisest. He notices next the brute creation, some of which, as elephants, dream. As the brutes dream, and wise men more seldom than the rudest idiots, Aristotle does not think it probable that dreams are divinely inspired. He denies, therefore, that they are sent from God, or divine, but asserts that they spring from the *Daimones*;[1] that is, he fancies them to be something between the natures of the Deity and the Daimones. We know the sense in which philosophers use that word, which, in Scripture, has usually a bad sense. He says that dreams were occasioned by those aërial inspirations, but are not from God ; because, he says, man's nature is not divine, but inferior ; and yet more than earthly, since it is angelic. Cicero discourses on this subject at great length, in his first book on Divination ; although he refutes in the second all he had said, while he was a disciple of the Academy.[2] For among other arguments in proof of the existence of deities, he adds dreams ;—if there is any divination in dreams, it follows that there is a Deity in heaven, for the mind of man cannot conceive of any dream without divine inspiration. Cicero's reasoning is valid ; if there is divination in dreams, then is there also a Deity. The distinction made by Macrobius is worthy of notice ; although he ignorantly confounds species and genera, through being a person of imperfect judgment, who strung together in rhapsodies whatever he read, without either discrimination or arrangement. This, then, should remain fixed,—the opinion concerning the existence of some kind of divine agency in dreams was not rashly implanted in the hearts of all men. Hence that expression of Homer's, a dream is from Jupiter.[3] He does not mean this generally and promiscuously of all dreams ; but he takes notice of it, when bringing the characters of his heroes before us, since they were divinely admonished in their sleep.

I now come to NEBUCHADNEZZAR'S DREAM. In this, two points are worthy of remark : First, all remembrance of its

---

[1] Calvin uses the Greek words ἐνύπνια, θεῖα, and δαιμόνια. The Greek *Daimones* corresponded with our idea of angels, and were said to be the origin of human souls. See most interesting passages in the Dialogues of Plato, also the DISSERTATION on this verse at the close of the Volume.

[2] De Divin., lib. i. § 21-23 ; and lib. ii. § 58, *et seq*.

[3] Iliad, book i. v. 63.

subject was entirely obliterated; and secondly, no interpretation was found for it. Sometimes the remembrance of a dream was not lost while its interpretation was unknown. But here Nebuchadnezzar was not only perplexed at the interpretation of the dream, but even the vision itself had vanished, and thus his perplexity and anxiety was doubled. As to the next point, there is no novelty in Daniel making known the interpretation; for it sometimes, but rarely, happens that a person dreams without a figure or enigma, and with great plainness, without any need of conjurors—a name given to interpreters of dreams. This indeed happens but seldom, since the usual plan of dreams is for God to speak by them allegorically and obscurely. And this occurs in the case of the profane as well as of the servants of God. When Joseph dreamt that he was adored by the sun and moon, (Gen. xxxvii. 9,) he was ignorant of its meaning; when he dreamt of his sheaf being adored by his brothers' sheaves, he understood not its meaning, but related it simply to his brothers. Hence God often speaks in enigmas by dreams, until the interpretation is added. And such was Nebuchadnezzar's dream.

We perceive, then, that God reveals his will even to unbelievers, but not clearly; because seeing they do not see, just as if they were gazing at a closed book or sealed letter; as Isaiah says,—God speaks to unbelievers in broken accents and with a stammering tongue. (Is. xxviii. 11, and xxix. 11.) God's will was so revealed to Nebuchadnezzar that he still remained perplexed and lay completely astonished. His dream would have been of no use to him, unless, as we shall see, Daniel had been presented to him as its interpreter. For God not only wished to hold the king in suspense, but he thus blotted out the remembrance of the dream from his mind, to increase the power of his sting. As mankind are accustomed to neglect the dreams which they do not remember, God inwardly fastened such a sting in the mind of this unbeliever, as I have already said, that he could not rest, but was always wakeful in the midst of his dreaming, because God was drawing him to himself by secret chains. This is the true reason why God denied him the immediate explanation of his dream, and blotted out the remembrance of it from his mind, until he should receive both from Daniel. We will leave the rest till to-morrow.

PRAYER.

Grant, Almighty God, since every perfect gift comes from thee, and since some excel others in intelligence and talents, yet as no one has anything of his own, but as thou deignest to distribute to man a measure of thy gracious liberality,—Grant that whatever intelligence thou dost confer upon us, we may apply it to the glory of thy name. Grant also, that we may acknowledge in humility and modesty what thou hast committed to our care to be thine own; and may we study to be restrained by sobriety, to desire nothing superfluous, never to corrupt true and genuine knowledge, and to remain in that simplicity to which thou callest us. Finally, may we not rest in these earthly things, but learn rather to raise our minds to true wisdom, to acknowledge thee to be the true God, and to devote ourselves to the obedience of thy righteousness; and may it be our sole object to devote and consecrate ourselves entirely to the glory of thy name throughout our lives, through Jesus Christ our Lord.—Amen.

Lecture Fifth.

WE yesterday saw the Magi sent for by the king's edict, not only in order to explain his dream to him, but also to narrate the dream itself which had slipt from his memory. But since four kinds of Magi are used here, or at least three, and their description is added in the fourth place, I shall briefly touch upon what seems to me their meaning. הרטמים, *Hartummim*, is usually explained by "soothsayers," and afterwards אשפים, *Assaphim*, they think, means "physicians." I am unwilling to contend against the first interpretation; but I see no reason for the second. They interpret it as "physicians," because they judge of men's health by feeling the pulse, but having no better reason than this, I adopt the opinion that it refers to astrologers. In the third place, מכשפים, *Mecasphim*, is used, meaning "sorcerers," though some change the signification, and say it means "star-gazers," who indicate future events and predict unknown ones from the position of the stars. I have nothing to bring forward more probable than this, except the uncertainty of what the Hebrews meant by the word: for since the matter itself is so buried in oblivion, who can distinguish between words which belong to the profession of an unknown art? כשדים, *Casdim*, is doubtless put for a race, for it is the name of a nation, yet on account of its excellence, the Magi appropriated it to themselves, as if the nobility and excellence of the whole nation was in their power; and this name is known to be in common use in Greece and Italy. All who professed their ability to predict future or hidden events from the stars or other conjectures, were called Chaldees. With respect to the three other words, I do not doubt their honourable meaning, and for this reason they called themselves Mathematicians, as if there were no science in the world except with them. Besides, although their principles were good, they were certainly stuffed with many superstitions, for they were soothsayers and diviners, and we know them to have given especial attention to augury. Although they were highly esteemed by their fellow-countrymen, yet they are condemned by God's law, for all their pretence to science was complete imposture. They are generally called Magi, and also Chaldeans, as shortly afterwards, when Daniel will repeat what they have spoken before the king, he will not enumerate those three species, but will simply call them Chaldees. It is surprising that Daniel and his companions were not called among them, for he ought to have been called among the first, since the king, as we have said, found these four to be ten times better than all the Magi and Diviners throughout his kingdom! Since their dexterity was not unknown to the king, why does he pass them completely by, while the other Magi are at hand and are called in to a case so arduous? Very probably the king omitted them because he trusted more in the natives; or suspected the captives, and was unwilling to entrust them with his secrets, as he had not yet sufficiently tried their fidelity and constancy. This might have been the reason, but it is better for us to consider the intention of the Almighty, for I have no doubt that this forgetfulness on the part of the king occurred by God's providence, as he was unwilling from the first to mingle his servant Daniel and the rest with the Magi and Soothsayers. This accounts for Daniel not being sent for with the rest; whence, as we shall see, his divination would afterwards become more illustrious. It now follows:

3. And the king said unto them, I have dreamed a dream, and my spirit was troubled to know the dream.

3 Et dixit illis rex, Somnium somniavi, et contritus est spiritus meus, ad sciendum[1] somnium.

I will add the next verse:

4. Then spake the Chaldeans to the king in Syriack, O king, live for ever: tell thy servants the dream, and we will shew the interpretation.

4. Et dixerunt Chaldæi regi Syriace, Rex in eternum vive: dic somnium servis tuis, et expositionem indicabimus.

Daniel relates first the great confidence of the Chaldeans, since they dared to promise the interpretation of a dream as yet unknown to them. *The king says he was troubled through desire to understand the dream;* by which he signifies that a kind of riddle was divinely set before him. He confesses his ignorance, while the importance of the object may be gathered from his words. Since, then, the king testifies his desire to inquire concerning a matter obscure and profound, and exceeding his comprehension, and since he clearly expresses himself to be contrite in spirit, some kind of fear and anxiety ought to have touched these Chaldeans; yet they securely promise to offer the very best interpretation of the dream as soon as they understood it. When they say, *O king, live for ever,* it is not a simple and unmeaning prayer, but they rather order the king to be cheerful and in good spirits, as they are able to remove all care and anxiety from his mind, because the explanation of the dream was at hand. We know how liberal in words those impostors always were; according to the language of an ancient poet, they enriched the ears and emptied the purses of others. And truly those who curiously court the breeze with their ears deserve to feed upon it, and to be taken in by such deceits. And all ages have proved that nothing

[1] For understanding.—*Calvin.*

exceeds the confidence of astrologers, who are not content with true science, but divine every one's life and death, and conjecture all events, and profess to know everything. We must hold generally that the art of conjecturing from dreams is rash and foolish; there is, indeed, a certain fixed interpretation of dreams, as we said yesterday, yet as we shall afterwards see, this ought not to be ascribed to a sure science, but to God's singular gift. As, therefore, a prophet will not gather what he has to say from fixed reasonings, but will explain God's oracles, so also he who will interpret dreams correctly, will not follow certain distinct rules; but if God has explained the meaning of the dream, he will then undertake the office of interpreting it according to his endowment with this gift. Properly speaking, these two things are opposite to each other and do not mutually agree, general and perpetual science, and special revelation. Since God claims this power of opening by means of a dream, what he has engraven on the minds of men, hence art and science cannot obtain it, but a revelation from the spirit must be waited for. When the Chaldeans thus boldly promise to become good interpreters of the dream, they not only betray their rashness, but become mere impostors, who pretend to be proficients in a science of which they know nothing, as if they could predict by their conjectures the meaning of the king's dream. It now follows:

5. The king answered and said to the Chaldeans, The thing is gone from me: if ye will not make known unto me the dream, with the interpretation thereof, ye shall be cut in pieces, and your houses shall be made a dunghill.

5. Respondit rex et dixit Chaldæis, Sermo a me exiit,[1] si non indicaveritis mihi somnium et interpretationem ejus, frusta efficiemini,[2] et domus vestræ ponentur sterquilinium.[3]

Here the king requires from the Chaldeans more than they professed to afford him; for although their boasting, as we have said, was foolish in promising to interpret any dream, yet they never claimed the power of narrating to any one his dreams. The king, therefore, seems to me to act unjustly

[1] Or, has departed.—*Calvin.*
[2] Some translate הדמין, *hedmin*, by "blood;" but the received meaning is better, and since there is little difference in the matter itself, I shall not trouble you concerning it.—*Calvin.*
[3] That is, shall be made a dunghill.—*Calvin.*

in not regarding what they had hitherto professed, and the limits of their art and science, if indeed they had any science! When he says—the matter or speech had departed from him, the words admit of a twofold sense, for מִלְּתָה, *millethah,* may be taken for an "edict," as we shall afterwards see; and so it might be read, *has flowed away;* but since the same form of expression will be shortly repeated when it seems to be used of the dream, (ver. 8,) this explanation is suitable enough, as the king says his dream had vanished: so I leave the point undecided. It is worth while noticing again what we said yesterday, that terror was so fastened upon the king as to deprive him of rest, and yet he was not so instructed that the least taste of the revelation remained; just as if an ox, stunned by a severe blow, should toss himself about, and roll over and over. Such is the madness of this wretched king, because God harasses him with dreadful torments; all the while the remembrance of the dream is altogether obliterated from his mind. Hence he confesses—*his dream had escaped him;* and although the Magi had prescribed the limits of their science, yet through their boasting themselves to be interpreters of the gods, he did not hesitate to exact of them what they had never professed. This is the just reward of arrogance, when men puffed up with a perverse confidence assume before others more than they ought, and forgetful of all modesty wish to be esteemed angelic spirits. Without the slightest doubt God wished to make a laughingstock of this foolish boasting which was conspicuous among the Chaldees, when the king sharply demanded of them to relate his dream, as well as to offer an exposition of it.

He afterwards adds threats, clearly tyrannical; *unless they expound the dream, their life is in danger.* No common punishment is threatened, but he says they should become "pieces"—if we take the meaning of the word to signify "pieces." If we think it means "blood,' the sense will be the same. This wrath of the king is clearly furious, nay, Nebuchadnezzar in this respect surpassed all the cruelty of wild beasts. What fault could be imputed to the Chaldeans if they did not know the king's dream?—surely, they had never professed this, as we shall afterwards see ; and no king had ever demanded what was beyond the faculty of man. We perceive how the king manifested a brutal rage when he denounced death and every cruel torture on the Magi and sorcerers. Tyrants, indeed, often give the reins to their lust, and think all things lawful to themselves ; whence, also, these words of the tragedian, Whatever he wishes is lawful. And Sophocles says, with evident truth, that any one entering a tyrant's threshold must cast away his liberty ; but if we were to collect all examples, we should scarcely find one like this. It follows, then, that the king's mind was impelled by diabolic fury, urging him to punish the Chaldees who, with respect to him, were innocent enough. We know them to have been impostors, and the world to have been deluded by their impositions, which rendered them deserving of death, since by the precepts of the law it was a capital crime for any one to pretend to the power of prophecy by magic arts. (Lev. xx. 6.) But, as far as concerned the king, they could not be charged with any crime. Why, then, did he threaten them with death ? because the Lord wished to shew the miracle which we shall afterwards see. For if the king had suffered the Chaldeans to depart, he could have buried directly that anxiety which tortured and excruciated his mind. The subject, too, had been less noticed by the people ; hence God tortured the king's mind, till he rushed headlong in his fury, as we have said. Thus, this atrocious and cruel denunciation ought to have aroused all men ; for there is no doubt that the greatest and the least trembled together when they heard of such vehemence in the monarch's wrath. This, therefore, is the complete sense, and we must mark the object of God's providence in thus allowing the king's anger to burn without restraint.[1] It follows :

[1] Calvin is correct in preferring the sense of "pieces" to that of "blood;" for הדם, *hedem*, is a Chaldee word, and the ן is the Chaldee plural ending ; his criticism, too, on מלה, *meleh*, is also correct ; for it is the Chaldee equivalent for דבר, *deber*, a "word" or thing, and justly rendered "edict." As great light has been thrown upon the meaning and derivation of single words since Calvin's time, we may often find that modern knowledge has rendered his derivations untenable ; still the soundness of his judgment is

6. But if ye shew the dream, and the interpretation thereof, ye shall receive of me gifts and rewards, and great honour: therefore shew me the dream, and the interpretation thereof.

6. Et si somnium, et interpretationem ejus indicaveritis, donum, et munus, et honorem, vel *pretium*, magnum accipietis a facie mea:[1] propterea somnium, et interpretationem ejus indicate mihi.

Here the king, on the other hand, desires to entice them by the hope of gain, to apply themselves to narrate his dream. He had already attempted to strike them with horror, that even if they are unwilling he may wrest the narration of the dream from them as well as its interpretation. Meanwhile, if they could be induced by flattery, he tries this argument upon them; for he promises *a gift, and reward, and honour*, that is, he promises a large remuneration if they narrated his dream, and were faithful interpreters. Hence we gather, what all history declares, that the Magi made a gain of their predictions and guesses. The wise men of the Indies, being frugal and austere in their manner of living, were not wholly devoted to gain; for they are known to have lived without any need of either money, or furniture, or anything else. They were content with roots, and had no need of clothing, slept upon the ground, and were thus free from avarice. But the Chaldeans, we know, ran hither and thither to obtain money from the simple and credulous. Hence the king here speaks according to custom when he promises a large reward. We must remark here, how the Chaldeans scattered their prophecies for the sake of gain; and when knowledge is rendered saleable, it is sure to be adulterated with many faults. As when Paul speaks of corruptors of the Gospel, he says,—they trafficked in it, (2 Cor. ii. 17,) because when a profit is made, as we have previously said, even honourable teachers must necessarily degenerate and pervert all sincerity by their lying. For where avarice reigns, there is flattery, servile obsequiousness, and cunning of all kinds, while truth is utterly extinguished. Whence it

worthy of notice. It may be added, too, that the perplexity is increased when Chaldee forms are used, although there is a uniform change of single letters observable in the two languages. Thus ש, *sh*, becomes ת, *th*, as in verses 7 and 14; the Hebrew ז, *z*, becomes ד, *d*, in ver. 26; so the צ, *tz*, becomes ע, *gn;* the final ה, *h*, is turned into א, *a*, and the final ם, *m*, into ן, *n*.

[1] That is, by me.—*Calvin*.

is not surprising if the Chaldeans were so inclined to deceit, as it became natural to them through the pursuit of gain and the lust for wealth. Some honest teachers may receive support from the public treasury; but, as we have said, when any one is drawn aside by lucre, he must necessarily pervert and deprave all purity of doctrine. And from this passage we gather, further, the anxiety of the king, as he had no wish to spare expense, if by this means he could elicit the interpretation of his dream from the Chaldeans; all the while he is furiously angry with them, because he does not obtain what the offered reward ought to procure. It now follows:

7. They answered again, and said, Let the king tell his servants the dream, and we will shew the interpretation of it.
8. The king answered and said, I know of certainty that ye would gain the time, because ye see the thing is gone from me.

7. Responderunt secundo, et dixerunt, Rex somnium exponat[1] servis suis, et interpretationem indicabimus.
8. Respondit rex et dixit. Vere[2] novi ego[3] quod tempus redimitis, quia scitis quod exierit sermo a me.[4]

We may add the following verse;

9. But if ye will not make known unto me the dream, *there is but* one decree for you; for ye have prepared lying and corrupt words to speak before me, till the time be changed: therefore tell me the dream, and I shall know that ye can shew me the interpretation thereof.

9. Propterea si somnium non indicaveritis mihi, una hæc sententia *est;* et sermonem mendacem[5] et corruptum præparastis ad dicendum coram me, donec tempus mutetur;[6] propterea somnium narrate mihi, et cognoscam quod interpretationem ejus mihi indicetis.[7]

Here the excuse of the Magi is narrated. They state the truth that their art only enabled them to discover the interpretation of a dream; but the king wished to know the dream itself. Whence he appears again to have been seized with prodigious fury and became quite implacable. Kings sometimes grow warm, but are appeased by a single admonition, and hence this sentiment is very true,—anger is assuaged by mild language. But since the fair re-

[1] Narrate.—*Calvin.* [2] In truth.—*Calvin.*
[3] Now I know.—*Calvin.*
[4] That is, that the dream has fallen out of my mind, or the sentence has gone out of my lips.—*Calvin.*
[5] Or, fallacious.—*Calvin.* [6] That is, pass by.—*Calvin.*
[7] That is, ye may be able to explain to me.—*Calvin.*

ply of the Magi did not mitigate the king's wrath, he was quite hurried away by diabolical vehemence. And all this, as I have said, was governed by God's secret counsel, that Daniel's explanation might be more noticed. They next ask the king—*to relate his dream*, and then they promise as before to interpret it directly. And even this was too great a boast, as we have said, and they ought to have corrected their own conceit and foolish boasting when in such a difficulty. But since they persist in that foolish and fallacious self-conceit, it shews us how they were blinded by the devil, just as those who have become entangled by superstitious deceptions confidently defend their own madness. Such an example we have in the Magi, who always claimed the power of interpreting dreams.

The king's exception now follows :—*I know*, says he, *that ye would gain time, since you are aware that the matter has gone from me,* or the word has been pronounced, if we adopt the former sense. The king here accuses them of more disgraceful cunning, since the Magi have nothing to offer, and so desire to escape as soon as they know that the king has lost all remembrance of his dream. It is just as if he had said—You promised me to be sure interpreters of my dream, but this is false ; for if I could narrate the dream, it would be easy to prove your arrogance, since ye cannot explain that enigma ; but as ye know I have forgotten my dream, for that reason ye ask me to relate it ; but *this is only to gain time,* says he ; thus ye manage to conceal your ignorance and retain your credit for knowledge. But if my dream still remained in my memory I should soon detect your ignorance, for ye cannot perform your boasting. We see, therefore, how the king here loads the Magi with a new crime, because they were impostors who deluded the people with false boastings ; and hence he shews them worthy of death, unless they relate his dream. The argument indeed is utterly vicious ; but it is not surprising when tyrants appear in the true colours of their cruelty. Meanwhile we must remember what I have said,—the Magi deserved this reproof, for they were puffed up with vanity and made false promises, through conjecturing the future from dreams, auguries, and the like. But in the king's case, nothing was more unjust than to invent such a crime against the Magi, since if they deceived others it arose from being self-deceived. They were blinded and fascinated by the foolish persuasion of their own wisdom, and had no intention of deceiving the king; for they thought something might immediately occur which would free his mind from all anxiety. But the king always pursued the blindest impulse of his rage. Meanwhile we must notice the origin of this feeling,—he was divinely tormented, and could not rest a single moment till he obtained an explanation of his dream. He next adds, *If ye do not explain my dream, this sentence alone remains for you,* says he; that is, it is already decreed concerning you all, I shall not inquire particularly which of you is in fault and which wishes to deceive me; but I will utterly cut off all the tribe of the Magi, and no one shall escape punishment, unless ye explain to me both the dream and its interpretation.

He adds again, *Ye have prepared a fallacious and corrupt speech to relate here before me,* as your excuse. Again, the king charges them with fraud and malice, of which they were not guilty; as if he had said, they purposely sought specious pretences for practising deceit. But he says, *a lying speech,* or fallacious *and corrupt;* that is, yours is a stale excuse, as we commonly say, and I loathe it. If there were any colourable pretext I might admit what ye say, but I see in your words nothing but fallacies, and those too which savour of corruption. Now, therefore, we observe the king not only angry because the Magi cannot relate his dream, but charging it against them, as a greater crime, that they brought a stale excuse and wished purposely to deceive him. He next adds, *tell me the dream and then I shall know it;* or then I shall know that ye can faithfully interpret its meaning. Here the king takes up another argument to convict the Magi of cunning. Ye boast, indeed, that you have no difficulty in interpreting the dream. How can ye be confident of this, for the dream itself is still unknown to you? If I had told it you, ye might then say whether ye could explain it or not; but when I now ask you about the dream of which both you and I are ignorant, ye say, when I have related the dream, the rest is in your power; I therefore shall prove you to be good and true interpreters of dreams if ye can tell me mine, since the one thing depends on the other, and ye are too rash in presuming upon what is not yet discovered. Since, therefore, ye burst forth so hastily, and wish to persuade me that ye are sure of the interpretation, you are evidently quite deceived in this respect; and your rashness and fraud are herein detected, because ye are clearly deceiving me. This is the substance —the rest to-morrow.

PRAYER.

Grant, Almighty God, since during our pilgrimage in this world we have daily need of the teaching and government of thy Spirit, that with true modesty we may depend on thy word and secret inspiration, and not take too much on ourselves,—Grant, also, that we may be conscious of our ignorance, blindness, and stupidity, and always flee to thee, and never permit ourselves to be drawn aside in any way by the cunning of Satan and of the ungodly. May we remain so fixed in thy truth as never to turn aside from it, whilst thou dost direct us through the whole course of our vocation, and then may we arrive at that heavenly glory which has been obtained for us through the blood of thine only begotten Son.—Amen.

Lecture Sixth.

10. The Chaldeans answered before the king, and said, There is not a man upon the earth that can shew the king's matter: therefore *there is* no king, lord, nor ruler, *that* asked such things at any magician, or astrologer, or Chaldean.

10. Responderunt Chaldæi coram rege, et dixerunt, Non est homo super terram qui sermonem[1] regis posset explicare; propterea nullus rex, princeps, vel prefectus rem consimilem excuisivit ab ullo mago, et astrologo, et Chaldæo.

THE Chaldeans again excuse themselves for not relating the king's dream. They say, in reality, this is not their peculiar art or science; and they know of no example handed down of wise men being asked in this way, and required to answer as well *de facto* as *de jure*, as the phrase is. They

[1] Or, the matter.—*Calvin.*

boasted themselves to be interpreters of dreams, but their conjectures could not be extended to discover the dreams themselves, but only their interpretation. This was a just excuse, yet the king does not admit it, but is impelled by his own wrath and by the divine instinct to shew the Magi, and sorcerers, and astrologers, to be mere impostors and deceivers of the people. And we must observe the end in view, because God wished to extol his servant Daniel, and to separate him from the common herd. They add, that no kings had ever dealt thus with Magi and wise men. It afterwards follows:—

11. And *it is* a rare thing that the king requireth; and there is none other that can shew it before the king, except the gods, whose dwelling is not with flesh.

11. Et sermo de quo rex inquirit pretiosus est;[1] et nullus est qui possit exponere coram rege, nisi dii, quorum habitatio cum carne non est ipsis.[2]

They add, that the object of the king's inquiry surpassed the power of human ingenuity. There is no doubt that they were slow to confess this, because, as we said before, they had acquired the fame of such great wisdom, that the common people thought nothing unknown to them or concealed from them. And most willingly would they have escaped the dire necessity of confessing their ignorance in this respect, but in their extremity they were compelled to resort to this subterfuge. There may be a question why they thought the matter about which the king inquired was precious; for as they were ignorant of the king's dream, how could they ascertain its value? But it is not surprising that men, under the influence of extreme anxiety and fear, should utter anything without judgment. They say, therefore,— *this matter is precious;* thus they mingle flattery with their excuses to mitigate the king's anger, hoping to escape the unjust death which was at hand. *The matter of which the king inquires is precious;* and yet it would probably be said, since the matter was uncommon, that the dream was divinely sent to the king, and was afterwards suddenly buried in oblivion. There certainly was some mystery here, and

[1] Or, rare.—*Calvin.*
[2] Many words are superfluous, through the nature of the language.— *Calvin.*

hence the Chaldeans very reasonably considered the whole subject to surpass in magnitude the common measure of human ability; therefore they add,—*there cannot be any other interpreters than gods or angels.* Some refer this to angels, but we know the Magi to have worshipped a multitude of gods. Hence it is more simple to explain this of the crowd of deities which they imagined. They had, indeed, lesser gods; for among all nations a persuasion has existed concerning a supreme God who reigns alone. Afterwards they imagined inferior deities, and each fabricated a god for himself according to his taste. Hence they are called "gods," according to common opinion and usage, although they ought rather to be denoted genii or demons of the air. For we know that all unbelievers were imbued with this opinion concerning the existence of intermediate deities. The Apostles contended strongly against this ancient error, and we know the books of Plato[1] to be full of the doctrine that demons or genii act as mediators between man and the Heavenly Deity.

We may, then, suitably understand these words that the Chaldeans thought angels the only interpreters; not because they imagined angels as the Scriptures speak of them clearly and sincerely, but the Platonic doctrine flourished among them, and also the superstition about the genii who dwell in heaven, and hold familiar intercourse with the supreme God. Since men are clothed in flesh, they cannot so raise themselves towards heaven as to perceive all secrets. Whence it follows, that the king acted unjustly in requiring them to discharge a duty either angelic or divine. This excuse was indeed probable, but the king's ears were deaf because he was carried away by his passions, and God also spurred him on by furies, which allowed him no rest. Hence this savage conduct which Daniel records.

12. For this cause the king was angry and very furious, and commanded to destroy all the wise *men* of Babylon.

12. Propterea rex in ira et indignatione magna edixit ut interficerent omnes sapientes Babylonis.

[1] A most interesting and singular allegory on this subject occurs in Plato's *Phædrus*, edit. Bekker, § 51; edit. Priestley. (Lond., 1826,) p. 71, *et seq.;* see also *Cic. Tusc. Quæst.* i. 16; *Aristot. Metaph.* i. 5; and *De anima*, i. 2; *Diog. Laert.*, viii. 83.

The former denunciation was horrible, but now Nebuchadnezzar proceeds beyond it; for he not merely threatens the Chaldeans with death, but commands it to be inflicted. Such an example is scarcely to be found in history; but the cause of his wrath must be noticed, since God wished his servant Daniel to be brought forward and to be observed by all men. This was the preparation by which it became generally evident that the wise men of Babylon were proved vain, through promising more than they could perform; even if they had been endowed with the greatest wisdom, they would still have been destitute of that gift of revelation which was conferred upon Daniel. Hence it happened that the king denounced death against them all by his edict; for he might then perhaps acknowledge what he had never perceived before, namely, that their boasting was nothing but vanity, and their arts full of superstitions. For when superstition fails of success, madness immediately succeeds,' and when those who are thought and spoken of as remarkably devout, perceive their fictitious worship to be of no avail, then they burst forth into the madness which I have mentioned, and curse their idols, and detest what they had hitherto followed. So it occurred here, when Nebuchadnezzar suspected imposture in so serious a matter, and no previous suspicion of it had entered his mind; but now, when he sees through the deception, in so perplexing a case, and in such great anxiety, when left destitute of the advice of those from whom he hoped all things, then he is a hundredfold more infuriated than if he had been previously in a state of perfect calmness. It afterwards follows:—

13. And the decree went forth that the wise *men* should be slain; and they sought Daniel and his fellows to be slain.

14. Then Daniel answered with council and wisdom to Arioch the captain of the king's guard, which was gone forth to slay the wise *men* of Babylon:

15. He answered and said to Arioch the king's captain, Why *is*

13. Et edictum exiit et sapientes interficiebantur: et quærebant Daniel et socios ejus ad interficiendum.

14. Et tunc Daniel sciscitatus est *de* consilio et edicto ab Arioch principe satellitum regis, qui exierat ad interficiendum sapientes Babylonis.

15. Respondit et dixit ipsi Arioch præfecto[1] regis, Ad quid edic-

---

[1] It is the same noun which was lately used.— *Calvin.*

the decree *so* hasty from the king? Then Arioch made the thing known to Daniel.	tum festinaṇ è conspectu regis? Tunc rem[1] patefecit Arioch ipsi Danieli.

It appears from these words that some of the wise men had been slain, for Daniel at first is not required for slaughter; but when the Magi and Chaldeans were promiscuously dragged out for punishment, Daniel and his companions were in the same danger. And this is clearly expressed thus— *when the edict had gone forth*, that is, was published, according to the Latin phrase, *and the wise men were slain*, then Daniel was also sought for; because the king would never suffer his decree to be despised after it had once been published; for if he had publicly commanded this to be done, and no execution had been added, would not this have been ridiculous? Hence, very probably, the slaughter of the Magi and Chaldeans was extensive. Although the king had no lawful reason for his conduct, yet they deserved their punishment; for, as we said yesterday, they deserved to be exterminated from the world, and the pest must be removed if it could possibly be accomplished. If Nebuchadnezzar had been like David, or Hezekiah, or Josiah, he might most justly have destroyed them all, and have purged the land from such defilements; but as he was only carried away by the fervour of his wrath, he was himself in fault. Meanwhile, God justly punishes the Chaldeans, and this admonition ought to profit the whole people. They were hardened in their error, and were doubtless rendered more excuseless by being blinded against such a judgment of God. Because Daniel was condemned to death, though he had not been called by the king, the injustice of the edicts of those kings who do not inquire into the causes of which they are judges, becomes more manifest.

Nebuchadnezzar had often heard of Daniel, and had been compelled to admire the dexterity of his genius, and the singular gift of his wisdom. How comes it, then, that he passed him by when he had need of his singular skill? Although the king anxiously inquires concerning the dream, yet we observe he does not act seriously; since it would

---

[1] Or, discourse.—*Calvin*.

doubtless have come into his mind, "Behold, thou hadst formerly beheld in the captives of Judah the incredible gift of celestial wisdom—then, in the first place, send for them!" Here the king's sloth is detected because he did not send for Daniel among the rest. We have stated this to be governed by the secret providence of God, who was unwilling that his servant should mix with those ministers of Satan, whose whole knowledge consisted in juggling and errors. We now see how the king had neglected the gift of God, and had stifled the light offered to him; but Daniel is next dragged to death. Therefore, I said, that tyrants are, for this reason, very unjust, and exercise a cruel violence because they will not undertake the labour and trouble of inquiry. Meanwhile we see that God wonderfully snatches his own people from the jaws of death, as it happened in Daniel's case; for we may be surprised at Arioch sparing his life when he slew the others who were natives. How can we account for Daniel meeting with more humanity than the Chaldeans, though he was a foreigner and a captive? Because his life was in the hand and keeping of God, who restrained both the mind and the hand of the prefect from being immediately savage with him. But it is said—Daniel *inquired concerning the counsel and the edict.* Some translate *prudently* and *cunningly:* and עֵטָא, *gneta,* signifies "prudence," just as טַעַם, *tegnem,* metaphorically is received for "intelligence" when it signifies taste.[1] But we shall afterwards find this latter word used for an edict, and because this sense appears to suit better, I therefore adopt it, as Daniel had inquired of the prefect the meaning of the edict and the king's design. Arioch also is called the Prince of Satellites. Some translate it of executioners, and others of cooks, for טְבַח, *tebech,* signifies "to slay," but the noun deduced from this means a cook. Thus Potiphar is called, to whom Joseph was sold. (Gen. xxxix. 1.) It seems to me a kind of absurdity to call him the prince of gaolers; and if we say the prefect of cooks, it is equally unsuitable to his office of being sent to slay the Chaldeans. I therefore

---

[1] So translated in Auth. Vers., Exod. xvi. 31; Num. xi. 8; Job vi. 6; and Jer. xlviii. 11.

prefer interpreting it more mildly, supposing him to be the prefect of the guards ; for, as I have said, Potiphar is called רב טבחים, *reb tebechim,* and here the pronunciation only is changed. It follows:

Daniel also had said, Whither does the edict hasten from before the king? It seems by these words, that Daniel obliquely blames the king's anger and ingratitude, because he did not inquire with sufficient diligence before he rushed forward to that cruel punishment. Then he seems to mark his ingratitude, since he is now undeservedly doomed to death without being sent for, though the king might have known what was in him. As he refers to haste, I do not doubt his expostulating with the king, since he was neither called for nor listened to, and yet was to be slain with the rest, as if he were guilty of the same fault as the Chaldeans. The conclusion is,—there was no reason for such haste, since the king would probably find what he desired, if he inquired more diligently. It is afterwards added, *Arioch explained the matter to Daniel.* Whence it appears that Daniel was formerly ignorant of the whole matter ; and hence we may conjecture the amount of the terror which seized upon the pious man. For he had known nothing about it, and was led to punishment suddenly and unexpectedly, as if he had been guilty. Hence, it was necessary for him to be divinely strengthened, that he might with composure seek the proper time from both the prefect and the king, for relating the dream and adding its interpretation. Daniel's power of acting so composedly, arose from God's singular gift, since terror would otherwise have seized on his mind ; for we are aware that in sudden events, we become deprived of all plan, and lose our presence of mind. Since nothing of this kind was perceived in Daniel, it becomes clear that his mind was governed by God's Spirit. It is afterwards added—

16. Then Daniel went in, and desired of the king that he would give him time, and that he would shew the king the interpretation.

16. Et Daniel ingressus est, et postulavit a rege, ut tempus daret sibi, et expositionem[1] afferret regi.

This verse contains nothing new, unless we must notice what is not expressed, namely, that the prefect was not en-

[1] Interpretation.—*Calvin.*

tirely without fear in giving Daniel an introduction to the king. For he knew the king to be very angry, and himself under serious displeasure, for not immediately executing the edict. But, as we have already said, God had taken Daniel into his confidence, and so bends and tames the mind of the prefect, that he no longer hesitates to introduce Daniel to the king. Another point is also gathered from the context, namely, Daniel's obtaining his request; for it is said, *he returned home*, doubtless, because he obtained a single day from the king with the view of satisfying his demands on the next day. And yet it is surprising that this favour was granted, since the king wished the dream narrated to him immediately. Although Daniel does not here relate the reasons which he used with the king, yet most probably he confessed what we shall afterwards observe in its own place, namely, that he was not endued with sufficient intelligence to expound the dream, but hoping in God's kindness, he would return next day with a new revelation. Otherwise the king would never have permitted this, if Daniel had petitioned doubtfully; or if he had not borne witness to his hopes of some secret revelation from God, he would have been rejected immediately, and would have provoked still further the anger of the king. The Hebrews very commonly mention afterwards, in the context, whatever they omit in its proper place. So when he modestly confesses his inability to satisfy the king, till he has received from the Lord a faithful message, the king grants him the required time, as we shall see more clearly afterwards. It follows—

17. Then Daniel went to his house, and made the thing known to Hananiah, Mishael, and Azariah, his companions:
18. That they would desire mercies of the God of heaven concerning this secret; that Daniel and his fellows should not perish with the rest of the wise *men* of Babylon.

17. Tunc Daniel in domum venit,[1] et Hananiæ, et Misaeli, et Azariæ sociis suis sermonem[2] patefecit.
18. Et misericordias ad petendum[3] a facie Dei cœlorum super arcano hoc, ut ne interficerentur Daniel et socii ejus cum residuo sapientum Babylonis.[4]

[1] Departed.—*Calvin.*   [2] Or, the matter.—*Calvin.*
[3] Verbally, to implore mercy.—*Calvin.*
[4] That is, with the rest of the wise men of Babylon.—*Calvin.*

We observe with what object and with what confidence Daniel demanded an extension of time. His object was to implore God's grace. Confidence was also added, since he perceived a double punishment awaiting him, if he disappointed the king; if he had returned the next day without a reply, the king would not have been content with an easy death, but would have raged with cruelty against Daniel, in consequence of his deception. Without the slightest doubt, Daniel expected what he obtained—namely, that the king's dream would be revealed to him. He therefore urges his companions to implore unitedly mercy from God. Daniel had already obtained the singular gift of being an interpreter of dreams, and as we have seen, he alone was a Prophet of God. God was accustomed to manifest his intentions to his Prophets by dreams or visions, (Numb. xii. 6,) and Daniel had obtained both. Since Misael, Hananiah, and Azariah were united with him in prayer, we gather that they were not induced by ambition, to desire anything for themselves; for if they had been rivals of Daniel, they could not have prayed in concord with him. They did not pray about their own private concerns, but only for the interpretation of the dream being made known to Daniel. We observe, too, how sincerely they agree in their prayers, how all pride and ambition is laid aside, and without any desire for their own advantage. Besides, it is worthy of notice why they are said *to have desired mercy from God.* Although they do not here come into God's presence as criminals, yet they hoped their request would be graciously granted, and hence the word "mercy" is used. Whenever we fly to God to bring assistance to our necessities, our eyes and all our senses ought always to be turned towards his mercy, for his mere good-will reconciles him to us. When it is said, at the close of the verse,—*they should not perish with the rest of the wise men of Babylon,* some explain this, as if they had been anxious about the life of the Magi, and wished to snatch them also from death. But although they wished all persons to be safe, clearly enough they here separate themselves from the Magi and Chaldeans; their conduct was far different. It now follows—

19. Then was the secret revealed unto Daniel in a night vision. Then Daniel blessed the God of heaven.

19. Tunc Danieli in visione noctis arcanum patefactum est: tunc Daniel benedixit Deum cœli.

Here it may be gathered, that Daniel did not vacillate nor pray with his companions through any doubt upon his mind. For that sentence of James ought to come into our memory, namely, Those who hesitate, and tremble, and pray to God with diffidence, are unworthy of being heard. Let not such a one, says James, think he shall obtain anything from the Lord, if he is driven about variously like the waves of the sea. (Chap. i. 6.) As God, therefore, shewed himself propitious to the prayers of Daniel, we conclude him to have prayed with true faith, and to be clearly persuaded that his life was in God's hands; hence, also, he felt that God did not vainly harass the mind of King Nebuchadnezzar, but was preparing some signal and remarkable judgment for him. Because Daniel was imbued with this firm persuasion, he exercises a sure confidence, and prays to God as if he had already obtained his request. On the other hand, we perceive that God never closes his ears when rightly and cordially invoked, as also it is said in the Psalms, (cxlv. 18,) He is near to all who pray to him in truth; for there cannot be truth when faith is wanting; but as Daniel brought faith and sincerity to his prayers, he was listened to, and the secret concerning the dream was made known to him in a vision by night. I cannot now proceed any further.

PRAYER.

Grant, Almighty God, since we are in danger every day and every moment, not merely from the cruelty of a single tyrant, but from the devil, who excites the whole world against us, arming the princes of this world, and impelling them to destroy us,—Grant, I pray thee, that we may feel and demonstrate, by experience, that our life is in thy hand, and that under thy faithful guardianship thou wilt not suffer one hair of our heads to fall. Do thou also so defend us, that the impious themselves may acknowledge that we do not boast this day in vain in thy name, nor invoke thee without success. And when we have experienced thy paternal anxiety, through the whole course of our life, may we arrive at that blessed immortality which thou hast promised us, and which is laid up for us in heaven, through Jesus Christ our Lord.—Amen.

Lecture Seventh.

20. Daniel answered and said, Blessed be the name of God for ever and ever: for wisdom and might are his.

20. Loquutus est[1] Daniel et dixit, Sit nomen Dei benedicitum a seculo et in seculum: ejus est sapientia, et robur ipsius.[2]

DANIEL here pursues his narrative and thanks God after King Nebuchadnezzar's dream had been made known to him, while he relates the sense of the words which he had used. *May God's name be blessed*, says he, *from age to age*. We ought daily to wish for this; for when we pray that God's name may be hallowed, continuance is denoted under this form of prayer. But Daniel here breaks forth into the praises of God with greater vehemence, because he acknowledges his singular benefit in being snatched away from death, together with his companions, beyond his expectation. Whenever God confers any remarkable blessing on his servants, they are the more stirred up to praise him, as David says, (Psalm xl. 3,) Thou hast put a new song into my mouth. And Isaiah also uses this form of speech twice, (chap. xlii. 10,) as if God had given him material for a new and unusual song, in dealing so wonderfully with his Church. So also, there is no doubt that Daniel here wished to praise God in a remarkable manner, since he had received a rare proof of his favour in being delivered from instant death. Afterwards he adds, *whose* (or *since his*) *is the wisdom and the strength;* for the relative is here taken for the causal particle, and the sentence ought to be so expressed; the additional particles may avail to strengthen the expression, and be taken exclusively, as if he had said,—to God alone ought the praise of wisdom and virtue to be ascribed. Without him, indeed, both are sought in vain; but these graces do not seem to suit the present purpose; for Daniel ought rather to celebrate God's praises, through this vision being opened, and this was enough to content him. But he may here speak of God's glory as well from his power as his

[1] Verbally, answered.—*Calvin.*
[2] These particles are superfluous: there is nothing obscure in the sense. —*Calvin.*

wisdom; as, where Scripture wishes to distinguish the true God from all fictions, it takes these two principles—first, God governs all things by his own hand, and retains them under his sway; and secondly, nothing is hid from him —and these points cannot be separated when his majesty is to be proved. We see mankind fabricating deities for themselves, and thus multiplying gods, and distributing to each his own office; because they cannot rest in simple unity, when God is treated of. Some fancy God retains but half his attributes; as for instance, the praters about bare foreknowledge. They admit nothing to be hidden to God, and his knowledge of all things; and this they prove by the prophecies which occur in the Scriptures. What they say is true; but they very much lessen the glory of God; nay, they tear it to pieces by likening him to Apollo, whose office it formerly was, in the opinion of the heathen, to predict future events. When they sought predictions of future events, they endued Apollo with the virtue of making known to them future occurrences. Many at the present time think God able to foresee all things, but suppose him either to dissemble or purposely withdraw from the government of the world.

Lastly, Their notion of God's foreknowledge is but a cold and idle speculation. Hence I said, they rob God of half his glory, and, as far as they can, tear him to pieces. But Scripture, when it wishes to assert what is peculiar to God, joins these two things inseparably; first, God foresees all things, since nothing is hidden from his eyes; and next, he appoints future events, and governs the world by his will, allowing nothing to happen by chance or without his direction. Daniel here assumes this principle, or rather unites the two, by asserting Israel's God alone to deserve the name, since both wisdom and strength are in his power. We must remember how God is defrauded of his just praise, when we do not connect these two attributes together—his universal foresight and his government of the world allowing nothing to happen without his permission. But as it would be too cold to assert that to God alone belongs wisdom and strength, unless his wisdom was

21. And he changeth the times and the seasons: he removeth kings, and setteth up kings: he giveth wisdom unto the wise, and knowledge to them that know understanding.

21. Et ipse¹ mutat tempora, et articulos temporum: constituit reges et admovet reges: dat sapientiam sapientibus, et scientiam iis qui scientiam cognoscunt.²

Daniel explains, in these words, what might have been obscure; for he teaches God to be the true fountain of wisdom and virtue, while he does not confine them to himself alone, but diffuses them through heaven and earth. And we must mark this diligently; for when Paul affirms God alone to be wise, his praise does not seem magnificent enough, (Rom. xvi. 27;) but when we think of God's wisdom, and set before our eyes all around and about us, then we feel more strongly the import of Paul's words, that God only is wise. God, therefore, as I have already stated, does not keep his wisdom confined to himself, but makes it flow throughout the whole world. The full sense of the verse is,—whatever wisdom and power exists in the world, is a testimony to the Almighty's. This is man's ingratitude; whenever they find anything worthy of praise in themselves or others, they claim it directly as their own, and thus God's glory is diminished by the depravity of those who obtain their blessings from him. We are here taught not to detract anything from God's wisdom and power, since wherever these qualities are conspicuous in the world, they ought rather to reflect his glory. We now perceive the Prophet's meaning—God places before our eyes, as in a glass, the proofs of his wisdom and power, when the affairs of the world roll on, and mankind become powerful through wisdom, and some are raised on high, and others fall to the ground. Experience teaches us these events do not proceed from human skill, or through the equable course of nature, while the loftiest kings are cast down and others elevated to the highest posts of honour. Daniel, therefore, admonishes us not to seek in heaven alone for God's wisdom and power, since it is apparent to us on earth, and proofs of it are daily presented

¹ Or, it is he who.—*Calvin.*
² That is, to those who are skilled in science.—*Calvin.*

to our observation. We now see how these two verses are mutually united. He had stated wisdom to belong exclusively to God; he now shews that it is not hidden within him, but is made manifest to us; and we may perceive by familiar experience, how all wisdom flows from him as its exclusive fountain. We ought to feel the same concurring power also.

It is he, then, *who changes times and portions of time.* We know it to be ascribed to fortune when the world passes through such uncertain changes that everything is daily changing. Hence the profane consider all things to be acted on by blind impulse, and others affirm the human race to be a kind of sport to God, since men are tossed about like balls. But, as I have already said, it is not surprising to find men of a perverse and corrupt disposition thus perverting the object of all God's works. For our own practical improvement we should consider what the Prophet is here teaching, how revolutions, as they are called, are testimonies of God's power, and point out with the finger to the truth that the affairs of men are ruled by the Most High. For we must of necessity adopt one or the other of these views, either that nature rules over human events, or else fortune turns about in every direction, things which ought to have an even course. As far as nature is concerned, its course would be even, unless God by his singular counsel, as we have seen, thus changes the course of the times. Yet those philosophers who assign the supreme authority to nature are much sounder than others who place fortune in the highest rank. For if we admit for a moment this latter opinion that fortune directs human affairs by a kind of blind impulse, whence comes this fortune? If you ask them for a definition, what answer will they make? They will surely be compelled to confess this, the word "fortune" explains nothing. But neither God nor nature will have any place in this vain and changeable government of the world, where all things throw themselves into distinct forms without the least order or connection. And if this be granted, truly the doctrine of Epicurus will be received, because if God resigns the supreme government of the world, so that all things are rashly mingled together, he is no longer God. But in this variety he rather displays his hand in claiming for himself the empire over the world. In so many changes, then, which meet us on every side, and by which the whole face of things is renewed, we must remember that the Providence of God shines forth; and things do not flow on in an even course, because then the peculiar property of God might with some shew of reason be ascribed to nature. God, I say, so changes empires, and times, and seasons, that we should learn to look up to him. If the sun always rose and set at the same period, or at least certain symmetrical changes took place yearly, without any casual change; if the days of winter were not short, and those of summer not long, we might then discover the same order of nature, and in this way God would be rejected from his own dominion. But when the days of winter not only differ in length from those of summer, but even spring does not always retain the same temperature, but is sometimes stormy and snowy, and at others warm and genial; and since summers are so various, no year being just like the former one; since the air is changed every hour, and the heavens put on new appearances—when we discern all these things, God rouses us up, that we may not grow torpid in our own grossness, and erect nature into a deity, and deprive him of his lawful honour, and transfer to our own fancy what he claims for himself alone. If then, in these ordinary events, we are compelled to acknowledge God's Providence, if any change of greater moment arises, as when God transfers empires from one hand to another, and all but transforms the whole world, ought we not then to be the more affected, unless we are utterly stupid? Daniel, therefore, very reasonably corrects the perverse opinion which commonly seizes upon the senses of all, that the world either rolls on by chance, or that nature is the supreme deity, when he asserts—God changes times and seasons.

It is evident from the context, that he is here properly speaking of empires, since *he appoints and removes kings.* We feel great difficulty in believing kings placed upon their thrones by a divine power, and afterwards deposed again, since we naturally fancy that they acquire their power by their own talents, or by hereditary right, or by fortuitous accident. Meanwhile all thought of God is excluded, when the industry, or valour, or success, or any other quality of man is extolled! Hence it is said in the Psalms, neither from the east nor the west, but God alone is the judge. (Psalm lxxv. 6, 7.) The Prophet there derides the discourses of those who call themselves wise, and who gather up reasons from all sides to shew how power is assigned to man, by either his own counsel and valour, or by good fortune or other human and inferior instruments. Look round, says he, wherever you please, from the rising to the setting of the sun, and you will find no reason why one man becomes lord of his fellow-creatures rather than another. God alone is the judge; that is, the government must remain entirely with the one God. So also in this passage, the Lord is said to appoint kings, and to raise them from the rest of mankind as he pleases. As this argument is a most important one, it might be treated more copiously; but since the same opportunity will occur in other passages, I comment but shortly on the contents of this verse; for we shall often have to treat of the state of kingdoms and of their ruin and changes. I am therefore unwilling to add anything more at present, as it is sufficient to explain Daniel's intention thus briefly.

He afterwards adds,—*he gives wisdom to the wise, and knowledge to those who are endued with it.* In this second clause, the Prophet confirms what we have already said, that God's wisdom is not shrouded in darkness, but is manifested to us, as he daily gives us sure and remarkable proofs of this. Meanwhile he here corrects the ingratitude of men who assume to themselves the praise of their own excellencies which spring from God, and thus become almost sacrilegious. Daniel, therefore, asserts that men have no wisdom but what springs from God. Men are, indeed, clever and intelligent, but the question arises, whether it springs from themselves? He also shews us how mankind are to be blamed in claiming anything as their own, since they have really nothing belonging to them, however they may be wrapt in admiration of themselves. Who then will boast of becoming wise by his own innate strength? Has he originated the intellect with which he is endowed? Because God is the sole author of wisdom and knowledge, the gifts by which he has adorned men ought not to obscure his glory, but rather to illustrate it. He afterwards adds—

22. He revealeth the deep and secret things: he knoweth what *is* in the darkness, and the light dwelleth with him.

22. Ipse patefecit profunda et abscondita cognoscit quod in tenebr s,[1] et lux cum eo habitat.[2]

He pursues the same sentiment, and confirms it,—that all mortals receive from God's Spirit whatever intelligence and light they enjoy but he proceeds a step further in this verse than in the last. He had said generally, that men receive wisdom and understanding by God's good will; but here he speaks specially; for when a man's understanding is rare and unusual, there God's gift shines forth more clearly; as if he had said—God not only distributes to every one according to the measure of his own liberality, whatever acuteness and ingenuity they possess, but he adorns some with such intelligence that they appear as his interpreters. He speaks, therefore, here, specially of the gift of prophecy; as if he had said, God's goodness is conspicuous, not only in the ordinary prudence of mankind, for no one is so made as to be unable to discover between justice and injustice, and to form some plan for regulating his life; but in Prophets there is something extraordinary, which renders God's wisdom more surprising. Whence, then, do Prophets obtain the power of prophesying concerning hidden events, and penetrating above the heavens, and surpassing all bounds? Is this common to all men? Surely this far exceeds the ordinary ability of man, while the Prophet here teaches that God's beneficence and power deserve more praise, *because he reveals hidden and secret things;* and in this sense he adds—*light dwells with God;* as if he had said,—God differs very much from us, since we are involved in many clouds and mists but to God all things are clear; he has no occasion to hesitate, or inquire, and has no need to be hindered through ignorance. Now, we fully understand the Prophet's meaning.

[1] Lies hid.—*Calvin.*   [2] Or, in his power. *Calvin.*

Let us learn from this passage to attribute to God that praise which the greater part of the world claims to itself with sacrilegious audacity, though God shews it to belong to himself. Whatever understanding or judgment we may possess, we should remember that it was first received from God. Hence, also, if we have but a small portion of common sense, we are still equally indebted to God, for we should be like stocks or stones unless by his secret instinct he endued us with understanding. But if any one excels others, and obtains the admiration of all men, he ought still modestly to submit himself to God, and acknowledge himself the more bound to him, because he has received more than others. For who knows himself fully but God? The more, therefore, he excels in understanding, the more he will lay aside all claims of his own, and extol the beneficence of God. Thirdly, let us learn that the understanding of spiritual things is a rare and singular gift of the Holy Spirit, in which God's power shines forth conspicuously. Let us guard against that diabolical pride by which we see almost the whole world to be swollen and intoxicated. And in this respect we should chiefly glorify God, as he has not only adorned us with ordinary foresight, enabling us to discern between good and evil, but raised us above the ordinary level of human nature, and so enlightened us that we can understand things far exceeding our capacities. When Daniel pronounces *light to be with God,* we must supply a tacit antithesis; since he indicates, as I have already said, that men are surrounded by thick darkness, and grope about in obscurity. The habitation of men is here obliquely contrasted with the sanctuary of God; as if the Prophet had said, there is no pure and perfect light but in God alone. Hence, when we remain in our natural state, we must necessarily wander in darkness, or at least be obscured by many clouds. These words naturally lead us not to rest satisfied in our own position, but to seek from God that light in which he only dwells. Meanwhile, we should remember how God dwells in light unapproachable, (1 Tim. vi. 16,) unless he deigns to stretch forth his hand to us. Hence, if we desire to become partakers of this divine light, let us be on our guard against audacity, and mindful of our ignorance; let us seek God's illumination Thus his light will not be inaccessible to us, when, by his Spirit, he shall conduct us beyond the skies. He afterwards adds—

23. I thank thee, and praise thee, O thou God of my fathers, who hast given me wisdom and might, and hast made known unto me now what we desired of thee: for thou hast *now* made known unto us the king's matter.

23. Tibi confiteor, Deus patrum meorum et laudo ego,[1] qui dedisti mihi sapientiam et robur, et nunc notificasti mihi quæ postulavimus abs te; qui negotium[2] regis patefecist. nobis.

Daniel turns his discourse to God. *I confess to thee,* says he, *O God of my fathers, and praise thee.* Here he more openly distinguishes the God of the Israelites from all the fictions of the nations. Nor does he use this epithet in vain, when he praises the God of his fathers; for he wishes to reduce to nothing all the fabrications of the Gentiles concerning a multitude of deities. Daniel rejects this as a vain and foolish thing, and shews how the God of Israel alone is worthy of praise. But he does not found the glory of God on the authority of their fathers, as the Papists, when they wish to ascribe the supreme power to either George, or Catharine, or any others, count up the number of ages during which the error has prevailed. Thus they wish whatever the consent of mankind has approved to be received as oracular. But if religion depended on the common consent of mankind, where would be its stability? We know nothing vainer than the minds of men. If man is weighed, says the Prophet, with vanity in a balance, vanity itself will preponderate. (Psalm lxii. 9.) Nothing, therefore, is more foolish than this principle of this king,—what has prevailed by the consent of many ages must be religiously true. But here Daniel partially commends the God of their fathers, as their fathers were the sons of God. For that sacred adoption prevailed among the Jews, by which God chose Abraham and his whole family for himself. Daniel, therefore, here does not extol the persons of men, as if they either could or ought to add anything they pleased to God; but this is the reason why he says, *the God of Israel is the God of their fathers,* since he was of that race which the Almighty had

---

[1] And I also praise thee.—*Calvin.* [2] Or, question.—*Calvin.*

adopted. On the whole, he so opposes the God of Israel to all the idols of the Gentiles, that the mark of separation is in the covenant itself, and in the celestial doctrine by which he revealed himself to the sacred fathers. For while the Gentiles have no certain vision, and follow only their own dreams, Daniel here deservedly sets forth *the God of their fathers.*

He afterwards adds, *because thou hast given me wisdom and strength.* As far as relates to wisdom, the reason is clear enough why Daniel thanks God, since he had obtained, as he soon afterwards says, the revelation of the dream. He had also formerly been endued with the prophetic spirit and with visions, as he related in the first chapter, (ver. 17.) We may here inquire what he means by *strength?* He was not remarkable for his honour among men, nor was he ever a commander in military affairs, and he had no superior gift of magnificent power to cause him to return thanks to God. But Daniel regards this as the principal point, that the God of Israel was then acknowledged as the true and only God; because, whatever wisdom and virtue exists in the world, it flows from him as its only source. For this reason he speaks of himself as well as of all others, as if he had said —If I have any strength or understanding, I ascribe it all to thee; it is thine entirely. And, truly, though Daniel was neither a king nor a prefect, yet that unconquered greatness of mind which we have seen was not to be esteemed as without value. Hence he very properly acknowledges something of this kind to have been conferred upon him by heaven. Lastly, his intention is to debase himself and to attribute to God his own; but he speaks concisely, as we have said, since under the phrases "power" and "wisdom" he had previously embraced the proof of his divinity. He afterwards adds, *Thou hast revealed to me what we demanded of thee; thou hast made known to us the king's inquiry.* There seems here a slight discrepancy, as he praises God for granting him a revelation of the dream, and then unites others to himself. Yet the revelation was not common to them, but peculiar to himself. The solution is easy; for he first expresses that this was given to himself specially, that he might know the king's dream and understand its interpretation. When he has confessed this, he extends the benefit to his companions, and deservedly so; because though they did not yet understand what God had conferred upon Daniel, yet he had obtained this in their favour,— they were all snatched from death, and all their prayers attended to. And this availed very much for the confirmation of their faith, as it assured them they had not prayed in vain. For we said that there was no ambition in their prayers, as if any one desired any peculiar gift by which he might acquire honour and estimation for himself in the world. Nothing of the kind. It was enough for them to shew forth God's name among unbelievers; because by his kindness, they had been delivered from death. Hence Daniel very properly says, the king's dream was made known to him with its interpretation; and this he will afterwards transfer to his companions.

PRAYER.

Grant, Almighty God, since we have so many testimonies to thy glory daily before our eyes, though we seem so blind as to shut out all the light by our ingratitude; grant I pray, that we may at length learn to open our eyes; yea, do thou open them by thy Spirit. May we reflect on the number, magnitude, and importance of thy benefits towards us; and while thou dost set before us the proof of thy eternal divinity, grant that we may become proficient in this school of piety. May we learn to ascribe to thee the praise of all virtues, till nothing remains but to extol thee alone. And the more thou deignest to declare thyself liberal towards us, may we the more ardently desire to worship thee. May we devote ourselves to thee without reserving the slightest self-praise, but caring for this only, that thy glory may remain and shine forth throughout all the world through Christ our Lord.—Amen.

Lecture Eighth.

24. Therefore Daniel went in unto Arioch, whom the king had ordained to destroy the wise men of Babylon:

24. Itaque ingressus est Daniel ad Arioch, quem prefecerat rex ad perdendum[1] sapientes Baby-

[1] To slay.—*Calvin.*

he went and said thus unto him, Destroy not the wise *men* of Babylon: bring me in before the king, and I will shew unto the king the interpretation.	lonis: venit ergo, et sic loquutus est ei, Sapientes Babylonis ne perdas: introduc me ad regem et interpretationem regi indicabo.

BEFORE Daniel sent his message to the king, as we saw yesterday, he discharged the duty of piety as he ought, for he testified his gratitude to God for revealing the secret. But he now says, *that he came to Arioch, who had been sent by the king to slay the Magi, and asked him not to kill them, for he had a revelation;* of which we shall afterwards treat. Here we must notice that some of the Magi were slain, as I have said. For after Arioch had received the king's mandate, he would never have dared to delay it even a few days; but a delay occurred after Daniel had requested a short space of time to be afforded him. Then Arioch relaxed from the severity of the king's order against the Magi; and now Daniel asks him to spare the remainder. He seems, indeed, to have done this with little judgment, because we ought to desire the utter abolition of magical arts, for we saw before that they were diabolical sorceries. It may be answered thus,—although Daniel, saw many faults and corruptions in the Magi and their art, or science, or false pretensions to knowledge, yet, since the principles were true, he was unwilling to allow what had proceeded from God to be blotted out. But it seems to me that Daniel's object was somewhat different, for although the Magi might have been utterly destroyed without the slightest difficulty, yet he looks rather to the cause, and therefore wished the persons to be spared. It will often happen that wicked men are called in question as well as those who have deserved a tenfold death; but if they are not punished for any just reason, we ought to spare their persons, not through their worthiness, but through our own habitual sense of equity and rectitude. It is therefore probable that Daniel, when he saw the king's command concerning the slaughter of the Magi to be so tyrannical, went out to meet him, lest they should all be slain with savage and cruel violence, without the slightest reason. I therefore think that Daniel spared the Magi, but not through any personal regard; he wished them to be safe, but for another purpose, namely, to await their punishment from God. Their iniquity was not yet ripe for destruction through the indignation of the king. It is not surprising, then, that Daniel wished, as far as possible, to hinder this cruelty. It afterwards follows,—

25. Then Arioch brought in Daniel before the king in haste, and said thus unto him, I have found a man of the captives of Judah that will make known unto the king the interpretation.

25. Tunc Arioch cum festinatione introduxit Danielem ad regem, et sic locutus est ei, Inveni virum ex filiis captivitatis Jehudah, qui interpretationem regi notam faciet.

It may here be a question, in what sense Arioch speaks of bringing Daniel before the king, as if it were something new. For Daniel had already requested from the king time for prayer, as we have seen. Why then does Arioch now boast of *having found a man of the captives of Judah*, as if he were speaking of an obscure and unknown person? But very probably Daniel requested the time for prayer from Arioch, since we learn from history how difficult it was to approach those kings; for they thought it a profanation of their majesty to be polite and humane. The conjecture, therefore, is probable, that Arioch was the channel through whom the king granted the time to Daniel; or, we may suppose the words of Arioch are not simply related, but that Daniel shews the great boasting of courtiers, who always praise their own good offices, and adorn them with the splendour of words. Hence Arioch reminds the king how he had met with Daniel, and had at length obtained what the king very urgently desired. I do not therefore dwell longer on this, since either Arioch then explained more clearly to the king that Daniel could interpret his dream; or he joined what had formerly been done; or else Daniel had obtained this before; or he had begged of the king that some time should be given to Daniel. He puts *sons of transmigration, or captivity*, a usual scriptural phrase for captives, although this noun is collective. It now follows,—

26. The king answered and said to Daniel, whose name *was* Belteshazzar, Art thou able to make known unto me the dream which I

26. Respondit rex, et dixit Danieli cujus nomen *erat* Baltesazzar, Estne tibi facultas ad notificandum[1] mihi somnium

[1] To declare.—*Calvin.*

have seen, and the interpretation thereof?	quod vidi, et interpretationem ejus?

The king uses these words through his despair of an interpretation, since he perceived all the Magi in this respect without judgment and understanding; for he was at first persuaded that the Magi alone were the possessors of wisdom. Since he had asked them in vain, the error with which he was imbued, as I have said, prevented him from hoping for anything better elsewhere. Through surprise, then, he here inquires, as if the thing were impossible, Have you that power? There is no doubt that God drew this interrogation from the proud king to render his grace in Daniel more illustrious. The less hope there was in the king himself, the more there was in the revelation of both dignity and reverence, as we shall afterwards see; for the king was astonished, and fell prostrate through stupor upon the earth before a captive! This is the reason why Daniel relates the use of this interrogation by the king. It now follows,—

27. Daniel answered in the presence of the king, and said, The secret which the king hath demanded cannot the wise men, the astrologers, the magicians, the soothsayers, shew unto the king;	27. Respondit Daniel regi, et dixit, Arcanum quod rex postulat sapientes, magi, astrologi, genethliasi non possunt indicare regi.
28. But there is a God in heaven that revealeth secrets, and maketh known to the king Nebuchadnezzar what shall be in the latter days. Thy dream, and the visions of thy head upon thy bed, are these.	28. Sed est Deus in cœlis, qui revelat arcana; et indicavit regi Nebuchadnezzar quid futurum sit in fine[1] dierum: somnium tuum, et visio capitis tui super lectum tuum, hæc est.

First, with respect to these names we need not trouble ourselves much, since even the Jews themselves are compelled to guess at them. They are very bold in their definitions and rash in their affirmations, and yet they cannot clearly distinguish how one kind of wise man differed from the others; hence it is sufficient for us to hold that the discourse now concerns those then esteemed "wise men," under the various designations of Magi, Soothsayers, and Astrologers. Now, as to Daniel's answer. He says it was not surprising that the king did not find what he hoped for among the Magi, since God had breathed into him this dream

[1] In the extremity.—*Calvin.*

beyond the comprehension of human intellect. I know not whether those interpreters are right who think magical arts here simply condemned; for I rather think a comparison is instituted between the king's dream and the substance of the science of the Magi. I always exclude superstitions by which they vitiated true and genuine science. But as far as the principles are concerned, we cannot precisely condemn astronomy and whatever belongs to the consideration of the order of nature. This appears to me the whole intention,—the king's dream was not subjected to human knowledge, for mortals have no such natural skill as to be able to comprehend the meaning of the dream, and God manifests those secrets which need the peculiar revelation of the Spirit. When Daniel says the Magi, Astrologers, and the rest cannot explain to the king his dream, and are not suitable interpreters of it, the true reason is, because the dream was not natural and had nothing in common with human conjectures, but was the peculiar revelation of the Spirit. As when Paul disputes concerning the Gospel, he collects into order every kind of intelligence among men, because those who are endued with any remarkable acuteness or ability think they can accomplish anything. But the doctrine of the Gospel is a heavenly mystery (1 Cor. ii. 14) which cannot be comprehended by the most learned and talented among men. The real sense of Daniel's words is this,—the Magi, Astrologers, and Soothsayers had no power of expounding the king's dream, since it was neither natural nor human.

This is clearly evident from the context, because he adds, *there is a God in heaven who reveals secrets* For I take ברם, *berem,* here for the adversative particle. He opposes therefore the revelation of God to the conjectures and interpretations of the Magi, since all human sciences are included, so to speak, within their own bounds and bolts. Daniel, therefore, says that the matter requires the singular gift of the Holy Spirit. The same God also who revealed the king's dream to Daniel, distributes to each of us ability and skill according to his own pleasure. Whence does it arise that some are remarkable for quickness and others for stupidity and sloth ?—that some become proficients in human arts and learning, and others remain utterly ignorant, unless God shews, by this variety, how by his power and will the minds of men become enlightened or remain blunt and stupid ? As the Almighty is the supreme origin of all intelligence in the world, what Daniel here says is not generally true; and this contrast, unless we come to particulars, is either cold or superfluous. We understand, therefore, why he said in the former verse that the Magi and Astrologers could not explain the king's dream, since the Almighty had raised King Nebuchadnezzar above the common level for the purpose of explaining futurity to him through his dream.

There is then *a God in heaven who reveals secrets; he shews to king Nebuchadnezzar what will come to pass.* He confirms what I have said, that the king was utterly unable to comprehend the meaning of his own dream. It often happens that men's minds move hither and thither, and thus make clever guesses; but Daniel excludes all human *media*, and speaks of the dream as proceeding directly from God. He adds, *what shall happen at the end* or extremity *of the days.* We may inquire what he means by the word "extremity." Interpreters think this ought to be referred to the advent of Christ; but they do not explain why this word signifies Christ's advent. There is no obscurity in the phrase; "the end of the days" signifies the advent of Christ, because it was a kind of renewal to the world. Most truly, indeed, the world is still in the same state of agitation as it was when Christ was manifest in the flesh; but, as we shall afterwards see, Christ came for the very purpose of renovating the world, and since his Gospel is a kind of perfection of all things, we are said to be "in the last days." Daniel compares the whole period preceding Christ's advent with this extremity of the days. God therefore wished to shew the king of Babylon what should occur after one monarchy had destroyed another, and also that there should be an end of those changes whenever Christ's kingdom should arrive. At present I touch but briefly on this point, since more must be said upon it by and bye.

This, says he, *is the dream and vision of thy head upon thy couch.* It may seem absurd for Daniel here to profess to explain to the king the nature of his dream and its interpretation, and yet to put in something else. But, as he will add nothing out of place, we ought not to question the propriety of his saying, this was the king's vision and his dream ; for his object was to rouse the king the more urgently to attend to both the dream and its interpretation. Here we must take notice how the Prophet persists in this, with the view of persuading the king that God was the author of the dream about which he inquired of Daniel ; for the words would be entirely thrown away unless men were thoroughly persuaded that the explanation given proceeded from God. For many in the present day will hear willingly enough what may be said about the Gospel, but they are not inwardly touched by it, and then all they hear vanishes away and immediately escapes them. Hence reverence is the principle of true and solid understanding. Thus Daniel does not abruptly bring forward either the explanation or the narration of the dream, but prepares the proud king to listen, by shewing him that he neither dreamt at random nor in accordance with his own thoughts, but was divinely instructed and admonished concerning hidden events. It now follows,—

29. (As for thee, O king, thy thoughts came *into thy mind* upon thy bed what should come to pass hereafter ; and he that revealeth secrets maketh known to thee what shall come to pass.

29. Tibi, rex, cogitationes tuæ super lectum tuum ascenderunt, quid futurum esset posthac ; et qui revelat arcana exposuit tibi quid futurum esset.

He again confirms what I have just touched upon, for he wished to impress this upon the king's mind—that God was the author of the dream, to induce the king to prepare for its interpretation with becoming sobriety, modesty, and docility. For unless he had been seriously affected, he would have despised Daniel's interpretation ; just as we see men fail to profit through their own pride or carelessness even when God addresses them familiarly. Hence we must observe this order, and be fully prepared to listen to God, and learn to put a bridle upon ourselves on hearing his sacred name, never rejecting whatever he proposes to us, but treating it with proper gravity. This is the true reason why Daniel repeats again that King Nebuchadnezzar was divinely instructed in future events. He says, in the first clause, *The king's thoughts ascended,*—the phrase is Hebrew and Chaldee. Thoughts are said to ascend when they are revolved in the brain or head, as we formerly saw—this vision was in thy head; since the seat of the reasoning faculty is in the head. Daniel therefore aserts the king to be anxious about futurity, as the greatest monarchs think of what shall happen after their death, and every one dreams about enjoying the empire of the whole world. So King Nebuchadnezzar was very probably indulging these thoughts. But it follows immediately, that his thoughts could not profit him unless God unveiled the future, because it was his peculiar office, says the Prophet, *to reveal secrets.* Here we see clearly how vainly men disturb themselves when they turn over and over again subjects which surpass their abilities. King Nebuchadnezzar might have fatigued himself for a long time without profit if he had not been instructed by the oracle. Hence there is weight in these words—*He who reveals secrets has explained to the king what shall happen;* that is, thou canst not understand the dream by thine own thoughts, but God has deemed thee worthy of this peculiar favour when he wished to make thee conscious of mysteries which had been otherwise altogether hidden from thee, for thou couldst never have penetrated to such a depth.

He afterwards adds—

| 30. But as for me, this secret is not revealed to me for *any* wisdom that I have more than any living, but for *their* sakes that shall make known the interpretation to the king, and that thou mightest know the thoughts of thy heart.) | 30. Et ego,[1] non in sapientia quæ sit in me præ cunctis viventibus, arcanum hoc patefactum *est* mihi;[2] sed ut interpretationem regi exponerem, et cogitationes cordis tui cognosceres. |

Here Daniel meets an objection which Nebuchadnezzar might make,—If God alone can reveal secrets, how, I pray thee, canst thou, a mere mortal, do it? Daniel anticipates this, and transfers the whole glory to God, and ingenuously

[1] That is, to me.—*Calvin.*
[2] The repetition is superfluous, but it does not obscure the sense.—*Calvin.*

confesses that he has no interpretation of his own to offer, but represents himself as led forward by God's hand to be its interpreter; and as having nothing by his own natural talents, but acting as God pleased to appoint him his servant for this office, and as using his assistance. *This secret,* then, says he, *has been made known to me.* By these words he sufficiently declares, how his undertaking to interpret the dream was God's peculiar gift. But he more clearly expresses this gift to be supernatural, as it is called, by saying, *not in the wisdom which belongs to me.* For if Daniel had surpassed the whole world in intelligence, yet he could never divine what the king of Babylon had dreamt! He excelled, indeed, in superior abilities and learning, and was endowed, as we have said, with remarkable gifts; yet he could never have obtained this power which he acquired from God through prayer, (I repeat it again,) through his own study or industry, or any human exertions.

We observe how Daniel here carefully excludes, not only what men foolishly claim as their own, but also what God naturally confers; since we know the profane to be endowed with singular talents, and other eminent faculties; and these are called natural, since God desires his gracious gifts to shine forth in the human race by such examples as these. But while Daniel acknowledges himself endowed with no common powers, through the good pleasure and discipline of God, though he confesses this, I say, yet he places this revelation on a higher footing. We observe also how the gifts of the Spirit mutually differ, because Daniel acted in a kind of twofold capacity with regard to the endowments with which it pleased God to adorn him. First of all, he made rapid progress in all sciences, and flourished much in intellectual quickness, and we have already clearly shewn this to be owing to the mere liberality of God. This liberality puts all things in their proper order, while it shews God's singular favour in the explanation of the dream.

This secret, then, was not made known to me on account of any wisdom in me beyond the rest of mankind. Daniel does not affirm himself to be superior to all men in wisdom, as some falsely twist these words, but he leaves this in doubt by saying, This ought not to be ascribed to wisdom, for if I were the acutest of all men, all my shrewdness would avail me nothing; and, again, if I were the rudest idiot, still it is God who uses me as his servant in interpreting the dream to you. You must not, therefore, expect anything human from me, but you must receive what I say to you, because I am the instrument of God's Spirit, just as if I had come down from heaven. This is the simple sense of the words. Hence we may learn to ascribe the praise to God alone, to whom it is due; for it is his peculiar office to illuminate our minds, so that we may comprehend heavenly mysteries. For although we are naturally endued with the greatest acuteness, which is also his gift, yet we may call it a limited endowment, as it does not reach to the heavens. Let us learn, then, to leave his own to God, as we are admonished by this expression of Daniel.

He afterwards adds, *But that I may make known to the king the interpretation, and thou mayest know the thoughts of thy heart.* Daniel uses the plural number, but indefinitely; as if he had said, God has left thee indeed hitherto in suspense; but yet he did not inspire thee with this dream in vain. These things, therefore, are mutually united, namely, —God has revealed to thee this secret, and has appointed me his interpreter. Thus we perceive Daniel's meaning. For Nebuchadnezzar might object, Why does God torment me thus? What is the meaning of my perplexity;—first I dream, and then my dream escapes me, and its interpretation is unknown to me? Lest, therefore, Nebuchadnezzar should thus argue with God, Daniel here anticipates him, and shews how neither the dream nor the vision occurred in vain; but God now grants what was there wanting, namely, the return of the dream to Nebuchadnezzar's memory, and at the same time his acknowledgment of its purport, and the reason of its being sent to him.

PRAYER.

Grant, Almighty God, since thou desirest us to differ from the brutes, and hence didst impress our minds with the light of intellect,—Grant, I pray thee, that we may learn to acknowledge and to magnify this singular favour, and may we exercise ourselves in the knowledge of those things which induce us to reverence thy sovereignty. Besides this, may we distinguish between that common sense which thou hast bestowed upon us, and the illumination of thy Spirit, and the gift of faith, that thou alone mayest be glorified by our being grafted by faith into the body of thine only-begotten Son. We entreat also from thee further progress and increase of the same faith, until at length thou bring us to the full manifestation of light. Then, being like thee, we shall behold thy glory face to face, and enjoy the same in Christ our Lord.—Amen.

Lecture Ninth.

31. Thou, O king, sawest, and behold a great image. This great image, whose brightness was excellent, stood before thee, and the form thereof was terrible.
32. This image's head was of fine gold, his breast and his arms of silver, his belly and his thighs of brass,
33. His legs of iron, his feet part of iron and part of clay.
34. Thou sawest till that a stone was cut out without hands, which smote the image upon his feet that were of iron and clay, and brake them to pieces.
35. Then was the iron, the clay, the brass, the silver, and the gold, broken to pieces together, and became like the chaff of the summer thrashing-floors; and the wind carried them away, that no place was

31. Tu rex videbas, et ecce imago una grandis, imago illa magna, et splendor ejus[1] pretiosus[2] stabat coram te, et species ejus terribilis.
32. Hujus imaginis caput ex auro bono,[3] pectus ejus et brachia ejus ex argento, venter ejus et femora ejus ex ære, œs.
33. Crura ejus ex ferro,[4] pedes ejus partim ex ferro, et partim testa.
34. Videbas, quousque excisus fuit lapis, qui non ex manibus,[5] et percussit imaginem ad pedes qui erant ex ferro et testa, et contrivit eos.
35. Tunc contrita sunt simul ferrum, testa, æs, argentum, et aurum: et fuerunt quasi quisquiliæ[6] ex area æstivali et abstulit ea ventus, et non inventus est locus eorum; et lapis qui percusserat imaginem,

---

[1] Or, appearance, in common language—its splendour, therefore.—*Calvin.*
[2] Or, excellent.—*Calvin.* [3] Pure gold.—*Calvin.*
[4] Iron.—*Calvin.*
[5] Which was cut out without human hands.—*Calvin.*
[6] Or, chaff.—*Calvin.*

found for them: and the stone that smote the image became a great mountain, and filled the whole earth. fuit in montem magnum, et implevit totam terram.

ALTHOUGH Daniel here records the dream, and does not touch on its interpretation, yet we must not proceed farther without discoursing on the matter itself. When the interpretation is afterwards added, we shall confirm what we have previously said, and amplify as the context may guide us. Here Daniel records how Nebuchadnezzar saw an image consisting of gold, silver, brass, and iron, but its feet were mixed, partly of iron and partly of clay. We have already treated of the name of the "Vision," but I briefly repeat again, —king Nebuchadnezzar did not see this image here mentioned, with his natural eyes, but it was a specimen of the revelation which he knew with certainty to have been divinely offered to him. Otherwise, he might have thrown off all care, and acted as he pleased; but God held him down in complete torment, until Daniel came as its interpreter.

Nebuchadnezzar then saw an image. All writers endowed with a sound judgment and candidly desirous of explaining the Prophet's meaning, understand this, without controversy, of the Four Monarchies, following each other in succession. The Jews, when pressed by this interpretation, confuse the Turkish with the Roman empire, but their ignorance and unfairness is easily proved. For when they wish to escape the confession of Christ having been exhibited to the world, they seek stale calumnies which do not require refutation; but still something must afterwards be said in its proper place. My assertion is perfectly correct, that interpreters of moderate judgment and candour, all explain the passage of the Babylonian, Persian, Macedonian, and Roman monarchies: and Daniel himself afterwards shews this sufficiently by his own words. A question, however, arises, why God represented these four monarchies under this image? for it does not seem to correspond throughout, as the Romans had nothing in common with the Assyrians. History has fully informed us how the Medes and Persians succeeded the Chaldeans; how Babylon was besieged by the enemy; and how Cyrus, after obtaining the victory, transferred the empire to the Medes and Persians. It may, perhaps, seem absurd that one image only should be proposed. But it is probable—nay, it may be shewn—that God does not here regard any agreement between these four monarchies, for there was none at all, but the state of the world at large. God therefore wished, under this figure, to represent the future condition of the world till the advent of Christ. This is the reason why God joined these four empires together, although actually different ; since the second sprang from the destruction of the first, and the third from that of the second. This is one point, and we may now inquire, secondly, why Daniel calls the kingdom of Babylon by the honourable term *golden*. For we know the extent of its tyranny and the character of the Assyrians, and their union with the Chaldeans. We are also aware of the destruction of Nineveh, and how the Chaldeans made Babylon their capital city, to preserve the seat of empire among themselves. If we consider the origin of that monarchy, we shall surely find the Assyrians like savage beasts, full of avarice, cruelty, and rapacity, and the Chaldeans superior to all these vices. Why, then, is that empire called *the head* —and why a *golden head ?*

As to the name, "head," since that monarchy arose first, there is nothing surprising in Daniel's assigning the highest place to it. And as to his passing by Nineveh, this is not surprising, because that city had been already cut off, and he is now treating of future events. The Chaldean empire, then, was first in the order of time, and is called " golden " by comparison ; because the world grows worse as it becomes older ; for the Persians and Medes who seized upon the whole East under the auspices of Cyrus, were worse than the Assyrians and Chaldeans. So profane poets invented fables about *The Four Ages,* the Golden, Silver, Brazen, and Iron. They do not mention the clay, but without doubt they received this tradition from Daniel. If any one object, that Cyrus excelled in the noblest qualities, and was of a heroic disposition, and celebrated by historians for his prudence and perseverance, and other endowments, I reply, we must not look here at the character of any one man, but at the continued state of the Persian empire. This is sufficiently probable on comparing the empire of the Medes and Persians with that of the Babylonians, which is called "silver;" since their morals were deteriorated, as we have already said. Experience also demonstrates how the world always degenerates, and inclines by degrees to vices and corruptions.

Then as to the Macedonian empire, it ought not to seem absurd to find it compared to brass, since we know the cruelty of Alexander's disposition. It is frivolous to notice that politeness which has gained him favour with historians; since, if we reflect upon his natural character, he surely breathed cruelty from his very boyhood. Do we not discern in him, when quite a boy, envy and emulation? When he saw his father victorious in war, and subduing by industry or depraved arts the cities of Greece, he wept with envy, because his father left him nothing to conquer. As he manifested such pride when a boy, we conclude him to have been more cruel than humane. And with what purpose and intention did he undertake the expedition by which he became king of kings, unless through being discontented not only with his own power, but with the possession of the whole world? We know also how he wept when he heard from that imaginative philosophy, that there were more worlds than this. "What," said he, "I do not possess even one world!" Since, then, one world did not suffice for a man who was small of stature, he must indeed put off all humanity, as he really appeared to do. He never spared the blood of any one; and wherever he burst forth, like a devouring tempest, he destroyed everything. Besides, what is here said of that monarchy ought not to be restricted to the person of Alexander, who was its chief and author, but is extended to all his successors. We know that they committed horrible cruelties, for before his empire was divided into four parts, constituting the kingdoms of Asia, Syria, Egypt, and Macedonia, how much blood was shed! God took away from Alexander all his offspring. He might have lived at home and begotten children, and thus his memory would have been noble and celebrated among all posterity; but God exterminated all his family from the world. His mother perished by the sword at the age of eighty years; also his wife and sons, as well as a brother of unsound mind. Finally, it was a horrible proof of God's anger against Alexander's offspring, for the purpose of impressing all ages with a sense of his displeasure at such cruelty. If then we extend the Macedonian empire to the period when Perseus was conquered, and Cleopatra and Ptolemy slain in Egypt, and Syria, Asia, and Egypt reduced under the sway of Rome—if we comprehend the whole of this period, we shall not wonder at the prophet Daniel calling the monarchy "brazen."

When he speaks of THE ROMAN EMPIRE as "iron," we must always remember the reason I have noticed, which has reference to the world in general, and to the depraved nature of mankind; whence their vices and immoralities always increase till they arrive at a fearful height. If we consider how the Romans conducted themselves, and how cruelly they tyrannized over others, the reason why their dominion is called "iron" by Daniel will immediately appear. Although they appear to have possessed some skill in political affairs, we are acquainted with their ambition, avarice, and cruelty. Scarcely any nation can be found which suffered like the Romans under those three diseases, and since they were so subject to these, as well as to others, it is not surprising that the Prophet detracts from their fame and prefers the Macedonians, Persians, Medes, and even Assyrians and Chaldeans to them.

When he says, *the feet of the image were partly of iron and partly of clay*, this ought to be referred to the ruin which occurred, when God dispersed and cut in pieces, so to speak, that monarchy. The Chaldean power fell first; then the Macedonians, after subduing the East, became the sole monarchs to whom the Medes and Persians were subservient. The same event happened to the Macedonians, who were at length subdued by the Romans; and all their kings who succeeded Alexander were cut off. But there was another reason why God wished to overthrow the Roman monarchy. For it fell by itself according to the prediction of this prophecy. Since, then, without any external force it fell to pieces by itself, it easily appears that it was broken up by

Christ, according to this dream of King Nebuchadnezzar. It is positively certain, that nothing was ever stable from the beginning of the world, and the assertion of Paul was always true—the fashion of this world passeth away. (1 Cor. vii. 31.) By the word "fashion" he means whatever is splendent in the world is also shadowy and evanescent: he adds, also, that all which our eyes gaze upon must vanish away. But, as I have said, the reason was different when God wished to destroy the empire of the Chaldees, the Persians, and the Macedonians; because this was more clearly shewn in the case of the Romans, how Christ by his advent took away whatever was splendid, and magnificent, and admirable in the world. This, therefore, is the reason why God assigns specially to the Romans *feet of clay*. Thus much, then, with respect to the four empires.

In the third place, it may be doubted why *Christ* is said *to have broken this image from the mountain*. For if Christ is the eternal wisdom of God (Prov. viii. 15) by whom kings reign, this seems scarcely to accord with it; for how, by his advent, should he break up the political order which we know God approves of, and has appointed and established by his power? I answer,—earthly empires are swallowed and broken up by Christ accidentally, as they say. (Ps. ii. 9.) For if kings exercise their office honestly, clearly enough Christ's kingdom is not contrary to their power. Whence, then, does it happen that Christ strikes kings with an iron sceptre, and breaks, and ruins, and reduces them to nothing? Just because their pride is untameable, and they raise their heads to heaven, and wish, if possible, to draw down God from his throne. Hence they necessarily feel Christ's hand opposed to them, because they cannot and will not subject themselves to God.

But another question may be raised:—When Christ was made manifest, those monarchies had fallen long previously; for the Chaldean, the Persian, and that of the successors of Alexander, had passed away. The solution is at hand, if we understand what I have previously mentioned—that under one image the whole state of the world is here depicted for us. Although all events did not occur at the same moment, yet we shall find the Prophet's language essentially true, that Christ should destroy all monarchies. For when the seat of the empire of the East was changed, and Nineveh destroyed, and the Chaldeans had fixed the seat of empire among themselves, this happened by God's just judgment, and Christ was already reigning as the king of the world. That monarchy was really broken up by his power, and the same may be said of the Persian empire. For when they degenerated from a life of austerity and sobriety into one of foul and infamous luxury; when they raged so cruelly against all mankind, and became so exceedingly rapacious, their empire necessarily passed away from them, and Alexander executed the judgment of God. The same occurred to Alexander and his successors. Hence the Prophet means, that before Christ appeared, he already possessed supreme power, both in heaven and earth, and thus broke up and annihilated the pride and violence of all men.

But Daniel says—the image perished when the Roman empire was broken up, and yet we observe in the East and the neighbouring regions the greatest monarchs still reigning with very formidable prowess. I reply, we must remember what we said yesterday—the dream was presented to King Nebuchadnezzar, that he might understand all future events to the renovation of the world. Hence God was not willing to instruct the king of Babylon further than to inform him of the four future monarchies which should possess the whole globe, and should obscure by their splendour all the powers of the world, and draw all eyes and all attention to itself; and afterwards Christ should come and overthrow those monarchies. God, therefore, wished to inform King Nebuchadnezzar of these events; and here we must notice the intention of the Holy Spirit. No mention is made of other kingdoms, because they had not yet emerged into importance sufficient to be compared to these four monarchies. While the Assyrians and Chaldeans reigned, there was no rivalry with their neighbours, for the whole of the East obeyed them. It was incredible that Cyrus, springing from a barbarous region, could so easily draw to himself such resources, and seize upon so many provinces in so short a time!

For he was like a whirlwind which destroyed the whole East. The same may be said of the third monarchy; for if the successors of Alexander had been mutually united, there was then no empire in the world which could have increased their power. The Romans were fully occupied in struggling with their neighbours, and were not yet at rest on their own soil; and afterwards, when Italy, Greece, Asia, and Egypt were obedient to them, no other empire rivalled their fame; for all the power and glory of the world was at that period absorbed by their arms.

We now understand why Daniel mentioned those four kingdoms, and why he places their close at the advent of Christ. When I speak of Daniel, this ought to be understood of the dream; for without doubt God wished to encourage the Jews not to despair, when first the brightness of the Chaldean monarchy, then that of the Persian, next the Macedonian, and lastly, the Romans overwhelmed the world. For what could they have determined by themselves at the time when Nebuchadnezzar dreamt about the four empires? The kingdom of Israel was then utterly destroyed, the ten tribes were exiles, the kingdom of Judah was reduced to desolation. Although the city Jerusalem was yet standing, still where was the kingdom? It was full of ignominy and disgrace; nay, the posterity of David then reigned precariously in the tribe of Judah, and even there over but a part of it; and afterwards, although their return was permitted, yet we know how miserably they were afflicted. And when Alexander, like a tempest, devastated the East, they suffered, as we know, the greatest distress; they were frequently ravaged by his successors; their city was reduced almost to solitude, and the temple profaned; and when their condition was at the best, they were still tributary, as we shall afterwards see. It was certainly necessary for their minds to be supported in so great and such confused perturbation. This, therefore, was the reason why God sent the dream about those monarchies to the king of Babylon. If Daniel had dreamt, the faithful would not have had so remarkable a subject-matter for the confirmation of their faith; but when the king's dream is spread abroad through almost the whole East, and when its interpretation is equally celebrated, the Jews might recover their spirits and revive their hopes at their own time, since they understood from the first that these four monarchies should not exist by any mere changes of fortune; for the same God who had foretold to King Nebuchadnezzar future events, determined also what he should do, and what he wished to take place.

The Jews knew that the Chaldeans were reigning only by the decree of heaven; and that another more destructive empire should afterwards arise; thirdly, that they must undergo a servitude under the Macedonians; lastly, that the Romans should be the conquerors and masters of the world—and all this by the decree of heaven. When they reflected on these things, and finally heard of the Redeemer, as according to promise, a perpetual King, and all the monarchies, then so refulgent as without any stability—all this would prove no common source of strength. Now, therefore, we understand with what intention God wished what had hitherto been hidden, to be everywhere promulgated; the Jews, too, would hand down to their sons and grandsons what they had heard from Daniel, and afterwards this prophecy would be extant, and become an admiration to them throughout all ages.

When we come to the words, he says, *one image was great and large, its splendour was precious, and its form terrible.* By this phrase, God wished to meet a doubt which might creep into the minds of the Jews, on perceiving each of those empires prosperous in its turn. When the Jews, captive and forlorn, saw the Chaldeans formidable throughout the whole world, and, consequently, highly esteemed and all but adored by the rest of mankind, what could they think of it? Why, they would have no hope of return, because God had raised their enemies to such great power that their avarice and cruelty were like a deep whirlpool. The Jews might thus conclude themselves to be drowned in a very deep abyss, whence they could not hope to escape. But when the empire was transferred to the Medes and Persians, although they were allowed the liberty of returning, still we know how small a number used this indulgence, and the rest were ungrateful. Whether or not this was so, few of the Jews returned to their country; and these had to make war upon their neighbours, and were subject to continual molestation. As far as common sense would guide them, it was easier for them not to stir a step from Chaldea, Assyria, and the other parts of the East, since their neighbours in their own country were all so hostile to them. As long as they were tributary and esteemed almost as serfs and slaves, and while their condition was so humiliating, the same temptation remained. For, if they were God's people, why did he not care for them so far as to relieve them from that cruel tyranny? Why did he not restore them to calmness, and render them free from such various inconveniences, and from so many injuries? When the Macedonian empire succeeded, they were more miserable than before; they were daily exposed as a prey, and every species of cruelty was practised towards them. Then, with regard to the Romans, we know how proudly they domineered over them. Although Pompey, at his first assault, did not spoil the temple, yet at length he became bolder, and Crassus shortly afterwards destroyed everything, till the most horrible and prodigious slaughter followed. As the Jews must suffer these things, this consolation must necessarily be offered to them—the Redeemer shall at length arrive, who shall break up all these empires.

As to Christ being called *the stone cut out without human hands*, and being pointed out by other phrases, I cannot explain them now.

PRAYER.

Grant, Almighty God, since we so travel through this world that our attention is easily arrested, and our judgment darkened, when we behold the power of the impious refulgent and terrible to ourselves and others: Grant, I say, that we may raise our eyes upwards, and consider how much power thou hast conferred upon thine only-begotten Son. Grant, also, that he may rule and govern us by the might of his Spirit, protect us by his faithfulness and guardianship, and compel the whole world to promote our salvation; thus may we rest calmly under his protection, and fight with that boldness and patience which he both commands and commends, until at length we enjoy the fruit of the victory which thou hast promised, and which thou wilt provide for us in thy heavenly kingdom.— Amen.

Lecture Tenth.

WE have already explained God's intention in offering to King Nebuchadnezzar the dream concerning the four monarchies, and the kingdom of Christ which should put an end to them. We have shewn it to have been not for the king's sake so much as for the consolation and support of the remnant of the faithful in those very severe troubles which awaited them, and were close at hand. For when redemption had been promised to them, and the Prophets had extolled that remarkable beneficence of God in magnificent terms, their confidence might fail them amidst those revolutions which afterwards followed. For God wished to sustain their spirits, so that amidst such agitations and tumults they might remain constant, and patiently and quietly wait for the promised Redeemer. Meanwhile God wished to render all the Chaldeans without excuse, because this dream of the king's was everywhere celebrated, and yet none of them profited by it, as far as Christ's eternal reign is concerned. But this was the principal point in the dream, as we shall afterwards see. But God wished, in the first place, to consult the interests of his elect, lest they should despond among those so-called revolutions, which might seem contrary to those numerous prophecies, by which not merely simple liberty was promised, but perpetual and continued happiness under God's hand. We now understand the end which God intended by this dream. We must now treat its explanation. We have already touched upon some points, but Daniel himself shall lead the way along which we are to proceed. First of all he says—

36. This *is* the dream; and we will tell the interpretation thereof before the king.

37. Thou, O king, art a king of kings: for the God of heaven hath given thee a

36. Hoc est somnium: et interpretationem ejus dicemus coram rege.

37. Tu rex, rex regum *es*, cui Deus cœlorum regnum, po-

kingdom, power, and strength, and glory.

38. And wheresoever the children of men dwell, the beasts of the field, and the fowls of the heaven, hath he given into thine hand, and hath made thee ruler over them all. Thou *art* this head of gold.

tentiam et robur dedit,[1] et gloriam tibi.[2]

38. Et ubicunque habitant filii hominum, bestia agri, et volucris cœlorum,[3] dedit in manum tuam, et præfecit te omnibus :[4] tu ipse caput *es* aureum.

Daniel here declares "the golden head of the image" to be the Babylonian kingdom. We know that the Assyrians were subdued before the monarchy was transferred to Babylon; but since they did not prevail sufficiently to be considered as supreme rulers in that eastern territory, the Babylonian empire is here mentioned first. It is also worth while to remark, that God was unwilling to refer here to what had already occurred, but he rather proposed that the people should in future depend on this prophecy and rest upon it. Here it would have been superfluous to say anything about the Assyrians, since that empire had already passed away. But the Chaldeans were still to reign for some time —say seventy or at least sixty years. Hence God wished to hold the minds of his own servants in suspense till the end of that monarchy, and then to arouse them by fresh hopes, until the second monarchy should pass away, so that afterwards they might rest in patience under the third and fourth monarchies, and might perceive at length the time of Christ's advent to be at hand. This is the reason why Daniel places the Chaldean monarchy here in the first rank and order. And in this matter there is no difficulty, because he states King Nebuchadnezzar to be the golden head of the image. We may gather the reason of his being called *the golden head* from the context, namely, because its integrity was then greater than under the empire of the Medes and Persians. It is very true that the Chaldeans were the most cruel robbers, and we know how Babylon was then detested by all the pious and sincere worshippers of God. Still, since things usually become worse by process of time, the state of the world was as yet tolerable under that sovereignty.

[1] Some translate the nouns by adjectives or epithets—a strong and powerful kingdom.—*Calvin.*

[2] The word לך, *lek*, "to thee," is redundant.—*Calvin.*

[3] That is, "birds;" there is a change of number.—*Calvin.*

[4] Verbally, has made thee ruler over them all.—*Calvin.*

This is the reason why Nebuchadnezzar is called " the head of gold ;" but this ought not to be referred to him personally, but rather extended to his whole kingdom, and all his successors, among whom Belshazzar was the most hateful despiser of God; and by comprehension he is said to form part of this head of gold. But Daniel shews that he did not flatter the king, since he assigns this reason for Nebuchadnezzar being the golden head—God had set him up above all the earth. But this seems to be common to all kings, since none of them reign without God's permission—a sentiment which is partially true, but the Prophet implies that Nebuchadnezzar was raised up in an especial manner, because he excelled all other sovereigns. It now follows—

39. And after thee shall arise another kingdom inferior to thee, and another third kingdom of brass, which shall bear rule over all the earth.	39. Et post te exsurget regnum aliud inferius te,[1] et regnum tertium aliud quod *erit* æneum: et dominabitur in tota terra.

In this verse Daniel embraces the Second and Third Monarchies. He says the second should be inferior to the Chaldean in neither power nor wealth; for the Chaldean empire, although it spread so far and so wide, was added to that of the Medes and Persians. Cyrus subdued the Medes first; and although he made his father-in-law, Cyaxares, his ally in the sovereignty, yet he had expelled his maternal grandfather, and thus obtained peaceable possession of the kingdom throughout all Media. Then he afterwards conquered the Chaldeans and Assyrians, as well as the Lydians and the rest of the nations of Asia Minor. We see then that his kingdom is not called inferior through having less splendour or opulence in human estimation, but because the general condition of the world was worse under the second monarchy, as men's vices and corruptions increase more and more. Cyrus was, it is true, a prudent prince, but yet sanguinary. Ambition and avarice carried him fiercely onwards, and he wandered in every direction, like a wild beast, forgetful of all humanity. And if we scan his disposition accurately, we shall discover it to be, as Isaiah says, very greedy of human blood. (Chap. xiii. 18.) And here we may remark, that

---

[1] That is, to thine.—*Calvin.*

he does not treat only of the persons of kings, but of their counsellors and of the whole people. Hence Daniel deservedly pronounces the second state of the kingdom inferior to the first; not because Nebuchadnezzar excelled in dignity, or wealth, or power, but because the world had not degenerated so much as it afterwards did. For the more these monarchies extend themselves, the more licentiousness increases in the world, according to the teaching of experience. Whence the folly and madness of those who desire to have kings very powerful is apparent, just as if any one should desire a river to be most rapid, as Isaiah says when combating this folly. (Chap. viii. 7.) For the swifter, the deeper, and the wider a river flows on, the greater the destruction of its overflow to the whole neighbourhood. Hence the insanity of those who desire the greatest monarchies, because some things will by positive necessity occur out of lawful order, when one man occupies so broad a space; and this did occur under the sway of the Medes and Persians.

The description of the Third Monarchy now follows. It is called *brazen*, not so much from its hardness as from its being worse than the second. The Prophet teaches how the difference between the second and third monarchies is similar to that between silver and brass. The rabbis confound the two monarchies, through their desire to comprehend under the second what they call the kingdom of the Greeks; but they display the grossest ignorance and dishonesty. For they do not err through simple ignorance, but they purposely desire to overthrow what Scripture here states clearly concerning the advent of Christ. Hence they are not ashamed to mingle and confuse history, and to pronounce carelessly on subjects unknown to them—unknown, I say, not because they escape men moderately versed in history, but through their being brutal themselves, and discerning nothing. For instead of Alexander the son of Philip, they put Alexander the son of Mammea, who possessed the Roman empire, when half its provinces had been already separated from it. He was a spiritless boy, and was slain in his tent with the greatest ignominy by his own soldiers; besides that, he never really governed, but lived as a minor under the sway of his mother. And yet the Jews are not ashamed to distort and twist what relates to the king of Macedon to this Alexander the son of Mammea. But their wickedness and ignorance is easily refuted by the context, as we shall afterwards see. Here Daniel states shortly that there shall be a third monarchy: he does not describe its character, nor explain it fully; but we shall see in another place the meaning of his prophecy. He now interprets the dream of the king of Babylon, as the vision of the four empires had been offered to him. But the angel afterwards confirms the same to him by a vision, and very clearly, too, as will be seen in its own place. Without doubt this narrative of the brazen image relates to the Macedonian kingdom. How, then, is all doubt removed? By the description of the fourth empire, which is much fuller, and clearly indicates what we shall soon see, that the Roman empire was like the feet, partly of clay and partly of iron. He says, therefore,—

40. And the fourth kingdom shall be strong as iron: forasmuch as iron breaketh in pieces and subdueth all *things;* and as iron that breaketh all these, shall it break in pieces and bruise.
41. And whereas thou sawest the feet and toes, part of potter's clay, and part of iron, the kingdom shall be divided; but there shall be in it of the strength of the iron, forasmuch as thou sawest the iron mixed with miry clay.
42. And *as* the toes of the feet *were* part of iron, and part of clay; *so* the kingdom shall be partly strong, and partly broken.
43. And whereas thou sawest iron mixed with miry clay, they shall mingle themselves with the seed of men: but they shall not cleave one to another, even as iron is not mixed with clay.

40. Et regnum quartum erit robustum instar ferri: quia sicuti ferrum conterit et comminuit omnia, et sicuti ferrum contundit omnia hæc, conteret et contundet.
41. Quod autem vidisti pedes et digitos partim ex luto fictili,[1] et partim ex ferro: regnum divisum erit: et de fortitudine ferri erit in eo, propterea vidisti ferrum mixtum cum testa luti.[2]
42. Et digiti pedum[3] partim ex ferro, et partim ex terra,[4] ex parte regnum *illud* erit robustum, et ex parte erit fragile.
43. Quòd vidisti ferrum commixtum testæ luteæ,[5] commiscebunt se inter se in semine hominis, et non cohærebunt alius cum alio, sicuti ferrum non miscetur cum testa.

Here the Fourth Empire is described, which agrees only

[1] Or, potter's clay.—*Calvin.*
[2] Or, moist clay.—*Calvin.*
[3] Or, if we repeat the verb, it is the accusative case.—*Calvin.*
[4] Or, of the clay which he mentioned.—*Calvin.*
[5] For vessels.—*Calvin.*

with the Roman, for we know that the four successors of Alexander were at length subdued. Philip was the first king of Macedon, and Antiochus the second; but yet Philip lost nothing from his own kingdom; he only yielded it to the free cities of Greece. It was, therefore, hitherto entire, except as it paid tribute to the Romans for some years on account of the expenses of the war. Antiochus, also, when compelled to adopt the conditions imposed by the conqueror, was driven beyond Mount Taurus; but Macedonia was reduced to a province when Perseus was overcome and captured. The kings of Syria and Asia suffered in the same way; and, lastly, Egypt was seized upon by Augustus. For their posterity had reigned up to that period, and Cleopatra was the last of that race, as is sufficiently known. When, therefore, the three monarchies were absorbed by the Romans, the language of the Prophet suits them well enough; for, as the sword diminishes, and destroys, and ruins all things, thus those three monarchies were bruised and broken up by the Roman empire. There is nothing surprising in his here enumerating that popular form of government among "monarchies," since we know how few were rulers among this people, and how customary it was to call every kind of government among them an empire, and the people themselves the rulers of the whole world! But the Prophet compares them to "iron," not only on account of its hardness, although this reason is clearly expressed, but also through another kind of similitude,—they were worse than all others, and surpassed in cruelty and barbarity both the Macedonians and the Medo-Persians. Although they boast much in their own prowess, yet if any one exercises a sound judgment upon their actions, he will discover their tyranny to be far more cruel than all the rest; although they boast in their senators being as great as ordinary kings, yet we shall find them no better than robbers and tyrants, for scarcely one in a hundred of them shewed a grain of equity, either when sent into any province or when discharging any magistracy; and with regard to the body of the empire itself, it was all horrible pollution. This, then, is the reason why the Prophet says that monarchy was partly composed of iron, and partly of potter's clay, since we know how they suffered under intestine disorders. The Prophet requires no other interpretation here, because, he says, this mixture of iron and clay, which unites so badly, is a sign of disunion, through their never mingling together.

The kingdom, therefore, *shall be divided,* and he adds yet another mixture — *they shall mingle themselves with the seed of men,* that is, they shall be neighbours to others, and that mutual interchange which ought to promote true friendship, shall become utterly profitless. The opinion of those who introduce the alliance of Pompey and Cæsar is farfetched, for the Prophet is speaking of a continued government. If stability is sought for in any kind of government, it surely ought to shine forth in a republic, or at least in an oligarchy in preference to a despotism; because, when all are slaves, the king cannot so confidently trust his subjects, through their constant fear for themselves. But when all unite in the government, and the very lowest receive some mutual advantage from their commonwealth, then, as I have said, superior stability ought to be conspicuous. But Daniel pronounces, that even if the superior power should reside in the senate and the people—for there is dignity in the senate, and majesty in the people—yet that empire should fall. Besides, although they should be mutually united in neighbourhood and kindred, yet this would not prevent them from contending with each other with savage enmity, even to the destruction of their empire. Here then the Prophet furnishes us with a vivid picture of the Roman empire, by saying *that it was like iron,* and also *mingled with clay,* or mud, as they destroyed themselves by intestine discord after arriving at the highest pitch of fortune. Thus far concerning the four monarchies.

We may now inquire why Daniel said, *The stone which was to be cut out of the mountain should destroy all these empires;* since it does not appear, at first sight, to suit the kingdom of Christ. The Babylonian monarchy had been previously abolished—the Medes and Persians had been utterly prostrated by Alexander—and after Alexander's conquests, had been divided into four kingdoms; the Romans subdued all those lands; and then it is objected that the Prophet's language is absurd, *a stone shall come out of a mountain which shall break up all empires.* The solution, as I have said above, is at hand. Daniel does not here state that the events shall happen together, but simply wishes to teach how the empires of the world shall fail, and one kingdom shall be eternal. He does not regard, therefore, when or why the empires of the Chaldees and of the Persians fell, but he compares the kingdom of Christ with all those monarchies which have been mentioned. And we must always remember what I have touched upon, that the Prophet speaks for the captive people, and accommodates his style to the faithful, to whom he wished to stretch forth the hand, and to strengthen them in those most serious concussions which were at hand. And hence, when he speaks of all lands and nations, if any one objects—there were then other empires in the world, the answer is easy, the Prophet is not here describing what should happen through all the ages of the world, but only what the Jews should see. For the Romans were the lords of many regions before they passed over into Greece; we know they had two provinces in Spain, and after the close of the second Punic war were masters of that upper sea, and held undisputed possession of all the islands, as well as of Cisalpine Gaul and other regions. No notice is taken of this empire, till it was made known to the Jews, as they might have given themselves up to utter despair, when they could not perceive an end to those storms which almost ruined the world; and, meanwhile, they were the most miserable of all men, because the various and continual calamities of the world never ceased. We must remember this view of things, as otherwise the whole prophecy would be cold and profitless to us. I now return to the kingdom of Christ.

THE KINGDOM OF CHRIST is said *to break up all the empires of the world,* not directly, but only accidentally, as the phrase is. For Daniel here assumes a principle, sufficiently understood by the Jews; namely, those monarchies were opposed to Christ's kingdom. For the Chaldees had overthrown God's temple, and had endeavoured as far as possible to extinguish the whole of his worship, and to exterminate piety from the world. As far as concerns the Medes and Persians, although by their kindness a permission to return was granted to the people, yet very soon afterwards the kings of the Medes and Persians raged against that most miserable people, until the greater part of them preferred remaining in exile to returning home. At length came the Macedonian fury; and although the Jews were spared for a short period, we know how impetuously the kings of Syria and Egypt overran Judea, how cruelly they treated the wretched people by rapine and plunder, and the shedding of innocent blood. Again, the extreme barbarity of Antiochus in ordering all the Prophetic Books to be burned, and in all but exterminating the religion itself (1 Macc. i. 59) is well ascertained.

No wonder, then, that Daniel here opposes the reign of Christ to such monarchies! Next, as to the Romans, we know how thoroughly and proudly they despised the name of "Christian!" nay, they endeavoured by all means to root out from the world the Gospel and the doctrine of salvation, as an abominable thing. With all this we are familiar. Hence, to inform the faithful of their future condition until Christ's advent, Daniel shews how all the empires of the world should be adverse to God, and all its most powerful kings and sovereigns should be his very worst and most cruel enemies, and should use every means in their power to extinguish true piety. Thus he exhorts them to bear their cross, and never to yield to those wretched and sorrowful spectacles, but to proceed steadily in the course of their calling, until the promised Redeemer should appear. We stated this to be "accidental," since all the kingdoms of this world are clearly founded on the power and beneficence of Christ; but a memorable proof of God's anger ought to exist against them all, because they raised themselves against the Son of God, the Supreme King, with such extreme fury and hostility.

Now, Christ is compared *to a stone cut out of a mountain.* Some restrict this, unnecessarily, to the generation of Christ, because he was born of a virgin, out of the usual course of nature. Hence he says, as we have seen, *that it was cut out of a mountain without the hand of man;* that is, he was divinely sent, and his empire was separated from all earthly ones, since it was divine and heavenly. Now, therefore, we understand the reason of this simile.

With respect to the word " stone," Christ is not here called a *stone* in the sense of the word in Ps. cxviii. 22, and Is. viii. 14, and Zechariah ix. 15, and elsewhere. For there the name of a stone is applied to Christ, because his Church is founded on it. The perpetuity of his kingdom is denoted there as well as here; but, as I have already said, these phrases ought to be distinguished. It must now be added, —Christ is called a stone cut out without human hands, because he was from the beginning almost without form and comeliness, as far as human appearance goes. There is also a silent contrast between its magnitude, which the Prophet will soon mention, and this commencement. *The stone cut out of the mountain shall descend, and it shall become a great mountain, and shall fill the whole earth.* We see how the Prophet here predicts the beginning of Christ's Kingdom, as contemptible and abject before the world. It was not conspicuous for excellence, as it is said in Isaiah, A branch is sprung from the root of Jesse. (xi. 1.) When the posterity of David were deprived of all dignity, the royal name was utterly buried, and the diadem trodden under foot, as it is said in Ezekiel. (xvii. 19.) Hence, Christ first appeared cast down and lowly; but the branch increased wonderfully and beyond all expectation and calculation, unto an immense size, till it filled the whole earth. We now perceive how appositely Daniel speaks of Christ's kingdom: but we must treat the rest to-morrow.

PRAYER.

Grant, Almighty God, that we may remember ourselves to be pilgrims in the world, and that no splendour of wealth, or power, or worldly wisdom may blind our eyes, but may we always direct our eyes and all our senses towards the kingdom of thy Son. May we always fix them there, and may nothing hinder us from hastening on in the course of our calling, until at length we pass over the course and reach the goal which thou hast set before us, and to which thou dost this day invite us by the heralding of thy gospel. Do thou at length gather us unto that happy eternity which has been obtained for us through the blood of the same, thy Son. May we never be separated from him, but, being sustained by his power, may we at last be raised by him to the highest heavens.—Amen.

Lecture Eleventh.

WE must now explain more clearly what we yesterday stated concerning the eternal kingdom of Christ. In relating the dream, the Prophet said—*The stone cut out of the mountain without hands is the fifth kingdom,* by which the four kingdoms were to be broken up and destroyed, according to the vision shewn to King Nebuchadnezzar. We must now see whether or not this is the kingdom of Christ. The Prophet's words are these :

44. And in the days of these kings shall the God of heaven set up a kingdom, which shall never be destroyed: and the kingdom shall not be left to other people, *but* it shall break in pieces and consume all these kingdoms, and it shall stand for ever.
45. Forasmuch as thou sawest that the stone was cut out of the mountain without hands, and that it brake in pieces the iron, the brass, the clay, the silver, and the gold; the great God hath made known to the king what shall come to pass hereafter : and the dream *is* certain, and the interpretation thereof sure.

44. Et in diebus illis regum illorum suscitabit Deus cœlorum regnum, quod in seculum non dissipabitur,[1] et regnum *hoc* populo alieno non dere inquetur: confringet et conteret omnia illa regna, et ipsum stabit perpetuo.
45. Propterea vidisti, nempe e monte excisum lapidem et absque manu, qui confregit[2] ferrum, æs, testam, argentum et aurum : Deus magnus patefecit regi quid futurum esset postero tempore : et verum est somnium, et fidelis interpretatio ejus.

The Jews agree with us in thinking this passage cannot be otherwise understood than of the perpetual reign of Christ, and willingly and eagerly ascribe to the glory of their own nation whatever is written everywhere throughout the Scriptures ; nay, they often cry down many testimonies of Scripture for the purpose of boasting in their own privileges. They do not therefore deny the dream to have been

[1] Or, shall not be destroyed.—*Calvin.*
[2] Verbally, " and broke," but the copula ought to be rendered as the relative.—*Calvin.*

sent to King Nebuchadnezzar concerning Christ's kingdom ; but they differ from us, in expecting a Christ of their own. Hence they are compelled in many ways to corrupt this prophecy ; because, if they grant that the fourth empire or monarchy was accomplished in the Romans, they must necessarily acquiesce in the Gospel, which testifies of the arrival of that Messiah who was promised in the Law. For Daniel here openly affirms that Messiah's kingdom should arrive at the close of the fourth monarchy. Hence they fly to the miserable refuge that by the fourth monarchy should be understood the Turkish empire, which they call that of the Ishmaelites ; and thus they confound the Roman with the Macedonian empire. But what pretence have they for making only one empire out of two such different ones? They say the Romans sprang from the Greeks ; and if we grant this, whence did the Greeks spring? Did they not arise from the Caspian Mountains and Higher Asia? The Romans referred their origin to Troy, and at the time when the prophecy ought to be fulfilled, this had become utterly obscure—but what is this to the purpose when they had no reputation for a thousand years afterwards? But the Turks a long time afterwards, namely 600 years, suddenly burst forth like a deluge. In such a variety of circumstances, and at such a distance of time, how can they form one single kingdom? Then they shew no difference between themselves and the rest of the nations. For they recall us to the beginning of the world, and in this way make one kingdom out of two, and this mixture is altogether without reason, or any pretension to it. There is no doubt then, that Daniel intended the Romans by the fourth empire, since we yesterday saw, how in a manner contrary to nature, that empire ultimately perished by intestine discord. No single monarch reigned there, but only a democracy. All thought themselves to be equally kings, for they were all related. This union ought to have been the firmest bond of perpetuity. But Daniel here witnesses beforehand, how, even if they were intimately related, that kingdom would not be social, but would perish by its own dissensions. Finally, it is now sufficiently apparent that the Prophet's words cannot be otherwise explained than of the Roman empire, nor can they be drawn aside, except by violence, to the Turkish empire.

I shall now relate what our brother Anthony has suggested to me, from a certain Rabbi Barbinel,[1] who seems to excel others in acuteness. He endeavours to shew by six principal arguments, that the fifth kingdom cannot relate to our Christ—Jesus, the son of Mary. He *first* assumes this principle, since the four kingdoms were earthly, the fifth cannot be compared with them, except its nature is the same. The comparison would be, he says, both inappropriate and absurd. As if Scripture does not always compare the celestial kingdom of God with these of earth! for it is neither necessary nor important for all points of a comparison to be precisely similar. Although God shewed to the king of Babylon the four earthly monarchies, it does not follow that the nature of the fifth was the same, since it might be very different. Nay, if we weigh all things rightly, it is necessary to mark some difference between those four and this last one. The reasoning, therefore, of that rabbi is frivolous, when he infers that Christ's kingdom ought to be visible, since it could not otherwise correspond with the other kingdoms. The *second* reason, by which he opposes us, is this,—if religion makes the difference between kingdoms, it follows that the Babylonian, and Persian, and Macedonian are all the same; for we know that all those nations worshipped idols, and were devoted to superstition! The answer to so weak an argument is easy enough, namely, these four kingdoms did not differ simply in religion, but God deprived the Babylonians of their power, and transfer-

---

[1] The Rabbi Barbinel, to whose opinion Calvin's attention was drawn, was the celebrated Jewish statesman and commentator, Isaac Abarbanel. He claimed descent from the family of King David, being born in Lisbon 1437, and died at Venice 1508. From Dr. M'Caul's preface to Tegg's *Prideaux*, (1845,) we learn that his "Commentary to Daniel" was entitled *Mayene ha-yeshuah*, and published after his death in 1551, 4to, and also at Amsterdam, 1647. The younger Buxtorf translated it into Latin, and it was refuted at length by Carpzov, Hulsius, and Varenius Several of his works are still unprinted. He was a strong opponent of the Christian interpretation of Daniel, and an equally determined combatant of the rationalistic views of Moses the Egyptian, the son of Maimon.

red the monarchy to the Medes and Persians; and by the same providence of God the Macedonians succeeded them; and then, when all these kingdoms were abolished, the Romans possessed the sway over the whole East. We have already explained the Prophet's meaning. He wished simply to teach the Jews this,—they were not to despair through beholding the various agitations of the world, and its surprising and dreadful confusion; although those ages were subject to many changes, the promised king should at length arrive. Hence the Prophet wished to exhort the Jews to patience, and to hold them in suspense by the expectation of the Messiah. He does not distinguish these four monarchies through diversity of religion, but because God was turning the world round like a wheel while one nation was expelling another, so that the Jews might apply all their minds and attention to that hope of redemption which had been promised through Messiah's advent.

The *third* argument which that rabbi brings forward may be refuted without the slightest trouble. He gathers from the words of the Prophet that the kingdom of our Christ, the son of Mary, cannot be the kingdom of which Daniel speaks, since it is here clearly expressed that there should be no passing away or change of this kingdom: *it shall not pass on to another* or a strange *people*. But the Turks, says he, occupy a large portion of the world, and religion among Christians is divided, and many reject the doctrine of the Gospel. It follows, then, that Jesus, the son of Mary, is not that king of whom Daniel prophesied—that is, about whom the dream which Daniel explained occurred to the king of Babylon. But he trifles very foolishly, because he assumes what we shall ever deny—that Christ's kingdom is visible. For however the sons of God are dispersed, without any reputation among men, it is quite clear that Christ's kingdom remains safe and sure, since in its own nature it is not outward but invisible. Christ did not utter these words in vain, "My kingdom is not of this world." (John xviii. 36.) By this expression he wished to remove his kingdom from the ordinary forms of government. Although, therefore, the Turks have spread far and wide, and the world is filled with impious despisers of God, and the Jews yet occupy a part of it, still Christ's kingdom exists and has not been transferred to any others. Hence this reasoning is not only weak but puerile.

A *fourth* argument follows:—It seems very absurd that Christ, who was born under Octavius or Augustus Cæsar, should be the king of whom Daniel prophesied. For, says he, the beginning of the fourth and fifth monarchy was the same, which is absurd; for the fourth monarchy ought to endure for some time, and then the fifth should succeed it. But here he not only betrays his ignorance, but his utter stupidity, since God so blinded the whole people that they were like restive dogs. I have had much conversation with many Jews: I have never seen either a drop of piety or a grain of truth or ingenuousness—nay, I have never found common sense in any Jew. But this fellow, who seems so sharp and ingenious, displays his own impudence to his great disgrace. For he thought the Roman monarchy began with Julius Cæsar! as if the Macedonian empire was not abolished when the Romans took possession of Macedon and reduced it to a province, when also Antiochus was reduced into order by them—nay, when the third monarchy, namely, the Macedonian, began to decline, then the fourth, which is the Roman, succeeded it. Reason itself dictates to us to reckon in this way, since unless we confess the fourth monarchy to have succeeded directly on the passing away of the third, how could the rest follow on? We must observe, also, that the Prophet does not look to the Cæsars when he treats of these monarchies; nay, as we saw concerning the mingling of races, this cannot in any way suit the Cæsars; for we shewed yesterday how those who restrict this passage to Pompey and Cæsar are only trifling, and are utterly without judgment in this respect. For the Prophet speaks generally and continuously of a popular state, since they were all mutually related, and yet the empire was not stable, through their consuming themselves internally by intestine warfare. Since this is the case, we conclude this rabbi to be very foolish and palpably absurd in asserting the Christ not to be the son of Mary who was born under Augustus, although I do not argue for the kingdom of Christ commencing at his nativity.

His *fifth* argument is this :—Constantine and other Cæsars professed the faith of Christ. If we receive, says he, Jesus the son of Mary as the fifth king, how will this suit? as the Roman Empire was still in existence under this king. For where the religion of Christ flourishes, where he is worshipped and acknowledged as the only King, that kingdom ought not to be separated from his. When therefore Christ, under Constantine and his successors, obtained both glory and power among the Romans, his monarchy cannot be separated from theirs. But the solution of this is easy, as the Prophet here puts an end to the Roman Empire when it began to be torn in pieces. As to the time when Christ's reign began, I have just said it ought not to be referred to the time of his birth, but to the preaching of the Gospel. From the time when the Gospel began to be promulgated, we know the Roman monarchy to have been dissipated and at length to vanish away. Hence the empire did not endure through Constantine or other emperors, since their state was different; and we know that neither Constantine nor the other Cæsars were Romans. From the time of Trojan the empire began to be transferred to strangers, and foreigners reigned at Rome. We also know by what monsters God destroyed the ancient glory[1] of the Roman people!—for nothing could be more abandoned or disgraceful than the conduct of many of the emperors. If any one will but run through their histories, he will discover immediately that no other people ever had such monsters for rulers as the Romans under Heliogabalus and others like him,—I omit Nero and Caligula, and speak only of foreigners. The Roman Empire was therefore abolished after the Gospel began to be promulgated and Christ became generally known throughout the world. Thus we observe the same ignorance in this argument of the rabbi as in the others.

The *last* assertion is,—The Roman empire as yet partially survives, hence what is here said of the fifth monarchy can-

[1] This word is omitted in the edition published at Geneva A.D. 1667, but is correctly inserted in that of Bart. Vincentius, A.D. 1571.—*Tr.*

not belong to the son of Mary ; it is necessary for the fourth empire to be at an end, if the fifth king began to reign when Christ rose from the dead and was preached in the world. I reply, as I have said already, the Roman empire ceased, and was abolished when God transferred their whole power with shame and reproach to foreigners, who were not only barbarians, but horrible monsters! It would have been better for the Romans to suffer the utter blotting out of their name, rather than submit to such disgrace. We perceive how this sixth and last reason vanishes away. I wished to collect them together, to shew you how foolishly those Jewish reasoners make war with God, and furiously oppose the clear light of the Gospel.

I now return to Daniel's words. He says, *A kingdom shall come and destroy all other kingdoms.* I explained yesterday the sense in which Christ broke up those ancient monarchies, which had come to an end long before his advent. For Daniel does not wish to state precisely what Christ would do at any one moment, but what should happen from the time of the captivity till his appearance. If we attend to this intention, all difficulty will be removed from the passage. The conclusion, therefore, is this; the Jews should behold the most powerful empires, which should strike them with terror, and utterly astonish them, yet they should prove neither stable nor firm, through being opposed to the kingdom of the Son of God. But Isaiah denounces curses upon all the kingdoms which do not obey the Church of God. (Chap. lx. 12.) As all those monarchs erected their crests against the Son of God and true piety, with diabolical audacity, they must be utterly swept away, and God's curse, as announced by the Prophet, must become conspicuous upon them. Thus Christ rooted up all the empires of the world. The Turkish empire, indeed, at this day, excels in wealth and power, and the multitude of nations under its sway; but it was not God's purpose to explain future events after the appearance of Christ. He only wished the Jews to be admonished, and prevented from sinking under the weight of their burden, since they would be in imminent danger through the rise of so many fresh tyrannies in the world, and the absence of all repose. God wished, therefore, to brace their minds by fortitude. One reason was this—to cause them to dwell upon the promised redemption, and to experience how evanescent and uncertain are all the empires of the world which are not founded in God, and not united to the kingdom of Christ. God, therefore, *will set up the kingdoms of the heavens, which shall never be dissipated.* It is here worth while to notice the sense in which Daniel uses the term "perpetuity." It ought not to be restricted to the person of Christ, but belongs to all the pious and the whole body of the Church. Christ is indeed eternal in himself, but he also communicates his eternity to us, because he preserves the Church in the world, and invites us by the hope of a better life than this, and begets us again by his Spirit to an incorruptible life. The perpetuity, then, of Christ's reign, is twofold, without considering his person. *First,* in the whole body of believers; for though the Church is often dispersed and hidden from men's eyes, yet it never entirely perishes; but God preserves it by his incomprehensible virtue, so that it shall survive till the end of the world. Then there is a *second* perpetuity in each believer, since each is born of incorruptible seed, and renewed by the Spirit of God. The sons of Adam are now not mortal only, but bear within them heavenly life; since the Spirit within them is life, as St. Paul says, in the Epistle to the Romans. (Chap. viii. 10.) We hold, therefore, that whenever Scripture affirms Christ's reign to be eternal, this is extended to the whole body of the Church, and need not be confined to his person. We see, then, how the kingdom from which the doctrine of the Gospel began to be promulgated, was eternal; for although the Church was in a certain sense buried, yet God gave life to his elect, even in the sepulchre. Whence, then, did it happen that the sons of the Church were buried, and a new people and a new creation required, as in Ps. cii. 18? Hence it easily appears that God is served by a remnant, although they are not evident to human observation.

He adds, *This kingdom shall not pass away to another people.* By this phrase the Prophet means that this sovereignty cannot be transferred, as in the other instances. Darius was conquered by Alexander, and his posterity was extinguished, till at length God destroyed that ill-fated Macedonian race, until no one survived who boasted himself to be sprung from that family. With respect to the Romans, although they continued to exist, yet they were so disgracefully subjected to the tyranny of strangers and barbarians, as to be completely covered with shame and utterly disgraced. Then, as to the reign of Christ, he cannot be deprived of the empire conferred upon him, nor can we who are his members lose the kingdom of which he has made us partakers. Christ, therefore, both in himself and his members, reigns without any danger of change, because he always remains safe and secure in his own person. As to ourselves, since we are preserved by his grace, and he has received us under his own care and protection, we are beyond the reach of danger; and, as I have already said, our safety is ensured, for we cannot be deprived of the inheritance awaiting us in heaven. We, therefore, who are kept by his power through faith, as Peter says, may be secure and calm, (1 Pet. i. 5,) because whatever Satan devises, and however the world attempts various plans for our destruction, we shall still remain safe in Christ. We thus see how the Prophet's words ought to be understood, when he says that this fifth empire is not to be transferred and alienated to another people. The last clause of the sentence, which is this, *it shall bruise and break all other kingdoms, and shall stand perpetually itself,* does not require any long exposition. We have explained the manner in which Christ's kingdom should destroy all the earthly kingdoms of which Daniel had previously spoken; since whatever is adverse to the only-begotten Son of God, must necessarily perish and utterly vanish away. A Prophet exhorts all the kings of the earth to kiss the Son. (Ps. ii. 12.) Since neither the Babylonians, nor Persians, nor Macedonians, nor Romans, submitted themselves to Christ, nay, even used their utmost efforts to oppose him, they were the enemies of piety, and ought to be extinguished by Christ's kingdom; because, although the Persian empire was not in existence when Christ appeared in the world, yet its remembrance was cursed before God. For Daniel does not here touch only on those things which were visible to men, but raises our minds higher, assuring us most clearly that no true support on which we can rest can be found except in Christ alone. Hence he pronounces, that without Christ all the splendour, and power, opulence, and might of the world, is vain, and unstable, and worthless. He confirms the same sentiment in the following verse, where God shewed the king of Babylon what should happen in the last times, when he pointed out *a stone cut out of the mountain without hands.* We stated Christ to be cut out of the mountain without hands, because he was divinely sent, so that men cannot claim anything for themselves in this respect, since God, when treating of the redemption of his own people, speaks thus, by Isaiah,—Since God saw no help in the world, he relied upon his own arm and his own power. (lxiii. v. 5.) As, therefore, Christ was sent only by his heavenly Father, he is said to be *cut out without hands.*

Meanwhile, we must consider what I have added in the second place, that the humble and abject origin of Christ is denoted, since it was like a rough and unpolished stone. With regard to the word "mountain," I have no doubt Daniel here wished to shew Christ's reign to be sublime, and above the whole world. Hence the figure of the mountain means, in my opinion,—Christ should not spring out of the earth, but should come in the glory of his heavenly Father, as it is said in the Prophet : And thou, Bethlehem Ephratah, art the least among the divisions of Judah; yet out of thee shall a leader in Israel arise for me, and his reign shall be from the days of eternity. (Micah v. 2.) Daniel, then, here condescends to those gross imaginations to which our minds are subjected. Because, at the beginning, Christ's dignity did not appear so great as we discern it in the kings of the world, and to this day it seems to some obscured by the shame of the cross, many, alas ! despise him, and do not acknowledge any dignity in him. Daniel, therefore, now raises aloft our eyes and senses, when he says *this stone should be cut out of the mountain.* Meanwhile, if any one prefers taking the mountain for the elect people, I will not object to it, but this seems to me not in accordance with the genuine sense of the Prophet. At length he adds, *And the dream is true, and its interpretation trustworthy.* Here Daniel securely and intrepidly asserts, that he does not bring forward doubtful conjectures, but explains faithfully to King Nebuchadnezzar what he has received from the Lord. Here he claims for himself the Prophetic authority, to induce the king of Babylon to acknowledge him a sure and faithful interpreter of God. We see how the prophets always spoke with this confidence, otherwise all their teaching would be useless. If our faith depended on man's wisdom, or on anything of the kind, it would indeed be variable. Hence it is necessary to determine this foundation of truth, —Whatever the Prophets set before us proceeds from God ; and the reason why they so constantly insist on this is, lest their doctrine should be supposed to be fabricated by men. Thus also in this place, Daniel first says, *the dream is true ;* as if he said, the dream is not a common one, as the poets fable concerning a gate of horn ; the dream is not confused, as men imagine when scarcely sane, or stuffed with meat and drink, or through bodily constitution, either melancholy or choleric. He states, therefore, the king of Babylon's dream to have been a true oracle ; and adds, *its interpretation is certain.* Where, as in the next clause, the Prophet again urges his own authority, lest Nebuchadnezzar should doubt his divine instructions to explain the truth of his dream. It now follows,—

46. Then the king Nebuchadnezzar fell upon his face, and worshipped Daniel, and commanded that they should offer an oblation and sweet odours unto him.

46. Tunc rex Nebuchadnezer cecidit in faciem suam, et Danielem adoravit : et oblationem, et suffitum odoriferum,[1] jussit illi sacrificari.

When the king of Babylon *fell upon his face,* it is partly to be considered as worthy of praise and partly of blame. It was a sign of both piety and modesty, when he prostrated himself before God and his Prophet. We know the fierceness and pride of kings ; nay, we see them act like madmen, because they do not reckon themselves among mortals, and become blinded with the splendour of their

[1] That is, a sweet-smelling fragrance.—*Calvin.*

greatness. Nebuchadnezzar was really a very powerful monarch, and it was difficult for him so to regulate his mind as to attribute the glory to God. Thus the dream which Daniel explained could not be pleasing to him. He saw his monarchy cursed before God, and about to perish in ignominy: others, too, which should succeed it were ordained in heaven; and though he might receive some comfort from the destruction of the other kingdoms, yet it was very harsh to delicate ears, to hear that a kingdom, which appeared most flourishing, and which all men thought would be perpetual, was of but short duration and sure to perish. As, therefore, the king so prostrated himself before Daniel, it is, as I have said, a sign of piety in thus reverencing God, and in embracing the prophecy, which would otherwise be bitter and distasteful. It was also a sign of modesty, because he humbled himself so before God's Prophet Thus far the king of Babylon is worthy of praise, and we will discuss tomorrow the deficiency in his reverence.

PRAYER.

Grant, Almighty God, since thou hast shewn us by so many, such clear and such solid testimonies, that we can hope for no other Redeemer than him whom thou hast set forth : and as thou hast sanctioned his divine and eternal power by so many miracles, and hast sealed it by both the preaching of the Gospel and the seal of thy Spirit in our hearts, and dost confirm the same by daily experience,—Grant that we may remain firm and stable in him. May we never decline from him: may our faith never waver, but withstand all the temptations of Satan: and may we so persevere in the course of thy holy calling, that we may be gathered at length unto that eternal blessedness and perpetual rest which has been obtained for us by the blood of the same, thy Son.—Amen.

Lecture Twelfth.

WE said yesterday that King Nebuchadnezzar was worthy of praise, because he prostrated himself before Daniel after he had heard the narration of his dream and the interpretation which was added. For he gave them some testimony of piety, since in the person of Daniel he adored the true God, as we shall mention hereafter. Hence he shewed himself teachable, since the prophecy might exasperate his mind; because tyrants can scarcely ever bear anything to detract from their power. But he cannot be entirely excused. Although he confesses the God of Israel to be the only God, yet he transfers a part of his worship to a mortal man. Those who excuse this do not sufficiently remember how profane men mingle heavenly and earthly things; though they occasionally have right dispositions, yet they relax immediately to their own superstitions. Without doubt the confession which we shall meet with directly was confined to this single occasion. Nebuchadnezzar was not really and completely converted to true piety, so as to repent of his errors, but he partially recognised the supreme power to be with the God of Israel. This reverence, however, did not correct all his idolatries, but by a sudden impulse, as I have said, he confessed Daniel to be a servant of the true God. At the same time he did not depart from the errors to which he had been accustomed, and he afterwards returned to greater hardness, as we shall find in the next chapter. So also we see Pharaoh giving glory to God, but only for a moment, (Exod. ix. 27, and x. 16;) meanwhile he continued determinately proud and cruel, and never put off his original disposition. Our opinion of the king of Babylon ought to be of the same kind, though different in degree. King Nebuchadnezzar's obstinacy was not equal to the pride of Pharaoh. Each, indeed, shewed some sign of reverence, but neither was truly and heartily submissive to the God of Israel. Hence he bows before Daniel, not thinking him a God, but mingling and confounding, as profane men do, black and white; and we know that from the beginning even the dullest men had some perception of the only God. For no one ever denied the existence of a Supreme Deity, but men afterwards fabricated for themselves a multitude of gods, and transferred a part of the divine worship to mortals. As King Nebuchadnezzar was involved in these errors, we are not surprised at his adoring Daniel, and at the same time confessing there is but one God! And at this day we see how all in the papacy confess this truth, and yet they tear up the name of God, not in word, but in reality; for they so divide the worship of God, that each has part of the spoil and the plunder. Daniel relates what experience even now teaches us. This adoration was, it is true, commonly received among the Chaldeans, since the Orientals were always extravagant in their ceremonies, and we know their kings to have been adored as gods. But since the word for sacrificing is here used, and the word מנחה, *mencheh*, for "offering" also occurs, it is quite clear that Daniel was worshipped without consideration, as if he had been a demigod dropped down from heaven. Hence we must conclude that King Nebuchadnezzar did wrong in offering this honour to Daniel.

There ought to be moderation in our respect for God's Prophets, as we should not extol them beyond their deserts; we know the condition on which the Lord calls us forth—that he alone may be exalted, while all his teachers, and prophets, and servants, should remain in their own position. A question arises concerning the Prophet himself,—Why did he allow himself to be worshipped? For if Nebuchadnezzar sinned, as we have said, the Prophet had no excuse for allowing it. Some commentators labour anxiously to excuse him; but if he passed this by in silence, we must be compelled to confess him in some degree corrupted by the allurements of the court, since it is difficult to be familiar there without immediately being subject to its contagion. The defence of any man, however perfect, ought never to interfere with this fixed principle—nothing must be subtracted from the honour of God, and—it is a mark of perverseness whenever and howsoever the worship which is peculiar to God is transferred to creatures. Perhaps Daniel decidedly refused this, and so restrained the folly of the king of Babylon; but I leave the point in doubt, as nothing is said about it. Although it is scarcely probable that he took no notice at the time, when he saw the honour of God partly transferred to himself; for this would have been to make himself a partaker of sacrilege and impiety.

A holy Prophet could scarcely fall into this snare. We know many things are omitted in the narrative, and Daniel does not record what was done, but what the king ordered. He prostrated himself on his face; but perhaps Daniel shewed this to be unlawful. When he ordered sacrifice to be offered, Daniel might have rejected it as a great sin. For Peter properly corrected the error of Cornelius, which was more tolerable, since he wished to adore Peter after the common fashion. If, therefore, the Apostle did not endure this, but boldly rebuked the deed, (Acts x. 26,) what must be said about the Prophet? But, as I have said, I dare not assert anything on either side, unless what conjecture renders probable, that God's servant rejected this preposterous honour. If, indeed, he allowed it, he had no excuse for his sin; but still, as we have said, it is very difficult for those who desire to retain their purity to have much intercourse with courts, without contracting some spots of corruption. We see this even in the person of Joseph. Although he was completely dedicated to God, yet in his language, as shewn by his swearing, he was tainted by the Egyptian custom. (Gen. xlii. 15.) And since this was sinful in him, the same may be said of Daniel. Let us go on:—

47. The king answered unto Daniel, and said, Of a truth *it is*, that your God *is* a God of gods, and a Lord of kings, and a revealer of secrets, seeing thou couldest reveal this secret.

47. Respondit rex Danieli, et dixit, Ex vero Deus vester ipse *est* Deus deorum, et dominus regum, et revelator arcanorum, quod potueris revelare arcanum hoc.

This confession is quite pious and holy, and is fraught with rectitude and sincerity; it may even be taken as a proof of true conversion and repentance. But, as I have lately reminded you, profane men are sometimes seized with an admiration of God; and then they profess largely and copiously whatever may be expected from God's true worshippers. Still this is but momentary, for all the while they remain wrapt up in their own superstitions. God, therefore, extorts this language from them, when they speak so piously; but they inwardly retain their faults, and afterwards easily fall back to their accustomed habits—as a memorable example will shortly prove to us. Whatever sense be adopted, God wished his glory to be proclaimed by the mouth of the profane king, and desired him to be the herald of his own power and influence. But this was peculiarly profitable to those Jews who still remained firm in their allegiance; for the greater part had revolted—notoriously enough, and had degenerated with great facility from the pure worship of God. When led into captivity, they became idolaters and apostates, and denied the living God; but a small number of the pious remained; God wished to promote their benefit, and to strengthen their minds when he drew this confession from the king of Babylon. But another object was gained, since the king as well as all the Chaldeans and Assyrians were rendered more excuseless. For if the God of Israel was truly God, why did Bel in the meantime retain his rank? *He is the God of gods*—then it must be added at once, he is the enemy of false gods. We observe how Nebuchadnezzar here mingles light with darkness, and black with white, while he confesses the God of Israel to be supreme among gods, and yet continues to worship other deities. For if the God of Israel obtains his right, all idols vanish away. Hence, Nebuchadnezzar contends with himself in this language. But, as I have said, he is seized by a violent impulse, and is not quite in his senses when he so freely declares the power of the only God.

As far then as words go, he says, *truly your God is himself a God of gods.* The particle *truly* is by no means superfluous here; it is strongly affirmative. For if any one had inquired of him whether Bel and other idols were to be worshipped as gods, he might answer, " yes ;" but doubtfully, and according to pre-conceived opinion, since all superstitious worshippers are perplexed, and if ever they defend their superstitions, they do so with the rashness which the devil suggests, but not according to their judgment. In truth, their minds are not composed when they dare to assert their own superstitions to be pious and holy. But Nebuchadnezzar seems here formally to renounce his own errors; as if he had said—Hitherto I acknowledged other gods, but I now change my opinion; I have discovered your God to be the chief of all gods. And, truly, if he really spoke his own mind, he might perceive he was doing injustice to his own idols, if there was any divinity in them; Israel's God was confessedly held in utter hatred and abomination by the profane nations. By extolling him above all gods, he degrades Bel and the whole crew of false gods which the Babylonians worshipped. But, as we have said, he was swayed by impulse and spoke without thinking. He was in a kind of enthusiasm, since God astonished him, and then drew him on to wonder at and to declare his own power. He calls him *Lord of kings,* by which eulogium he claims for him the supreme dominion over the world; he means to assert that Israel's God not only excels all others, but holds the reins of government over the world. For if he is the Lord of kings, all people are under his hand and dominion! and the multitude of mankind cannot be drawn away from his empire, if he rules their very monarchs. We understand, therefore, the meaning of these words, namely, whatever deity is worshipped is inferior to the God of Israel, because he is high above all gods; then his providence rules over the world, while he is Lord of all peoples and kings, and governs all things by his will.

He adds, *he is a revealer of secrets.* This is our proof of Divinity, as we have said elsewhere. For Isaiah, when wishing to prove the existence of only one God, takes these two principles, viz., Nothing happens without his permission; and his foreseeing all things. (Chap. xlviii. 3-5.) These two principles have been inseparably united. Although Nebuchadnezzar did not understand what was the true peculiarity of Divinity, yet he is here impelled by the secret instinct of God's Spirit clearly to set forth God's power and wisdom. Hence he confesses the God of Israel to excel all gods, since he obtains power in the whole world, and nothing whatever is concealed from him. He adds the reason— *Daniel could reveal that secret.* This reason does not seem a very good one; for he infers the world to be governed by one God, because Daniel made this secret known. But then "this has no reference to his power." The answer to this remark is easy; we shewed elsewhere how we ought not to imagine a god like Apollo who can only predict future events. And, truly, it is far too insipid to attribute to God simple prescience, as if the events of the world had any other dependence than upon his power; for God is said to have a previous knowledge of future events, because he determined what he wished to have done. Hence Nebuchadnezzar concluded the dominion of the whole world to be in God's hands, because he could predict futurity; for unless he had the full power over the future, he could not predict anything with certainty. As, therefore, he really predicts future events, this clearly determines all things to be ordained by him, and disproves the existence of chance, while he fulfils whatever he has decreed.

Let us learn from this passage, how insufficient it is to celebrate God's wisdom and power with noisy declamation, unless we at the same time reject all superstitions from our minds, and so cling to the only God as to bid all others heartily farewell. No fuller verbal confession can be required than is here set before us; and yet we observe how Nebuchadnezzar was always involved in Satan's impostures, because he wished to retain his false gods, and thought it sufficient to yield the first place to the God of Israel. Let us learn again, to do our best in purging the mind from all superstitions, that the only God may pervade all our senses. Meanwhile, we must observe how severe and dreadful a judgment awaits Papists, and all like them, who at least ought to be imbued with the rudiments of piety, while they confess the existence of but one supreme God, and yet mingle together a great multitude of deities, and dishonour both his power and wisdom, and at the same time observe what is here said by a profane king. For the Papists not only divide God's power, by distributing it in parts to each of their saints; but also when they speak of God himself, they fancy him as knowing all things beforehand, and yet leaving all things contingent on man's free will; first creating all things, and then leaving every event in suspense. Hence heaven and earth, as they bear either men's merits or crimes, at one time become useful, and at another adverse to mankind. Truly enough, neither rain, nor heat, nor cloudy nor serene weather, nor anything else happens without God's permission; and whatever is adverse is a sign of his curse; whatever is prosperous and desirable is the sign of his favour. This, indeed, is true, but when the Papists lay their foundation in the will of man, we see how they deprive God of his rights. Let us learn, then, from this passage, not to attribute to God less than was conceded by this profane king.

| 48. Then the king made Daniel a great man, and gave him many great gifts, and made him ruler over the whole province of Babylon, and chief of the governors over all the wise men of Babylon. | 48. Tunc rex Danielem magnificavit, et munera præclara, et magna dedit ei,[1] et constituit eum super totam povinciam Babylonis, et magistrum procerum super omnes sapientes Babylonis. |

Here also another point is added, namely, how King Nebuchadnezzar raised God's Prophet and adorned him with the highest honours. We have spoken of that preposterous worship which he himself displayed and commanded others to offer. As far as concerns gifts and the discharge of public duties, we can neither condemn Nebuchadnezzar for honouring God's servant, nor yet Daniel for suffering himself to be thus exalted. All God's servants ought to take care not to make a gain of their office, and we know how very pestilent the disease is when prophets and teachers are addicted to gain, or easily receive the gifts offered them. For where there is no contempt of money, many vices necessarily spring up, since all avaricious and covetous men adulterate God's word and make a traffic of it. (2 Cor. ii. 17.) Hence all prophets and ministers of God ought to watch against being covetous of gifts. But as far as Daniel is concerned, he might receive what the king offered him just as Joseph could lawfully undertake the government of the whole of Egypt. (Gen. xli. 40.) There is no doubt that Daniel had other views than his private and personal advantage. We must not believe him covetous of gain while he bore his exile so patiently, and, besides this, when at the hazard of his life he had preferred abstinence from the royal food to alienating himself from the people of God. As he manifestly preferred the shame of the cross by which God's people were then oppressed, to opulence, luxury and honour, who will think him blinded by avarice through receiving gifts?

[1] Or, gave him many gifts, as some translate.—*Calvin.*

But since he saw the sons of God miserably and cruelly oppressed by the Chaldeans, he wished as far as he could to succour them in their miseries. As he well knew this would afford some consolation and support to his race, he allowed himself to be made prefect of a province. And the same reason influenced him to seek some place of authority for his companions, as follows,—

49. Then Daniel requested of the king, and he set Shadrach, Meshach, and Abed-nego, over the affairs of the province of Babylon: but Daniel *sat* in the gate of the king.

49. Et Daniel petiit a rege; et constituit super opus[1] provinciæ Babylonis Sidrach, Mesach, et Abed-nego: Daniel autem *erat* in porta regis.

Some ambition may be noticed here in the Prophet, since he procures honours for his own companions. For when the king spontaneously offers him a command, he is obliged to accept it; he need not offend the mind of the proud king. There was a necessity for this, because he himself seeks from the king prefectships for others. What shall we say was the origin of this conduct? As I have already hinted, Daniel may be here suspected of ambition, for it might be charged against him as a crime that he made a gain of the doctrine which he had been divinely taught. But he rather regarded his people, and wished to bring some comfort to them when oppressed. For the Chaldeans treated their slaves tyrannically, and we are aware how the Jews were utterly hated by the whole world. When therefore Daniel, through the feeling of pity, seeks some consolation from the people of God, there is no reason for accusing him of any fault, because he was not drawn aside by private advantage, and did not desire honours for either himself or his companions; but he was intent on that object to enable his companions to succour the Jews in their troubles. Hence the authority which he obtains for them has no other object than to cause the Jews to be treated a little more humanely, as their condition would not be so harsh and bitter while they have prefects of their own people who should study to treat them as brethren. We now see how Daniel may be rightly acquitted of this charge without any difficulty or argument; for the

[1] Or, administration.—*Calvin.*

matter itself is sufficiently clear, and we may readily collect that Daniel was both pious and humane, and free from all charge of sin. From the words—*was in the king's gate*, we ought not to understand his being a gate-keeper. Some suppose this phrase to be used, because they were accustomed to exercise justice there; but they transfer to the Chaldeans what Scripture teaches us of the Jews. I take it more simply. Daniel was chief over the king's court, since he held the supreme command there; and that sense is more genuine. Besides, we are fully aware of the custom of the Chaldeans and Assyrians to make the approach to the king difficult. Daniel is therefore said *to be at the gate*, to prevent any entrance into the king's palace, unless by his permission. It now follows,—

CHAPTER THIRD.

1. Nebuchadnezzar the king made an image of gold, whose height *was* threescore cubits, *and* the breadth thereof six cubits: he set it up in the plain of Dura, in the province of Babylon.

1. Nebuchadnezer rex fecit imaginem ex auro, altitudo ejus cubitorum sexaginta, latitudo cubitorum sex: erexit eam in planitie Dura,[1] in provincia Babylonis.

Very probably this statue was not erected by King Nebuchadnezzar within a short period, as the Prophet does not notice how many years had passed away; for it is not probable that it was erected within a short time after he had confessed the God of Israel to be the Supreme Deity. Yet as the Prophet is silent, we need not discuss the matter. Some of the rabbis think this statue to have been erected as an expiation; as if Nebuchadnezzar wished to avert the effect of his dream by this charm, as they say. But their guess is most frivolous. We may inquire, however, whether Nebuchadnezzar deified himself or really erected this statue to Bel the principal deity of the Chaldeans, or invented some new-fangled divinity? Many incline to the opinion that he wished to include himself in the number of the deities, but

[1] Some make this word a noun appellative, and translate it, "habitable land," but the following translation is more correct:—He placed an image on the plains of Dura.—*Calvin.*

this is not certain—at least I do not think so. Nebuchadnezzar seems to me rather to have consecrated this statue to some of the deities; but, as superstition is always joined with ambition and pride, very likely Nebuchadnezzar was also induced by vain glory and luxury to erect this statue. As often as the superstitious incur expense in building temples and in fabricating idols, if any one asks them their object, they immediately reply—they do it in honour of God! At the same time they are all promoting their own fame and reputation. All the superstitious reckon God's worship valueless, and rather wish to acquire for themselves favour and estimation among men. I readily admit this to have been Nebuchadnezzar's intention, and indeed I am nearly certain of it. But at the same time some pretence to piety was joined with it; for he pretended that he wished to worship God. Hence, also, what I formerly mentioned appears more clear, namely,—King Nebuchadnezzar was not truly and heartily converted, but rather remained fixed in his own errors, when he was attributing glory to the God of Israel. As I have already said, that confession of his was limited, and he now betrays what he nourished in his heart; for when he erected the statue he did not return to his own natural disposition, but rather his impiety, which was hidden for a time, was then detected. For that remarkable confession could not be received as a proof of change of mind. All therefore would have said he was a new man, if God had not wished it to be made plain that he was held bound and tied by the chains of Satan, and was still a slave to his own errors. God wished then to present this example to manifest Nebuchadnezzar to be always impious, although through compulsion he gave some glory to the God of Israel.

PRAYER.

Grant, Almighty God, since our minds have so many hidden recesses that nothing is more difficult than thoroughly to purge them from all fiction and lying,—Grant, I say, that we may honestly examine ourselves. Do thou also shine upon us with the light of thy Holy Spirit; may we truly acknowledge our hidden faults and put them far away from us, that thou mayest be our only God, and our true piety may obtain the palm of thine approbation. May we offer thee pure and spotless worship, and meanwhile may we conduct ourselves in the world with a pure conscience; and may each of us be so occupied in our duties as to consult our brother's advantage as well as our own, and at length be made partakers of that true glory which thou hast prepared for us in heaven through Christ our Lord.—Amen.

Lecture Thirteenth.

WE began in the last Lecture to treat of THE GOLDEN STATUE which Nebuchadnezzar erected, and placed in the plain or open country of Dura. We stated this statue to have been erected for a religious reason, when the ambition of that king or tyrant was at its full sway, which we may always observe in the superstitious. For although they always put forward the name of God, and persuade themselves that they are worshipping God, yet pride always impels them to desire the approbation of the world. Such was the desire of King Nebuchadnezzar in erecting this statue, as its very magnitude displays. For the Prophet says, *the height of the statue was sixty cubits, and its breadth six cubits.* Such a mass must have cost much expense, for the image was made of gold. Probably this gold was acquired by much rapine and plunder; but whether it was so or not, we may here view, as I have said, the profane king so worshipping God as to propagate the remembrance of his own name to posterity. The region in which he placed the image seems to imply this. Without doubt the Prophet here points out some celebrated place which men were accustomed to frequent for the sake of merchandise and other necessities. But as far as the king's special intention is concerned, we stated their conjecture to be out of place who think the statue to have been erected for the sake of expiating his dream. It is more probable, since the Jews were dispersed throughout Assyria and Chaldea, that this image was erected, lest those foreigners who were exiles from their country should introduce any novelty. This conjecture carries some weight with it; for Nebuchadnezzar knew the Jews to be so attached to the God of their fathers as to be averse to all the superstitions of the Gentiles. He feared, therefore, lest they should seduce others to their own opinions, and he wished to counteract this by erecting a new statue, and commanding all his subjects to bow down to it. Meanwhile, we see how quickly the acknowledgment of Israel's God, whose glory and power he had so lately celebrated, had vanished from his mind! Now this trophy is erected to reproach him, as if he had been vanquished as well as the idols of the heathen. But, we have said elsewhere, Nebuchadnezzar never seriously acknowledged the God of Israel, but by a sudden impulse was compelled to confess him to be the Supreme and only God, though he was all the while drowned in his own superstitions. Hence his confession was rather the result of astonishment, and did not proceed from true change of heart. Let us now come to the remainder:

2. Then Nebuchadnezzar the king sent to gather together the princes, the governors, and the captains, the judges, the treasurers, the counsellors, the sheriffs, and all the rulers of the provinces, to come to the dedication of the image which Nebuchadnezzar the king had set up.

2. Tunc Nebuchadnezer rex misit ad congregandum satrapas, duces, et quæstores, primates, *vel proceres*, judices, magistratus, optimates, et omnes præfectos provinciarum, ut venirent ad dedicationem imaginis, quam erexerat Nebuchadnezer rex.

I do not know the derivation of the word "Satrap;" but manifestly all these are names of magistracies, and I allow myself to translate the words freely, since they are not Hebrew, and the Jews are equally ignorant of their origin. Some of them, indeed, appear too subtle; but they assert nothing but what is frivolous and foolish. We must be content with the simple expression—*he sent to collect the satraps.*

3. Then the princes, the governors, and captains, the judges, the treasurers, the counsellors, the sheriffs, and all the rulers of the provinces, were gathered together unto the dedication of the image that Nebuchadnezzar the king had set up; and they stood before the image that Nebuchadnezzar had set up.

3. Tunc congregati sunt satrapæ, duces, proceres, quæstores, magistratus, judices, optimates, et omnes præfecti provinciarum ad dedicationem imaginis, quam erexerat Nebuchadnezer rex: et steterunt coram imagine quam erexerat Nebuchadnezer.

Let us add the context, as the subject is continued:

4. Then an herald cried aloud, To you it is commanded, O people, nations, and languages,

5. That at what time ye hear the sound of the cornet, flute, harp, sackbut, psaltery, dulcimer, and all kinds of music, ye fall down and worship the golden image that Nebuchadnezzar the king hath set up.

4. Et præco clamabat in fortitudine:[1] Vobis edicitur, populi, gentes, et linguæ,[2]

5. Simulac audieritis vocem cornu, *vel, tubæ,* fistulæ, citharæ, sambucæ, psalterii, symphoniæ, et omnia instrumenta musices: ut procidatis, et adoretis imaginem auream, quam erexit Nebuchadnezer rex.

I do not know of what kind these musical instruments were.

6. And whoso falleth not down and worshippeth, shall the same hour be cast into the midst of a burning fiery furnace.

7. Therefore at that time, when all the people heard the sound of the cornet, flute, harp, sackbut, psaltery, and all kinds of music, all the people, the nations, and the languages, fell down *and* worshipped the golden image that Nebuchadnezzar the king had set up.

6. Et quisquis non prociderit[3] et adoraverit, eadem hora,[4] projicietur in medium fornacem ignis ardentis, *vel, ardentem.*

7. Itaque simulatque, *eadem hora atque,* audierint omnes populi vocem cornu, fistulæ, citharæ, sambucæ, psalterii, et omnium instrumentorum musices, prociderunt omnes populi, gentes et linguæ adorantes imaginem auream, quam erexerat Nebuchadnezer rex.

We see how Nebuchadnezzar wished to establish among all the nations under his sway a religion in which there should be no mixture of foreign novelty. He feared dissension as a cause of disunion in his empire. Hence we may suppose the king to have consulted his own private ease and advantage, as princes are accustomed to consult their own wishes rather than God's requirements in promulgating edicts concerning the worship of God. And from the beginning, this boldness and rashness have increased in the world, since those who have had supreme power have always dared to fabricate deities, and have proceeded beyond this even to ordering the gods which they have invented to be worshipped. The different kinds of gods are well known as divided into three—the PHILOSOPHICAL, the POLITICAL, and the POETICAL. They called those gods "PHILOSOPHICAL" which natural reason prompts men to worship. Truly, indeed, philosophers are often foolish when they dispute about the essence

---

[1] Or, in the midst of the multitude; for חיל, *hil,* may be explained both ways.— *Calvin.*
[2] That is, nations of all languages.—*Calvin.*
[3] That is, shall not bend the knee.—*Calvin.*
[4] That is, instantly.—*Calvin.*

or worship of God; but since they follow their own fancies they are necessarily erroneous. For God cannot be apprehended by human senses, but must be made manifest to us by his own word; and as he descends to us, so we also in turn are raised to heaven. (1 Cor. ii. 14.) But yet philosophers in their disputes have some pretexts, so as not to seem utterly insane and irrational. But the poets have fabled whatever pleases them, and thus have filled the world with the grossest and at the same time the foulest errors. As all theatres resounded with their vain imaginations, the minds of the vulgar have been imbued with the same delusions; for we know human dispositions are ever prone to vanity. But when the devil adds fire to the fuel, we then see how furiously both learned and unlearned are carried away. So it happened when they persuaded themselves of the truth of what they saw represented in their theatres. Thus, that religion which was founded on the authority of the Magi was considered certain by the heathen, as they called those gods "POLITICAL" which were received by the common consent of all. Those also who were considered prudent said it was by no means useful to object to what the philosophers taught concerning the nature of the gods, since this would tear asunder all public rites, and whatever was fixed without doubt in men's minds. For both the Greeks and Latins, as well as other barbarous nations, worshipped certain gods as the mere offspring of opinion, and these they confessed to have once been mortal. But philosophers at least retained this principle—the gods are eternal; and if the philosophers had been listened to, the authority of the Magi would have fallen away. Hence the most worldly-wise were not ashamed, as I have mentioned, to urge the expulsion of philosophy from sacred things.

With regard to the POETS, the most politic were compelled to succumb to the petulance of the common people, and yet they taught at the same time what the poets feigned and fabled concerning the nature of the gods was pernicious. This, then, was the almost universal rule throughout the world as to the worship of God, and the very foundation of piety—namely, no deities are to be worshipped except those which have been handed down from our forefathers. And this is the tendency of the oracle of Apollo which Xenophon[1] in the character of Socrates so greatly praises, namely, every city ought to worship the gods of its own country! For when Apollo was consulted concerning the best religion, with the view of cherishing the errors by which all nations were intoxicated, he commanded them not to change anything in their public devotions, and pronounced that religion the best for every city and people which had been received from the furthest antiquity. This was a wonderful imposture of the devil, as he was unwilling to stir up men's minds to reflect upon what was really right, but he retained them in that old lethargy—"Aha! the authority of your ancestors is sufficient for you!" The greatest wisdom among the profane was, as I have said, to cause consent to be taken for reason. Meanwhile, those who were supreme either in empire, or influence, or dignity, assumed to themselves the right of fashioning new deities; for we see how many dedicated temples to fictitious deities, because they were commanded by authority. Hence it is by no means surprising for Nebuchadnezzar to take this license of setting up a new deity. Perhaps he dedicated this statue to Bel, who is considered as the Jupiter of the Chaldeans; but yet he wished to introduce a new religion by means of which his memory might be celebrated by posterity. Virgil[2] derides this folly when he says:

And he increases the number of deities by altars. For he means, however men may erect numerous altars on earth, they cannot increase the number of the gods in heaven. Thus, therefore, Nebuchadnezzar increased the number of the deities by a single altar, that is, introduced a new rite to make the statue a monument to himself, and his own name famous as long as that religion flourished. Here we perceive how grossly he abused his power; for he did not consult his own Magi as he might have done, nor even reflect within himself whether that religion was lawful or not; but

[1] Xenophon in Comment., et Cicero de Legibus, lib. ii. § 8.
[2] Æneid, lib. vii. 211, "... et numerum Divorum altaribus addit." Heyne reads "*addit;*" Calvin, "*auget.*"

through being blinded by pride, he wished to fetter the minds of all, and to compel them to adopt what he desired. Hence we gather how vain profane men are when they pretend to worship God, while at the same time they wish to be superior to God himself. For they do not admit any pure thought, or even apply themselves to the knowledge of God, but they make their will law, just as it pleases them. They do not adore God, but rather their own fiction. Such was the pride of King Nebuchadnezzar, as appears from his own edict:

King Nebuchadnezzar sent to collect all the satraps, generals, and prefects, to come to the dedication of the image, which King Nebuchadnezzar had erected. The name of the king is always added, except in one place, as though the royal power raised mortals to such a height that they could fabricate deities by their own right! We observe how the king of Babylon claimed the right of causing the statue to be worshipped as a god, while it was not set up by any private or ordinary person but by the king himself. While the royal power is rendered conspicuous in the world, kings do not acknowledge it to be their duty to restrain themselves within the bounds of law, so long as they remain obedient to God. And at this day we see with what arrogance all earthly monarchs conduct themselves. For they never inquire what is agreeable to the word of God, and in accordance with sincere piety; but they defend the errors received from their forefathers, by the interposition of the royal name, and think their own previous decision to be sufficient, and object to the worship of any god, except by their permission and decree. With respect to the dedication, we know it to have been customary among the heathens to consecrate their pictures and statues before they adored them. And to this day the same error is maintained in the Papacy. For as long as images remain with the statuary or the painter, they are not venerated; but as soon as an image is dedicated by any private ceremony, (which the Papists call a "devotion,") or by any public and solemn rite, the tree, the wood, the stone, and the colours become a god! The Papists also have fixed ceremonies among their exorcisms in consecrating statues and pictures. Nebuchadnezzar, therefore, when he wished his image to be esteemed in the place of God, consecrated it by a solemn rite, and as we have said, this usage was customary among the heathen. He does not here mention the common people, for all could not assemble in one place; but the prefects and elders were ordered to come, and they would bring numerous attendants with them: then they bring forward the king's edict, and each takes care to erect some monument in his own province, whence it may spread the appearance of all their subjects worshipping as a god the statue which the king had erected.

It now follows—*All the satraps, prefects, generals, elders, treasurers, and magistrates came and stood before the image which King Nebuchadnezzar had set up.* It is not surprising that the prefects obeyed the king's edict, since they had no religion but what they had received from their fathers. But obedience to the king weighed with them more then reverence for antiquity; as in these times, if any king either invents a new superstition, or departs from the papacy, or wishes to restore God's pure worship, a sudden change is directly perceived in all prefects, and in all countries, and senators. Why so? Because they neither fear God nor sincerely reverence him, but depend on the king's will and flatter him like slaves, and thus they all approve, and if need be applaud, whatever pleases the king. It is not surprising then if the Chaldean elders, who knew nothing experimentally of the true God or of true piety, are so prone to worship this statue. Hence also, we collect the great instability of the profane, who have never been taught true religion in the school of God. For they will bend every moment to any breezes, just as leaves are moved by the wind blowing among trees; and because they have never taken root in God's truth, they are necessarily changeable, and are borne hither and thither with every blast. But a king's edict is not simply a wind, but a violent tempest, and no one can oppose their decrees with impunity; consequently those who are not solidly based upon God's word, do not act from true piety, but are borne away by the strength of the storm.

It is afterwards added—*A herald cried out lustily,* or among the multitude. This latter explanation does not suit so well—the herald crying amidst the multitude—since there were a great concourse of nations, and the kingdom of Babylon comprehended many provinces: *The herald, therefore, cried with a loud voice, An edict is gone forth for you, O nations, peoples, and tongues.* This would strike them with terror, since the king made no exception to his command for every province to worship his idol; for each person would observe the rest, and when every one sees the whole multitude obedient, no one would dare to refuse; hence all liberty is at an end. It now follows,—*When ye hear the sound of the trumpet,* or horn, *harp, pipe, psaltery, sackbut,* &c., *ye must fall down and adore the image. But whoever did not fall down before it, should be cast the same hour into a burning fiery furnace.* This would excite the greater terror, since King Nebuchadnezzar sanctioned this impious worship with a punishment so severe; for he was not content with a usual kind of death, but commanded every one who did not worship the statue to be cast into the fire. Now, this denunciation of punishment sufficiently demonstrates how the king suspected some of rebellion. There would have been no dispute if Jews had not been mixed with Chaldeans and Assyrians, for they always worshipped the same gods, and it was a prevailing custom with them to worship those deities whom their kings approved. Hence it appears that the statue was purposely erected to give the king an opportunity of accurately ascertaining whether the Jews, as yet unaccustomed to Gentile superstitions, were obedient to his command. He wished to cause the sons of Abraham to lay aside sincere piety, and to submit to his corruptions, by following the example of others, and framing their conduct according to the king's will and the practice of the people among whom they dwelt. But we shall treat this hereafter.

Respecting the required adoration, nothing but outward observance was needed. King Nebuchadnezzar did not exact a verbal profession of belief in this deity, that is, in the divinity of the statue which he commanded to be worshipped;

it was quite sufficient to offer to it merely outward worship. We here see how idolatry is deservedly condemned in those who pretend to worship idols, even if they mentally refrain and only act through fear and the compulsion of regal authority. That excuse is altogether frivolous. We see, then, how this king or tyrant, though he fabricated this image by the cunning of the devil, exacted nothing else than the bending the knees of all the people and nations before the statue. And truly he had in this way alienated the Jews from the worship of the one true God, if this had been extorted from them. For God wishes first of all for inward worship, and afterwards for outward profession. The principal altar for the worship of God ought to be situated in our minds, for God is worshipped spiritually by faith, prayer, and other acts of piety. (John iv. 24.) It is also necessary to add outward profession, not only that we may exercise ourselves in God's worship, but offer curselves wholly to him, and bend before him both bodily and mentally, and devote ourselves entirely to him, as Paul teaches. (1 Cor. vii. 34; 1 Thess. v. 23.) Thus far, then, concerning both the adoration and the penalty.

It follows again,—*As soon as the burst of the trumpets was heard and the sound of so many instruments, all nations, peoples, and tongues fell down and adored the image which King Nebuchadnezzar had set up.* Here I may repeat what I said before—all men were very obedient to the injunctions of their monarchs; whatever they ordered was obeyed, so long as it did not cause complete ruin; and they often bore the heaviest burdens with the view of perfect conformity. But we must remark how our propensities have always a vicious tendency. If King Nebuchadnezzar had commanded the God of Israel to be worshipped, and all temples to be overthrown, and all altars throughout his empire to be thrown down, very great tumults would doubtless have arisen; for the devil so fascinates men's minds that they remain pertinaciously fixed in the errors which they have imbibed. Hence the Chaldeans, Assyrians, and others would never have been induced to obey without the greatest difficulty. But now, on the appearance of the signal, they directly fall down and adore the golden statue. Hence we may learn to reflect upon our own character, as in a mirror, with the view of submitting ourselves to God's Word, and of being immovable in the right faith, and of standing unconquered in our consistency, whatever kings may command. Although a hundred deaths may threaten us, they must not weaken our faith, for unless God restrain us by his curb, we should instantly start aside to every species of vanity; and especially if a king introduces corruptions among us, we are immediately carried away by them, and, as we said, are far too prone to vicious and perverse modes of worship. The Prophet repeats again the king's name to shew us how little the multitude thought of pleasing God; never considering whether the worship was sacred and sound, but simply content with the king's nod. The Prophet deservedly condemns this easy indifference.

We should learn also from this passage, not to be induced by the will of any man to embrace any kind of religion, but diligently to inquire what worship God approves, and so to use our judgment as not rashly to involve ourselves in any superstitions. Respecting the use of musical instruments, I confess it to be customary in the Church even by God's command; but the intention of the Jews and of the Chaldeans was different. For when the Jews used trumpets and harps and other instruments in celebrating God's praises, they ought not to have obtruded this custom on God as if it was the proof of piety; but it ought to have another object, since God wished to use all means of stirring men up from their sluggishness, for we know how cold we grow in the pursuits of piety, unless we are aroused. God, therefore, used these stimulants to cause the Jews to worship him with greater fervour. But the Chaldeans thought to satisfy their god by heaping together many musical instruments. For, like other persons, they supposed God like themselves, for whatever delights us, we think must also please the Deity. Hence the immense heap of ceremonies in the Papacy, since our eyes delight in such splendours; hence we think this to be required of us by God, as if he delighted in what pleases us. This is, indeed, a gross error. There is no doubt that the harp, trumpet, and other musical instruments with which Nebuchadnezzar worshipped his idol, formed a part of his errors, and so also did the gold. God, indeed, wished his sanctuary to manifest some splendour; not that gold, silver, and precious stones please him by themselves, but he wished to commend his glory to his people, since under this figure they might understand why everything precious should be offered to God, as it is sacred to him. The Jews, indeed, had many ceremonies, and much of what is called magnificent splendour in the worship of God, and still the principle of spiritual worship yet remained among them. The profane, while they invented gross deities which they reverenced according to their pleasure, thought it a proof of perfect sanctity, if they sang beautifully, if they used plenty of gold and silver, and if they employed showy utensils in these sacrifices. I must leave the rest for to-morrow.

PRAYER.

Grant, Almighty God, since we always wander miserably in our thoughts, and in our attempts to worship thee we only profane the true and pure reverence of thy Divinity, and are easily drawn aside to depraved superstition,—Grant that we may remain in pure obedience to thy word, and never bend aside from it in any way. Instruct us by the unconquered fortitude of thy Spirit. May we never yield to any terrors or threats of man, but persevere in reverencing thy name even to the end. However the world may rage after its own diabolic errors, may we never turn out of the right path, but continue in the right course in which thou invitest us, until, after finishing our race, we arrive at that happy rest which is laid up for us in heaven, through Christ our Lord.—Amen.

Lecture Fourteenth.

8. Wherefore at that time certain Chaldeans came near, and accused the Jews.

8. Itaque statim,[1] appropinquarunt viri Chaldæi, et vociferati sunt accusationem contra Iudæos.[2]

[1] The same hour.—*Calvin.*

[2] That is, accused them clamorously and with tumult. Others translate, "brought forward an accusation." For אכל, *akel*, signifies to "devour," and they say that it is used metaphorically for "to accuse" when

9. They spake, and said to the king Nebuchadnezzar, O king, live for ever.
10. Thou, O king, hast made a decree, that every man that shall hear the sound of the cornet, flute, harp, sackbut, psaltery, and dulcimer, and all kinds of music, shall fall down and worship the golden image:
11. And whoso falleth not down and worshippeth, *that* he should be cast into the midst of a burning fiery furnace.
12. There are certain Jews, whom thou hast set over the affairs of the province of Babylon, Shadrach, Meshach, and Abed-nego: these men, O king, have not regarded thee; they serve not thy gods, nor worship the golden image which thou hast set up.

9. Loquuti sunt, et dixerunt Nebuchadnezer regi, Rex, in æternum vive.
10. Tu, rex, posuisti edictum, ut omnis homo cum audiret vocem cornu, *vel, tubæ*, fistulæ, citharæ, sambucæ, psalterii, et symphoniæ, et omnium instrumentorum musices, procideret, et adoraret imaginem auream.
11. Et qui non prociderit, et adoraverit, projiciatur in medium, *vel, intra*, fornacem ignis ardentis.
12. Sunt viri Iudæi, quos ipsos posuisti, *id est, præfecisti*, super administrationem, *vel, opus*, provinciæ Babylonis, Sadrach, Mesach, et Abednego, viri isti non posuerunt ad te, rex, cogitationem,[1] deum tuum[2] non colunt, et imaginem auream quam tu erexisti non adorant.

Although their intention is not here expressed who accused Shadrach, Meshach, and Abed-nego, yet we gather from this event that the thing was most probably done on purpose when the king set up the golden image. We see how they were observed, and, as we said yesterday, Nebuchadnezzar seems to have followed the common practice of kings. For although they proudly despise God, yet they arm themselves with religion to strengthen their power, and pretend to encourage the worship of God for the single purpose of retaining the people in obedience. When, therefore, the Jews were mingled with Chaldeans and Assyrians, the king expected to meet with many differences of opinion, and so he placed the statue in a celebrated place by way of trial and experiment, whether the Jews would adopt the Babylonian rites. Meanwhile this passage teaches us how the king was probably instigated by his counsellors, as they were indignant at strangers being made prefects of the province of Babylon while they were slaves; for they had become exiles by the right of warfare. Since then the Chal-

joined to this noun. But since it also signifies "to cry out," this sense is suitable, as the accusers were clamorous.—*Calvin.*
[1] Others translate, "reason."—*Calvin.*
[2] Or, "thy gods," but there is not much difference.—*Calvin.*

deans were indignant, they were impelled by envy to suggest this advice to the king. For how did they so suddenly discover that the Jews paid no reverence to the statue, and especially Shadrach, Meshach, and Abed-nego? Truly, the thing speaks for itself. These men watched to see what the Jews would do; and hence we readily ascertain how they, from the beginning, laid the snare by advising the king to fabricate the statue. And when they tumultuously accuse the Jews, we perceive how they were filled with envy and hatred. It may be said, they were inflamed with jealousy, since superstitious men wish to impose the same law upon all, and then their passion is increased by cruelty. But simple rivalry, as we may perceive, corrupted the Chaldeans, and caused them clamorously to accuse the Jews.

It is uncertain whether they spoke of the whole nation generally, namely, of all the exiles, or pointed out those three persons only. The accusation was probably restricted to Shadrach, Meshach, and Abed-nego. If these three could be broken down, the victory over the rest was easy. But few could be found in the whole people hardy enough to resist. We may well believe these clamourers wished to attack those whom they knew to be spirited and consistent beyond all others, and also to degrade them from those honours which they could not bear them to enjoy. It may be asked, then, why did they spare Daniel, since he would never consent to dissemble by worshipping the statue which the king commanded to be set up? They must have let Daniel alone for the time, since they knew him to be in favour with the king; but they brought the charge against these three, because they could be oppressed with far less trouble. I think them to have been induced by this cunning in not naming Daniel with the other three, lest his favour should mitigate the king's wrath. The form of accusation is added—*O king, live for ever!* It was the common salutation. *Thou, O king!*—this is emphatic, as if they had said, "Thou hast uttered this edict from thy royal authority, *whoever hears the sound of the trumpet,* or horn, *harp, pipe, psaltery, and other musical instruments, shall fall down before the golden statue; whoever should refuse to do this should be cast into the burning fiery furnace. But here are some Jews whom thou hast set over the administration of the province of Babylon.* They add this through hatred, and through reproving the ingratitude of men admitted to such high honour and yet despising the king's authority, and inducing others to follow the same example of disrespect. We see then how this was said to magnify their crime. *The king has set them over the province of Babylon, and yet these men do not adore the golden image nor worship thy gods.* Here is the crime. We see how the Chaldeans, throughout the whole speech, condemn Shadrach, Meshach, and Abed-nego of this single crime—a refusal to obey the king's edict. They enter into no dispute about their own religion, for it would not have suited their purpose to allow any question to be raised as to the claim their own deities had to supreme adoration. They omit, therefore, everything which they perceive would not suit them, and seize upon this weapon—the king is treated with contempt, because Shadrach, Meshach, and Abed-nego do not worship the image as the king's edict ordered them to do.

Here, again, we see how the superstitious do not apply their minds to the real inquiry how they should piously and properly worship God; but they neglect this duty and follow their own audacity and lust. Since therefore the Holy Spirit sets before us such rashness, as in a mirror, let us learn that God cannot approve of our worship unless it be offered up with truth. Here human authority is utterly unavailing, because unless we are sure that our religion is pleasing to God, whatever man can do for us will only add to our weakness. While we observe those holy men charged with the crime of ingratitude and rebellion, we in these times ought not to be grieved by it. Those who calumniate us reproach us with despising the edicts of kings who wish to bind us by their errors; but, as we shall see by and bye, our defence is obvious and easy. Meanwhile we ought to undergo this infamy before the world, as if we were disobedient and unmanageable; and with respect to ingratitude, even if a thousand wicked men should load us with reproaches, we must bear their calumnies for the time patiently, until the

Lord shall shine upon us as the assertor of our innocence. It now follows,—

13. Then Nebuchadnezzar, in his rage and fury, commanded to bring Shadrach, Meshach, and Abed-nego. Then they brought these men before the king.

14. Nebuchadnezzar spake, and said unto them, *Is it* true, O Shadrach, Meshach, and Abed-nego, do not ye serve my gods, nor worship the golden image which I have set up?

15. Now, if ye be ready, that at what time ye hear the sound of the cornet, flute, harp, sackbut, psaltery, and dulcimer, and all kinds of music, ye fall down and worship the image which I have made, *well:* but if ye worship not, ye shall be cast the same hour into the midst of a burning fiery furnace; and who *is* that God that shall deliver you out of my hands?

13. Tunc Nebuchadnezer cum iracundia et excandescentia,[1] jussit adduci Sadrach, Mesach, et Abednego: viri autem illi adduxerunt coram rege.[2]

14. Loquutus est Nebuchadnezer, et dixit illis, Verumne, Sadrach, Mesach, et Abednego, deos meos non colitis,[3] et imaginem auream quam statui,[4] non adoratis?

15. Nunc ecce parati eritis,[5] simulac audiveritis vocem cornu, *vel, tubœ,* fistulœ, citharœ, sambucœ, psalterii, symphoniæ, et omnium instrumentorum musices, ut procidatis, et adoretis imaginem quam feci. Quoad si non adoraveritis, eadem hora projiciemini in medium fornacis ignis ardentis: et quis ille Deus qui eruat vos e manu mea?

This narrative clearly assures us, how kings consult only their own grandeur by a show of piety, when they claim the place of their deities. For it seems very wonderful for King Nebuchadnezzar to insult all the gods, as if there was no power in heaven unless what he approved of. *What god,* says he, *can pluck you out of my hand?* Why then did he worship any deity? Simply to retain the people by a curb, and thus to strengthen his own power, without the slightest affection of piety abiding within his mind. At the beginning Daniel relates how the king was inflamed with wrath. For nothing is more troublesome to kings than to see their authority despised; they wish every one to be obedient to themselves, even when their commands are most unjust. After the king is cool again, he asks Shadrach, Meshach, and Abed-nego, whether they were prepared to worship his god and his golden image? Since he addresses them doubtfully, and gives them a free choice, his words imply moderation. He seems to free them from all blame, if they will

---

[1] Some translate, fury.—*Calvin.*
[2] We must understand, them.—*Calvin.*
[3] Or rather, my god.—*Calvin.*   [4] Or, I have erected.—*Calvin.*
[5] Some read it interrogatively, Are ye prepared?—*Calvin.*

only bow themselves down hereafter. He now adds directly, *if ye are not prepared, behold I will throw you into a furnace of burning fire;* and at length breaks forth into that sacrilegious and dreadful blasphemy—There is no god who can deliver the saints alive out of his hand!

We see, then, in the person of Nebuchadnezzar, how kings swell with pride, while they pretend some zeal for piety; since in reality no reverence for God influences them, while they expect all men to obey every command. And thus, as I have said, they rather substitute themselves for God, than desire to worship him and promote his glory. This is the meaning of the words, *the statue which I have created, and which I have made;* as if he had said, You are not allowed to deliberate about worshipping this image or not; my orders ought to be sufficient for you. I have erected it purposely and designedly; it was your duty simply to obey me. We see then how he claims the supreme power, by fashioning a god. Nebuchadnezzar is not now treating matters of state policy; he wishes the statue to be adored as a deity, because he had decreed it, and had promulgated his edict. And we must always remember what I have touched upon, namely, this example of pride is set before us, to shew us not to attach ourselves to any religion with rashness, but to listen to God and depend on his authority and commands, since if we listen to man, our errors would be endless. Although kings are so proud and ferocious, yet we must be guided by this rule—Nothing pleases God but what he has commanded in his word; and the principle of true piety is the obedience which we ought to render to him alone. With respect to blasphemy, it clearly demonstrates my previous assertion, however kings put forward some desire for piety, yet they despise every deity, and think of nothing but extolling their own magnificence. Hence, they traffic in the name of God to attract greater reverence towards themselves; but at the same time, if they choose to change their deities a hundred times a-day, no sense of religion will hinder them. Religion, then, is to the kings of the earth nothing but a pretext; but they have neither reverence nor fear of God in their minds, as the language of this profane king proves. *What*

God? says he, clearly there is no God. If any one reply—he speaks comparatively, since he here defends the glory of his own god whom he worshipped, still he utters this blasphemy against all gods, and is impelled by intolerable arrogance and diabolical fury. We are now coming to the principal point where Daniel relates the constancy with which Shadrach, Meshach, and Abed-nego were endued.

16. Shadrach, Meshach, and Abed-nego, answered and said to the king, O Nebuchadnezzar, we *are* not careful to answer thee in this matter.

17. If it be *so*, our God, whom we serve, is able to deliver us from the burning fiery furnace; and he will deliver *us* out of thine hand, O king.

18. But if not, be it known unto thee, O king, that we will not serve thy gods, nor worship the golden image which thou hast set up.

16. Responderunt Sadrach, Mesach, et Abednego, et dixerunt regi; Nebuchadnezzr, non sumus soliciti super hoc sermone,[1] quid respondeamus tibi.[2]

17. Ecce est Deus noster, quem nos colimus, potens, *id est, potest*, liberare nos e fornace ignis ardentis, et e manu tuâ, rex eruet.

18. Et si non, notum sit tibi, O rex, quod deos tuos nos non colimus, et imaginem auream quam erexisti, non adorabimus.

In this history it is necessary to observe with what unbroken spirit these three holy men persisted in the fear of God, though they knew they were in danger of instant death. When, therefore, this kind of death was placed straight before their eyes, they did not turn aside from the straightforward course, but treated God's glory of greater value than their own life, nay, than a hundred lives, if they had so many to pour forth, and opportunity had been given them. Daniel does not relate all their words, but only their import, in which the unconquered virtue of that Holy Spirit, by which they had been instructed, is sufficiently evident; for that denunciation was certainly dreadful, when the king said, *If ye are not prepared to fall down at the sound of the trumpet before the image, it is all over with you, and ye shall be directly cast into a furnace of fire.* When the king had so fulminated, they might have winced, as men usually do, since life is naturally dear to us, and a dread of death seizes upon our senses. But Daniel relates all these circumstances, to assure us of the great fortitude of God's servants when they are led by his Spirit, and yield to no threats, and succumb to no

[1] Or, business.—*Calvin*.

[2] Others translate, we ought not to answer thee about this business; and they think ל, the letter L, to be superfluous, as it often is.—*Calvin*.

terrors. They answer the king, We do not need any long deliberation. For when they say they care not, they mean by this word, the matter is settled; just as that sentence of Cyprian is related by Augustine,[1] when courtiers persuaded him to preserve his life, for it was with great reluctance that the emperor devoted him to death, when flatterers on all sides urged him to redeem his life by the denial of piety, he answered, There can be no deliberation in a matter so sacred! Thus those holy men say, *We do not care*, we do not enter into the consideration of what is expedient or useful, no such thing! for we ought to settle it with ourselves never to be induced by any reason to withdraw from the sincere worship of God.

If you please to read—*we ought not to answer you*, the sense will be the same. They imply that the fear of death was set before them in vain, because they had determined and resolved in their inmost souls, not to depart a single inch from the true and lawful worship of God. Besides they here give a double reason for rejecting the king's proposal. They say God has sufficient power and strength to liberate them; and then, even if they must die, their life is not of so much value as to deny God for the sake of preserving it. Hence they declare themselves prepared to die, if the king persists in urging his wish for the adoration of the image. This passage is therefore worthy of the greatest attention. First of all, we must observe the answer—for when men entice us to deny the true God we must close our ears, and refuse all deliberation; for we have already committed an atrocious insult against God, when we even question the propriety of swerving from the purity of his worship through any impulse or any reason whatever. And I heartily wish every one would observe this! How excellent and striking is the glory of God, and how everything ought to yield to it, whenever there is danger of its being either diminished or obscured. But at this day, this fallacy deceives the multitude, since they think it lawful to debate whether it is allowable to swerve from the true worship of God for a time,

---

[1] Cyprian was martyred under the edict of Valerian, A.D. 257.—See Euseb. Eccl. Hist., lib. vii. chap. 10.

whenever any utility presents itself on the opposite side. Just as in our days, we see how hypocrites, of whom the world is full, have pretences by which they cloak their delinquencies, when they either worship idols with the impious, or deny at one time openly, and at another obliquely, true piety. "Oh! what can happen?—such a one will say—of what value is consistency? I see some evident advantage if I can only dissemble a little, and not betray what I am. Ingenuousness is injurious not only to me privately, but to all around me!" If a king has none around him who endeavour to appease his wrath, the wicked would give way to their passions, and by their greater license would drive him to the extremity of cruelty. It is, therefore, better to have some mediators on the watch to observe whether the wicked are planning anything. Thus, if they cannot openly, they may covertly avert danger from the heads of the pious. By such reasoning as this, they think they can satisfy God. As if Shadrach, Meshach, and Abed-nego, had not the same excuse; as if the following thought would not occur to them —"Behold! we are armed with some power in favour of our brethren; now what barbarity, what cruelty will be exercised against them, if the enemies of the religion which they profess succeed us? For as far as they can, they will overthrow and blot out our race and the very remembrance of piety. Is it not better for us to yield for a time to the tyranny and violent edict of the king than to leave our places empty?— which the furious will by and bye occupy, who will utterly destroy our wretched race which is now dreadfully oppressed." Shadrach, Meshach, and Abed-nego might, I say, collect all these pretences and excuses to palliate their perfidy if they had bent the knee before the golden image for the sake of avoiding danger; but they did not act thus. Hence, as I have already said, God retains his rights entire when his worship is upheld without the slightest doubt, and we are thoroughly persuaded that nothing is of such importance as to render it lawful and right to swerve from that profession which his word both demands and exacts.

On the whole, that security which ought to confirm the pious in the worship of God is opposed here to all those tortuous and mistaken counsels which some men adopt, and thus, for the sake of living, lose life itself, according to the sentiment of even a profane poet. For of what use is life except to serve God's glory? but we lose that object in life for the sake of the life itself—that is, by desiring to live entirely to the world, we lose the very purpose of living! Thus, then, Daniel opposes the simplicity which ought to mark the sons of God to all those excuses which dissemblers invent with the view of hiding their wickedness by a covering. We *are not anxious*, say they, and why not? Because we have already determined God's glory to be of more consequence than a thousand lives, and the gratification of a thousand senses. Hence, when this magnanimity flourishes, all hesitation will vanish, and those who are called upon to incur danger through their testimony for the truth need never trouble themselves; for, as I before said, their ears are closed to all the enticements of Satan.

And when they add—*God is sufficiently powerful to preserve us; and if not, we are prepared for death*, they point out to us what ought to raise our minds above all trials, namely, the preciousness of our life in God's sight, since he can liberate us if he pleases. Since, therefore, we have sufficient protection in God, let us not think any method of preserving our life better than to throw ourselves entirely on his protection, and to cast all our cares upon him. And as to the second clause, we must remark this, even if the Lord should wish to magnify his own glory by our death, we ought to offer up this as a lawful sacrifice; and sincere piety does not flourish in our hearts unless our minds are always prepared to make this sacrifice. Thus I wished to remark these things shortly now, and with God's permission, I will explain them fully to-morrow.

PRAYER.

Grant, Almighty God, since we see the impious carried away by their impure desires with so strong an impulse; and while they are so puffed up with arrogance, may we learn true humility, and so subject ourselves to thee that we may always depend upon thy word and always attend to thy instructions. When we have learned what worship pleases thee, may we constantly persist unto the end, and never be moved by any threats, or dangers, or violence, from our position, nor drawn aside from our course; but by persevering obedience to thy word, may we shew our alacrity and obedience, until thou dost acknowledge us as thy sons, and we are gathered to that eternal inheritance which thou hast prepared for all members of Christ thy Son.—Amen.

Lecture Fifteenth.

WE said yesterday that the constancy of Shadrach, Meshach, and Abed-nego, was based upon these two reasons:— Their certain persuasion that God was the guardian of their life, and would free them from present death by his power if it were useful. And also their determination to die boldly and fearlessly, if God wished such a sacrifice to be offered. What Daniel relates of these three men belongs to us all. Hence we may gather this general instruction. When our danger for the truth's sake is imminent, we should learn to place our life in God's hand, and then bravely and fearlessly devote ourselves to death. As to the *first* point, experience teaches us how very many turn aside from God and the profession of faith, since they do not feel confidence in God's power to liberate them. It may be said with truth of us all —God takes care of us, since our life is placed in his hand and will; but scarcely one in a hundred holds this deeply and surely fixed in his heart, since every one takes his own way of preserving his life, as if there were no virtue in God. Hence he has made some proficiency in God's word who has learnt to place his life in God's care, and to consider it safe under his protection. For if he has made progress thus far, he may be in danger a hundred times, yet he will never hesitate to follow wherever he is called. This one feeling frees him from all fear and trembling, since God can extricate his servants from a thousand deaths, as it is said in the Psalm, (lxviii. 20,) The issues of death are in his power. For death seems to consume all things; but God snatches from that whirlpool whom he pleases. So this persuasion ought to inspire us with firm and unassailable constancy, since it is necessary for those who so repose the whole care of their life and safety upon God, to be thoroughly conscious and undoubtedly sure that God will defend a good cause. And this is also expressed by these words of Shadrach, Meshach, and Abed-nego: *Behold our God whom we worship.* When they bring forward God's worship, they bear testimony to the sureness of their support, when they undertake nothing rashly, but are worshippers of the true God, and labour for the defence of piety. For this is the difference between martyrs and malefactors, who are often compelled to suffer the penalty of their madness for attempting to overthrow all things. We see, indeed, the majority tossed about by their own intemperance. If they happen to suffer punishment, they are not to be reckoned among God's martyrs; for, as Augustine says, the martyr is made by his cause, and not by his punishment. Hence the weight of these words, when these three men attest their worship of God, since in this way they boast in their power of enduring any urgent danger not rashly, but only as supported by the sure worship of God. I now come to the *second* point.

If God be unwilling to deliver us from death, be it known to thee, O king, we will not worship thy gods. I said first of all, we should be constantly prepared to undergo every conflict, to commit our life to his charge, to submit to his will and hand, and to the protection of his custody. But the desire of this earthly and fading life ought not to retain its hold upon us, and to hinder us from the free and candid confession of the truth. For God's glory ought to be more precious to us than a hundred lives. Hence we cannot be witnesses for God without we lay aside all desire of this life, and at least prefer God's glory to it. Meanwhile, we must remark the impossibility of doing this, without the hope of a better life drawing us towards itself. For where there is no promise of any eternal inheritance implanted in our hearts, we shall never be torn away from this world. We are naturally desirous of existence, and that feeling cannot be eradicated, unless faith overcome it; as Paul says, Not that we wished to be unclothed, but clothed upon. (2 Cor. v. 4.) Paul confesses that men cannot be naturally induced to wish for departure from the world, unless, as we have said, through the power of faith. But when we understand our inheritance to be in heaven, while we are strangers upon earth, then we put off that clinging to the life of this world to which we are too much devoted.

These then are the two points which prepare the sons of God for martyrdom, and remove hesitation as to their offering their life in sacrifice to God. *First*, if they are persuaded that God is the protector of their life and will certainly liberate them should it be expedient; and *secondly*, when they live above the world and aspire to the hope of eternal life in heaven, while prepared to renounce the world. This magnanimity is to be remarked in their language, when they say, *Be it known to thee, O king, that we do not worship thy gods nor adore the statue which thou hast set up.* Here they obliquely accuse the king of arrogating too much to himself, and of wishing religion to stand or fall by his own will. *Thou hast erected the statue,* but thy authority is of no moment to us, since we know it to be a fictitious deity whose image thou wishest us to worship. The God whom we worship has revealed himself to us; we know him to be the maker of heaven and earth, to have redeemed our fathers from Egypt, and to intend our chastisement by driving us into exile. Since, therefore, we have a firm foundation for our faith, hence we reckon thy gods and thy sway valueless. It follows:

19. Then was Nebuchadnezzar full of fury, and the form of his visage was changed against Shadrach, Meshach, and Abed-nego: *therefore* he spake, and commanded that they should heat the furnace one seven times more than it was wont to be heated.

20. And he commanded the most mighty men that *were* in his army to bind Shadrach, Meshach, and

19. Tunc Nebuchadnezer repletus fuit iracundia, et forma faciei ejus mutata fuit[1] erga Sadrach, Mesach, et Abednego: loquutus est, jussit, *vel, edixit,* accendi fornacem uno septies. *hoc est, septuplo,* magis quam solebat accendi.

20. Et viris præstantibus robore, *vel, robustis virtute,* qui erant in ejus satellitio[2] mandavit ut vincirent

---

[1] צלם, *tzelem,* is here taken in a different sense from its previous one, for Daniel sometimes uses it for "image," but here for the "figure" or "countenance" of the king, which was changed.—*Calvin.*

[2] היל, *hil,* is here used for "attendants," or "servants," properly it means "army," but as the king is not at war, it doubtless means "attendants;" he chose, therefore, the strongest of his attendants.—*Calvin.*

A'bed-nego, *and* to cast *them* into the burning fiery furnace.	Sadrach, Mesach, et Abednego, ut projicerent *illos* in fornacem ignis ardentis.

Here, at first sight, God seems to desert his servants, since he does not openly succour them. The king orders them to be thrown into a furnace of fire: no help from heaven appears for them. This was a living and remarkably efficacious proof of their faithfulness. But they were prepared, as we have seen, to endure everything. These bold answers were not prompted simply by their trust in God's immediate help, but by a determination to die; since a better life occupied their thoughts, they willingly sacrificed the present life. Hence they were not frightened at this terrible order of the king's, but followed on their course, fearlessly submitting to death for the worship of God. No third way was opened for them, when a choice was granted either to submit to death, or apostatize from the true God. By this example we are taught to meditate on our immortal life in times of ease, so that if God pleases, we may not hesitate to expose our souls by the confession of the true faith. For we are so timorous when we are attacked by calamity, we are seized with fear and torpor, and then when we are not pressed by any urgency we feign for ourselves a false security. When we are allowed to be at ease, we ought to apply our minds to meditation upon a future life, so that this world may become cheap to us, and we may be prepared when necessary to pour forth our blood in testimony to the truth. And this narrative is not set before us simply to lead us to admire and celebrate the courage of these three holy ones, but their constancy is proposed to us as an example for imitation.

With reference to King Nebuchadnezzar, Daniel here shews, as in a glass, the pride and haughtiness of kings when they find their decrees disobeyed. Surely a mind of iron ought to grow soft by the answer which we have just narrated, on hearing Shadrach, Meshach, and Abed-nego committing their lives to God; but when it heard how they could not be drawn aside from their faithfulness by the fear of death, its anger was only increased. In considering this fury, we ought to take into account the power of Satan in seizing and occupying the minds of men. For there is no moderation in them, even if they shew some great and remarkable hope of virtues,—for, as we have seen, Nebuchadnezzar was endued with many virtues; but as Satan harassed him, we discern nothing but cruelty and barbarity. Meanwhile, let us remember how pleasing our constancy is to God, though it may not produce any immediate fruit before the world. For many indulge in pleasure through thinking they would be rash in devoting themselves to death, without any apparent utility. And on this pretext, they excuse themselves from not contending more boldly for the glory of God, by supposing they would lose their labour, and their death would be fruitless. But we hear what Christ pronounces, namely, this sacrifice is pleasing to God, when we die for the testimony of the heavenly doctrine, although the generation before which we bear witness to God's name is adulterous and perverse, nay, even hardened by our constancy. (Matt. v. 11, and x. 32, and Mark viii. 38.)

And such an example is here set before us in these three holy men; because, although Nebuchadnezzar was more inflamed by the freedom of their confession, yet that liberty pleased God, and they did not repent of it, though they did not discern the fruit of their constancy which they wished. The Prophet also expresses this circumstance to demonstrate the king's fury, since *he ordered the furnace to be heated seven times hotter than before;* and then, *he chose from his own servants the strongest of all to bind these holy men, and cast them into the furnace of fire.*

But from the result it is very evident, that this did not occur without God's secret impulse; for the devil will sometimes throw discredit on a miracle, unless all doubt is removed. Since therefore the king ordered the furnace to be heated sevenfold more than before, next when he chose the strongest attendants, and commanded them to follow him, God thus removed all doubts, by liberating his servants, because light emerges more clearly from the darkness, when Satan endeavours to shut it out. Thus God is accustomed to frustrate the impious; and the more impious they are in opposing his glory, the more he makes his honour and doctrine conspicuous. In like manner, Daniel here paints, as in a picture, how King Nebuchadnezzar passed nothing by, when he wished to strike terror into the minds of all the Jews by this cruel punishment. And yet he obtained nothing else by his plans than a clearer illustration of God's power and grace towards his servants. It now follows:—

21. Then these men were bound in their coats, their hosen, and their hats, and their *other* garments, and were cast into the midst of the burning fiery furnace.
22. Therefore because the king's commandment was urgent, and the furnace exceeding hot, the flame of the fire slew those men that took up Shadrach, Meshach, and Abednego.
23. And these three men, Shadrach, Meshach, and Abed-nego, fell down bound into the midst of the burning fiery furnace.

21. Tunc viri illi vincti sunt, *vel*, *ligati*, in suis chlamydibus,[1] et cum tiaris suis:[2] in vestitu suo: et projecti sunt in fornacem ignis ardentis.
22. Propterea quod urgebat, *vel*, *festinabat, ad verbum*, præceptum regis, et fornacem vehementer jusserat accendi, viros illos qui extulerant Sadrach, Mesach, et Abednego occidit favilla, *alii vertunt flammam*, ignis.
23. Et viri illi tres Sadrach, Mesach, et Abednego ceciderant in medium fornacis ignis,[3] ardentis vincti.

Here Daniel relates the miracle by which God liberated his servants. It has two parts: first, these three holy men walked untouched in the midst of the flame; and the fires consumed those attendants who cast them into the furnace. The Prophet diligently enumerates whatever tends to prove the power of God. He says, *since the king's command was urgent,* that is, since the king ordered in such anger the furnace to be heated, the flames devour the men who executed his orders. For in Job, (xviii. 5,) שביב, *shebib,* means " spark," or the extremity of a flame. The sense of the Prophet is by no means obscure, since the extremity of the flame consumed those strong attendants by playing round them, while Shadrach, Meshach, and Abed-nego walked through the fuel in

---

[1] Some translate sandals, or, shoes, others hose; but the majority take the second noun for hose; but we need not trouble ourselves too much about the words, if we only understand the thing itself.—*Calvin.*
[2] We know that the Orientals then wore turbans as they do now, for they wrap up the head; and though we do not see many of them, yet we know the Turkish dress; then the general name is added.—*Calvin.* See also the note on this passage in Wintle's translation, which is full of good explanatory notes.
[3] That is, within the furnace of fire.—*Calvin.*

the fire and flame. They were not in the extremity of the flame; for it is as if the Prophet had said,—the king's slaves were consumed by the very smoke, and the fire was without the slightest effect on the servants of God. Hence he says, *these three fell down in the furnace of fire.* By saying *they fell,* it means they could not take care of themselves or attempt to escape; for he adds, *they were bound.* This might at first naturally suffocate them, till they were immediately consumed; but they remained untouched, and then walked about the furnace loose. We hereby see how conspicuous was God's power, and how no falsehood of Satan's could obscure it. And next, when the very points of the flame, or the fiery sparks, devour the servants, here again the deed is proved to be of God. Meanwhile, the result of the history is the preservation of these three holy men, so surprisingly beyond their expectation.

This example is set before us, to show us how nothing can be safer than to make God the guardian and protector of our life. For we ought not to expect to be preserved from every danger because we see those holy men delivered; for we ought to hope for liberation from death, if it be useful, and yet we ought not to hesitate to meet it without fear, if God so please it. But we should gather from our present narrative the sufficiency of God's protection, if he wishes to prolong our lives, since we know our life to be precious to him; and it is entirely in his power, either to snatch us from danger, or to withdraw us to a better existence, according to his pleasure. We have an example of this in the case of Peter; for he was on one day led forth from prison, and the next day put to death. Even then God shewed his care of his servant's life, though Peter at length suffered death. How so? Because he had finished his course. Hence, as often as God pleases, he will exert his power to preserve us; if he leads us onwards to death, we must be assured it is best for us to die, and injurious to us to enjoy life any longer. This is the substance of the instruction which we may receive from this narrative. It now follows:—

24. Then Nebuchadnezzar the

24. Tunc Nebuchadnezer rex con-

king was astonied, and rose up in haste, *and* spake, and said unto his counsellors, Did not we cast three men bound into the midst of the fire? They answered and said unto the king, True, O king.

25. He answered and said, Lo, I see four men loose, walking in the midst of the fire, and they have no hurt; and the form of the fourth is like the Son of God.

tremuit,[1] et surrexit in festinatione, celeriter: loquutus est, et dixit consiliariis suis:[2] An non viros tres projecimus in fornacem ligatos? *vinctos?* Responderunt, et dixerunt regi, Vere, rex.

25. Respondit, et dixit, Atqui ego video viros quatuor solutos, ambulantes in igne, et nulla noxa in ipsis est: et facies quarti similis est filio Dei.

Here Daniel relates how God's power was manifest to the profane—to both the king and his courtiers, who had conspired for the death of these holy men. He says, then, *the king trembled* at that miracle; since God often compels the impious to acknowledge his power, and when they stupify themselves, and harden all their senses, they are compelled to feel God's power whether they will or not. Daniel shews how this happened to King Nebuchadnezzar. *He trembled, says he, and rose up quickly, and said to his companions, Did we not cast three men bound into the fire?* When they say, *It is so,* Nebuchadnezzar was doubtless impelled by a Divine impulse, and a secret instinct, to inquire of his companions to extract this confession from them. For Nebuchadnezzar might easily approach the furnace, but God wished to extract this confession from his enemies, that both they and the king might allow the rescue of Shadrach, Meshach, and Abed-nego, to have proceeded from no earthly medium, but from the admirable and extraordinary power of God. We may here remark, how the impious are witnesses to God's power, not willingly, but because God placed this question in the king's mouth, and also in his not permitting them to escape or turn aside from the confession of the truth. But Nebuchadnezzar says, *four men walked in the fire, and the face of the fourth is like the son of a god.* No doubt God here sent one of his angels, to support by his presence the minds of his saints, lest they should faint. It was indeed a formidable spectacle to see the furnace so hot, and to be cast

---

[1] Or, was terrified.—*Calvin.*

[2] Some translate, to his companions; and the word may be derived from either *consilium* or *consuetudo:* hence it might mean companions who were around the king; but soon afterwards it means counsellors, and there is no need of variety.—*Calvin.*

into it. By this consolation God wished to allay their anxiety, and to soften their grief, by adding an angel as their companion. We know how many angels have been sent to one man, as we read of Elisha. (2 Kings vi. 15.) And there is this general rule—He has given his angels charge over thee, to guard thee in all thy ways ; and also, The camps of angels are about those who fear God. (Ps. xci. 11, and xxxiv. 7.) This, indeed, is especially fulfilled in Christ ; but it is extended to the whole body, and to each member of the Church, for God has his own hosts at hand to serve him. But we read again how an angel was often sent to a whole nation. God indeed does not need his angels, while he uses their assistance in condescension to our infirmities. And when we do not regard his power as highly as we ought, he interposes his angels to remove our doubts, as we have formerly said. A single angel was sent to these three men ; Nebuchadnezzar calls him a son of God ; not because he thought him to be Christ, but according to the common opinion among all people, that angels are sons of God, since a certain divinity is resplendent in them ; and hence they call angels generally sons of God. According to this usual custom, Nebuchadnezzar says, *the fourth man is like a son of a god.* For he could not recognise the only-begotten Son of God, since, as we have already seen, he was blinded by so many depraved errors. And if any one should say it was enthusiasm, this would be forced and frigid. This simplicity, then, will be sufficient for us, since Nebuchadnezzar spoke in the usual manner, as one of the angels was sent to those three men— since, as I have said, it was then customary to call angels sons of God. Scripture thus speaks, (Ps. lxxxix. 6, and elsewhere,) but God never suffered truth to become so buried in the world as not to leave some seed of sound doctrine, at least as a testimony to the profane, and to render them more inexcusable—as we shall treat more at length in the next lecture.[1]

[1] See DISSERTATION XIII. at the end of this volume.

PRAYER.

Grant, Almighty God, since our life is only for a moment, nay, is only vanity and smoke, that we may learn to cast all our care upon thee, and so to depend upon thee, as not to doubt thee as our deliverer from all urgent perils, whenever it shall be to our advantage. Grant us also to learn to neglect and despise our lives, especially for the testimony of thy glory; and may we be prepared to depart as soon as thou callest us from this world. May the hope of eternal life be so fixed in our hearts, that we may willingly leave this world and aspire with all our mind towards that blessed eternity which thou hast testified to be laid up for us in heaven, through the gospel, and which thine only-begotten Son has procured for us through his blood.—Amen.

Lecture Sixteenth.

26. Then Nebuchadnezzar came near to the mouth of the burning fiery furnace, *and* spake, and said, Shadrach, Meshach, and Abed-nego, ye servants of the most high God, come forth, and come *hither*. Then Shadrach, Meshach, and Abed-nego came forth of the midst of the fire.

26. Tunc accessit Nebuchadnezer ad ostium fornacis ignis ardentis : loquutus est et dixit, Sadrach, Mesach, et Abednego servi Dei excelsi, egredimini, et venite. Tunc egressi sunt Sadrach, Mesach, et Abednego e medio ignis.

HERE a sudden change is described in the mood of this cruel and proud king. We have already seen how confidently he exacted worship from the servants of God, and when he saw them disobedient to his command, how mightily he raged against them. Now Daniel shews in how short a time this pride was subdued and this cruelty appeased; but we must remark that the king was not so changed as entirely to put off his disposition and manners. For when he was touched with this present miracle, he gave God the glory, but only for a moment; and still he did not return to wisdom. We cannot take too diligent notice of examples of this kind, as many estimate the characters of others from a single action. But the worst despisers of God can submit to him for a short time, not merely by feigning to do so before men, but in real seriousness, since God compels them by his power, but meanwhile they retain their pride and ferocity within their breasts. Of this kind, then, was the conversion of King Nebuchadnezzar. For when astonished by the miracle, he could no longer resist the Almighty, he was still inconsistent, as we shall afterwards see. We may also notice how the impious, who are unregenerate by God's Spirit, are often impelled to worship God; but this is only temporary, and this equable tenor never remains through their whole life. But when God renews his own, he undertakes to govern them even to the end; he animates them to perseverance, and confirms them by his Spirit.

We must here remark how God's glory is illustrated by this temporary and vanishing conversion of the reprobate; because, whether they will or not, yet they yield to God for a time, and thus the greatness of his power is acknowledged. God, therefore, turns an event which does not profit the reprobate to his own glory, and at the same time punishes them more severely. For Nebuchadnezzar's conduct was less excusable after his once acknowledging the God of Israel to be the supreme and only God, and then relapsing into his former superstitions. He says, therefore,— *He approached the door of the furnace, and spoke thus,— Shadrach, Meshach, and Abed-nego, servants of the most high God, come forth and come hither.* A short time before, he wished his own statue to be worshipped, and his own name to be esteemed the only one in heaven and earth, since this was pleasing to him. We then saw how he claimed the right of subjecting the religion and worship of God to his own will and lust; but now, as if he were a new man, he calls Shadrach, Meshach, and Abed-nego, servants of the most high God! What place, then, was left to him and to all the Chaldeans? How could they now worship those fictitious gods and idols which they had fabricated? But God extracted these words from the proud and cruel king, as when criminals are compelled, by tortures, to say what they would otherwise refuse. Thus Nebuchadnezzar confessed God to be *the most high God of Israel,* as if he had been tortured, but not of his own accord, or in a composed state of mind. He does not pretend this before men, as I have said; but his mind was neither pure nor perfect, since it was in a ferment with this temporary commotion. And this must also be added—the instinct was rather violent than voluntary.

Daniel afterwards relates—*His companions came forth from the midst of the fire.* By these words he again confirms the miracle; for God could extinguish the fire of the furnace, but he wished it to burn in the sight of all, to render the power of this deliverance the more conspicuous. Meanwhile we must notice *the three men walking in the furnace,* until the king commanded them to come forth, because God had issued no command. They saw themselves perfectly safe and sound in the midst of the furnace; they were content with God's present benefit, but still they had no free departure, until fetched by the king's voice. As when Noah, in the ark, saw safety prepared for him in that tomb, yet he did not try anything until commanded to come forth. (Gen. viii. 16.) So also Daniel asserts that his companions did not come forth from the furnace till the king commanded them. Then at length they understood how what they had heard from the king was pleasing to God; not because he was a Prophet or teacher, but because they were cast into the furnace by his command. So also when he recalls them, they know the end of their cross to be arrived, and thus they pass from death unto life. It follows—

27. And the princes, governors, and captains, and the king's counsellors, being gathered together, saw these men, upon whose bodies the fire had no power, nor was an hair of their head singed, neither were their coats changed, nor the smell of fire had passed on them.

27. Et congregati sunt satrapæ, duces, præfecti, et consiliarii regis[1] ad conspiciendos viros illos, quod non dominatus esset ignis corporibus eorum, et pilus capitis eorum non adustus esset, et vestibus eorum non esset mutatus, et odor ignis non pervasisset, *vel, non penetrasset,* ad eos.[2]

Daniel relates how the satraps were gathered together with the leaders, prefects, and councillors of the king. The gathering was simply a collection of numbers, and if they deliberated about anything of importance, they all agreed. And this confirms the miracle, since if they had been stupi-

[1] Some translate the last "prefects," but badly: it properly signifies either counsellors or familiar friends, as appears from many passages.—*Calvin.*

[2] Or, "to them," for the relative may apply either to their persons or their clothing, and it is of little consequence to which.—*Calvin.*

fied, how could the great power of God be proposed to the eyes of the blind? Although they were so astonished, they were not altogether foolish. And Daniel implies this by saying, *they were assembled together.* After they had discussed the matter, he says, they came to behold that specimen of the incredible power of God. Then he enumerates many reasons, which clearly shew these three men not to have been preserved by any other means than God's singular good will. He says, *The fire had no power over their bodies:* then, *a hair of their head was not burnt:* thirdly, *their garments were unchanged:* lastly, *the smell of fire had not penetrated to themselves or their garments.* He expresses more by the word *smell* than if he had simply said,—the fire had not penetrated. For fire must naturally consume and burn up whatever is submitted to it; but when not even the smell of fire has passed over any substance, the miracle is more conspicuous. Now, we understand the Prophet's intention. On the whole, he shews how the benefit of freedom was no small one, since *Shadrach, Meshach, and Abed-nego came safe out of the furnace.* Besides, these satraps, prefects, and governors, were witnesses of the power of God. Their testimony would be the more valuable, as all the Jews were spectators of this grace of God, which even they scarcely believed. But since these men were clearly and professedly enemies to true piety, they would willingly have concealed the miracle, had it been in their power. But God draws them against their wills, and compels them to be eye-witnesses, and they are thus obliged to confess what cannot be in the slightest degree doubtful. It follows—

28. *Then* Nebuchadnezzar spake, and said, Blessed *be* the God of Shadrach, Meshach, and Abed-nego, who hath sent his angel, and delivered his servants that trusted in him, and have changed the king's word, and yielded their bodies, that they might not serve nor worship any god except their own God.

28. Loquutus est Nebuchadnezer, et dixit, Benedictus Deus ipsorum, nempe Sadrach, Mesach, et Abed-nego, cui misit angelum suum, et eripuit, *servavit,* servos suos, qui confisi sunt in ipso, et verbum regis mutarunt,[1] et tradiderunt corpora sua, ne colerent, vel adorarent omnem deum,[2] præter Deum suum.

[1] Transgressed, that is, deprived the king's edict of its confidence and authority.—*Calvin.*
[2] That is, adore any other god.—*Calvin.*

This, indeed, is no common confession, but the event proved how suddenly King Nebuchadnezzar was acted on by impulse, without having the living root of the fear of God in his heart. And I repeat this again, to shew that repentance does not consist in one or two works, but in perseverance, as Paul says,—"If ye live in the Spirit, walk also in the Spirit." (Gal. v. 25.) Here he requires constancy in the faithful, by which they may shew themselves to be truly born again of God's Spirit. Nebuchadnezzar celebrated the God of Israel as if inspired by an enthusiasm, but at the same time he mingled his idols with the true God, so that there was no sincerity in him. So when the impious feel God's power, they do not dare to proceed with obstinacy against him, but wish to appease him by a false repentance, without putting off their natural disposition. Thus we readily conclude Nebuchadnezzar to be always the same, although God extracted from him this confession,—*Blessed*, says he, *be the God of Shadrach, Meshach, and Abed-nego!* Why does he not rather speak of him as his own God? This may be excused, had he really devoted himself to the God of Israel, and abjured his former superstitions. As he does not act thus, his confession is worthless; not because he wished to obtain men's favour or good opinion by what he said, but he deceived himself after the manner of hypocrites. He pronounces the God of Shadrach, Meshach, and Abed-nego to be blessed: if he really felt this, he must at the same time curse his idols, for the glory of the one true God cannot be extolled without all idols being reduced to nothing. For how can God's praise exist without his being solely conspicuous? If any other deity is opposed to him, his majesty is already buried in complete obscurity. Hence we may collect that Nebuchadnezzar was not touched with true repentance when he blessed the God of Israel. He adds, *Who sent his angel, and delivered his servants.* Here Daniel shews more clearly the absence of conversion in Nebuchadnezzar, and his failure to embrace the God of Israel, and worship him with sound and complete surrender of his affections. Why so? Because piety is always founded upon the knowledge of the true God, and this requires instruction. Nebuchadnezzar knew the God of Israel to be majestic from the display of his power, for he had such a spectacle presented to him as he could not despise, if he wished. Here he confesses that Israel's God was mighty, since he was taught it by a miracle; but this, as I have reminded you, is not sufficient for solid piety, unless instruction is added, and occupies the first place. I allow, indeed, that miracles prepare men to believe, but if miracles only occurred without the knowledge of God being added from his Word, faith will vanish away—as the example sufficiently remarkable here sets before us. We term the faith of Nebuchadnezzar to be but momentary, because, while his senses were fixed upon the miracle, he was content with the spectacle without inquiring into the character of the God of Israel, and the bearing of his law. He was not anxious about a Mediator; hence he neglected the chief point of piety, and rashly seized upon one part of it only. We clearly observe this in many profane men, for God often humbles them, to induce them suppliantly to fly to him for safety; but meanwhile they remain perplexed by their own senses; they do not deny their own superstitions, nor regard the true worship of God. To prove our obedience to God, we must uphold this principle—nothing pleases him which does not spring from faith. (Rom. xiv. 23.) But faith cannot be acquired by any miracle, or any perception of the Divine power; it requires instruction also. The miracles avail only to the preparation for piety or for its confirmation; they cannot by themselves bring men to worship the true God. This is surprising indeed, when a profane king says *the angel was sent by God.*

It is sufficiently evident from heathen writings that something was always known about angels. This was, as it were, a kind of anticipation and previous persuasion, since all people are persuaded that angels exist, so that they had some idea of angels, although but a partial one. For, when a short time ago Daniel said the fourth appearance in the furnace was called by the king of Babylon "a son of a god," then, as I have explained it, Nebuchadnezzar professed some belief in angels. He now says more expressly, *God sent his angel.* As angels afford supplies to the elect and the faithful, I treat the subject here but shortly, since I am not in the habit of dwelling upon ordinary passages. It is enough for the present passage to shew how the impious, who have learnt nothing from either God himself or from piety at large, were yet imbued with these principles, since God is accustomed to use the assistance of angels to preserve his people. For this reason Nebuchadnezzar now says, *the angel was sent by God to deliver his servants.* He next adds, *who trusted in him;* and this is worthy of notice, since it is added as a reason why these three men were so wonderfully preserved, through reposing all their hopes on God. Although Nebuchadnezzar was very like a log or a stone with relation to the doctrine of faith, yet God wished by means of this stone and log to instruct us, to inspire us with shame, and to reprove us of incredulity, since we are unable to conform our lives to his will, and to approach all dangers boldly, whenever it becomes necessary. For if we are thoroughly persuaded that God is the guardian of our life, surely no threats, nor terrors, nor death itself, should hinder us from persevering in our duty. But distrust is the cause of slothfulness, and whenever we deflect from a straightforward course, we deprive God of his honour, by becoming backsliders, while some want of faith betrays itself and is palpably apparent. Hence let us learn, if we wish our life to be protected by God's hand, to commit ourselves entirely to him, since he will never disappoint us when we confide in him. We saw how doubtful about the event Shadrach, Meshach, and Abed-nego were; but their doubt did not diminish their hope and confidence. They were placed in this alternative—either God will take us from the furnace, or, if we must die, he will preserve us for some better state, and gather us into his kingdom. Although they dared not persuade themselves that he would notice them, yet they reposed their lives in the hand and care of God. Hence they are deservedly complimented by Nebuchadnezzar, when he said,—*They trusted in their God,* and afterwards, *they changed the king's edict,* that is, reduced it to nothing, and abrogated it, because they were endued with greater power. For whoever rests in God, easily despises all mankind, and whatever is lofty and magnificent in the world. And this context is worthy of observation, since faith ought to be put as a foundation, and then fortitude and constancy must be added, with which Shadrach, Meshach, and Abed-nego were endowed; because any one who reposes upon God can never be moved aside from the discharge of his duty; and however numerous the impediments which may occur, he will be borne aloft on the wings of his confidence. He who knows God to be on his side, will be superior to the whole world, and will neither wonder at the sceptre and diadems of kings, nor dread their power, but rather surpass all the majesty of the earth which may oppose him, and never to turn aside from this course.

He afterwards adds, *they delivered up their bodies instead of worshipping or adoring any god except their own God.* That very thing which the king is compelled to praise in these three men, at this day many who boast themselves to be Christians wish to escape. For they fancy their faith to be buried in their hearts, and bring forth no fruit of their profession. There is no doubt God wished these things to be related by his Prophet, to shew the detestable cunning of those who wish to defraud God of his lawful honour, and at the same time shelter themselves from his gaze, lest he should notice their insult. Such as these are unworthy of being convinced by the word of God, but Nebuchadnezzar is here appointed their master, censor, and judge. And we must diligently remark this,—Nebuchadnezzar praises these three, because they refused to worship any other god except their own. Why then did he mingle together a great multitude of deities? For he did not depart from his own errors and give himself up entirely to the God of Israel, and embrace his worship in its purity. Why then does he praise in others what he does not imitate? But this is far too common; for we see virtue praised and yet frozen to death, as in this instance, for many are willing to offer him lip-service. (Juvenal, Sat. i.) Although Nebuchadnezzar seemed here to speak seriously, yet he did not consider himself; but he took away all pretext for excuse, since he could not afterwards pretend ignorance and error, after asserting with his own mouth that no other god ought to be worshipped. Hence he may cause those who now wish to be called Christians to be ashamed, unless they depart far away from all superstitions, and consecrate themselves entirely to God, and retain his worship in its sincerity. We must remember then how King Nebuchadnezzar does not simply praise the constancy of these three men, because he does not acknowledge any god, for he does reckon the God of Israel to be a true deity. Hence it follows, that all others were fictitious and utterly vain. But he spoke to no purpose, because God did not thereby touch his heart, as he usually works in his elect when he regenerates them. It follows,—

29. Therefore I make a decree, That every people, nation, and language, which speak anything amiss against the God of Shadrach, Meshach, and Abed-nego, shall be cut in pieces, and their houses shall be made a dunghill; because there is no other God that can deliver after this sort.

29. Et a me positum est, *hoc est, ponitur,* edictum,[1] ut omnis populus, natio,[2] et lingua quæ protulerit *aliquid* transversum,[3] contra Deum ipsorum, nempe Sadrach, Mesach, et Abednego, in frusta fiet, et domus ejus *in* latrinam, *vel, in sterquilinium,* redigetur: quia non est Deus alius qui possit servare hoc modo.

Here Nebuchadnezzar is urged further forward—for we must use this phrase—since he does not take up the worship of one God from his heart, and bid his errors finally farewell. Hence it is as if God was thrusting him violently forward, while he promulgates this edict. The edict is by itself pious and praiseworthy; but, as we have already said, Nebuchadnezzar is borne along by a blind and turbulent impulse, because piety had no root in his heart. Though he is always intent on this miracle, his faith is only momentary, and his fear of God but partial. Why then is Nebuchadnezzar now seen as the patron of God's glory? Because he was frightened by the miracle, and thus being acted on by impulse alone, he could not be soundly restrained by the fear of God alone. And finally, this desire which he expresses is nothing but an evanescent movement. It is useful to remark this, since we see many borne along by impetuous zeal and rage to vindicate God's glory; but they lack tact and judgment, so that

[1] Or, decree,—we have already explained this word.—*Calvin.*
[2] Some translate, family.—*Calvin.*
[3] שלה, *sheleh,* signifies to err; hence the noun is derived, which many translate error, and others rashness; but it means a perverse speech—whoever, therefore, utters a perverse speech.—*Calvin.*

they deserve no praise. And many wander still further—as we see in the Papacy—when many edicts of kings and princes fly about; and if any one should ask them why they are so eager as not to spare even human blood, they put forth indeed a zeal for God, but it is mere madness without a spark of true knowledge. We must hold, therefore, that no law can be passed nor any edict promulgated concerning religion and the worship of God, unless a real knowledge of God shines forth. Nebuchadnezzar indeed had a reason for this edict, but, as I have already said, there was a special motive for his conduct. Some, indeed, now wish to be thought Christian princes, and yet are only inflamed by a hypocritical zeal, and so they pour forth innocent blood like cruel beasts. And why so? Because they make no distinction between the true God and idols. But I shall discuss this point at greater length to-morrow, and so pass over casually what I shall treat at length, when the fit opportunity arrives.

Every people, therefore, and nation, and language, which shall have offered a perverse speech against their God. Nebuchadnezzar again extolled the God of Israel, but how was he taught the majesty of God? By this one proof of his power, for he neglected the chief point—the ascertaining from the law and the prophets the nature of God and the power of his will. Thus we see, on one side, how God's glory is asserted here, and yet the principal point in his worship, and in true piety, is neglected and omitted. No light punishment is added— *he must be cut in pieces, next, his house must be turned into a dunghill, since he has spoken reproachfully of the God of Israel.* Hence we gather how this severity is not to be utterly condemned, when God's worship is defended by severe punishments; yet a correct sentence ought to be passed in each case. But I put this off also till to-morrow. It is now added, *because there is no other God who can deliver after this manner;* and this confirms what I have formerly touched upon, namely, King Nebuchadnezzar does not regard the law in his edict, nor yet the other requisites of piety; but he is only impelled and moved by the miracle, so as not to bear or desire anything to be said opprobriously against the God of Israel. Hence the edict is deserving of blame in this point, since he does not inquire what God's nature is, with the view of obtaining a sufficient reason for issuing it. It is added at length,—

30. Then the king promoted Shadrach, Meshach, and Abed-nego, in the province of Babylon.

30. Tunc rex prosperare fecit,[1] Sadrach, Mesach, et Abednego, in provincia Babylonis.

This seems to be of slight consequence; but yet it was not added in vain. We are to understand that the miracle was confirmed throughout the whole province and region, because all the Chaldeans knew those three men were cast into the furnace, and then afterwards shared in the imperial sway and were restored to their former honours. In consequence of this event, God's power could not be unknown. It was just as if God had sent forth three heralds through the whole region, who everywhere proclaimed how they were wonderfully delivered from death by God's special interposition. Whence, also, it would be understood how worthless were all the deities then worshipped in Chaldea, and how that great deity whose statue Nebuchadnezzar had set up had been despised, and how the true God proved his consistency in snatching his servants from death.

PRAYER.

Grant, Almighty God, since thou hast instructed us by the doctrine of thy law and Gospel, and dost daily deign to make known thy will to us with familiarity, that we may remain fixed in the true obedience of this teaching, in which thy perfect justice is manifested; and may we never be moved away from thy worship. May we be prepared, whatever happens, rather to undergo a hundred deaths than to turn aside from the profession of true piety, in which we know our safety to be laid up. And may we so glorify thy name as to be partakers of that glory which has been acquired for us through the blood of thine only-begotten Son.—Amen.

[1] Verbally, for צלח, *tzelech*, signifies "to prosper;" hence the word is deduced, which signifies "to rest in a state of prosperity;" that is, he caused those three men to become prosperous.—*Calvin.*

Lecture Seventeenth.

CHAPTER FOURTH.

1. Nebuchadnezzar the king, unto all people, nations, and languages, that dwell in all the earth; Peace be multiplied unto you.
2. I thought it good to shew the signs and wonders that the high God hath wrought toward me.
3. How great *are* his signs! and how mighty *are* his wonders! his kingdom *is* an everlasting kingdom, and his dominion *is* from generation to generation.

1. Nebuchadnezer rex omnibus populis, nationibus, et linguis; quæ habitant in tota terra, pax vobiscum multiplicetur.
2. Signa et mirabilia quæ fecit mecum Deus excelsum pulchrum coram me enarrare.
3. Signa ejus quam magna *sunt!* et mirabilia ejus quam fortia! regnum ejus regrum seculare,[1] et dominatio ejus cum ætate, et ætate.

SOME join these verses to the end of the third chapter, but there is no reason for this; and it will clearly appear from the context that the edict is here set forth in the king's name, and other events are inserted. Daniel, therefore, here speaks in the person of the king; he afterwards narrates what happened to the king, and then returns to his own person. Those who separate these three verses from the context of the fourth chapter, do not seem to have sufficiently considered the intention and words of the Prophet. This passage may seem harsh and rough, when Daniel introduces the king of Babylon as speaking—then speaks in his own name—and afterwards returns to the person of the king. But since this variety does not render the sense either doubtful or obscure, there is no reason why it should trouble us. We now see how all the sentences which we shall explain in their places are mutually united.

The contents of this chapter are as follow: Nebuchadnezzar was sufficiently instructed in the worship of the God of Israel as one God, and was compelled at the time to confess this; yet he did not depart from his own superstitions; his conceptions of the true God were but momentary, and hence he suffered the punishment due to such great ingratitude. But God intended him to become more and more blinded, as he is accustomed to treat the reprobate

---
[1] That is, perpetual.—*Calvin*.

and even his elect at times. When men add sin to sin, God loosens his reins and allows them to destroy themselves. Afterwards he either extends his hand towards them, or withdraws them by his hidden virtue, or reduces them to order by his rod, and completely humbles them. He treated the king of Babylon in this way. We shall afterwards discuss the dream; but we must here briefly notice the king's admonition, that he might feel himself without excuse when he was so utterly broken down. God indeed might justly punish him as soon as he saw he was not truly converted; but before he inflicted the final chastisement—as we shall see in its place—he wished to admonish him, if there were any hope of his repentance. Although he seemed to receive with the greatest modesty what God had manifested by his dream through Daniel's interpretation of it, yet he professed with his mouth what he did not really possess. And he shews this sufficiently, because, when he ought to be afraid and cautious, he does not lay aside his pride, but glories in himself as a king of kings, and in Babylon as the queen of the whole world! Since, then, he spoke so confidently after being admonished by the Prophet, we perceive how little he had profited by his dream. But God wished in this way to render him more inexcusable, and although he did not bring forth fruit immediately, yet a long time afterwards, when God touched his mind, he very properly recognised this punishment to have been divinely inflicted. Hence this dream was a kind of entrance and preparation for repentance, and as seed seems to lie putrid in the earth before it brings forth its fruit, and God sometimes works by gentle processes, and provides for the teaching, which seemed for a long time useless, becoming both efficacious and fruitful.

I now come to the words themselves; the preface to the edict is, *Nebuchadnezzar the king to all peoples, nations, and languages, which dwell in the whole earth,* namely, under his sway. He does not mean this to be extended to Scythia, or Gaul, or other distant regions; but since his empire extended far and wide, he spoke boastingly. Thus we see the Romans, whose sway did not reach near so far, called Rome itself the seat of the empire of the whole world! Here Nebuchadnezzar now predicts the magnificence and mightiness of his own monarchy. Hence he sends his edict *to all peoples, and nations, and languages, which dwell on the earth.* He afterwards adds, *it seemed to me good to relate the signs and wonders which the mighty God hath wrought with me.* No doubt he feels himself to have paid the penalty of his ingratitude, since he had so punctiliously ascribed the glory to one true God, and yet had relapsed into his own superstitions, and had never really said farewell to them. We see how often King Nebuchadnezzar was chastised before he profited by the rod of the Almighty. Hence we need not be suprised if God often strikes us with his hand, since the result of experience proves us to be dull, and, to speak truly, utterly slothful. When God, therefore, wishes to lead us to repentance, he is compelled to repeat his blows continually, either because we are not moved when he chastises us with his hand, or we seem roused for the time, and then we return again to our former torpor. He is therefore compelled to redouble his blows. And we perceive this in the narrative before us, as in a glass. But the singular benefit of God was this, Nebuchadnezzar, after God had often chastised him, yielded at length. It is unknown whether or not this confession proceeded from true and genuine repentance: I must leave it in doubt. Yet without the slightest doubt Daniel recited this edict, to shew the king so subdued at length, as to confess the God of Israel to be the only God, and to bear witness to this among all people under his sway.

Meanwhile we must remark, how this edict of the king of Babylon receives the testimony of the Spirit; for Daniel has no other object or purpose in relating the edict, than to shew the fruit of conversion in King Nebuchadnezzar. Hence, without doubt, King Nebuchadnezzar bore witness to his repentance when he celebrated the God of Israel among all people, and when he proclaimed a punishment to all who spoke reproachfully against God. Hence this passage is often cited by Augustine against the Donatists.[1] For they wished to grant an act of impunity to themselves, when they disturbed the Church with rashness and corrupted pure doc-

[1] Ep. clxvi. ad Donat. et alibi.

trine, and even permitted themselves to attack it like robbers. For some were then discovered to have been slain by them, and others mutilated in their limbs. Since, then, they allowed themselves to act so licentiously and still desired to commit crimes with impunity, yet they held this principle as of first importance. No punishment ought to be inflicted on those who differ from others in religious doctrine; as we see in these days, how some contend far too eagerly about this subject. What they desire is clear enough. If any one carefully observes them, he will find them impious despisers of God; they wish to render everything uncertain in religion, and as far as they can they strive to tear away all the principles of piety. With the view then of vomiting forth their poison, they strive eagerly for freedom from punishment, and deny the right of inflicting punishment on heretics and blasphemers.

Such is that dog Castalio[1] and his companions, and all like him, such also were the Donatists; and hence, as I have mentioned, Augustine cites this testimony in many places, and shews how ashamed Christian princes ought to be of their slothfulness, if they are indulgent to heretics and blasphemers, and do not vindicate God's glory by lawful punishments, since King Nebuchadnezzar who was never truly converted, yet promulgated this decree by a kind of secret instinct. At all events, it ought to be sufficient for men of moderate and quiet tastes to know how King Nebuchadnezzar's edict was praised by the approval of the Holy Spirit. If this be so, it follows that kings are bound to defend the worship of God, and to execute vengeance upon those who profanely despise it, and on those who endeavour to reduce it to nothing, or to adulterate the true doctrine by their errors, and so dissipate the unity of the faith and disturb the Church's peace. This is clear enough from the Prophet's context; for Nebuchadnezzar says at first, *it pleases me to relate the signs and wonders which God has*

---

[1] Sebastian Castalio is here referred to. He was an opponent of Calvin, and banished from Geneva by his influence. Being a man of extensive learning he was appointed Greek professor at Basil. See Mosheim, cent. xvi. sec. iii. pt. 2, and the authorities there quoted.

prepared for me. He had already explained how wonderfully God had treated him; but this had passed away. Now God seizes him a second and even a third time, and then he confesses it to be his boast to explain the wonderful signs of God. He afterwards breaks forth into the exclamation, *How mighty are his signs! How remarkable his miracles! His kingdom is a kingdom of an age, and his dominion is from age to age.* Without doubt Nebuchadnezzar wished to excite his subjects to the attentive perusal of this edict, and to the acknowledgment of its value, and thus to subject themselves to the true and only God. He calls him *The High God,* meaning, doubtless, the God of Israel; meanwhile, we do not know whether he cast away his superstitions. I however incline to the opposite conjecture, since he did not put off his errors, but was compelled to give glory to the Most High God. He so acknowledged the God of Israel as to join inferior deities with him as allies and companions, just as all unbelievers, while admitting one supreme deity, imagine a multitude of others. So also Nebuchadnezzar confessed Israel's God to be Most High; yet he did not correct the idolatry which still flourished under his sway; nay, he mingled and confused the false gods with the God of Israel. Thus he did not leave behind his own corruptions. He celebrates indeed with magnificence the glory of the supreme God, but this is not sufficient without abolishing all superstitions, and promoting that religion alone which is prescribed by the word of God, and causing his pure and perfect worship to flourish.

In fine, this preface might seem a proof of an important conversion; but we shall directly see how far Nebuchadnezzar was from being entirely purged of his errors. It ought, indeed, to affect us exceedingly to behold the king wrapt up in so many errors, and yet seized with admiration of the Divine virtue, since he cannot express his thoughts, but exclaims,—*His signs how mighty! his wonders how powerful!* He added, *His kingdom is a perpetual kingdom, and his dominion is from age to age.* Here he confesses God's power not to be dependent upon man's will, since he had just before said, the statue which he had erected was to be worshipped, because he had chosen so to decree it. Now, however, he remits much of this pride by confessing God's kingdom to be a perpetual one. The narrative now follows. Thus far we have merely a preface, because the edict was diffused among his subjects to render them attentive to the most important subjects.

4. I Nebuchadnezzar was at rest in mine house, and flourishing in my palace:

5. I saw a dream which made me afraid, and the thoughts upon my bed, and the visions of my head, troubled me.

6. Therefore made I a decree to bring in all the wise *men* of Babylon before me, that they might make known unto me the interpretation of the dream.

4. Ego Nebuchadnezer quietus, *aut, felix*, eram domi meæ, et florens, *aut, viridis*, in palatio meo.

5. Somnium vidi, et exterruit me,[1] et cogitationes super cubile meum et visiones capitis mei conturbaverunt me.

6. Et a me positum fuit decretum, ut adducerentur, *hoc est, accerserentur*, coram me omnes sapientes Babylonis, qui interpretationem somnii patefacerent mihi.

Nebuchadnezzar here explains how he acknowledged the Supreme God. He does not relate the proofs which he had previously received; but since his pride was subdued in this last dream, he makes a passing allusion to it. Meanwhile, as he doubtless recalled his former dreams to mind, and condemned himself for his ingratitude, in burying in oblivion this great power of God, and in wiping away the remembrance of those benefits by which God had adorned him. Here, however, he speaks only of his last dream, which we shall see in its own place. But before he comes as far as the dream, he says, *he was at rest.* שְׁלֵה, *seleh*, signifies " rest " and " happiness ;" and since prosperity renders men secure, it is metaphorically used for "security." David, when he pronounces the same sentence upon himself, uses the same words, (Ps. xxx. 6,) " I said in my prosperity," or rest ; שַׁלְוָה, *selueh*, which some translate "abundance;" but it rather signifies a quiet or prosperous state. Nebuchadnezzar, therefore, here marks the circumstance of time; hence we may know him to have been divinely seized, because prosperous fortune had rendered him stupid and drunken. There is nothing surprising in this, for the old and common proverb is, "fulness is the parent of ferocity,"

[1] Or, I was terrified. The copula may be resolved into the relative pronoun, " I saw a dream which frightened or terrified me."—*Calvin.*

as we see horses when too much fed, prance about and throw their riders. Thus also it happens with men. For if God treats them rather indulgently and liberally, they become fierce and insolent towards all men, and strike off God's yoke, and forget themselves to be but men. And when this happened to David, what shall happen to the profane and to others who are still too much devoted to the world? For David confesses himself to have been so deceived by his quiet and felicity, as to determine within himself that he had nothing else to fear,—" I said in my happiness," or my quiet, " I shall not be removed;" and he afterwards adds, " O Lord, thou didst chastise me, and I was laid low." (Ps. xxxviii. 7.) Since, therefore, David promised himself perpetual quiet in the world, because God spared him for a time, how ought our tranquillity to be suspected lest we should grow torpid on our lees? Nebuchadnezzar, then, does not recite this in vain—*I was quiet at home, I flourished in my palace,* since this was the cause of his confidence and pride, and of his carelessly despising God. He afterwards adds, he *saw a dream and was disturbed.* He, doubtless, wished here to distinguish his dreams from common ones, which often arise from either a disturbance of the brain, or our daily thoughts, or other causes, as we have elsewhere seen. It is not necessary to repeat what we have already treated more copiously. It is sufficient to state, briefly, how this dream, in which God previously informed him of the future punishment at hand, is separated from others which are either troubled, or fluctuating, or without reason. He says, therefore, *he saw a dream, and was disturbed,* while he was awake. He adds, *his thoughts were upon his bed;* and then, *he was disturbed by visions of the head.* These expressions only look towards that heavenly oracle, or vision, or dream, of which we shall afterwards speak more fully. It follows, *he put forth a decree to summon all the wise men of Babylon to explain,* or make manifest, *the interpretation of the dream.* Doubtless the king often dreamt, and did not always call together the Magi and soothsayers, and astrologers, and others who were skilled in the science of divination, or at least professed to be so. He did not consult them on all his dreams; but because God had inscribed in his heart a distinct mark by which he had denoted this dream, hence the king could not rest till he heard its interpretation. As we previously saw the authority of the first dream about the Four Monarchies and the Eternal Kingdom of Christ confirmed, so the king perceived this one to have proceeded from heaven. There is another difference between this dream and the one formerly explained. For God blotted out the remembrance of the dream about the Four Monarchies from King Nebuchadnezzar, so that it became necessary for Daniel to bring his dream before the king, and at the same time to add the interpretation. Daniel was then more obscure, for although he proved himself to have excelled all the Chaldeans, yet King Nebuchadnezzar would have wondered at him less if he had only been an interpreter of a dream. God wished, therefore, to acquire greater reverence for his Prophet and his doctrine, when he enjoined upon him two duties; first, the divination of the dream itself, and then the explanation of its sense and purpose. In this second dream Daniel is only an interpreter. God had already sufficiently proved him to be endued with a heavenly spirit, when Nebuchadnezzar not only called him among the rest of the Magi, but separated him from them all. He afterwards says:

7. Then came in the magicians, the astrologers, the Chaldeans, and the soothsayers: and I told the dream before them; but they did not make known unto me the interpretation thereof.

7. Tunc ingressi sunt magi, astrologi, Chaldæi, *hoc est, sapientes,* et physici, *vel, mathematici,* et somnium, *inquit,* exposui ego coram ipsis, et interpretationem ejus non patefecerunt mihi.

With respect to the words used above, we have formerly freed ourselves from all trouble, because we cannot accurately define what science each professed. Clearly enough they covered their shamelessness by honourable titles, although they gave themselves up to every possible imposture. They called themselves by the usual name of learned men, when they were really unacquainted with any art or science, and deluded mankind by miserable predictions; hence, by these words, Daniel comprehended all the Magi, soothsayers, astrologers, and augurs, who professed the art of divination. Here Nebuchadnezzar confesses that he sent for these men in vain. Hence it follows, this whole science was a fallacy, or, at least, Daniel's exposition of the dream was not by human skill, but by revelation from heaven. I embrace this opinion, since Nebuchadnezzar wished clearly to express that Daniel's power of interpreting his dream did not spring from man, but was a singular gift of the Spirit. He had considered it a settled point that, if any knowledge or skill in divination existed, it must belong to the Magi, soothsayers, augurs, and other Chaldeans who boasted in the possession of perfect wisdom. This, therefore, was without controversy—that the astrologers and the rest were most powerful in divination, and as far as human faculties would allow, nothing escaped them. Hence it follows, on the other hand, that Daniel was divinely instructed, since if he had been only an astrologer or magician, he must, like others, have required a long apprenticeship to this science. Nebuchadnezzar, therefore, wishes here to extol Daniel beyond all the Magi, as if he had said—He is a heavenly Prophet! And this, also, will appear better from what is added, as follows:

8. But at the last Daniel came in before me, (whose name *was* Belteshazzar, according to the name of my god, and in whom *is* the spirit of the holy gods,) and before him I told the dream, *saying*,

9. O Belteshazzar, master of the magicians, because I know that the spirit of the holy gods *is* in thee, and no secret troubleth thee, tell me the visions of my dream that I have seen, and the interpretation thereof.

8. Quousque tandem coram me introductus est Daniel cujus nomen Beltsazar secundum nomen dei mei, et in quo spiritus deorum sanctorum: et somnium coram ipso narravi.

9. Beltsazar princeps, *vel, magister*, majorum, quia ego novi quod spiritus deorum sanctorum in te *sit*, et nullum arcanum te anxium reddit,[1] visiones somnii mei quod vidi, et interpretationem ejus expone.

Here the king of Babylon addresses Daniel kindly, since he saw himself deserted by his own teachers. And hence we gather that no one comes to the true God, unless impelled by necessity. Daniel was not either unknown or far off; for we saw him to have been in the palace. Since then the king had Daniel with him from the first, why did he pass him over? Why did he call the other Magi from all quarters by

[1] Some translate, "may be troublesome to thee," but I shall treat this word by and bye.—*Calvin.*

his edict? Hence, as I have said, it clearly appears he would never have given glory to God, unless when compelled by extreme necessity. Hence he never willingly submitted to the God of Israel; and his affections were clearly but momentary, whenever they manifested any sign of piety. Because he besought Daniel so imploringly, we see his disposition to have been servile; just as all proud men swell out when they do not need any one's help, and become overbearing in their insolence; but when they are reduced to extremity, they would rather lick the dust than not obtain the favour which they need. Such was the king's disposition, since he willingly despised Daniel, and purposely preferred the Magi. But as soon as he saw himself left in difficulties, and unable to find any remedy except in Daniel, this was his last refuge; and he now seems to forget his own loftiness while speaking softly to God's holy Prophet. But I shall proceed with the rest to-morrow.

PRAYER.

Grant, Almighty God, since thou here proposest a remarkable example before our eyes, that we may learn thy power to be so great as not to be sufficiently celebrated by any human praises: and since we hear how its herald was a profane king, nay, even a cruel and proud one, and thou hast afterwards deigned to manifest thyself to us familiarly in Christ,—Grant, that in the spirit of humility we may desire to glorify thee, and to cleave entirely to thee. May we declare thee to be ours, not only in mouth and tongue, but also in works; not only as our true and only God, but our Father, since thou hast adopted us in thine only-begotten Son, until at length we enjoy that eternal inheritance which is laid up for us in heaven by the same Christ our Lord.—Amen.

Lecture Eighteenth.

9. *O Belteshazzar, master of the Magi, since I know that the spirit of the holy gods is in thee, and no secret can escape thee*—or overcome thee, as I shall soon explain the word—*relate the visions of my sleep which I saw, and their interpretation.* We yesterday shewed King Nebuchadnezzar to be a suppliant to Daniel, when reduced to extremity. He

did not seek him at first, but consulted his Magicians, and he is now compelled to venerate the person whom he had despised. He calls him *Belteshazzar*, and doubtless the name severely wounded the Prophet's mind; for another name had been imposed upon him by his parents from his earliest infancy; whence he could recognise himself as a Jew, and could draw his origin from a holy and elect nation. For his change of name was doubtless made by the tyrant's cunning, as we have previously said, as to cause him to forget his own family. King Nebuchadnezzar wished, by changing his name, to render this holy servant of God degenerate. Hence, as often as he was called by this name, he was clearly offended in no slight degree. But this evil could not be remedied, since he was a captive, and knew he had to deal with a people victorious, proud, and cruel. Thus, in the last verse, Nebuchadnezzar had used this name according to the name of his god. Since then Daniel had a name of his own, which his parents had given him by God's appointment, Nebuchadnezzar wished to blot out that sacred name, and so called him as a mark of respect Belteshazzar, which we may believe to have been deduced from the name of an idol. Hence this doubled the Prophet's grief, when he was stained with that base spot in bearing an idol's mark on his name; but it was his duty to endure this scourge of God among his other trials. Thus God exercised his servant in every way by enduring a cross.

He now calls him *Prince of the Magi*, and this doubtless wounded the holy Prophet's feelings. He wished nothing better than separation from the Magi, who deceived the world by their impostures and soothsaying. For although they were skilled in the science of astrology, and knew some principles worthy of praise, yet we are sure they corrupted all the sciences. Hence Daniel did not willingly hear himself included among them; but he could not free himself from this infamy. Thus we see his patience to have been divinely proved in various ways. Now, Nebuchadnezzar adds, *because I know the spirit of the holy gods to be in thee*. Many understand this of angels; and this interpretation is not objectionable, as I have hinted elsewhere. For the existence of a supreme God was known to all the nations, but they fancied angels to be inferior deities. Whatever be the true meaning, Nebuchadnezzar here betrays his own ignorance, since he had made no real progress in the knowledge of the true God; because he was entangled in his former errors, and retained many gods, as from the beginning he had been imbued with that superstition. This passage might have been translated in the singular number, as some do, but it would be too forced, and the reason for such a translation is too weak; for they think Nebuchadnezzar to have been truly converted; but the vanity of this is proved by the whole context; and being occupied by this opinion, they wish to relieve him from all fault. But since it is clear that in this edict of Nebuchadnezzar many proofs of his old ignorance are comprehended, there is no reason why we should depart from the simple sense of the words. Hence he attributes a divine spirit to Daniel, but meanwhile imagines many gods. Since, therefore, *the spirit of the holy gods is in thee*, he says, *and no secret overcomes thee.* Some translate אנס, *anes*, to be troublesome; it properly signifies to compel, or to force; for those who translate "there is no secret which can surpass thee," depart from the correct sense. Others translate it, "to be troublesome." This would be a more tolerable translation, but they would do better by translating, "no secret renders thee anxious or perplexed." If the rules of grammar would allow the א, *aleph*, to be a servile letter, the sense would be more suitable. For נסה, *neseh*, signifies to try, or prove, and also to elevate. We may translate it, "No secret is loftier than thy understanding;" or, "No secret proves thee;" if he had said,—Daniel was endued with a divine spirit;—he does not examine any proposition, and has no need to make an experiment in any science, since his answer is easy and at hand. But it is necessary to remember what I said,—No secret renders thee anxious, or confounds thee. Nebuchadnezzar knew this. Then why did he not directly call him to himself in his perplexity? As Daniel could free him from all perplexity, the king's ingratitude is proved, because he admitted the Magi to his counsels, and neglected Daniel. We see then how he always endeavoured to avoid God, till he was drawn along by a violent hand, and thereby displayed the absence of conversion. For repentance is voluntary, and those only are said to repent who willingly return by a change of mind to the God from whom they had revolted; and this cannot be done without faith and the love of God. He then asks him *to relate his dream and its interpretation.* But the dream was not unknown, and he relates it to Daniel. There is, therefore, something superfluous in these words, but no doubt about the sense—as Nebuchadnezzar only asks for the explanation of his dream. It follows :—

10. Thus *were* the visions of mine head in my bed: I saw, and behold a tree in the midst of the earth, and the height thereof *was* great.

11. The tree grew, and was strong, and the height thereof reached unto heaven, and the sight thereof to the end of all the earth:

12. The leaves thereof *were* fair, and the fruit thereof much, and in it *was* meat for all: the beasts of the field had shadow under it, and the fowls of the heaven dwelt in the boughs thereof, and all flesh was fed of it.

10. Visiones autem capitis mei super cubile meum, Videbam, et ecce arborem in medio terræ, et altitudo ejus magna.

11. Crevit, *multiplicata est,* arbor, et invaluit, et altitudo ejus pertigit, *hoc est, ut altitudo ejus pertingeret,* ad cœlos, et conspectus ejus ad extremum totius, *vel, universæ,* terræ.

12. Ramus ejus pulcher, et fructus ejus copiosus,[1] et esca omnibus in ea: sub ea umbrabat[2] bestia agri: et in ramis ejus habitabant[3] aves cœlorum, et ex ea alebatur omnis caro.

The following verses ought to be joined on :—

13. I saw in the visions of my head upon my bed, and, behold, a watcher and an holy one came down from heaven:

14. He cried aloud, and said thus, Hew down the tree, and cut off his branches, shake off his leaves, and scatter his fruit: let the beasts get away from under it, and the fowls from his branches:

15. Nevertheless, leave the stump of his roots in the earth, even with

13. Videbam *etiam* in visionibus capitis mei super cubile meum, et ecce vigil et sanctus descendit e cœlis.

14. Clamavit in fortitudine, *hoc est, forriter,* et ita loquutus est, Succidite arborem, et diripite folia ejus,[4] excutite ramos ejus, et dispergite fructus ejus: fugiat bestia ex umbra ejus, *de subtus, ad verbum,* et aves ex frondibus ejus, *vel ex ramis ejus.*

15. Tandem imum radicum ejus in terra relinquite, et in vinculo ferri,

---

[1] שׂגיא, *segia*, signifies large, or much.—*Calvin.*
[2] Verbally, took shelter.—*Calvin.*   [3] Or, nestled.—*Calvin.*
[4] It is better not to repeat boughs twice, as some do. I confess the word עֲנָף, *gnef*, here used, means leaf as well as bough, but עֲנָף, *gnefa*, means bough; hence the repetition is not superfluous—seize or cut off its leaves.—*Calvin.*

a band of iron and brass, in the tender grass of the field; and let it be wet with the dew of heaven, and *let* his portion *be* with the beasts in the grass of the earth:

16. Let his heart be changed from man's, and let a beast's heart be given unto him; and let seven times pass over him.

hoc est, ferreo, et æneo, in herba agri, et pluvia cœlorum irrigetur, et cum bestia sit portio ejus in herba terræ.

16. Cor ejus ab humano, *simpliciter, ab homine,* mutent,[1] et cor bestiæ detur ei : et septem tempora transeant super eam.

Here Nebuchadnezzar relates his dream, of which the interpretation will follow in its place. Yet because this narrative is cold and useless unless we should say something of the subject itself, it is necessary to make some remarks—the rest shall be deferred. First of all, under the figure of a tree Nebuchadnezzar himself is intended, not because it fully represents the king's office, but because God appointed the existence of governments in the world for this purpose—to be like trees on whose fruits all men feed, and under whose shadow they rest. Hence this ordinance of God flourishes, because tyrants, however they are removed from the exercise of just and moderate dominion, whether they wish it or not, are compelled to be like trees; since it is better to live under the most cruel tyrant than without any government at all. Let us suppose all to be on one equal level, what would such anarchy bring forth? No one would wish to yield to others; every one would try the extent of his powers, and thus all would end in prey and plunder, and in the mere license of fraud and murder, and all the passions of mankind would have full and unbridled sway. Hence I have said, tyranny is better than anarchy, and more easily borne, because where there is no supreme governor there is none to preside and keep the rest in check. Wherefore they philosophize too minutely who think this to be a description of a king endued with superior virtues; for there was no such superiority in justice and equity in King Nebuchadnezzar. God principally wished to shew, by this figure, with what intention and with what political order he desires the world to be governed; and why he sets over it kings and monarchies and other magistrates. Then he desired to shew, *secondly,* although tyrants and other princes forget their

---

[1] That is, shall be changed, as elsewhere appears.—*Calvin.*

duty, it is still divinely enjoined upon them, and yet God's grace always shines forth in all governments. Tyrants endeavour to extinguish the whole light of equity and justice, and to mingle all things; but the Lord meanwhile restrains them in a secret and wonderful manner, and thus they are compelled to act usefully to the human race, whether they will or not. This then is the meaning of the figure or image of the tree.

It is now added, *the birds of heaven dwelt amidst the branches, and the beasts lived by its sustenance*—which ought to be referred to mankind. For although even the beasts of the field profit by political order, yet we know society to have been ordained by God for the benefit of men. There is no doubt at all of the whole discourse being metaphorical, —nay, properly speaking, it is an allegory since an allegory is only a continued metaphor. If Daniel had only represented the king under the figure of a tree, it would have been a metaphor; but when he pursues his own train of thought in a continuous tenor, his discourse becomes allegorical. He says, therefore, *the beasts of the field dwelt under the tree,* because we are sheltered by the protection of magistrates; and no heat of the sun so parches and burns up miserable men as living deprived of that shade under which God wished them to repose. *The birds of heaven also nestled in its boughs and leaves.* Some distinguish, with too much subtlety, between birds and beasts. It is sufficient for us to observe the Prophet noticing how men of every rank feel no small utility in the protection of princes; for if they were deprived of it, it were better for them to live like wild beasts than mutually to confide in each other. Such protection is needful, if we reflect upon the great pride natural to all, and the blindness of our self-love, and the furiousness of our lusts. As this is the case, God shews, in this dream, how all orders among us need the protection of magistrates; while *pasture* and *food* and *shelter* signify the various forms of usefulness which political order provides for us. For some might object—they have no need of government either for one reason or another; for if we discharge properly all the duties of life, we shall always find God's blessing sufficient for us.

It is now added, *its height was great;* then, *it grew till it reached even to heaven, and its aspect extended itself to the furthest bounds of the land.* This is restricted to the Babylonian monarchy, for there were then other empires in the world, but they were either powerless or but slightly important. The Chaldeans, also, were then so powerful that no prince could approach to such majesty and power. Since, therefore, King Nebuchadnezzar was so pre-eminent, the loftiness of the tree here described is not surprising, though it reached to heaven; while the altitude rendered it visible throughout the whole land. Some of the rabbis place Babylon in the middle of the earth, because it was under the same line or parallel with Jerusalem—which is very foolish. Those also who place Jerusalem in the centre of the earth are equally childish; although Jerome, Origen, and other ancient authors, treat Jerusalem as in the centre of the world. In this conjecture of theirs they deserve the laughter of the Cynic who, when asked to point out the middle of the earth, touched the ground with his staff immediately under his feet! Then when the questioner objected to this determination of the centre of the earth, he said, "Then do you measure the earth!" As far as concerns Jerusalem, their conjectures are not worth mentioning. That proud Barbinel [Abarbanel] wished to seem a philosopher, but nothing is more insipid than the Jews when they depart from their own rules of grammar; and the Lord so blinded them and delivered them up to a reprobate sense, when he wished them to be spectacles of horrible blindness and prodigious stupidity,—and in a small and minute matter that silly fellow shews his absurdity.

He now says, *Its boughs were beautiful, and its fruit copious.* This must be referred to the common opinion of the vulgar; for we know men's eyes to be dazzled by the splendour of princes. For if any one excels others in power, all men adore him and are seized with admiration, and are incapable of judging correctly. When the majesty of a general or a king comes before them, they are all astonished and perceive nothing, and they do not think it lawful for them to inquire strictly into the conduct of princes. Since, then, the power and wealth of King Nebuchadnezzar were so great, no wonder the Prophet says, *His branches were beautiful, and their fruit copious*. But meanwhile we must remember what I lately said, namely, God's blessing shines forth in princes, even if they materially neglect their duty, because God does not suffer all his grace in them to be extinguished; and hence they are compelled to bring forth some fruit. It is much better, therefore, to preserve the existence of some kind of dominion than to have all men's condition equal, when each attracts the eyes of his neighbours. And this is the meaning of what I have said—*there was food and provision for all*, as I have lately explained it.

The *second* part of the dream follows here. Hitherto Nebuchadnezzar has described the beauty and excellency of his state under the figure of a lofty tree which afforded shade to the beasts and on whose fruit they fed, and next as giving nests to the birds of heaven under its boughs. The cutting down of the tree now follows. *I saw*, says he, *in the visions of my head upon my couch, and, behold, a watcher and a holy one came down from heaven*. No doubt we ought to understand an angel by a watcher. He is called "a holy one," which is only another form of expression for an angel; and they are worthy of this name, because they are perpetually watchful in the performance of God's commands. They are not subject to slumber, they are not nourished by either food or drink, but live a spiritual life; hence they have no use for sleep, which is the result of drink and food. Lastly, as angels have no bodies, their very spiritual nature makes them watchful. But this phrase not only expresses their nature but also their duty; because God has them at hand to fulfil his bidding, and destines them to the performance of his commands, hence they are called "watchers." (Psalm ciii. 20.) In this Psalm angels are said to do his bidding, because, by an agility incomprehensible to us, they run about hither and thither, and fly directly from heaven to earth, from one end of the world to another—from the rising even to the setting sun. Since, therefore, angels can so easily and promptly fulfil God's orders, they are deservedly called "watchers." They are called "holy ones," because they are not infected by human infirmities. But we are filled with many sins, not merely because we are earthly, but since we have contracted pollution from our first parents, which vitiates alike the whole body and mind. By this expression, then, Nebuchadnezzar desired to distinguish between angels and mortals. For although God here sanctifies his elect, yet as long as they dwell in the prison of the body they never arrive at the holiness of angels. Here then we mark the difference between angels and men. Nebuchadnezzar could not understand this by himself, but he was taught of God to perceive the destruction of the tree to arise not from man but from the Almighty.

He afterwards adds—*the angel cried with a loud voice, cut down the tree, strip off the leaves, cut off its boughs, scatter its fruits,* (or throw them away,) *and let the beasts flee from its shadow, and the birds of heaven dwell no longer under its branches.* By this figure God meant to express that King Nebuchadnezzar should be for a time like a beast. This ought not to seem absurd, although it is but rough to speak of a tree being deprived of a human heart, since men know trees to have no other life than that usually called vegetable. The dignity or excellence of the tree cannot be lessened by its being without a human heart, for it never had one originally. But though this is rather a rough mode of expression, yet it contains in it nothing absurd, although Daniel bends a little aside from the strictness of the allegory; nay, Nebuchadnezzar himself had an allegorical dream, and yet God mingled something with it by which he might comprehend the meaning veiled under the image of a tree. The angel, then, orders the tree to be deprived of its human heart, and its bough and fruit to be torn down and cast away, after it had been cut down; next he orders the heart of a beast to be given to it, and thus its portion might be with the wild animals of the woods. But as this must be repeated elsewhere, I now pass it by rather hastily. The general meaning is this; King Nebuchadnezzar was to be deprived for a time not only of his empire but even of his human sense, and to be in no way different from the beasts, since he was unworthy of holding even the lowest place among mankind. Although he seemed to surpass the human race in his elevation, yet he must be cast down and thrown below even the lowest mortals!

The reason for this punishment follows, when it is added, *seven times shall pass over him;* and then, *do not cut off its lowest root, but let the rain of heaven water it;* and next, *his portion shall be with the wild beasts.* Although the chastisement is hard and horrible, when Nebuchadnezzar is expelled from the society of men, and rendered like wild beasts; but it is something in his favour when God does not tear him up by the roots, but allows the root to remain for the tree to spring up again and flourish, and be planted again in its own place, and recover new vigour through its roots. Here Daniel reviews the punishment inflicted on King Nebuchadnezzar, in which God afforded a specimen of his clemency, in sparing him and not utterly cutting him down, but in allowing his root to remain. Some here discourse about the mitigation of penalties when God sees those repent whom he has chastised with rods; but I do not think it applicable here. There was no true conversion in King Nebuchadnezzar, as we said before, and shall see again more clearly. God did not wish to press him too hard, and this we must attribute to his clemency; because when he seems to set no bounds to his punishment of men's sins, yet in all temporal punishments he allows men to taste his pity; so that ever the reprobate remain without excuse. The assertion of some—that punishments are not remitted without the fault being excused, is false, as we see in the example of Ahab. For God remitted the fault to the impious king, but because he seemed to shew some signs of repentance, God abstained from greater punishment. (1 Kings xxi. 29.) So also we may see the same in the case of Nebuchadnezzar. God was unwilling utterly to root him out—for the metaphor of the tree shews this—but he desired *seven times to pass over him.* Some understand seven weeks, others seven years; but we shall treat this point more copiously by and bye. Lastly, we must notice this: in the midst of the time during which God's wrath seemed to rage against this wretched king, his benefits were also mingled with it. We learn this from the words, *his portion shall be with the beasts of the field;* that is, he shall feed upon some food by which life shall be preserved; and then, *it shall be watered* or irrigated *with the rain of heaven.* For God signifies—though he wished to punish King Nebuchadnezzar, and to render him a remarkable example of his wrath—his knowledge of what he could bear; hence, he so tempers his punishment as to leave hope remaining for the future. Thus he took his food even with the beasts of the earth, but he is not deprived of the irrigation of the dew of heaven.

PRAYER.

Grant, Almighty God, since we see it so difficult for us to bear prosperity without injury to the mind, that we may remember ourselves to be mortal—may our frailty be ever present to our eyes, and render us humble, and lead us to ascribe the glory to thee. Being advised by thee, may we learn to walk with anxiety and fear, to submit ourselves to thee, and to conduct ourselves modestly towards our brethren. May none of us despise or insult his brother, but may we all strive to discharge our duties with moderation, until at length thou gatherest us into that glory which has been obtained for us by the blood of thine only-begotten Son.—Amen.

Lecture Nineteenth.

17. This matter *is* by the decree of the watchers, and the demand by the word of the holy ones; to the intent that the living may know that the most High ruleth in the kingdom of men, and giveth it to whomsoever he will, and setteth up over it the basest of men.

17. In decreto vigilum verbum,[1] et in sermone sanctorum postulatio, ut cognoscant viventes, quod dominator *sit* excelsus in regno hominum: et cui voluerit tradet illud, et humilem,[2] hominum[3] eriget super ipsum.

In this verse God confirms what he had shewn to the king of Babylon by means of a dream. He says, then, the king was instructed in a certain thing; since it had been so determined before God and his angels. The full meaning is this,—Nebuchadnezzar must know it to be impossible to escape the punishment whose image he had seen in the dream. There is, however, some ambiguity in the words,

---

[1] Or, edict, for it may be conveniently translated so.—*Calvin.*
[2] Or, abject.—*Calvin.*   [3] Or, among men.—*Calvin.*

since interpreters find great difficulties with the second clause; for they say the angels ask the question, to afford proof to the king of Babylon, and that all men may acknowledge the supreme power of the one God. But this seems to me too forced. As far as the word פִּתְגָמָא, *pethegma*, is concerned, it signifies "word" in Chaldee; but here I think it properly used for "edict," as in the first chapter of Esther, (ver. 20;) and this is a very suitable sense, as the edict was promulgated in the decree so that the "word" or vision might not prove vain and inefficient; since God wished to point out to the king what was already fixed and determined in heaven. We now understand the Prophet's intention. But a new question still remains, because it seems absurd to attribute power and authority to those angels, lest in this way they seem to be equal to God. We know God to be judge alone, and hence it is his proper office to determine what pleases him; and if this is transferred to angels, it seems as if it lessened his supreme authority, because it is not becoming to make them companions of his Majesty. But we know it to be no new thing in Scripture for God to join angels with himself, not as equals but as attendants, and to attribute to them so much honour as to deign to call them into counsel. Hence angels are often called God's counsellors. As in this place they are said to decree together with God; and not by their own will or pleasure, as they say, but because they subscribe to God's judgment. Meanwhile, we must remark the double character assigned to them. In the first clause, Daniel makes them subscribe to the decree, and afterwards uses the word *demand*. And this suits the sense well enough; because the angels urge God by their prayers to humble all mortals and to exalt himself alone. Thus, whatever obscures his glory may be reduced into order. It is right for angels constantly to desire this, since we know them to desire nothing in comparison with the adoration of God by themselves in alliance with all mankind. But when they see God's authority diminished by man's pride and audacity, the object of their demand is that God would reduce under his yoke the proud who erect their crests against him.

We now see why Daniel says, *this was declared in the decree of the watchers, and was demanded in their speech;* as if he should say, "thou hast all angels opposed to thee; for by one consent and with one mouth they accuse thee before God, for as far as possible thou obscurest his glory; and God, assenting to their prayers, has determined to cast thee away, and to render thee an object of contempt and reproach before the whole world; and this decree has been signed by all the angels, as if it were common between him and them. For by their subscription and agreement he might prevail in confirming the confidence of the profane king. Without doubt God, after his usual manner, accommodated the vision to the understanding of a man who never was taught in his law, but only imbued with a confused notion of his divinity, so that he could not distinguish between God and angels. Meanwhile, this sentiment is true—the edict was promulgated at the united consent and demand of the whole celestial host; for angels bear with the greatest reluctance whatever detracts from God's glory, and all the folly of mankind when they wish to draw and attract to themselves the peculiar attributes of the only God. This seems to be the genuine sense. The following sentence flows very suitably, —*mortals must know God to be a ruler in the kingdoms of men.* For Daniel marks the end of the demand, since angels desire God's rights to remain entire, and to be quite unaffected by the ingratitude of mankind. But men cannot ascribe even the slightest merit to themselves without detracting from God's praise; hence angels continually seek from God the casting down of all the proud, and that he will not permit himself to be defrauded of his proper rights, but maintain in all its integrity his own sovereign powers. This also must be diligently observed—*mortals should notice how the Lord reigns in the kingdoms of men.* For even the worst of men confess the mighty power of God; they dare not draw him down from his heavenly throne by their blasphemies, but they imagine themselves able to obtain and defend their worldly kingdoms, by either their exertions or their wealth, or by some other means. Unbelievers, therefore, willingly shut up God in heaven, just as Epicurus fancied him to be enjoying his own delights at his ease. Hence Daniel shews God to be deprived of his rights, *unless he is recognised as a ruler in the kingdoms of men*, that is, on earth to humble all whom he pleases. So also it is said in the Psalms, (lxxv. 7,) Power springs not from either the east or the west, but from heaven; and elsewhere, God raises the poor out of the mire, (Ps. cxiii. 6.) Then in the sacred Canticle of the Virgin, he casts down the proud from their seat, and exalts the abject and the humble. (Luke i. 52.) All indeed confess this, but scarcely one in a hundred feels in his mind the dominion of God over the earth, and that no man can raise himself, or remain in any post of honour, since this is the peculiar gift of God. Because men are persuaded of this with difficulty, Daniel eloquently expresses it, *the Lord shall be lofty in the kingdoms of men;* that is, shall not only exercise his power in heaven, but also govern the human race, and assign to every one his own grade and position. *He will give it to whom he wills.* He speaks of different empires in the singular number; just as if God had said, some are raised up by God's will, and others are cast down; and the whole happens according to God's pleasure. The meaning is this—every one has his own condition divinely assigned to him; and thus a man's ambition, or skill, or prudence, or wealth, or the help of others, do not profit men in aspiring to any altitude, unless God raises them by his stretched out hand. Paul also teaches the same thing in other words; there is no power but from God, (Rom. xiii. 1,) and afterwards Daniel often repeats the same sentiment.

He adds, *he raises up the humble man above himself.* In a change so remarkable as this, God's power shines forth better while he raises from the dust those who were formerly obscure and contemptible, and even sets them above kings. When this happens, profane men say, God is playing with them, and rolls men about like balls in his hand, which are first tossed upwards and then thrown down upon the ground. But they do not consider the reason why God by open proofs wishes to shew how we are under his absolute power, on which our condition entirely depends; when we do not comprehend this of our own accord, examples are necessarily set before us by which we are compelled to perceive what almost all are willingly ignorant of. We now understand the whole intention of the Prophet. Angels seek from God by continual prayers to declare his own power to mortals, and thus to lay prostrate the proud who think to excel by their own power and industry, or else by chance, or by the help of men. To induce God to punish men for their sacrilegious deeds, the angels desire him to prostrate them, and thus to shew himself to be not only the king and ruler of heaven, but also of earth. Now, this not only happens in the case of a single king, but we know history to be full of such proofs. Whence, then, or from what order have kings often been created? And when there was no greater pride in the world than in the Roman empire, we see what happened. For God brought forward certain monsters which caused the greatest astonishment among the Greeks and all the Orientals, the Spaniards, Italians, and Gauls; for nothing was more monstrous than some of the emperors. Then their origin was most base and shameful, and God could not shew more clearly how empires were not transferred by the will of man, nor even acquired by valour, counsel, and powerful troops, but remained under his own hand to bestow upon whomsoever he pleased. Let us go on:

18. This dream I king Nebuchadnezzar have seen. Now thou, O Belteshazzar, declare the interpretation thereof, forasmuch as all the wise *men* of my kingdom are not able to make known unto me the interpretation: but thou *art* able; for the spirit of the holy gods *is* in thee.	18. Hoc somnium vidi ego Rex Nebuchadnezer: et tu Beltsazar, interpretationem enarra,[1] quoniam cuncti sapientes regni mei non potuerunt interpretationem patefacere mihi: tu vero potes: quia spiritus deorum sanctorum in te.

Here Nebuchadnezzar repeats what he had formerly said about seeking an interpretation for his dream. He understood the figure which was shewn to him, but he could not understand God's intentions nor even determine its relation to himself. On this point he implores Daniel's confidence; he affirms his vision in a dream to induce Daniel to pay great attention to its interpretation. Then he adds, with the same purpose, *All the wise men of his kingdom could not*

[1] Verbally, say.—*Calvin.*

explain the dream; where he confesses all the astrologers, and diviners, and others of this kind to be utterly vain and fallacious, since they professed to know everything. For some were augurs, some conjecturers, some interpreters of dreams, and others astrologers, who not only discoursed on the course, distances, and orders of the stars, and the peculiarities of each, but wished to predict futurity from the course of the stars. Since, therefore, they boasted so magnificently in their superior knowledge of all events, Nebuchadnezzar confesses them to have been impostors. But he ascribes this power in reality to Daniel, because he was endued by the divine Spirit. Hence he excludes all the wise men of Babylon from so great a gift through his having proved them destitute of God's Spirit. He does not assert this in so many words, but this meaning is easily elicited from his expressions implying all the variety of the Chaldean wise men. Then in the second clause he exempts Daniel from their number, and states the reason to be his excelling in the divine Spirit. Nebuchadnezzar, therefore, here asserts what is peculiar to God, and acknowledges Daniel to be his Prophet and minister. When he calls angels *holy deities,* we have mentioned this already as an expression which ought not to seem surprising in a heathen, uninstructed in the true doctrine of piety, and only just initiated in its elements. But we know this common opinion respecting angels being mingled together with the one God. Hence Nebuchadnezzar speaks in the ordinary and received language when he says, the spirit of the holy gods dwells in Daniel. It now follows:

19. Then Daniel (whose name *was* Belteshazzar) was astonied for one hour, and his thoughts troubled him. The king spake, and said, Belteshazzar, let not the dream, or the interpretation thereof, trouble thee. Belteshazzar answered and said, My lord, the dream *be* to them that hate thee, and the interpretation thereof to thine enemies.

19. Tunc Daniel, cui nomen Beltsazar, obstupefactus fuit circiter horam unam: et cogitationes ejus turbabant eum. Respondit rex et dixit, Beltsazar, somnium et interpretatio *ejus* ne conturbet te, *terreat.* Respondit Beltsazar et dixit, Domine mi, somnium *sit* inimicis tuis, et interpretatio ejus hostibus tuis.

Here Daniel relates how he was in some sense astonished. And I refer this to the sorrow which the holy Prophet had endured from that horrible punishment which God had shewn under a figure; nor ought it to seem surprising for Daniel to be grievously afflicted on account of the calamity of the king of Babylon; for although he was a cruel tyrant, and had harassed and all but destroyed God's Church, yet since he was under his sway, he was bound to pray for him. But God had clearly taught the Jews this, by means of Jeremiah, Pray ye for the prosperous state of Babylon, because your peace shall be in it. (Jer. xxix. 7.) At the close of seventy years it was lawful for the pious worshippers of God to beg him to free them; but until the time predicted by the Prophet had elapsed, it was not lawful either to indulge in hatred against the king, or to invoke God's wrath upon him. They knew him to be the executor of God's just vengeance, and also to be their sovereign and lawful ruler. Since then Daniel was treated kindly by the king when by the rights of warfare he was dragged into exile, he ought to be faithful to his own king, although he exercised tyranny against the people of God. This was the reason why he suffered so much sorrow from that sad oracle. Others think he was in an ecstasy; but this seems to suit better because he does not simply speak of being astonished, but even disturbed and terrified in his thoughts. Meanwhile, we must remark, how variously the Prophets were affected when God uses them in denouncing his approaching judgments. Whenever God appointed his Prophets the heralds of severe calamities, they were affected in two ways; on the one side, they condoled with those miserable men whose destruction they saw at hand, and still they boldly announced what had been divinely commanded; and thus their sorrow never hindered them from discharging their duty freely and consistently. In Daniel's case we see both these feelings. The sympathy, then, was right in his condoling with his king and being silent for about an hour. And when the king commands him to be of good courage and not to be disturbed, we have here depicted the security of those who do not apprehend the wrath of God. The Prophet is terrified, and yet he is free from all evil; for God does not threaten him, nay, the very punishment which he sees prepared for the king, afforded the hope of future deliverance. Why then is he frightened? because the faithful, though God spares them and shews himself merciful and propitious, cannot view his judgments without fear, for they acknowledge themselves subject to similar penalties, if God did not treat them with indulgence. Besides this, they never put off human affections, and so pity takes possession of them, when they see the ungodly punished or even subject to impending wrath. For these two reasons they suffer sorrow and pain. But the impious, even when God openly addresses and threatens them, are not moved, but remain stupid, or openly deride his power and treat his threats as fabulous, till they feel them seriously. Such is the example which the Prophet sets before us in the king of Babylon.

Belteshazzar, he says, *let not thy thoughts disturb thee; let not the dream and its interpretation frighten thee!* Yet Daniel was afraid for his sake. But as I have already said, while the faithful are afraid though they feel God to be propitious, yet the impious sleep in their security, and are unmoved and unterrified by any threats. Daniel adds the cause of his grief,—*O my lord,* he says, *may the dream be for thine enemies, and its interpretation to thy foes!* Here Daniel explains why he was so astonished — because he wished so horrible a punishment to be turned away from the person of the king; for although he might deservedly have detested him, yet he reverenced the power divinely assigned to him. Let us learn, therefore, from the Prophet's example, to pray for blessings on our enemies who desire to destroy us, and especially to pray for tyrants if it please God to subject us to their lust; for although they are unworthy of any of the feelings of humanity, yet we must modestly bear their yoke, because they could not be our governors without God's permission; and not only for wrath, as Paul admonishes us, but for conscience' sake, (Rom. xiii. 5,) otherwise we should not only rebel against them, but against God himself. But, on the other hand, Daniel shews the impossibility of his being changed or softened by any sentiment of pity, and thus turned from his intended course:

20. The tree that thou sawest, which grew, and was strong, whose	20. Arborquam vidisti, quæ magna *erat* et robusta, et cujus magnitudo

height reached unto the heaven, and the sight thereof to all the earth:

21. Whose leaves *were* fair, and the fruit thereof much, and in it *was* meat for all; under which the beasts of the field dwelt, and upon whose branches the fowls of the heaven had their habitation:

22. It *is* thou, O king, that art grown and become strong: for thy greatness is grown, and reacheth unto heaven, and thy dominion to the end of the earth.

pertingebat ad cœlos, et aspectus ejus ad totam terram.

21. Et folium ejus pulchrum erat,[1] et fructus ejus copiosus: et in qua,[2] cibus cunctis: sub qua habitabant bestiæ agri, et in cujus ramis quiescebant aves cœli.

22. Tu *es* ipse rex, qui multiplicatus es et roboratus,[3] ita ut magnitudo tua multiplicata fuerit, et pertigerit ad cœlos, et potestas tua ad fines terræ.

Here we see what I have touched upon, namely, how Daniel acted respectfully to the king, and thus was mindful of his prophetic duty, while he punctually discharged the commands of God. We must notice this distinction, for nothing is more difficult for ministers of the Word than to maintain this middle course. Some are always fulminating through a pretence of zeal, and forget themselves to be but men: they shew no sign of benevolence, but indulge in mere bitterness. Hence they have no authority, and all their admonitions are hateful. Next, they explain God's Word with pride and boasting, when they frighten sinners without either humanity, or pain, or sympathy. Others, again, who are wicked and perfidious flatterers, gloss over the grossest iniquities; they object to both Prophets and Apostles, esteeming the fervour of their zeal to have driven away all human affections! Thus they delude miserable men, and destroy them by their flattery. But our Prophet, as all the rest, here shews how God's servants ought to take a middle course. Thus Jeremiah, when prophesying adversity, feels sorrow and bitterness of spirit, and yet does not turn aside from unsparing reproof of the severest threats, as both sprang from God. (Jer. ix. 1.) The rest of the prophets also act in the same manner. Here Daniel, on the one hand, pities the king, and on the other, through knowing himself to be the herald of God's anger, he is not frightened by any danger while setting before the king the punishment which he had despised. Hence we gather why he was not astonished.

[1] That is, whose leaves were beautiful.—*Calvin.*
[2] Verbally, "in it."—*Calvin.*
[3] That is, who hast become great and strong.—*Calvin.*

He felt no fear of the tyrant, although many do not dare to discharge their duty when an odious message is entrusted to them, which stimulates the impious and the unbelievers to madness. Daniel, however, was not astonished with any fear of this kind; he only wished God to act mercifully towards his king. For he says here *Thou art king thyself.* He does not speak with any doubt or hesitation, neither does he use obscurity nor a number of excuses, but plainly announces king Nebuchadnezzar to be intended by the tree which he saw. Hence *the tree which thou sawest is large and strong, under the shade of which the beasts of the field were dwelling, and in the boughs of which the birds of the air were making their nests: thou,* says he, *art the king.* Why so? *Thou hast become great and strong; thy magnitude has extended to the heavens, and thy power to the ends of the earth.* Now, what follows?

23. And whereas the king saw a watcher and an holy one coming down from heaven, and saying, Hew the tree down, and destroy it; yet leave the stump of the roots thereof in the earth, even with a band of iron and brass, in the tender grass of the field; and let it be wet with the dew of heaven, and *let* his portion *be* with the beasts of the field, till seven times pass over him;

24. This *is* the interpretation, O king, and this *is* the decree of the most High, which is come upon my lord the king.

23. Et quod vidit rex, vigilem, et sanctum descendere è cœlis, qui dixit:[1] Succidite arborem, et dispergite eam: tantummodo imum radicum ejus in terra relinquite: et *sit* in vinculo ferri et æris in herba agri, et rore cœlorum proluatur, et cum bestiis agri portio ejus, donec septem tempora transeant super eam.

24. Hæc interpretatio, rex, et decretum excelsi est, quod spectat ad dominum meum regem.

Daniel follows up what he had begun with perseverance, shewing judgment to be overhanging the king of Babylon. He calls him lord, indeed, with cordiality; meanwhile he was the ambassador of the Supreme King, he did not hesitate to elevate his discourse above the king's command—as all the prophets do who rise up against mountains and hills, as Jeremiah does in chap. i. 10. Thus this sentence is worthy of notice,—" I have appointed thee over kingdoms and peoples, to pluck them up and to plant them, to build and to destroy." God, therefore, wishes to assert so great a reverence for his Word, because there is nothing in the

[1] Verbally, "and he said," for the copula ought to be resolved into the relative pronoun.—*Calvin.*

world so magnificent or splendid which does not yield to it. Daniel, then, as far as concerns human events and political order, confesses the king to be his master; but meanwhile he goes on with the embassy entrusted to him. *The king then*, says he, *saw a watcher descend from heaven.* He always speaks of an angel.[1] We have stated why Scripture calls angels "watchers," since they are at hand to perform God's commands; and we know God executes his decrees by their agency: I said angels always discharge this duty, and keep watch over the faithful. But the name "watcher" is a general one, and implies the promptness with which angels are endued, to enable them to discharge with the utmost celerity whatever God enjoins upon them. *Thou hast seen, then, one descend from heaven, who said, Cut down the tree, and scatter it abroad.* He repeats what he had said before, namely, the time of his punishment was defined here, because God would destroy the king of Babylon and all remembrance of him. An exception is then added,— *Until seven times pass over.* I have said nothing of those times, but their opinion is probable who take it for an indefinite number, meaning, until a long time shall pass away. Others think months denoted; others, years; but I willingly incline to this interpretation, since God wishes for no short time to punish King Nebuchadnezzar. It may not seem customary, indeed, but as he wished to put forth an example for all ages, he desired to prolong his punishment. This, therefore, seems the meaning of the seven years; for we know the number seven years to signify a long time in Scripture, since it denotes perfection.

PRAYER.

Grant, Almighty God, since thou settest before us our sins, and at the same time announcest thyself as our judge, that we may not abuse thy forbearance and lay up for ourselves a treasure of greater wrath through our sloth and torpor. Grant, also, that we may fear thee reverently, and be anxiously cautious ourselves: may we be frightened by thy threats, and enticed by thy sweetness, and be willing and submissive to thee: may we never desire more than to consecrate ourselves entirely to obey thee, and to glorify thy name through Jesus Christ our Lord.— Amen.

---

[1] See DISSERTATION XIV. at the end of this Vol.

Lecture Twentieth.

25. That they shall drive thee from men, and thy dwelling shall be with the beasts of the field, and they shall make thee to eat grass as oxen, and they shall wet thee with the dew of heaven, and seven times shall pass over thee, till thou know that the most High ruleth in the kingdom of men, and giveth it to whomsoever he will.

25. Et te expellent ab hominibus, et cum bestiis agrestibus erit habitatio tua: et herba sicut boves te pascent, et rore cœlorum te irrigabunt: et septem tempora transibunt super te, donec cognoscas, quod dominator *sit* excelsus in regno hominum, et cui voluerit det illud.

DANIEL proceeds with the explanation of the king's dream, to whom the last verse which I explained yesterday applies. This ought to be expressed, because this message was sorrowful and bitter for the king. We know how indignantly kings are usually compelled not only to submit to orders, but even to be cited before God's tribunal, where they must be overwhelmed in shame and disgrace. For we know how prosperity intoxicates the plebeian race. What, then, can happen to kings except forgetfulness of the condition of our nature when they attempt to free themselves from all inconvenience and trouble? For they do not consider themselves subject to the common necessities of mankind. As, therefore, Nebuchadnezzar could scarcely bear this message, here the Prophet admonishes him in a few words concerning the cutting down of the tree as the figure of that ruin which hung over him. He now follows this up at length, when he says, *They shall cast thee out from among men, and thy habitation shall be with the beasts of the field.* When Daniel had previously discoursed upon the Four Monarchies, there is no doubt about the king's mind being at first exasperated; but this was far more severe, and in the king's opinion far less tolerable, as he is compared to wild beasts, and cut off from the number of mankind, and then he was driven into the fields and woods to feed with the wild beasts. If Daniel had only said the king was to be despoiled of his royal dignity, he would have been greatly offended by that disgrace, but when he was subject to such extreme shame, he was, doubtless, inwardly maddened by it. But God still restrained his fury lest he should desire to be revenged upon the supposed injury which he suffered. For we shall afterwards see from the context that he did not grow wise again. Since, therefore, he always cherished the same pride, there is no doubt of his cruelty, for these two vices were united; but the Lord restrained his madness, and spared his holy Prophet. Meanwhile, the constancy of God's servant is worthy of observation, as he does not obliquely hint at what should happen to the king, but relates clearly and at length how base and disgraceful a condition remained for him. *They shall cast thee out,* says he, *from among men.* If he had said, thou shalt be as it were one of the common herd, and shalt not differ from the very dregs of the people, this would have been very severe. But when the king is ejected from the society of mankind, so that not a single corner remains, and he is not allowed to spend his life among ox-herds and swineherds, every one may judge for himself how odious this would be; nor does Daniel here hesitate to pronounce such a judgment.

The following clause has the same or at least similar weight,—*Thy dwelling,* says he, *shall be with the beasts of the field, and its herb shall feed thee.* The plural number is used indefinitely in the original; and hence it may be properly translated, "Thou shalt feed on grass; thou shalt be watered by the dew of heaven; thy dwelling shall be with wild beasts." I do not wish to philosophize with subtlety, as some do, who understand angels. I confess this to be true; but the Prophet simply teaches punishment to be at hand for the king of Babylon, while he should be reduced to extreme ignominy, and differ in nothing from the brutes. This liberty, therefore, as I have said, is worthy of notice, to shew us how God's servants, who have to discharge the duty of teaching, cannot faithfully act their part unless they shut their eyes and despise all worldly grandeur. Hence, by the example of the king, let us learn our duty, and not be stubborn and perverse when God threatens us. Although, as we have said, Nebuchadnezzar did not grow wise, as the context will shew us, yet we shall see how he bore the terrible judgment denounced against him. If, therefore, we, who are but as refuse compared to him, cannot bear God's threats when they are set before us, he will be our witness and judge, who, though possessed of such mighty power, dared nothing against the Prophet. Now, at the end of the verse, the sentence formerly explained is repeated,—*Until thou dost acknowledge,* says he, *how great a Lord there is in the kingdom of men, who delivers it to whomsoever he will.* This passage teaches us again how difficult it is for us to attribute supreme power to God. In our language, indeed, we are great heralds of God's glory, but still every one restricts his power, either by usurping something to himself, or by transferring it to some one else. Especially when God raises us to any degree of dignity, we forget ourselves to be men, and snatch away God's honour from him, and desire to substitute ourselves for him. This disease is cured with difficulty, and the punishment which God inflicted on the king of Babylon is an example to us. A slight chastisement would have been sufficient unless this madness had been deeply seated in his bowels and marrow, since men claim to themselves the peculiar property of God. Hence they have need of a violent medicine to learn modesty and humility. In these days, monarchs, in their titles, always put forward themselves as kings, generals, and counts, by the grace of God; but how many falsely pretend to apply God's name to themselves, for the purpose of securing the supreme power! For what is the meaning of that title of kings and princes—" by the grace of God?" except to avoid the acknowledgment of a superior. Meanwhile, they willingly trample upon that God with whose shield they protect themselves,—so far are they from seriously thinking themselves to reign by his permission! It is mere pretence, therefore, to boast that they reign through God's favour. Since this is so, we may easily judge how proudly profane kings despise God, even though they make no fallacious use of his name, as those triflers who openly fawn upon him, and thus profane the name of his grace! It now follows:

26. And whereas they commanded to leave the stump of the tree roots; thy kingdom shall be sure unto thee, after that thou shalt have known that the heavens do rule.

26. Et quod dixerunt de relinquenda radice stirpium arboris, regnum tuum tibi stabit, ex quo cognoveris quod potestas *sit* cœlorum.[1]

[1] Or, that there is dominion in the heavens.—*Calvin.*

Here Daniel closes the interpretation of the dream, and shews how God did not treat King Nebuchadnezzar so severely by not giving way to clemency. He mitigates, indeed, the extreme rigour of the punishment, to induce Nebuchadnezzar to call upon God and repent, through indulging the hope of pardon, as a clearer exhortation will afterwards follow. But Daniel now prepares him for penitence, by saying *His kingdom should stand.* For God might cast him out from intercourse with mankind, and thus he would always remain among wild beasts. He might instantly remove him from the world; but this is a mark of his clemency, since he wished to restore him, not to a merely moderate station, but to his former dignity, as if it had never been trenched upon. We see, therefore, how useful the dream was to King Nebuchadnezzar, so long as he did not despise the Prophet's holy admonition, through ingratitude towards God; because Daniel not only predicted the slaughter which was at hand, but brought at the same time a message of reconciliation. God, therefore, had instructed the king to some purpose, unless he had been unteachable and perverse, like the majority of mankind. Besides, we may gather from this the general doctrine of our being invited to repentance when God puts an end to his chastisements; since he sets before us a taste of his clemency to induce in us the hope of his being entreated, if we only fly to him heartily and sincerely. We must notice also what Daniel adds in the second part of the verse, *from which thou mayest know that there is power in heaven:* for under these words the promise of spiritual grace is included. Since God will not only punish the king of Babylon, to humble him, but will work in him and change his mind, as he afterwards fulfilled, though at a long interval.

From which thou shalt know, then, says he, *that power is in heaven.* I have stated the grace of the Spirit to be here promised, as we know how badly men profit, even if God repeats his stripes an hundredfold. Such is the hardness and obstinacy of our hearts—for we rather grow more and more obdurate, while God calls us to repentance. And, doubtless, Nebuchadnezzar had been like Pharaoh, unless

God had humbled him, not only with outward penalties, but had added also the inward instinct of his Spirit, to allow himself to be instructed, and to submit himself to the judgment and power of heaven. Daniel means this when he says, *Wherefore thou shalt know;* for Nebuchadnezzar would never have acquired this knowledge of his own accord, unless he had been touched by the secret movement of the Spirit. He adds, *That there is power in heaven;* meaning, God governs the world and exercises supreme power; for he here contrasts heaven with earth, meaning all mankind. For if kings see all things tranquil around them, and if no one causes them terror, they think themselves beyond all chance of danger, as they say; and through being desirous of certainty in their station, they look round on all sides, but never raise their eyes upwards to heaven, as if God did not concern himself to behold the kingdoms of the earth, and to set up whom he would, and to prostrate all the proud. The princes of this world never consider their power to be from heaven, as if this were entirely out of God's hands; but, as I have said, they look right and left, before and behind. This is the reason why Daniel said, Power is from heaven. There is a contrast then between God and all mankind, as if he had said, Thou shalt know God reigns—as we have formerly seen. It follows:

27. Wherefore, O king, let my counsel be acceptable unto thee, and break off thy sins by righteousness, and thine iniquities by shewing mercy to the poor; if it may be a lengthening of thy tranquillity.

27. Proptzrea, rex, consilium meum placeat apud te,[1] et peccata tua[2] justitia redimas,[3] et iniquitatem tuam in misericordia erga pauperes: ecce erit prolongatio paci tuæ.[4]

Since interpreters do not agree about the sense of these words, and as the doctrine to be derived from them depends partly upon that, we must remark, in the *first* place, that מלכי, *meleki,* means "my counsel." Some translate it "my

---

[1] שפר, *shepher,* signifies to be beautiful; but it is metaphorically transferred to approbation or complacency, as the phrase is, "therefore my counsel shall please thee."—*Calvin.*

[2] Or, "that" for ו, *vau,* may be used in this way.—*Calvin.*

[3] So it is usually translated: we shall discuss the word by and bye.—*Calvin.*

[4] The Greeks translate—if by chance—or a medicine for their error.—*Calvin.*

king," and both words are derived from the same root מֶלֶךְ, *melek,* signifying " to reign ;" but it also signifies " counsel." There is no doubt that this passage ought to be explained thus :—*May my counsel therefore please thee, and mayest thou redeem thy sins.* The word פְּרוּק, *peruk,* is here translated " to redeem ;" it often signifies " to break off," or " separate," or " abolish." In this passage it may conveniently be translated, " separate or break off thy sins" by pity and humanity; as if he had said, Thus thou shalt make an end of sin, and enter upon a new course, and thus thy cruelty may be changed into clemency, and thy tyrannical violence into pity. But this is not of much consequence. The verb often signifies to free and to preserve ; the context does not admit the sense of preserving, and it would be harsh to say, Free thy sins by thy righteousness. Hence I readily embrace the sense of Daniel exhorting the king of Babylon to a change of life, so as to break off his sins in which he had too long indulged. With respect to the clause at the end of the verse, *behold there shall be a cure for thine error,* as I have mentioned, the Greeks translate, " if by chance there should be a cure ;" but the other sense seems to suit better ; as if he had said, " this is the proper and genuine medicine," some translate, " a promulgation," since אֲרַךְ, *arek,* signifies " to produce ;" and at the same time they change the signification of the other noun, for they say, " there shall be a prolongation to thy peace or quiet." That sense would be tolerable, but the other suits better with the grammatical construction ; besides, the more received sense is, *this medicine may be suitable to the error.* A different sense may be elicited without changing the words at all ; *there shall be a medicine for thine errors;* meaning, thou mayest learn to cure thine errors. For length of indulgence increases the evil, as we have sufficiently noticed. Hence this last part of the verse may be taken, and thus Daniel may proceed with his exhortation ; as if he had said,—it is time to cease from thine errors, for hitherto thou hast deprived thyself of all thy senses by giving unbridled license to thy lusts. If, therefore, there is any moderation in thine ignorance, thou mayest open thine eyes and understand at length how to repent.

I now return to the substance of the teaching. *May my counsel please thee!* says he. Here Daniel treats the profane king more indulgently than if he had addressed his own nation; for he used the prophetic office. But because he knew the king did not hold the first rudiments of piety, he here undertakes only the office of a counsellor, since he was not an ordinary teacher. As to Nebuchadnezzar sending for him, this was not a daily thing, nor did he do this, because he wished to submit to his doctrine. Daniel therefore remembers the kind of person with whom he was treating, when he tempers his words and says, *may my counsel be acceptable to thee!* He afterwards explains his counsel in a few words,—*Break away,* says he, *thy sins*—or cast them away—*by righteousness, and thy iniquities by pity to the poor.* There is no doubt that Daniel wished to exhort the king to repentance; but he touched on only one kind, which we know was very customary with the Prophets. For when they recall the people to obedience by repentance, they do not always explain it fully, nor define it generally, but touch upon it by a figure of speech, and treat only of the outward duties of penitence. Daniel now follows this custom. If inquiry is made concerning the nature of repentance, it is the conversion of man towards God, from whom he had been alienated. Is this conversion then only in the hands, and feet, and tongue? Does it not rather begin in the mind and the heart, and then pass on to outward works? Hence true penitence has its source in the mind of men, so that he who wished to be wise must set aside his own prudence, and put away his foolish confidence in his own reason. Then he must subdue his own depraved affections and submit them to God, and thus his outward life will follow the inward spirit. Besides this, works are the only testimonies to real repentance; for it is a thing too excellent to allow its root to appear to human observation. By our fruits therefore we must testify our repentance. But because the duties of the second table, in some sense, open the mind of man; hence the Prophets in requiring repentance, only set before us the duties of charity, as Daniel says. *Redeem,* therefore, *thy sins,* says he, or break away, or cast them away—but how? namely, by righteousness. Without doubt the word "justice" means here the same as "grace" or "pity." But those who here transfer "grace" to "faith," twist the Prophet's words too violently; for we know of nothing more frequent among the Hebrews than to repeat one and the same thing under two forms of speech. As, therefore, Daniel here uses sins and iniquities in the same sense, we conclude justice and pity ought not to be separated, while the second word expresses more fully the sense of justice. For when men see their life must be changed, they feign for themselves many acts of obedience which scarcely deserve the name. They have no regard for what pleases God, nor for what he commands in his word; but just as they approve of one part or another, they thrust themselves rashly upon God, as we see in the Papacy. For what is a holy and religious life with them? To run about here and there; to undertake pilgrimages imposed by vows; to set up a statue; to found masses, as they call it; to fast on certain days; and to lay stress on trifles about which God has never said a single word. As, therefore, men err so grossly in the knowledge of true righteousness, the Prophet here adds the word "pity" by way of explanation; as if he had said, Do not think to appease God by outward pomps, which delight mankind because they are carnal and devoted to earthly things, and fashion for themselves a depraved idea of God according to their own imagination; let not then this vanity deceive you; but learn how true justice consists in pity towards the poor. In this second clause, then, only a part of the idea is expressed, since true justice is not restricted simply to the meaning of the word, but embraces all the duties of charity. Hence we ought to deal faithfully with mankind, and not to deceive either rich or poor, nor to oppress any one, but to render every one his own. But this manner of speaking ought to be familiar to us, if we are but moderately versed in the prophetic writings.

The meaning of the phrase is this:—Daniel wished to shew the king of Babylon the duty of living justly, and cultivating faith and integrity before men, without forgetting the former table of the law. For the worship of God is more precious than all the righteousness which men cultivate among themselves. But true justice is known by its outward proofs, as I have said. But he treats here the second table rather than the first: for, while hypocrites pretend to worship God by many ceremonies, they allow themselves to commit all kinds of cruelty, rapine, and fraud, without obeying any law of correct living with their neighbours. Because hypocrites cover their malice by this frivolous pretence, God sets before them a true test to recall them to the duties of charity. This, then, is the meaning of the verse from which we have elicited a double sense. If we retain the future time, *behold, there shall be a medicine!* it will be a confirmation of the former doctrine; as if he had said, We must not travel the long and oblique circuits—there is this single remedy: or, if we are better pleased with the word of exhortation, the context will be suitable; may there be a medicine for thine errors! Mayest thou not indulge thyself hereafter as thou hast hitherto done, but thou must open thine eyes and perceive how miserably and wickedly thou hast lived, and so desire to heal thine errors. As the Papists have abused this passage, to shew God to be appeased by satisfactions, it is too frivolous and ridiculous to refute their doctrine; for when they speak of satisfactions, they mean works of supererogation. If any one could fulfil God's law completely, yet he could not satisfy for his sins. The Papists are compelled to confess this; what then remains?—The offering to God more than he demands, which they call works not required! But Daniel does not here exact of King Nebuchadnezzar any work of supererogation; he exacts justice, and afterwards shews how a man's life cannot be justly spent unless humanity prevails and flourishes among men, and especially when we are merciful to the poor. Truly there is no supererogation here! To what end then serves the law? Surely this has no reference to satisfactions, according to the ridiculous and foolish notions of the Papists! But if we grant them this point, still it does not follow that their sins are redeemed before God, as if works compensated either their fault or penalty, as they assert; for they confess their fault not to be redeemed by satisfactions—this is one point gained—and then as to the penalty, they say it is redeemed; but we must see whether this agrees with the Prophet's intention.

I will not contend about a word; I will allow it to mean "to redeem"—Thou mayest redeem thy sins; but we must ascertain, whether this redemption is in the judgment of God or of man? Clearly enough, Daniel here regards the conduct of Nebuchadnezzar as unjust and inhuman, in harassing his subjects, and in proudly despising the poor and miserable. Since, therefore, he had so given himself up to all iniquity, Daniel shews the remedy; and if this remedy is treated as a redemption or liberation, there is nothing absurd in saying, we redeem our sins before men while we satisfy them. I redeem my sins before my neighbour, if after I have injured him, I desire to become reconciled to him, I acknowledge my sins and seek for pardon. If, therefore, I have injured his fortunes, I restore what I have unjustly taken, and thus redeem my transgression. But this does assist us in expiating sin before God, as if the beneficence which I put in practice was any kind of expiation. We see, therefore, the Papists to be foolish and silly when they wrest the Prophet's words to themselves. We may now inquire in the last place, to what purpose Daniel exhorted King Nebuchadnezzar to break away from or redeem his sins? Now this was either a matter of no consequence—which would be absurd—or it was a heavenly decree, as the king's dream was a promulgation of the edict, as we have formerly seen. But this was determined before God, and could not be changed in any way; it was therefore superfluous to wish to redeem sins. If we follow a different explanation, no difficulty will remain; but even if we allow the Prophet to be here discoursing of the redemption of sins, yet the exhortation is not without its use.

In whatever way Nebuchadnezzar ought to prepare to bear God's chastisement, yet this would prove most useful to him, to acknowledge God to be merciful. And yet the time might be contracted, during which his obstinate wickedness should extend; not as if God changed his decree, but because he always warns by threatening, for the purpose of treating men more kindly, and tempering vigour with his wrath, as is evident from many other examples. This would not have been without its use to a teachable disposition, nor yet without fruit, when Daniel exhorted King Nebuchadnezzar to redeem his sins, because he might obtain some pardon, even if he had paid the penalty, since not even a single day had been allowed out of the seven years. Yet this was a great progress, if the king had at last humbled himself before God, so as to be in a fit state for receiving the pardon which had been promised. For as a certain time had been fixed beforehand, or at least shewn by the Prophet, hence it would have profited the king, if through wishing to appease his judge he had prepared his mind for obtaining pardon. This doctrine was therefore in every way useful, because the same reason avails with us. We ought always to be prepared to suffer God's chastisements; yet it is no slight or common alleviation of our sufferings, when we so submit ourselves to God, as to be persuaded of his desire to be propitious to us, when he sees us dissatisfied with ourselves, and heartily detesting our transgressions.

PRAYER.

Grant, Almighty God, that we may learn to bear patiently all adverse misfortunes, and know that thou exercisest towards us the duties of a judge, as often as we are afflicted in this world. Thus may we prevent thy wrath, and so condemn ourselves with true humility, that trusting in thy pity we may always flee to thee, relying upon the mediation of thy only-begotten Son, which thou hast provided for us. Grant, also, that we may beg pardon of thee, and resolve upon a true repentance, not with vain and useless fictions, but by true and serious proofs, cultivating true charity and faith among ourselves, and testifying in this way our fear of thy name, that thou mayest be truly glorified in us by the same our Lord.—Amen.

Lecture Twenty-first.

28. All this came upon the king Nebuchadnezzar.	28. Hoc totum impletum fuit, *vel, incidit,* super Nebuchadnezer regem
29. At the end of twelve months	29. In fine mensium duodecim,[1]

[1] That is, after twelve months.—*Calvin.*

he walked in the palace of the kingdom of Babylon.

30. The king spake, and said, Is not this great Babylon, that I have built for the house of the kingdom, by the might of my power, and for the honour of my majesty?

31. While the word *was* in the king's mouth, there fell a voice from heaven, *saying*, O king Nebuchadnezzar, to thee it is spoken; The kingdom is departed from thee:

32. And they shall drive thee from men, and thy dwelling *shall be* with the beasts of the field: they shall make thee to eat grass as oxen, and seven times shall pass over thee, until thou know that the most High ruleth in the kingdom of men, and giveth it to whomsoever he will.

in palatio regni, quod est in Babylone, deambulabat.

30. Loquutus est rex et dixit, An non hæc est Babylon magna, quam ego ædificavi in domum regni,[1] in robore fortitudinis meæ, et in pretium, *vel, excellentiam,* decoris mei?

31. Adhuc sermo *erat* in ore regis,[2] vox e cœlis cecidit, Tibi dicunt, rex Nebuchadnezer, regnum *tuum* migravit, *vel, discessit,* abs te.

32. Et ex hominibus te ejicient, et cum bestia agri habitatio tua: herbam sicuti boves gustare te facient:[3] et septem tempora transibunt super te, donec cognoscas quod dominator *sit* excelsus in regno hominum, et cui voluerit det illud.

After Nebuchadnezzar has related Daniel to be a herald of God's approaching judgment, he now shews how God executed the judgment which the Prophet had announced. But he speaks in the third person, according to what we know to be a common practice with both the Hebrews and Chaldees. Thus Daniel does not relate the exact words of the king, but only their substance. Hence he first introduces the king as the speaker, and then he speaks himself in his own person. There is no reason why this variety should occasion us any trouble, since it does not obscure the sense. In the first verse, Nebuchadnezzar shews the dream which Daniel had explained not to have been in vain. Thus the miracle shews itself to be from heaven, by its effects; because dreams vanish away, as we know well enough. But since God fulfilled, at his own time, what he had shewn to the king of Babylon by his dream, it is clear there was nothing alarming in the dream, but a sure revelation of the future punishment which fell upon the king. Its moderation is also expressed. Daniel says, when a year had passed away, and the king was walking in his own palace, and boasting in his greatness, at that moment a voice came down from heaven, and repeated what he had already heard in

---

[1] That is, that it may be a royal seat.—*Calvin.*
[2] That is, when the speech was in the king's mouth.—*Calvin.*
[3] Or, the grass shall feed thee as it does oxen.—*Calvin.*

the dream. He afterwards relates how he had been expelled from human society, and dwelt for a long time among the brutes, so as to differ from them in nothing. As to the use of words, since מהלך, *mehelek,* occurs here, some think that he walked upon the roof of his palace, whence he could behold all parts of the city. The inhabitants of the east are well known to use the roofs of their houses in this way; but I do not interpret the phrase with such subtlety, since the Prophet seems to wish nothing else than to shew how the king enjoyed his own ease, luxury, and magnificence. There is nothing obscure in the rest of the language.

I now approach the matter before us. Some think Nebuchadnezzar to have been touched with penitence when instructed by God's anger, and thus the time of his punishment was put off. This does not seem to me probable, and I rather incline to a different opinion, as God withdrew his hand till the end of the year, and thus the king's pride was the less excusable. The Prophet's voice ought to have frightened him, just as if God had thundered and lightened from heaven. He now appears to have been always like himself. I indeed do not deny that he might be frightened by the first message, but I leave it doubtful. Whichever way it is, I do not think God spared him for a time, because he gave some signs of repentance. I confess he sometimes indulges the reprobate, if he sees them humbled. An example of this, sufficiently remarkable, is displayed in King Ahab. (1 Kings xxi. 29.) He did not cordially repent, but God wished to shew how much he was pleased with his penitence, by pardoning a king impious and obstinate in his wickedness. The same might be said of Nebuchadnezzar, if Scripture had said so; but as far as we can gather from these words of the Prophet, Nebuchadnezzar became prouder and prouder, until his sloth arrived at its height. The king continued to grow proud after God had threatened him so, and this was quite intolerable. Hence his remarkable stupidity, since he would have been equally careless had he lived an hundred years after he heard that threat! Finally, I think although Nebuchadnezzar perceived some dreadful and horrible punishment to be at hand, yet, while frightened for the time, he did not lay aside his pride and haughtiness of mind. Meanwhile, he might think this prediction to be in vain; and what he had heard probably escaped from his mind for a long time, because he thought he had escaped; just as the impious usually abuse God's forbearance, and thus heap up for themselves a treasure of severer vengeance, as Paul says. (Rom. ii. 5.) Hence he derided this prophecy, and hardened himself more and more. Whatever sense we attach to it, nothing else can be collected from the Prophet's context, than the neglect of the Prophet's warning, and the oracle rendered nugatory by which Nebuchadnezzar had been called to repentance. If he had possessed the smallest particle of soundness of mind, he ought to flee to the pity of God, and to consider the ways in which he had provoked his anger, and also to devote himself entirely to the duties of charity. As he had exercised a severe tyranny towards all men, so he ought to study benevolence; yet when the Prophet exhorted him, he did not act thus, but uttered vain boastings, which shew his mind to have been swollen with pride and contempt for God. As to the space of time here denoted, it shews how God suspended his judgments, if perchance those who are utterly deplorable should be reclaimed; but the reprobate abuse God's humanity and indulgence, as they make this an occasion of hardening their minds, while they suppose God to cease from his office of judge, through his putting it off for a time. *At the end,* then, *of twelve months, the king was walking in his palace; he spoke, and said.* This doubling of the phrase shews us how the king uttered the feelings of premeditated pride. The Prophet might have said more simply, The king says,—but he says, *he spoke, and said.* I know how customary it is with both the Hebrews and Chaldees to unite these words together; but I think the repetition emphatic in this place, since the king then uttered what he had long ago conceived and concealed in his mind; *Is not this great Babylon, which I have built for a royal palace, and that too in the mightiness of my valour; as I have built it in the splendour of my excellency?* In these words we do not see any open blasphemy which could be very offensive to God, but we must consider the king by this language to claim to himself supreme power, as if he were God! We may gather this from the verse, "Is not this great Babylon?" says he. He boasts in the magnitude of his city, as if he wished to raise it giant-like to heaven; *which I,* says he— using the pronoun with great emphasis—*which I have built, and that too in the greatness of my valour.* We see that by claiming all things as his own, he robs God of all honour.

Before I proceed further, we must see why he asserts Babylon to have been founded by himself. All historians agree in the account of the city being built by Semiramis. A long time after this event, Nebuchadnezzar proclaims his own praises in building the city. The solution is easy enough. We know how earthly kings desire, by all means in their power, to bury the glory of others, with the view of exalting themselves and acquiring a perpetual reputation. Especially when they change anything in their edifices, whether palaces or cities, they wish to seem the first founders, and so to extinguish the memory of those by whom the foundations were really laid. We must believe, then, Babylon to have been adorned by King Nebuchadnezzar, and so he transfers to himself the entire glory, while the greater part ought to be attributed to Semiramis or Ninus. Hence this is the way in which tyrants speak, as all usurpers and tyrants do, when they draw towards themselves the praises which belong to others. *I,* therefore, says he, *have built it, by the strength of my hand.* Now it is easy to see what had displeased God in this boasting of the king of Babylon, namely, his sacrilegious audacity in asserting the city to have been built by his own mightiness. But God shews this praise to be peculiar to himself and deservedly due to him. Unless God builds the city, the watchman watches but in vain. (Psalm cxxvii. 1.) Although men labour earnestly in founding cities, yet they never profit unless God himself preside over the work. As Nebuchadnezzar here extols himself and opposes the strength of his fortitude to God and his grace, this boasting was by no means to be endured. Hence it happened that God was so very angry with him. And thus we perceive how this example proves to us what Scripture always inculcates,—God's resistance of the proud, his humbling their superciliousness, and his detestation of their arrogance. (Psalm xviii. 27.) Thus God everywhere announces himself as the enemy of the proud, and he confirms it by the present example, as if he set before us in a mirror the reflection of his own judgment. (James iv. 6; 1 Peter v. 5.) This is one point. The reason also must be noticed why God declares war on all the proud, because we cannot set ourselves up even a little, without declaring war on God; for power and energy spring from him. Our life is in his hands; we are nothing and can do nothing except through him. Whatever, then, any one assumes to himself he detracts from God. No wonder then if God testifies his dislike of the haughty superciliousness of men, since they purposely weary him when they usurp anything as their own. Cities, indeed, are truly built by the industry of men, and kings are worthy of praise who either build cities or adorn them, so long as they allow God's praise to be inviolate. But when men exalt themselves and wish to render their own fortitude conspicuous, they bury as far as they can the blessing of God. Hence it is necessary for their impious rashness to be judged by God, as we have already said. The king also confesses his vanity when he says, *I have built it for a royal palace, and for the excellency of my splendour.* By these words he does not dissemble how completely he looked at his own glory in all those buildings by which he hoped to hand down his name to posterity. Hence, on the whole, he wishes to be celebrated in the world, both during his life and after his death, so that God may be nothing in comparison with himself, as I have already shewn how all the proud strive to substitute themselves in the place of God.

It now follows,—*While the speech was in the mouth of the king, a voice descended from heaven—They say unto thee, O King Nebuchadnezzar, thy kingdom has departed from thee!* God does not now admonish the king of Babylon by either the mouth of a Prophet or a dream by night; but he sends forth his own voice from heaven; and as if he had not tamed down the pride by which the king was puffed up, a voice is now heard from heaven which inspires greater terror than either the Prophet's oracle or interpretation. Thus God is in the habit of dealing with the hardened and impenitent, since he causes his own prophets to denounce the penalty which hangs over them. Besides, when he sees them untouched or unaffected, he doubles the terror, until the final execution follows, as in the case of this tyrant. *The word was in the king's mouth when the voice was heard.* We see how God restrains in a moment the madness of those who raise themselves extravagantly. But it is not surprising that the voice was so suddenly heard, because time for repentance was allowed to King Nebuchadnezzar. In the form of speech, *they say to thee,* it is not necessary to inquire anxiously to whom these words apply. Some restrict them to angels; but I do not agree to this; it seems rather to be used in the customary way, *they say*—meaning "it is said," as if sanctioned by common consent. Hence *they say to thee, O King Nebuchadnezzar;* God does not simply call him by his name, but uses the word king—not for the sake of honour, but of ridicule, and to strike away from the king all the allurements by which he deceived himself. Thou indeed art intoxicated by thy present splendour, for while all adore thee, thou art forgetful of thy frailty ; but this royal majesty and power will not hinder God from laying thee prostrate ; for since thou wilt not humble thyself, thy kingdom shall be taken from thee! This indeed appeared incredible, since Nebuchadnezzar had the tranquil possession of the kingdom in his hand ; no one dared to shew himself his enemy ; he had subdued all his neighbours; his monarchy was terrible to all nations; hence God pronounces, *The kingdom has passed away from thee!* And this shews the certainty of the oracle; and thus Nebuchadnezzar may know the time to be fulfilled, and the punishment to be no longer delayed, because he had trifled with God's indulgence.

It follows,—*They shall expel thee from among men, and thy habitation shall be with the beasts of the field*—or of the country,—*they shall make thee eat grass like oxen!* Some think Nebuchadnezzar to have been changed into a beast ; but this is too harsh and absurd. We need not fancy any change of nature ; but he was cut off from all intercourse with men, and with the exception of a human form, he did not differ from the brutes,—nay, such was his deformity in his exile that, as we shall afterwards see, he became a horrid spectacle ;—all the hairs of his body stood up and grew like eagles' feathers ; his claws were like those of birds. In these points he was like the beasts, in others like the rest of mankind. It is uncertain whether God struck this king with madness, causing him to escape and lie hid for a length of time, or whether he was cast forth by a tumult and conspiracy of nobles, or even the consent of the whole people. All this is doubtful, since the history of those times is unknown to us. Whether, then, Nebuchadnezzar was snatched away by madness, and while he continued a maniac was separated from the society of men, or was cast forth as many tyrants have been, his dwelling with beasts for a time, becomes a memorable example to us. He was probably rendered stupid, by God's leaving him a human form while he deprived him of reason, as the context will make evident to us. *They shall cast thee out from human society ; thy dwelling shall be with wild beasts ; they shall make thee eat grass like an ox!* that is, when deprived of all delight, nay, of the commonest and plainest food, thou wilt find no other sustenance than that of oxen. Thou shalt eat the grass like an animal, *and seven times shall pass over thee.* Of the "seven times" we have spoken before. Some restrict this to days, but this is contrary not only to every reason, but to every pretext. Nor do I explain it of months ; the space of time would have been much too short. Hence the opinion of those who extend it to seven years is more probable. If Nebuchadnezzar had been cast out by a tumult, he would not have been so quickly recalled : then, since God wished to make an example of him for all generations, I suppose him to have been driven out from common society for a length of time. For if the penalty had been for seven months only, we see how coolly God's judgments would be received in the world. Hence, with the view of engraving this penalty more deeply in the hearts of all, he wished to protract it longer—I will not say to seven years, since I have previously expounded the certain number as put for an uncertain one, implying a long space of time.

Seven years, then, *shall pass away,* says he, *until thou shalt know that there is a lofty ruler in the kingdoms of men.* This is the end of the punishment, as we have previously said, for I need not repeat my former remarks. But we must remember this—God mitigates the bitterness of the penalty by making it temporary. Then he proposed this end to induce Nebuchadnezzar to repent, as he required many blows for this purpose, according to the old proverb about the fool who can never be recalled to a sound mind without suffering calamity. Thus King Nebuchadnezzar ought to be beaten with stripes, to render him submissive to God, as he never profited by any holy admonition or any heavenly oracle. God does not treat all in this way. Hence we have here a special example of his clemency, which provides for the punishment inflicted on King Nebuchadnezzar, being both useful and profitable. For the reprobate are more and more hardened against God, and are ever stirred up and excited to madness. It was an act, then, of special grace, when Nebuchadnezzar was chastised for the time by the hand of God, to cause his repentance and his owning God's entire sway over the whole world.

He says, *that God may be Lord in the kingdom of men;* because nothing is more difficult than to persuade tyrants to submit to the power of God. On the one side they confess themselves to reign by his grace; but at the same time, they suppose their own sway to be obtained by either valour or good fortune, and to be retained by their own guards, counsels, and wealth. Hence, as far as they can, they shut God out from the government of the world, while they are puffed up with a false conceit of themselves, as if all things were maintained in their present state by their valour or advice. This, then, was an ordinary effect when Nebuchadnezzar began to feel *God to be the ruler in the kingdom of men,* since kings wish to place him somewhere between themselves and the multitude. They confess the people to be subject to God's power, but think themselves exempt from the common order of events, and in possession of a privilege in favour of their lusts, relieving them from the hand and empire of God. Hence, as I have said, it was no common thing for Nebuchadnezzar to acknowledge *God to reign in the earth;* for tyrants usually enclose God in heaven, and think him content with his own happiness, and careless about mingling in the concerns of men. Hence *thou mayest know him to be the ruler.* He afterwards adds the kind of dominion, *because God raises up whomsoever he pleases, and casts down others:* God is not only supreme in the sense of sustaining all things by his universal providence, but because no one without his will obtains empire at all. He binds some with a belt, and looseth the bonds of others, as it is said in the book of Job. (Chap. xii. 18.) We ought not, therefore, to imagine God's power to be at rest, but we should join it with present action, as the phrase is. Whether tyrants obtain power, or sovereigns are pious and just, all are governed by God's secret counsel, since otherwise there could be no king of the world. It follows:

33. The same hour was the thing fulfilled upon Nebuchadnezzar; and he was driven from men, and did eat grass as oxen, and his body was wet with the dew of heaven, till his hairs were grown like eagles' *feathers*, and his nails like birds' *claws*.

33. In illa hora sermo completus fuit super Nebuchadnezer, et ab hominibus ejectus est, et herbam tanquam boves comedit, et rore cœlorum corpus ejus irrigatum fuit, donec pilus ejus quasi aquilæ crevit, et ungues ejus quasi avium.

The Prophet concludes what he had said: As soon as the voice had come down from heaven, Nebuchadnezzar was cast out from mankind! Some occasion of expelling him might have preceded this; but since the divination is uncertain, I had rather leave undetermined what the Holy Spirit has not revealed. I only wished to touch upon this point shortly, when he boasted in the foundation of Babylon by the fortitude of his own energy; since his own nobles must have become disgusted when they saw him carried away with such great pride; or he might have spoken in this way when he thought snares were prepared for him, or when he felt some crowds moved against him. Whatever be the meaning, God sent forth his voice, and the same moment he expelled King Nebuchadnezzar from the company of mankind. Hence, *in the same hour,* says he, *the speech was fulfilled.* If a long period had interposed, it might have been ascribed to either fortune or other inferior means, as a reason; but when such is the connection between the language and its effect, the judgment is too clear to be obscured by the malignity of mankind. He says, therefore, *He was cast forth and fed with herbs,* differing in nothing from oxen : *his body was soaked in rain,* since he lay out in the open air. We are ourselves often subject to the drenching shower, and in the fields are sure to meet with it, and travellers often reach their inn wet through. But the Prophet speaks of the continuance of God's judgment, since he had no roof to shelter him, and always lay out in the fields. Hence he says, *he was moistened by the dew of heaven until,* says he, *his nails became claws, and his hair like the wings of eagles.* This passage confirms what has been said concerning the explanation of the seven times as a long period, for his hair could not have grown so in seven months, nor could such great deformity arise. Hence this change, thus described by the Prophet, sufficiently shews King Nebuchadnezzar to have suffered his punishment for a length of time, for he could not be so quickly humbled, because pride is not easily tamed in a man of moderate station, how much less then in so great a monarch ! It afterwards follows :

34. And at the end of the days I Nebuchadnezzar lifted up mine eyes unto heaven, and mine understanding returned unto me, and I blessed the most High, and I praised and honoured him that liveth for ever, whose dominion *is* an everlasting dominion, and his kingdom *is* from generation to generation.

34. Et a fine dierum,[1] ego Nebuchadnezer oculos meos in cœlum extuli, et intellectus meus ad me rediit, et excelsum benedixi, et viventem *in* secula laudavi et glorificavi, quia potestas ejus potestas seculi,[2] et regnum ejus cum ætate et ætate.[3]

The Prophet again introduces King Nebuchadnezzar as the speaker. He says, then, *After that time had elapsed, he raised his eyes to heaven.* Without doubt, he means those seven years. As to his then beginning to raise his eyes to heaven, this shews how long it takes to cure pride, the disease under which he laboured. For when any vital part of the body is corrupt and decaying, its cure is difficult and tedious ; so also when pride exists in men's hearts, and gains an entrance within the marrow, and infects the inmost soul,

---

[1] That is, when the time was passed over.—*Calvin.*
[2] That is, eternal.—*Calvin.*
[3] That is, of perpetual duration.—*Calvin.*

it is not easily plucked out ; and this is worthy of notice.
Then we are taught how God by his word so operated upon
King Nebuchadnezzar, as not immediately and openly to
withdraw the effect of his grace. Nebuchadnezzar profited
by being treated disgracefully during those seven years or
times, and by being driven from the society of mankind ;
but he could not perceive this at once till God opened his
eyes. So, therefore, God often chastises us, and invites us
by degrees, and prepares us for repentance, but his grace
is not immediately acknowledged. But lest I should be too
prolix, I will leave the rest till to-morrow.

PRAYER.

Grant, Almighty God, (since we are nothing in ourselves, and yet
we cease not to please ourselves, and so are blinded by our vain
confidence, and then we vainly boast in our virtues, which are
worthless,) that we may learn to put off these perverse affections.
May we so submit to thee as to depend upon thy mere favour :
may we know ourselves, to stand and be sustained by thy strength
alone : may we learn so to glorify thy name that we may not
only obey thy word with true and pure humility, but also earnestly implore thy assistance, and distrusting ourselves, may rely
upon thy favour as our only support, until at length thou gatherest us into thy heavenly kingdom, where we may enjoy that
blessed eternity which has been obtained for us by thine only-
begotten Son —Amen.

Lecture Twenty-second.

I SHALL now continue the comments which were interrupted yesterday. From Nebuchadnezzar saying, *he raised
his eyes to heaven, and his intellect returned to him*, we
understand him to have been for the time deprived of his
mind. He is much astonished, in my opinion, by feeling his
own evils, but meanwhile he bites the bit and is like a
madman. Some think him to have been a complete maniac ;
I do not contend about this ; it is enough for me to know
he was deprived of his senses and was altogether like the
brutes. But it is probable there was no intelligence remain-

ing, to cause him to feel torture at his slaughter. Meanwhile, he did not raise his eyes to heaven until God drew him to himself. God's chastisements do not profit us unless they work inwardly by his Spirit, as we said yesterday. The phrase only means, he began to think God to be a just judge. For while at the time he felt the sting of his own disgrace, yet as it is said elsewhere, he did not regard the hand of the striker. (Is. ix. 13.) He began, therefore, to acknowledge God to be the avenger of pride, after the aforesaid time had elapsed. For those who cast their eyes down to the earth raise their eyes to heaven. As Nebuchadnezzar ought to awake from his stupor and rise up towards God, of whom he had been formerly forgetful, so he ought to prostrate himself to the earth, as he had already received the reward of his haughtiness. He had dared to raise his head above the lot of man, when he assumed to himself what was peculiar to God. He does not raise his eyes to heaven by any vain confidence, as he had formerly been intoxicated by the splendour of his monarchy; but he looked up to God, while mentally cast down and prostrate.

He afterwards adds, *and I blessed him on high, and praised and glorified him living for ever.* This change shews the punishment to have been chiefly and purposely inflicted on King Nebuchadnezzar, since he spoiled God of his just honour. He here describes the fruit of his repentance. If this feeling flowed from repentance, and Nebuchadnezzar really blessed God, it follows that he was formerly sacrilegious, as he had deprived God of lawful honour and wished to raise himself into his place, as we have already said. Hence, also, we must learn what the true praise of God really is; namely, when reduced to nothing, we acknowledge and determine all things to be according to his will; for, as we shall afterwards see, he is the Governor of heaven and earth, and we should esteem his will as the source of law and reason, and the final appeal of justice. For we may sometimes celebrate the praises of God with ostentation, but it will then be mere pretence; for no one can sincerely and heartily praise him, without ascribing to him all the properties which we shall afterwards see. First of all, Nebuchadnezzar says, *Because his power is eternal, and his kingdom from age to age.* In the first place, he here confesses God to be an eternal king; which is a great step. For human frailty is opposed to this perpetuity; because the greatest monarchs, who excel in power, have nothing firm; they are not only subject to chance and change, as profane men express it— or rather depend upon the will of God—but they utterly fade away through their vanity. We see the whole world fluctuating like the waves of the sea. If there be any tranquillity, in one direction or another, yet every moment something new and sudden may happen, quite unexpectedly. As a tempest arises directly in a calm and serene sky, so also we see it occur in human affairs. Since it is so, no condition upon earth is firm, and monarchs especially disturb themselves by their own turbulent agitations. This is, therefore, the perpetuity which is here predicted by King Nebuchadnezzar; because God as an absolute sovereign rules his own empire for himself, and is thus beyond all danger of change. This is the first point. It now follows:

| 35. And all the inhabitants of the earth *are* reputed as nothing: and he doeth according to his will in the army of heaven, and *among* the inhabitants of the earth; and none can stay his hand, or say unto him, What doest thou? | 35. Et omnes habitatores terræ quasi nihil reputantur, et secundum voluntatem suam facit in exercitu cœlorum, et *in* habitatoribus terræ; et non est qui prohibeat manum ejus,[1] et dicat ei, Quid fecisti?[2] |

Now the opposite clause is added to complete the contrast, because though it follows that nothing is firm or solid in mankind, yet this principle flourishes, namely, God is eternal; yet few reason thus, because in words all allow God to be firm and everlasting, yet they do not descend into themselves and seriously weigh their own frailty. Thus, being unmindful of their own lot, they rage against God himself. The explanation then which occurs here is required; for after Nebuchadnezzar praises God, because his power is eternal, he adds by way of contrast, *all the dwellers on the earth are considered as nothing.* Some take כלה, *keleh,* for a single word, meaning "anything complete," for

[1] Or, who can abolish; for מחא, *mecha,* signifies either to blot out or to prohibit.—*Calvin.*
[2] Or, why hast thou done so?—*Calvin.*

כלה, *keleh*, is to "finish," or "complete;" it also signifies to "consume" sometimes, whence they think the noun to be derived, because men are limited within their own standard, but God is immense. This is harsh; the more received opinion is, that ה *he*, is put for א, *a*, here; and thus Nebuchadnezzar says, men are esteemed as of no value before God. Already, then, we see how suitably these two clauses agree together; for God is an eternal king, and men are as nothing in comparison with him. For if anything is attributed to men as springing from themselves, it so far detracts from the supreme power and empire of God. It follows, then, that God does not entirely receive his rights, until all mortals are reduced to nothing. For although men make themselves of very great importance, yet Nebuchadnezzar here pronounces himself by the Spirit's instinct, to be of no value before God; for otherwise they would not attempt to raise themselves, unless they were utterly blind in the midst of their darkness. But when they are dragged into the light they feel their own nothingness and utter vanity. For whatever we are, this depends on God's grace, which sustains us every moment, and supplies us with new vigour. Hence it is our duty to depend upon God only; because as soon as he withdraws his hand and the virtue of his Spirit, we vanish away. In God we are anything he pleases, in ourselves we are nothing.

It now follows: *God does according to his pleasure in the army of the heavens, and among the dwellers upon earth.* This may seem absurd, since God is said to act according to his will, as if there were no moderation, or equity, or rule of justice, with him. But we must bear in mind, what we read elsewhere concerning men being ruled by laws, since their will is perverse, and they are borne along in any direction by their unruly lust; but God is a law to himself, because his will is the most perfect justice. As often, then, as Scripture sets before us the power of God, and commands us to be content with it, it does not attribute a tyrannical empire to God, according to the calumnies of the impious. But because we do not cease to cavil against God, and oppose our reason to his secret counsels, and thus strive with him, as if he did not act justly and fairly when he does anything which we disapprove; hence God pronounces all things to be done according to his own will, so that the Holy Spirit may restrain this audacity. We should remember then, when mention is made of God, how impossible it is for anything either perverse or unjust to belong to him; his will cannot be turned aside by any affection, for it is the perfection of justice. Since this is so, we should remember how extremely unbridled and perverse our rashness is, while we dare object to anything which God does; whence the necessity of this teaching which puts the bridle of modesty upon us is proved, since God does all things according to his will, as it is said in Psalm cxv. 3, Our God in heaven does what he wishes. From this sentence we gather that nothing happens by chance, but every event in the world depends on God's secret providence. We ought not to admit any distinction between God's permission and his wish. For we see the Holy Spirit—the best master of language—here clearly expresses two things; *first*, what God does; and *next*, what he does by his own will. But *permission*, according to those vain speculators, differs from *will;* as if God unwillingly granted what he did not wish to happen! Now, there is nothing more ridiculous than to ascribe this weakness to God. Hence the efficacy of action is added; *God does what he wishes*, says Nebuchadnezzar. He does not speak in a carnal but in a spiritual sense, or instinct, as we have said; since the Prophet must be attended to just as if he had been sent from heaven. Now, therefore, we understand how this world is administered by God's secret providence, and that nothing happens but what he has commanded and decreed; while he ought with justice to be esteemed the Author of all things.

Some object here to the apparent absurdity of saying God is the author of sin, if nothing is done without his will; nay, if he himself works it! This calumny is easily answered, as the method of God's action differs materially from that of men. For when any man sins, God works in his own manner, which is very different indeed from that of man, since he exercises his own judgment, and thus is said to blind and to harden. As God therefore commands both the reprobate and the evil one, he permits them to indulge in all kinds of licentiousness, and in doing so, executes his own judgments. But he who sins is deservedly guilty, and cannot implicate God as a companion of his wickedness. And why so? Because God has nothing in common with him in reference to sinfulness. Hence we see how these things which we may deem contrary to one another, are mutually accordant, since God by his own will governs all events in the world, and yet is not the author of sin. And why so? Because he treats Satan and all the wicked with the strict justice of a judge. We do not always see the process, but we must hold this principle with firmness—supreme power is in God's hands; hence we must not cavil at his judgments, however inexplicable they may appear to us. Wherefore this phrase follows, *There is no one who can hinder his hand, or can say unto him, Why dost thou act thus?* When Nebuchadnezzar says, God's hand cannot be hindered, he uses this method of deriding human folly which does not hesitate to rebel against God. Already they raise their finger to prevent, if possible, the power of his hand; and even when convicted of weakness, they proceed in their own fury. Nebuchadnezzar, then, deservedly displays their ridiculous madness in conducting themselves so intemperately in wishing to restrain the Almighty, and to confine him within their bounds, and to fabricate chains for the purpose of restricting him. When mankind thus burst forth into sacrilegious fury, they deserve to be laughed at, and this is here the force of Daniel's words.

He afterwards adds, *No one can say, Why dost thou act thus?* We know how they gave way to the language of extreme petulance; since scarcely one man in a hundred restrains himself with such sobriety as to attribute the glory to God, and to confess himself just in his works. But Nebuchadnezzar does not here consider what men are accustomed to do, but what they ought to do. He says therefore, and with strict justice, God cannot be corrected; since however the reprobate chatter, their folly is self-evident, for it has neither reason nor the pretence of reason to support it.

The whole sense is—God's will is our law, against which we strive in vain ; and then, if he permits us sufficient license, and our infirmity breaks forth against him, and we contend with him, all our efforts will be futile. God himself will be justified in his judgments, and thus every human countenance must submit to him. (Ps. li. 6.) This is the general rule.

We must now notice the addition, *God's will must be done as well in the army of heaven as among the inhabitants of earth.* By "the army of heaven" I do not understand, as in other places, the sun, moon, and stars, but angels and even demons, who may be called heavenly without absurdity, if we consider their origin, and their being "princes of the air." Hence Daniel means to imply angels, demons, and men, to be equally governed by God's will ; and although the impious rush on intemperately, yet they are restrained by a secret bridle, and are prevented from executing whatever their lusts dictate. God therefore is said *to do in the army of the heavens and also among men whatsoever he wishes ;* because he has the elect angels always obedient to him, and the devils are compelled to obey his command, although they strive in the contrary direction. We know how strongly the demons resist God, but yet they are compelled to obey him, not willingly, but by compulsion. But God acts among angels and demons just as among the inhabitants of the earth. He governs others by his Spirit, namely, his elect, who are afterwards regenerated by his Spirit, and they are so treated by him that his justice may truly shine forth in all their actions. He also acts upon the reprobate, but in another manner ; for he draws them headlong by means of the devil ; he impels them with his secret virtue ; he strikes them by a spirit of dizziness ; he blinds them and casts upon them a reprobate spirit, and hardens their hearts to contumacy. Behold how God does all things according to his own will among men and angels ! There is also another mode of action, as far as concerns our outward condition ; for God raises one aloft and depresses another. (Ps. cxiii. 7.) Thus we see the rich made poor, and others raised from the dunghill, and placed in the highest stations of honour. The profane call this the sport of fortune! But the moderation of God's providence is most just, although incomprehensible. Thus God acts according to his will among men and angels; but that interior action must be put in the first place, as we have said. It now follows:

36. At the same time my reason returned unto me; and, for the glory of my kingdom, mine honour and brightness returned unto me: and my counsellors and my lords sought unto me; and I was established in my kingdom; and excellent majesty was added unto me.

36. Et in tempore illo intellectus meus rediit ad me, et ad excellentiam regni mei,[2] decor meus et dignitas mea reversa est ad me: et me consiliarii mei et proceres mei requisierunt: et in regno meo confirmatus sum, et dignitas mea amplior aucta[3] fuit mihi.

Here Nebuchadnezzar explains at length what he had previously touched upon but shortly; for he had recovered his soundness of mind, and thus commends God's mercy in being content with a moderate and temporary chastisement; and then he stretched forth his hand, and out of a beast formed a man again! He was not changed into a brute, as we have said, but he was treated with such ignominy, and made like wild beasts, and pastured with them. This deformity, then, was so dreadful, that his restoration might be called a kind of new creation. Hence with very good reason Nebuchadnezzar celebrates this grace of God. *At that time,* therefore, *my intellect returned to me;* he had said this once before, but since understanding and reason are inestimable blessings of God, Nebuchadnezzar inculcates this truth, and confesses himself to have experienced God's singular grace, because he had returned to a sound mind. And at the same time he adds, *he had returned to the honour and glory of his kingdom; because he had been consulted again by his counsellors and elders.* How this was accomplished is unknown, since the memory of those times is buried, unless the princes of his kingdom were inclined to clemency—which is very probable—and desired among them the king who had been cast out. We do not say this was done by them on purpose, because God made use of them,

---

[1] Although זמנא, *zemena,* properly is a time fixed before hand and determined.—*Calvin.*
[2] Namely, "I returned;" for the phrase is elliptical.—*Calvin.*
[3] Was added.—*Calvin.*

and they were ignorantly carrying out his purposes. They had heard the voice from heaven, *O King Nebuchadnezzar, to thee it is said, thy kingdom is departed from thee!* This indeed would be universally known and understood among all men; but we know how easily oblivion creeps over men when God speaks. These princes, then, were unaware of their doing God's work when they demanded their king. In this way he returned to the dignity of his kingdom; and even additional dignity was next conferred upon him. At length it follows:

37. Now I Nebuchadnezzar praise, and extol, and honour the King of heaven, all whose works *are* truth, and his ways judgment: and those that walk in pride he is able to abase.	37. Nunc ego Nebuchadnezer laudo, et extollo, et glorifico Regem cœlorum : quia omnia opera ejus veritas, et viæ ejus judicium: et eos qui ambulant in superbia potest humiliare.[1]

At the close of the edict, Nebuchadnezzar joins the ingenuous confession of his faults with the praises of God! What he says of the proud, he doubtless applies properly to himself; as if he had said, God wished to constitute me a remarkable monument of his method of humbling the proud for the instruction of all mankind. For I was inflated with pride, and God corrected this by so remarkable a punishment, that my example ought to profit the world at large. Hence I said, King Nebuchadnezzar does not simply return thanks to God, but at the same time confesses his fault, for though subdued with deserved harshness, yet his haughtiness could not be arrested by any lighter remedy. First of all he says, *I praise, extol, and glorify the king of heaven!* This heaping together of words doubtless proceeded from vehement affection. At the same time a contrast must be understood, on the principle formerly mentioned; since God is never rightly praised unless the ignominy of men is detected; he is not properly extolled, unless their loftiness is cast down; he is never glorified unless men are buried in shame and lie prostrate in the dust. Hence, while Nebuchadnezzar here praises, extols, and glorifies God, he also confesses himself and all mortals to be nothing—as he did before—to deserve no praise but rather the utmost ignominy.

[1] That is, for humbling the proud.—*Calvin.*

He adds, *since all his works are truth.* Here קשוט, *kesot,* is taken for "rectitude or integrity." For דיני־אמת, *diniameth,* mean true judgments, but refer here to equity. *God's works are* therefore *all truth,* that is, all integrity, as if he had said, none of God's works deserve blame. Then the explanation follows, *All his ways are judgments.* We see here the praise of God's perfect justice; this ought to be referred to Nebuchadnezzar personally, as if he had said, God does not deal with me too strictly; I have no reason for expostulating with him, or for murmuring as if he were too severe with me. I confess, therefore, that I deserve whatever punishment I sustain. And why so? *All his ways are justice;* meaning the highest rectitude. Then, *All his works are truth;* that is, nothing contrary to equity is found there, nothing crooked, but everywhere the highest justice will shine forth. We see then how Nebuchadnezzar by this language condemns himself out of his own mouth by declaring God's justice to be in all his works. This general form of expression does not prevent Nebuchadnezzar from openly and freely confessing himself a criminal before God's tribunal; but it acquires greater force by his example, which admonishes us by the general confession of God's justice, rectitude, and truthfulness in whatever he does. And this is worthy of notice, since many find no difficulty in celebrating God's justice and rectitude when they are treated just as they like; but if God begins to treat them with severity, they then vomit forth their poison and begin to quarrel with God, and to accuse him of injustice and cruelty. Since therefore Nebuchadnezzar here confesses God to be just and true in all his works, without any exception, notwithstanding his own severe chastisements, this confession is not feigned; for he necessarily utters what he says from the lowest depths of his heart, through his having experienced the rigour of the divine judgment.

He now adds at last, *He can humble those who walk in pride.* Here Nebuchadnezzar more openly displays his own disgrace, for he is not ashamed to confess his fault before the whole world, because his punishment was known to every one. As God then wished his folly to be universally detested, by making so horrible an example of him by his punishment, so Nebuchadnezzar now brings his own case forward, and bears witness to the justice of the penalty, in consequence of his extreme pride. Here then we see God's power joined with his justice, as we have previously mentioned. He does not attribute to God a tyranny free from all law; for as soon as Nebuchadnezzar had confessed all God's ways to be just, he condemns himself of pride directly afterwards. Hence he does not hesitate to expose his disgrace before mankind, that God may be glorified. And this is the true method of praising God, not only by confessing ourselves to be as nothing, but also by looking back upon our failings. We ought not only to acknowledge ourselves inwardly guilty before him, but also openly to testify the same before all mankind whenever it is necessary. And when he uses the word "humility," this may be referred to outward dejection; for Nebuchadnezzar was humbled when God cast him out into the woods to pass his life in company with the wild beasts. But he was also humbled for another reason, as if he had been a son of God. Since this humbling is twofold, Nebuchadnezzar wishes here to express the former kind, because God prostrates and throws down the proud. This is one kind of humiliation; but it becomes profitless unless God afterwards governs us by a spirit of submission. Hence Nebuchadnezzar does not here embrace the grace of God, which was worthy of no common praise and exaltation; and in this edict he does not describe what is required of a pious man long trained in God's school; yet he shews how he had profited under God's rod, by attributing to him the height of power. Besides this, he adds the praise of justice and rectitude, while he confesses himself guilty, and bears witness to the justice of the punishment which had been divinely inflicted on him.

PRAYER.

Grant, Almighty God, since the disease of pride remains fixed in us all through our original corruption in our father Adam,—Grant, I say, that we may learn to mortify our spirits, and to be displeased with our conduct, as we ought; may we feel ourselves to be deprived of all wisdom and rectitude without thee alone. May we fly to thy pity, and confess ourselves utterly subject to eternal death; may we rely on thy goodness which thou hast deigned to offer us through thy Gospel; may we trust in that Mediator whom thou hast given us; may we never hesitate to fly to thee, to call upon thee as our Father, and having been renewed by thy Spirit, may we walk in true humility and modesty, till at length thou shalt raise us to that heavenly kingdom which has been obtained for us by the blood of thine only-begotten Son.—Amen.

Lecture Twenty-third.

CHAPTER FIFTH.

1. Belshazzar the king made a great feast to a thousand of his lords, and drank wine before the thousand.

1. Beltsazar rex fecit convivium magnum proceribus suis mille, et coram mille vinum bibit.

DANIEL here refers to the history of what happened at the taking of Babylon; but meanwhile he leaves those judgments of God to the consideration of his readers, which the Prophets had predicted before the people had become exiles. He does not use the prophetic style, as we shall afterwards see, but is content with simple narrative; while the practice of history may be learnt from the following expressions. It is our duty now to consider how this history tends towards building us up in the faith and fear of God. First of all we notice the time at which Belshazzar celebrated this banquet. Seventy years had passed away from the time when Daniel had been led into exile with his companions. For although Nebuchadnezzar will soon be called the father of Belshazzar, yet it is clear enough that Evil-Merodach lived between them; for he reigned twenty-three years. Some reckon two kings before Belshazzar; for they place Regassar after Labassardach; and these two will occupy eight years. Metasthenes has stated it so, and he has many followers. But Nebuchadnezzar the Great, who took Daniel captive, and was the son of the first king of that name, evidently reigned forty-five years. Some transfer two years to the reign of his father; at any rate, he held the regal power for forty-five years; and if the twenty-three years of Evil-Merodach are added, they will make sixty-eight years—in which Belshazzar had reigned eight years. We see, then, how seventy-two years had passed away from the period of Daniel being first led captive. Metasthenes reckons thirty years for the reign of Evil-Merodach; and then, if we add eight years, this makes more than eighty years—which appears probable enough, although Metasthenes seems to be in error in supposing different kings instead of only different names.[1] For Herodotus does not call Belshazzar, of whom we are now speaking, a king, but calls his father Labynetus, and gives him the same name.[2] Metasthenes makes some mistakes in names, but I readily embrace his computation of time, when he asserts Evil-Merodach to have reigned thirty years. For when we treat of the seventy years which Jeremiah had formerly pointed out, we ought not to begin with Daniel's exile, nor yet with the destruction of the city, but with the slaughter which occurred between the first victory of king Nebuchadnezzar, and the burning and ruin of the temple and city. For when the report concerning the death of his father was first spread abroad, as we have elsewhere said, he returned to his own country, lest any disturbance should occur through his absence. Hence we shall find the seventy years during which God wished the people's captivity to last, will require a longer period for the reign of Evil-Merodach than twenty-three years; although there is not any important difference, for soon after Nebuchadnezzar returned, he carried off the king, leaving the city untouched. Although the temple was then standing, yet God had inflicted the severest punishment upon the people, which was like a final slaughter, or at least nearly equal to it. However this was, we see that Belshazzar was celebrating this banquet just as the time of the deliverance drew nigh.

Here we must consider the Providence of God, in arranging the times of events, so that the impious, when the time of their destruction is come, cast themselves headlong of their own accord. This occurred to this wicked king. Wonderful

---

[1] See the DISSERTATIONS at the end of this volume, in which these historical points are treated at length.
[2] Herod., lib. i. sect. 188. Comp. *Cyropœd.*, lib. iv. and vii.

indeed was the stupidity which prepared a splendid banquet filled with delicacies, while the city was besieged. For Cyrus had begun to besiege the city for a long time with a large army. The wretched king was already half a captive; and yet, as if in spite of God, he provided a rich banquet, and invited a thousand guests. Hence we may conjecture the extent of the noise and of the expense in that banquet. For if any one wishes to entertain only ten or twenty guests, it will occasion him much trouble, if he wishes to treat them splendidly. But when it was a royal entertainment, where there were a thousand nobles with the king's wife and concubines, and so great a multitude assembled together, it became necessary to obtain from many quarters what was required for such a festival; and this may seem incredible! But Xenophon though he related many fables and preserved neither the gravity nor the fidelity of a historian, because he desired to celebrate the praises of Cyrus like a rhetorician; although he trifles in many things, yet here had no reason or occasion for deception. He says a treasure was laid up, so that the Babylonians could endure a siege of even ten or more years. And Babylon was deservedly compared to a kingdom; for its magnitude was so large as to surpass belief. It must really have been very populous, but since they drew their provisions from the whole of Asia, it is not surprising that the Babylonians had food in store, sufficient to allow them to close their gates, and to sustain them for a long period. But in this banquet it was most singular that the king, who ought to have been on guard, or at least have sent forth his guards to prevent the city from being taken, was as intent upon his delicacies as if he had been in perfect peace, and exposed to no danger from any outward enemy. He had a contest with a strong man, if any man ever was so. Cyrus was endued with singular prudence, and in swiftness of action by far excelled all others. Since, then, the king was so keenly opposed, it is surprising to find him so careless as to celebrate a banquet. Xenophon, indeed, states the day to have been a festival. The assertion of those Jews who think the Chaldeans had just obtained a victory over the Persians, is but trifling. For Xenophon—who may be trusted whenever he does not falsify history in favour of Cyrus, because he is then a very grave historian, and entirely worthy of credit; but when he desires to praise Cyrus, he has no moderation—is here historically correct, when he says the Babylonians were holding a usual annual festival. He tells us also how Babylon was taken, viz., by Gobryas and Gadatas his generals. For Belshazzar had castrated one of these to his shame, and had slain the son of the other in the lifetime of his father. Since then the latter burnt with the desire of avenging his son's death, and the former his own disgrace, they conspired against him. Hence Cyrus turned the many channels of the Euphrates, and thus Babylon was suddenly taken. The city we must remember was twice taken, otherwise there would not have been any confidence in prophecy; because when the Prophets threaten God's vengeance upon the Babylonians, they say their enemies should be most fierce, not seeking gold or silver, but desiring human blood; and then they narrate every kind of atrocious deed which is customary in war. (Jer. l. 42.) But nothing of this kind happened when Babylon was taken by Cyrus; but when the Babylonians freed themselves from the Persian sway by casting off their yoke, Darius recovered the city by the assistance of Zopyrus, who mutilated his person, and pretended to have suffered such cruelty from the king as to induce him to betray the city. But then we collect how hardly the Babylonians were afflicted, when 3000 nobles were crucified! And what usually happens when 3000 nobles are put to death, and all suspended on a gallows—nay, even crucified? Thus it easily appears, how severely the Babylonians were punished at the time, although they were then subject to a foreign power, and treated shamefully by the Persians, and reduced to the condition of slaves. For they were forbidden the use of arms, and were taught from the first to become the slaves of Cyrus, and dare not wear a sword. We ought to touch upon these things shortly to assure us of the government of human events by the judgment of God, when he casts headlong the reprobate when their punishment is at hand. We have an illustrious example of this in King Belshazzar.

The time of the deliverance predicted by Jeremiah was at hand—the seventy years were finished—Babylon was besieged. (Jer. xxv. 11.) The Jews might now raise up their heads and hope for the best, because the arrival of Cyrus approached, contrary to the opinion of them all; for he had suddenly rushed down from the mountains of Persia when that was a barbarous nation. Since, therefore, the sudden coming of Cyrus was like a whirlwind, this change might possibly give some hope to the Jews; but after a length of time, so to speak, had elapsed in the siege of the city, this might cast down their spirits. While king Belshazzar was banqueting with his nobles, Cyrus seems able to thrust him out in the midst of his merriment and hilarity. Meanwhile the Lord did not sit at rest in heaven; for he blinds the mind of the impious king, so that he should willingly incur punishments, yet no one drew him on, for he incurred it himself. And whence could this arise, unless God had given him up to his enemy? It was according to that decree of which Jeremiah was the herald. Hence, although Daniel narrates the history, it is our duty, as I have said, to treat of things far more important; for God who had promised his people deliverance, was now stretching forth his hand in secret, and fulfilling the predictions of his Prophets. (Jer. xxv. 26.)

It now follows—*King Belshazzar was drinking wine before a thousand.* Some of the Rabbis say, " he strove with his thousand nobles, and contended with them all in drinking to excess;" but this seems grossly ridiculous. When he says, *he drank wine before a thousand,* he alludes to the custom of the nation, for the kings of the Chaldeans very rarely invited guests to their table; they usually dined alone, as the kings of Europe now do; for they think it adds to their dignity to enjoy a solitary meal. The pride of the kings of Chaldea was of this kind When, therefore, it is said, *Belshazzar drank wine before a thousand,* something extraordinary is intended, since he was celebrating this annual banquet contrary to his ordinary custom, and he deigned to treat his nobles with such honour as to receive them as his guests. Some, indeed, conjecture that he drank wine openly, as he was accustomed to become intoxicated when there were no witnesses present; but there is no force in this comment: the word *before* means in the presence or society of others. Let us go on:

2. Belshazzar, whiles he tasted the wine, commanded to bring the golden and silver vessels which his father Nebuchadnezzar had taken out of the temple which *was* in Jerusalem; that the king and his princes, his wives and his concubines, might drink therein.

2. Beltsazar præcepit[1] in gustu, vel, sapore, vini, ut afferrent vasa auri et argenti,[2] quæ asportaverat, vel, extulerat, Nebuchadnezer pater ejus ex templo quod *est* in Jerusalem, ut biberent in illis rex, et proceres ejus, uxores et concubinæ.[3]

Here king Belshazzar courts his own punishment, because he furiously stirred up God's wrath against himself, as if he was dissatisfied with its delay while God put off his judgment for so long a period. This is according to what I have said. When the destruction of a house is at hand, the impious remove the posts and gates, as Solomon says. (Prov. xvii. 19.) God therefore, when he wishes to execute his judgments, impels the reprobate by a secret instinct to rush forward of their own accord, and to hasten their own destruction. Belshazzar did this. His carelessness was the sign of his stupidity, and also of God's wrath, when in the midst of his own pride and crimes he could delight in revelling. Thus his blindness more clearly points out God's vengeance, since he was not content with his own intemperance and excesses, but must openly declare war against God. *He ordered,* therefore, says he, *the gold and silver vessels to be brought to him which he had taken away from Nebuchadnezzar.* These vessels appear to have been laid up in the treasury; hence Nebuchadnezzar had never abused these vessels in his lifetime; we do not read that Evil-Merodach did anything of this kind, and Belshazzar now wishes purposely to inflict this insult on God. There is no doubt he brought forth those vessels by way of ridicule, for the purpose of triumphing over the true God, as we shall afterwards see.

[1] Verbally it means said, but here it signifies commanded.—*Calvin.*
[2] Made of gold and silver.—*Calvin.*
[3] Some translate his wife, since there was one principal wife, who alone was the king's companion, and she received the name of Queen, as we shall afterwards see.—*Calvin.*

We have already explained the sense in which the Prophet calls Nebuchadnezzar the father of Belshazzar, since it is usual in all languages to speak of ancestors as fathers; for Belshazzar was of the offspring of Nebuchadnezzar, and being really his grandson, he is naturally called his son; and this will occur again. There are some who think Evil-Merodach was stricken with that grievous affliction mentioned in the last chapter: possibly his name was Nebuchadnezzar, but there is no reason for adopting their opinion;[1] it is frivolous to fly directly to this conjecture when the name of the father occurs. The Prophet says *Belshazzar committed this under the influence of wine.* Since טעם, *tegnem*, signifies "to taste," no doubt he here speaks of tasting; and since this may be metaphorically transferred to the understanding, some explain it to mean being impelled by wine, and thus his drunkenness took the place of reason and judgment. Nights and love and wine, says Ovid, have no moderation in them.[2] This explanation I think too forced; it seems simply to mean, when Belshazzar grew warm with wine, he commanded the vessels to be brought to him; and this is the more usual view. When, therefore, the savour of the wine prevailed,—that is, when it seized upon the king's senses, *then he ordered the vessels to be brought.* It is worth while to notice this, to induce us to be cautious concerning intemperance in drinking, because nothing is more common than the undertaking many things far too rashly when our senses are under the influence of wine. Hence we must use wine soberly, that it may invigorate not only the body but the mind and the senses, and may never weaken, or enervate, or stupify our bodily or mental powers. And this is, alas! too common, since the vulgar proverb is well known—pride springs from drunkenness. For this reason the poets supposed Bacchus to have horns, since intemperate men are

---

[1] This is the view of the Duke of Manchester; it is ably supported in his learned volume on "The Times of Daniel." As we have had occasion to review the general argument elsewhere, we merely allude to it here.— See DISSERTATIONS.

[2] Ars. Amor., Eleg. vi. The French translation is worthy of notice,—
"La nuiet, l'amour, le boire sans mesure,
N'induit a rien sinon a toute ordure."—*Ed.*

always puffed up, and the most wretched fancy themselves kings. What then must happen to monarchs, when in their forgetfulness they dream themselves kings of kings, and even deities? The Prophet wishes to mark this fault when he says, *Belshazzar, under the influence of wine, ordered vessels to be brought to him.* It now follows,—

3. Then they brought the golden vessels that were taken out of the temple of the house of God which *was* at Jerusalem; and the king and his princes, his wives and his concubines, drank in them.	3. Tunc attulerunt vasa aurea quæ extulerant ex templo domus Dei quæ erat in Jerusalem: et biberunt in illis rex, et proceres ejus, et uxor,[1] et concubinæ ipsius.

The Prophet uses the word "golden," probably, because the most precious vessels were brought; silver might also have been added, but the more splendid ones are noticed. He does not say that Nebuchadnezzar carried them off, but implies it to be the common act of all the Babylonians. They obtained the victory under the direction of this king, hence he used the spoils; and since they were all engaged in the victory, the Prophet speaks of them all. In using the phrase, "the temple," he expresses more than before, by saying, not from Jerusalem only but from the temple of God's house.

4. They drank wine, and praised the gods of gold, and of silver, of brass, of iron, of wood, and of stone.	4. Biberunt vinum, et laudarunt deos aureos, et argenteos, æreos, ferreos, ligneos, et lapideos.

Here the Prophet shews more distinctly and clearly how the king insulted the true and only God, by ordering his vessels to be brought to him. For when they had been brought forth, *they praised,* says he, *all their gods of gold and silver;* meaning in defiance of the true God they celebrated the praises of their false deities, and thanked them, as we find in Habakkuk. (Ch. i. 16.) Although there is no doubt they sacrificed heartily the produce of their industry, as the Prophet there expresses it, yet they exalted their own gods, and thus obliterated the glory of the true God. And this is the reason why the Prophet now takes pains to state those vessels to have been brought *from the temple of God's house.* For he here strengthens the impiety of the king and his

---

[1] Or, "wives," in the plural number.—*Calvin.*

nobles for erecting their horns against the God of Israel. There is then a great contrast between God who commanded his temple to be built at Jerusalem, and sacrifices to be offered to him and false gods. And this was the head and front of Belshazzar's offending, because he thus purposely rose up against God, and not only tyrannically and miserably oppressed the Jews, but triumphed over their God—the Creator of heaven and earth. This madness accelerated his ultimate destruction, and it occurred for the purpose of hastening the time of their deliverance. Hence I have represented him to have been drawn by God's great instinct to such madness that vengeance might be ripened.

They drank, says he, *wine, and praised their gods.* The Prophet does not ascribe the praise of their gods to drunkenness, but he obliquely shews their petulance to have been increased by drink. For if each had been sober at home, he would not have thus rashly risen up against God; but when impiety exists in the heart, intemperance becomes an additional stimulus. The Prophet seems to me to mean this, when he repeats, *they were drinking;* for he had said, *the king and his nobles, his wife, and concubines, were drinking.* He now inculcates the same thing in similar words, but adds, *they drank wine,*—meaning their madness was the more inflamed by the excitement of the wine. *Then they praised the gods of silver,* &c. The Prophet here reproachfully mentions *gods of gold, silver, brass, wood, and stone,* since we know God to have nothing in common with either gold or silver. His true image cannot be expressed in corruptible materials; and this is the reason why the Prophet calls all the gods which the Babylonians worshipped, *golden, silver, brazen, wooden, and stone.* Clearly enough the heathen never were so foolish as to suppose the essence of Deity to reside in gold, or silver, or stone; they only called them images of their deities; but because in their opinion the power and majesty of the deity was included within the material substance, the Prophet is right in so completely condemning their criminality, because we hear how carefully idolaters invent every kind of subtlety. In the present times, the Papacy is a glaring proof how men cling to gross superstitions when they desire to excuse their errors; hence the Prophet does not here admit those vain pretences by which the Babylonians and other heathens disguise their baseness, but he says, *their gods were of silver and gold.* And why so? for although they orally confessed that gods reign in heaven, (so great was the multitude and crowd of their deities that the supreme God was quite shrouded in darkness,) although therefore the Babylonians confessed their gods to have dwelt in heaven, yet they fled to statues and pictures. Hence the Prophet deservedly chides them *for adoring gods of gold and silver.* As to his saying, *then the vessels were brought,* it shews how the slaves of tyrants obey them in the worst actions, because no delay intervened in bringing the vessels from the treasury. Daniel therefore signifies how all the king's servants were obedient to his nod, and desirous of pleasing a person brutish and drunken; at the same time he shews the shortness of that intemperate intoxication; for he says,—

5. In the same hour came forth fingers of a man's hand, and wrote over against the candlestick upon the plaster of the wall of the king's palace; and the king saw the part of the hand that wrote.

5. In illa hora egressi sunt digiti manus hominis, et scribebant e regione lucernæ[1] super calcem parietis[2] palatii regis, et rex cernebat palmam[3] manus scribentis.

Here Daniel begins his narration of the change which took place, for at that instant the king acknowledged something sorrowful and disturbing to be at hand. Yet, as he did not at once understand what it was, God gave him a sign as an omen of calamity, according to the language of the profane. In this way God sent him warning when he saw the king and his nobles raging with mad licentiousness. *There appeared,* then, *the hand of a man,* says the Prophet, using this expression from its similitude and form. We are sure it was not a man's hand; it had the appearance of one, and hence was called so. Scripture often uses this method of expression, especially when treating external symbols.

[1] Or, "candlestick;" some explain it, "window."—*Calvin.*
[2] Some consider it the surface, others the roof, which is probable.—*Calvin.*
[3] Others translate it "finger."—*Calvin.*

This is, then, a sacramental form of speech,[1] if I may use the expression. God, indeed, wrote the inscription by his own power, but he shews King Belshazzar the figure as if a man had written it on the wall; hence *the fingers of a hand were put forth.* This expression conduces in no slight degree to the reality of the miracle; for if Belshazzar had seen this on the wall from the very first, he might have supposed some artifice had placed the hand there; but when the wall was previously bare, and then the hand suddenly appeared, we may readily understand the hand to have been a sign from heaven, through which God wished to shew something important to the king. *The fingers of a hand,* then, *were put forth, and wrote from the midst of the candlestick,* or lamp. Clearly, then, this was a feast by night, and Babylon was taken in the midst of the night. No wonder their banquets were protracted to a great length, for intemperance has no bounds. When men are accustomed to spend the day in luxury, I confess indeed they do not usually continue their banquets till midnight; but when they celebrate any splendid and remarkable feast, they do not find the daylight sufficient for their festivites and the grosser indulgences of the table.

Hence *the hand appeared from the candlesticks* to render it the more conspicuous. That hand, says the Prophet, wrote on the surface of the palace wall. If any one had announced to the king this appearance of a human hand, he might have doubted it; but he says the king was an eye-witness, for God wished to terrify him, as we shall afterwards see, and hence he set before him this spectacle. *The king,* then, *perceived it;* perhaps his nobles did not; and we shall afterwards see how the terror operated upon the king alone, unless, indeed, some others trembled with him. When, therefore, they saw his countenance changed and exhibiting proofs of terror, they began to fear, although they were all desirous of affording him some consolation. Hence God wished to summon this impious king to His tribunal when the hand of a man appeared before him in the act of writing. We shall see what it wrote in its proper place.

[1] This phrase is worthy of notice. The Latin is "*sacramentalis locutio;*" the French, "*est aussi sacramentale.*" See our *Ezekiel,* vol. ii., p. 312 and note, where the Sabbath is termed *a Sacrament.*

PRAYER.

Grant, Almighty God, since we are so prone to forgetfulness and to our own indulgence in the desires and pleasures of the flesh,— Grant, I say, to each of us to be recalled to the contemplation of thy judgments; and may we be anxious to walk as in thy sight. May we be afraid of thy just vengeance, be careful not to provoke it by our petulance and other vices; but may we submit ourselves to thee, be held up, and propped up by thy hands, and proceed in the sacred course of thy calling, until at length thou shalt raise us to thy heavenly kingdom, which has been acquired for us by the blood of thine only-begotten Son.— Amen.

Lecture Twenty-fourth.

6. Then the king's countenance was changed, and his thoughts troubled him, so that the joints of his loins were loosed, and his knees smote one against another.

6. Tunc Regis vultus[1] mutatus est: et cogitationes ejus terruerunt eum, et ligamina lumborum ejus solvebantur,[2] et poplites ejus invicem collisi sunt.

HERE Daniel shews how the king's mind was struck with fear, lest any one should think his fright without foundation. But he expresses, by many circumstances, how disturbed the king was, and thus the sufficiency of the reason would easily appear. It was needful for him to be so struck, that all might understand how God was seated on his throne, and summoned him as a criminal. We mentioned before how Daniel impresses us with the pride of this king, and his careless security is a clear proof of it. When the daily siege of the city ought to have rendered him anxious, he was celebrating his usual banquets, as if in profound peace. Whence he appears to be corrupted by a kind of spiritual drunkenness, so as not to feel his own calamities. This, then, is the reason why God roused him up and awakened him from his lethargy, because no ordinary means were effectual in recalling him to soundness of mind. The fear which he experienced might seem a convenient preparation for penitence.

[1] "The form or figure," verbally.—*Calvin.*
[2] "His hip-joints," for the Hebrews and Chaldees use roundabout expressions.—*Calvin.*

But we see the same thing in this case as we do in that of Esau; for he was not only touched with contrition when he saw himself cut off, but he uttered a loud and piercing lamentation when seeking his father's "blessing," and yet he was too late. (Gen. xxvii. 34.) A similar occurrence is related here of King Belshazzar, but we must remark upon everything in order. Daniel says, *The king's countenance was changed;* then, *the joints of his limbs were loosened, and he was disturbed,* or frightened, *in his thoughts;* and lastly, he adds, *his knees smote together.* The word properly signifies, to strike one against another. By these signs the Prophet shews how King Belshazzar was frightened by the vision already mentioned. Without doubt, as I have just said, God inspired him with this terror, for we know even when God has openly ascended to his own tribunal, how stupid the reprobate remain, and how immovable! But God wished to affect the mind of this impious king, and to render his ignorance without excuse.

Here we may remark, generally, in how many ways God touches men's hearts—not those of the reprobate only, but also of his elect, for we see even the best men slow and slothful when God summons them to his judgment-seat. It becomes necessary to chastise them with rods, otherwise they never approach God of their own accord. He might, indeed, move their minds without violence; but he wishes to set before us, as in a glass, our slowness and slothfulness, since we do not obey his word with natural willingness. Hence he tames his children with cords when they will not profit by his word. With regard to the reprobate, he often chides their obstinacy, because, before he undertakes the office of judge, he kindly entices them; when they do not profit by this, he threatens; and when his threats are useless and devoid of efficacy, he then calls them to his tribunal. Respecting the fate of the King of Babylon, God had suffered Daniel to be silent, for his ingratitude and pride had closed the door, so as to prevent Daniel from undertaking the office of a teacher as he was prepared to do; hence the King of Babylon continued without one. But God suddenly appeared as a judge, by the writing of which we have shortly spoken, and of which we shall say more in the proper place. Whatever its meaning may be, we see King Belshazzar not only admonished by an outward sign of his approaching death, but inwardly stirred up to acknowledge himself to be dealing with God. For the reprobate often enjoy their own pleasures, as I have said, although God shews himself to be their judge. But he treats King Belshazzar differently: he desires to inspire him with terror, to render him more attentive to the perusal of the writing. This time was, as I have said, a preparation for repentance; but he failed in the midst of his course, as we see too many do who tremble at the voice of God and at the signs of his vengeance, as soon as he admonishes them; but these feelings are but evanescent; thus proving how little they have learnt of the necessary lesson.

The example of Esau is similar to this, since he despised God's grace when he heard himself deprived of the inheritance divinely promised him. (Gen. xxv. 33.) He treated the blessing as a fable till he found it a serious matter; he then began to lament, but all in vain. Such also was the fright of King Belshazzar, as we shall soon perceive. Even when Daniel explained the writing to him, he was by no means moved by it, but adorned Daniel with royal tokens of regard. Yet the object and use of this was totally different, for when the nobles were moved, and the reality became manifest, God in this way demonstrated his glory: and Darius, who took the city, with his son-in-law Cyrus, understood how his own valour and perseverance were not the sole cause of his victory, and how the satraps, Gobryas and Gadata, would not have assisted him so materially unless the whole affair had been under God's auspices. Thus God shewed himself as in a glass to be the avenger of his people, as he had promised seventy years previously. It now follows:—

7. The king cried aloud to bring in the astrologers, the Chaldeans, and the soothsayers. *And* the king spake, and said to the wise *men* of Babylon, Whosoever shall read this writing, and shew me the interpretation thereof, shall be clothed with

7. Clamavit rex fortiter, ut introducerentur magi, Chaldæi, et astrologi,[1] et loquutus est rex, et dixit sapientibus Babylonis, Quisquis legerit scripturam hanc, et interpretationem ejus indicaverit mihi, purpura vestietur, et torques ex

[1] We have previously explained these words.—*Calvin.*

scarlet, and *have* a chain of gold about his neck, and shall be the third ruler in the kingdom.

auro, *hoc est, aureus,* super collum ejus, et tertius in regno dominabitur.

The Prophet narrates how King Belshazzar sought a remedy for his anxiety; hence we gather how his mind was so immediately wounded, and how he felt he could not escape God's hand, otherwise he would not have called the wise men so suddenly in the midst of the banquet. Again, when the Prophet says, *He cried out loudly,* he was clearly so astonished as to forget his being king, for to cry out at table was not consistent with his dignity. But God expelled all pride from him, by compelling him to burst forth into a cry, like a man completely beside himself. We must now consider the remedy to which he resorted: he ordered the *Chaldeans, and magi, and astrologers to be called.* We learn from this how exceedingly prone men are to vanity, lying, and falsehood. Daniel ought to have been first, even among the Chaldeans, for that was an answer worthy of remembrance which he had given to the grandfather of this king, when he predicted his becoming like the beasts of the forest. Since this prophecy was verified by the event, his authority ought to have flourished even to a thousand years. He was daily in the king's sight, and yet he was neglected, while the king sent for all the Chaldeans, and astrologers, and diviners, and magi. Truly enough, these men were then in so great repute that they deservedly obscured the fame of Daniel, for they were indignant at a captive being preferred to native teachers, when they knew their own glory amongst all peoples depended upon the persuasion of their being the only wise men. As, therefore, they wished to retain their good opinion, as being God's counsellors, no wonder they despised this stranger. But this feeling cannot avail for a moment before God: for what can be urged in defence of the king's impiety? His grandfather was a memorable instance of God's vengeance, when rejected from the company of men, and compelled to dwell among the wildest beasts of the forest. This, truly, could not appear a matter of chance. God, then, had first admonished him by a dream, and next sent his own Prophet as the interpreter of the oracle and the vision. As I have said, the fame of this event ought to have been perpetual among the Chaldeans, yet the grandson of King Nebuchadnezzar had forgotten his example, insulted the God of Israel, profaned the vessels of the temple, and triumphed with his idols! When God sets before him the sign of his judgment, he calls together the magi and the Chaldeans, and passes by Daniel. And what possible excuse can he have for this? We have seen, as I have said, how very prone men are to be deluded by Satan's impostures, and the well-known proverb becomes true,—The world loves to be deceived!

This, also, is worthy of notice, because in the present day, and in troublous times, many protect themselves behind the shield of their ignorance. But the explanation is at hand—they are willingly blind; they shut their eyes amidst the clearest light; for if God considered King Belshazzar without excuse when the Prophet was once presented to him, what excuse can the blind of these days allege? Oh! if I could determine what God's will is for me, I would submit myself instantly to it, because God daily and openly calls to us and invites us, and shews us the way; but none answer him, none follow him, or at least how very few! Hence we must diligently consider the example of the King of Babylon when we see him full of anxiety, and yet not seeking God as he ought. And why so? He wanders about in great hesitation; he sees himself constrained, and yet he cannot fly from the judgment of God, but seeks consolation in magi, Chaldeans, and other impostors; for, as we have seen, they had been once or twice proved so, and this ought to have been sufficiently celebrated and notorious to all men. We see, then, how blind King Belshazzar was, since he closed his eyes to the light offered him. So in the present day almost all the world continues in blindness; it is not allowed to wander in darkness, but when light shines upon it, it closes its eyes, rejects God's grace, and purposely desires to cast itself headlong. This conduct is far too common.

Now the Prophet says,—*The king promised the wise men a present of a chain of gold to whoever read the writing;* and besides this, *raiment of purple, and the third rank in the kingdom!* This shews him not to have been sincerely touched by the fear of God. And this repugnance is worthy of observation in the wicked, who dread God's judgments, and yet the pride of their hearts is not corrected and subdued, as we saw in the case of this king. For *his knees smote one against the other, and the joints of his loins were loosened:* he trembles throughout his entire frame, and becomes half dead with fear, because God's terror seizes on all his senses. Meanwhile, we see a hidden pride lurking in his mind, which breaks forth in the promise, *whoever shall interpret the writing, shall be the third in rank in the kingdom!* God had already deprived him of his royal dignity; yet he still wishes to raise others on high in defiance of God! What, then, is the meaning of this? We see how often the wicked are terrified, and how deeply they cherish a hidden contumacy, so that God never subdues them. They shew, indeed, many signs of repentance; but if any one carefully weighs all their words and deeds, he will find the Prophet's narration concerning King Belshazzar completely verified, because they rage against God, and are never teachable or obedient, but utterly stupified. We saw this partly in a former verse, and shall see it again more clearly at the end of the chapter. As to the latter clause of the verse, *he shall rule as third in the kingdom,* it is uncertain whether he promises the third portion or the third rank; for many think the queen, of whom mention will soon be made, was the wife of King Nebuchadnezzar, and grandmother of King Belshazzar. It follows:—

8. Then came in all the king's wise *men:* but they could not read the writing, nor make known to the king the interpretation thereof. 9. Then was king Belshazzar greatly troubled, and his countenance was changed in him, and his lords were astonied.	8. Tunc ingressi sunt omnes sapientes regis, et non potuerunt scripturam legere, et interpretationem ejus patefacere regi. 9. Tunc rex Beltsazar multum territus fuit, et vultus ejus mutatus fuit super eum, *in eo:* et principes ejus *fuerunt* obstupefacti.[1]

Here Daniel relates how deceived the king was in his opinion, in hoping for any interpretation of the writing from either the magi or the astrologers, the Chaldeans or the

[1] Or, anxious.—*Calvin.*

soothsayers; for none of them could read it. Hence he pays here the punishment of his ingratitude in passing over God's Prophet, while he knew he had predicted truth to his grandfather just as it had happened, as well as Daniel's general excellence in wisdom. Hence the proofs of his calling were sufficiently numerous and trustworthy. Since, then, he had so despised God's unparalleled benefit, he is destitute of counsel, and sees himself call in vain upon all the Chaldeans and astrologers. For Daniel says, *There was no one who could read the writing or reveal its interpretation to the king.* Because this seems absurd, many Rabbis have hazarded various conjectures. Some think the letters were transposed; others guess that they were changed into their counterparts and equivalents; and others think the characters were changed. But we have elsewhere shewn how bold the Jews are in their conjectures, whenever they have no certain guide. We do not require their guesses, because, very probably, the writing was visible to the king and concealed from all the Chaldeans, or else they were so blind that they could see nothing; just as God denounced against the Jews a stupor of this kind. We see what he pronounces, by Isaiah, (xxix. 11,) "Your law shall be like a sealed book: If it shall be said to any one, 'Read it,' he shall say, 'The book is sealed, I cannot:' or the book may be opened and ye shall all become blind: even those who seem to be sharper than all others, shall say they are ignorant and unlettered men." Whatever God threatened against the Jews we know was fulfilled, and is fulfilled to this day, since a veil is put before their eyes, as Paul says. (2 Cor. iii. 14.) Hence they were blind in the midst of the brightest light. What wonder then if the same thing happened to the Chaldeans, so that they could not read the writing? There is no necessity to conjecture any transposition of letters, or any inversion of their order, or any change of one into another; for the word תקל, *tekel*, went first, and afterwards מנא, מנא, *Mena, Mena.* These guesses then are frivolous; and thus much is certain, God wished the king to be made aware of his approaching destruction; next, his soul was moved, not with repentance, but only enough to render his sloth without excuse ; and hence, whether willingly or not, he was compelled to send for some remedy, since he knew himself to be dealing with God.

Now, with regard to the writing itself, God could not be a free agent unless he possessed the power of addressing one man at one time, and a number of men at another. He wished King Belshazzar to be conscious of this writing, while the magi were all as unable to read it as if they were blind. And then, with reference to the interpretation, their perplexity need not surprise us. For God spoke enigmatically, when he said MENE, MENE, and then TEKEL, that is *weighed*, and PERES, *divided*. If the magi could have read these words a hundred times over, they could never either conjecture or comprehend their true meaning. The prophecy was allegorical, until an interpreter was divinely ordained for it. So far as the mere letters are concerned, there is no reason why we should be surprised at the eyes of the magi being blinded, since God pleased it to be so, and wished to cite the king to his tribunal, as we have already said. The Prophet says, *The king was frightened, his countenance was changed, and the princes also were disturbed.* The publicity of the event ought to have increased the sense of God's judgment, for, as we shall afterwards see, King Belshazzar himself was slain that very night. Cyrus entered while the Babylonians were feasting, and enjoying their luxuries in security. So remarkable an example of God's justice might have been instantly buried in that drunken revel, had it not been rendered conspicuous to many bystanders. Hence Daniel repeats, *The king was disturbed,* after he saw no prospect of either aid or advice from his magi and astrologers. He says also, *his princes were astonished,* because not only the king ought to be troubled but the whole Court, and the report ought to flow forth not only through the city, but to foreign nations, since there is no doubt that Cyrus was afterwards informed of this prophecy; for he would not have courted Daniel so much, nor honoured him so remarkably, unless this occurrence had been made known to him. It afterwards follows :

10. *Now* the queen, by reason of the words of the king and his lords, came into the banquet-house; *and* the queen spake, and said, O king, live for ever: let not thy thoughts trouble thee, nor let thy countenance be changed:

11. There is a man in thy kingdom in whom *is* the spirit of the holy gods; and in the days of thy father, light and understanding, and wisdom, like the wisdom of the gods, was found in him; whom the king Nebuchadnezzar thy father, the king, I *say*, thy father, made master of the magicians, astrologers, Chaldeans, *and* soothsayers.

10. Regina propter verba regis et procerum in domum symposii,[1] ingressa est, loquuta est et dixit, Rex, in æternum vive: ne terreant te cogitationes tuæ, et vultus tuus ne mutetur.

11. Est vir in regno tuo, in quo spiritus *est* deorum sanctorum: et in diebus patris tui intelligentia,[2] et scientia, et sapientia quasi sapientia deorum reperta est in eo: et Rex Nebuchadnezer pater tuus magistrum magorum,[3] astrologorum, Chaldæorum, aruspicum constituit ipsum, pater tuus rex, *inquam.*

Here Daniel relates the occasion of his being brought before the king, as the reader and interpreter of the writing. The queen, he says, did this. It is doubtful whether it was the wife of King Belshazzar, or his grandmother. She was probably an old woman, as she refers to events in the time of King Nebuchadnezzar. This conjecture has no sufficient foundation, and hence it is better to suspend our judgment than to assert anything rashly; unless, as we before saw, his wife was at table with him. As far as we can gather the words of the Prophet with certainty, we must diligently notice them, and thus convict the king of ingratitude, because he did not admit Daniel among the magi, Chaldeans, and astrologers. The holy man had no wish to be reckoned in that company; he would have deserved to lose God's prophetic spirit had he thus mingled with impostors; and he is clearly to be distinguished from them. King Nebuchadnezzar had set him over all the magi; he had no wish to exercise this honour, unless, as I have just said, he would deprive himself of the singular gift of prophecy; for we must always take care how far we can go. We know how very prone we are to be enticed by the blandishments of the world, especially when ambition blinds us and disturbs all our senses. No plague is worse than this, because when any

[1] It must be translated in this way, because the noun is derived from שתה, *shetheh,* to drink.—*Calvin.*
[2] Verbally, "light," used metaphorically.—*Calvin.*
[3] I do not stop to explain these words.—*Calvin.*

one sees a prospect of the acquisition of either profit or honour, he does not regard either what he ought to do or what God permits, but is hurried on by a blind fury. This would have happened to Daniel, unless he had been restrained by a sense of true piety, and hence he repudiated the honour offered him by King Nebuchadnezzar. He never wished to be reckoned among soothsayers, and astrologers, and impostors of this kind, who deluded that nation with prodigies. Here the queen enters and mentions Daniel; but this does not render the king without excuse; for, as we have already said, Daniel had acquired a name of renown among men of all ages, and God wished to signalize him by a distinct mark, to fix the minds of all upon him, as if he were an angel from heaven. As King Belshazzar was ignorant of the existence of such a Prophet in his kingdom, this was the result of his gross and brutish indifference. God, therefore, wished King Belshazzar to be reproved by a woman, who said, *Let not thy thoughts disturb thee!* She calms him quietly, because she saw how frightened he was; but, meanwhile, she shews him the grossness of his error in wandering about in uncertainty, when the way was plain before him. God had put his torch in the Prophet's hand for the very purpose of lighting the king, unless he wilfully desired to wander in darkness, as all the wicked do. Hence, we may learn from the example of this king, the common fault of our nature; for no one runs out of the right way, unless he indulges in his own ignorance, and desires all light to be extinct within him. As to the language of the queen, *The spirit of the holy gods is in Daniel!* we have elsewhere explained its meaning. It is not surprising that the profane use this language, since they cannot discern between the one God and angels. Hence they promiscuously call anything divine and celestial, *a god* Thus also the queen calls angels, *holy gods,* and places the true God among them. But it is our privilege to acknowledge the true God as shining forth alone, and the angels as all taking their own ranks without any excellence in heaven or earth to obscure the glory of the only God. The writing has this tendency—the exaltation of God in the highest degree, and the magnifying of his excellency and his majestic supremacy. We here see how needful it is for us to be instructed in the essential unity of God, since from the very beginning of the world men have always been persuaded of the existence of some Supreme Deity; but after they became vain in their imaginations, this idea entirely escaped them, and they mingled God and angels in complete confusion. Whenever we perceive this, let us feel our need of Scripture as a guide and instructor which shines on our path, urging us to think of God as inviting us to himself and willingly revealing himself to us.

PRAYER.

Grant, Almighty God, since thou dost constantly address us by thy Prophets, and permittest us not to wander in the darkness of error, —Grant us, I say, to be attentive to thy voice, and make us docile and tractable towards thee; especially when thou settest before us a Master in whom are included all treasures of wisdom and knowledge. Grant us further, I pray thee, to be subject to thine only-begotten Son, to hold on in the right course of our holy calling, and to be always pressing onwards to that goal to which thou callest us, until we are successful in all our contests with this world, and at length arrive at that blessed rest which thou hast obtained for us through the blood of the same thy Son.—Amen.

Lecture Twenty-fifth.

WE began yesterday to explain the passage where Daniel relates how the queen advised King Belshazzar to send for the Prophet. We shewed how the king was here convicted of ingratitude, in suffering such a Prophet of God to be in obscurity so long, because that memorable prophecy, already treated, ought to have been well known and in everybody's mouth, as conferring a permanent authority on the holy man. Now, when Daniel says, *the queen entered the banqueting-room;* very probably she was not the king's wife, but his grandmother. I have expressed my intention of not contending the point, since in doubtful cases every one ought to enjoy his own unbiassed judgment. But it is incongruous to say, The king was feasting with his wife and concubines, and then to add, "the queen entered the banqueting-room." Hence we suppose her to be called Queen, through the honour, rank, and respect which she still enjoyed, without any power. The testimony of Herodotus confirms this view, for he praises the queen of King Nebuchadnezzar for her singular prudence, calling him Labynetus and her Nitocris.[1] It is far more probable that this matron was absent from a banquet unsuitable to her age and gravity, since she would scarcely be feasting with those who were thus devoting themselves to luxury. When she enters the room, she reminds the king of Daniel, and she now gives the reason why he surpasses all the magi and soothsayers, the diviners and the Chaldees.

12. Forasmuch as an excellent spirit, and knowledge, and understanding, interpreting of dreams, and shewing of hard sentences, and dissolving of doubts, were found in the same Daniel, whom the king named Belteshazzar: now let Daniel be called, and he will shew the interpretation.

12. Propterea quod spiritus excellens, et intelligentia, et cognitio, interpretatio somniorum, et arcanorum revelatio, et solutio nodorum[2] inventa est in eo, *nempe* Daniel, cui rex imposuerit nomen Beltsazar: et nunc Daniel vocetur, et interpretationem patefaciat.

The queen here assigns the reason why Daniel had obtained the honour of being esteemed the prince and master of all the wise men; because she said, *An excellent spirit was found in him, as he interpreted dreams, revealed secrets, and solved difficulties.* The three gifts in which Daniel excelled are here enumerated, and this proves him to have surpassed the other magi, since none of them could be compared with him. The magi boasted in their ability to interpret dreams, to solve all difficulties, and explain enigmas; but this boast of theirs was twice shewn to be vanity and folly. The queen therefore deservedly claims these three qualities for Daniel, while shewing his superiority to all others. Hence she reasons with authority when she says, A name was imposed upon him by the king. We have already spoken of this

[1] Herod., lib. i. c. 185 and 188.
[2] That is, he resolved difficulties by prudence and knowledge, as I said previously. I read it all in one context, though verbs and nouns are intermingled, for I wish to make it simple, and to avoid ambiguity.—*Calvin.*

name, Belteshazzar; but the queen now refers to this name, to inform the king in what great esteem and honour he was held by his grandfather. The name of his father is here expressed, since Belshazzar might despise all strangers; yet reason would dictate the propriety of deferring to the judgment of his grandfather, whom every one knew to be a most remarkable character, whom God humbled for a time, as we saw, and as Daniel will now allude to it. Let us proceed,—

13 Then was Daniel brought in before the king. *And* the king spake, and said unto Daniel, *Art* thou that Daniel, which *art* of the children of the captivity of Judah, whom the king my father brought out of Jewry?
14. I have even heard of thee, that the spirit of the gods *is* in thee, and *that* light, and understanding, and excellent wisdom, is found in thee.
15. And now the wise *men*, the astrologers, have been brought in before me, that they should read this writing, and make known unto me the interpretation thereof: but they could not shew the interpretation of the thing:
16. And I have heard of thee, that thou canst make interpretations, and dissolve doubts: now, if thou canst read the writing, and make known to me the interpretation thereof, thou shalt be clothed with scarlet, and *have* a chain of gold about thy neck, and shalt be the third ruler in the kingdom.

13. Tunc Daniel adductus est coram rege: loquutus est rex, et dixit Danieli, Tu *ne es*[1] ille Daniel, qui, ex filiis captivitatis Jehudah, quem abduxit rex pater meus e Jehudah.
14. Et audivi de te, quod spiritus deorum in te, et intelligentia, et cognitio, et sapientia excellens, inventa sit in te.
15. Et nunc producti sunt coram me sapientes, arioli,[2] qui scripturam hanc legerent, et interpretationem ejus patefacerent mihi: et non potuerunt interpretationem sermonis indicare.
16. Et ego audivi de te, quod possis nodos solvere, et arcana explicare: nunc si poteris scripturam legere et interpretationem ejus patefacere mihi, purpura vestieris, et torques ex auro super collum tuum, et tertius in regno dominaberis.

Here the king does not acknowledge his own folly, but without any modesty he interrogates Daniel, and that, too, as a captive,—*Art thou that Daniel, of the captives of Judah, whom my father led away?* He seems to speak contemptuously here, to keep Daniel in servile obedience; although we may read this sentence as if Belshazzar inquired, *Are you that Daniel? In truth, I have heard of thee!* He had heard before, and had said nothing; but now, when extreme necessity urges him, he pays the greatest respect to Daniel. *I have heard*, therefore, *that the spirit of the gods is in thee, since thou*

[1] If we read it interrogatively; or, " Thou art Daniel?"—*Calvin.*
[2] Or, conjurors. I do not dwell on this as I said before.—*Calvin.*

canst unravel intricacies and reveal secrets. With regard to the spirit of the gods, we have already mentioned how King Belshazzar, by the common custom of all nations, promiscuously mingled angels with God; because those miserable ones could not extol God as they ought, and treat angels as entirely under his feet. But this sentence shews men never were so brutal as not to ascribe all excellence to God, as we see in profane writers; whatever promotes human advantage, and is remarkable for superiority and dignity, they treat as benefits derived from the gods. Thus the Chaldeans called the gift of intelligence a spirit of the gods, being a rare and singular power of penetration; since men acknowledge they do not acquire and attain to the prophetic office by their own industry, but it is a heavenly gift. Hence men are compelled by God to assign to him his due praise; but because the true God was unknown to them, they speak implicitly, and, as I have said, they called angels gods, since in the darkness of their ignorance they could not discern which was the true God. Whatever be the meaning, Belshazzar here shews in what estimation he holds Daniel, saying, he depends on the reports received from others, and thus displaying his own slothfulness. He ought to have known the Prophet by personal experience; but from his being content with simple rumour, he proudly neglected the teacher offered to him, and neither reflected upon nor wished to confess his own disgrace. But thus God often extracts a confession from the impious, by which they condemn themselves, even if they wish exceedingly to escape censure.

The following phrase has the same meaning:—*All the wise men were brought before me, and the soothsayers or diviners, to read this writing to me, and to reveal its interpretation; and they could not do it,* said he; for God punished him by shewing how profitless were all the Chaldeans and soothsayers, in whom he trusted at the moment of his extremity. While he was thus disappointed in his hopes, he acknowledges himself to have been deceived; and when he preferred the magi and soothsayers, he thought himself fortified by their counsel, as long as they were on his side. Meanwhile his rejection of the holy Prophet was deservedly intolerable to God. Belshazzar confesses this without intending to do so; hence I said his confession was not ingenuous or voluntary, but violently extorted by the secret instinct of God. He also promises Daniel what he had previously promised the magi,—*Thou shalt be clothed in purple if thou canst read this writing, and wear a golden chain round thy neck, and thou shalt reign as the third person in the kingdom.* But the end of his reign was now close at hand, and yet in security he offers this dignity to Daniel. This shews how rapidly the terror which God had occasioned him had vanished away. He is agitated by the greatest uneasiness, just like madmen, for they having no certainty exult amidst their terror, and wish to leap or fly towards heaven itself. Thus also this tyrant though he trembles at God's judgment, yet retains a hidden obstinacy in his heart, and imagines his kingdom will permanently continue, while he promises wealth and honours to others. It now follows,—

17. Then Daniel answered and said before the king, Let thy gifts be to thyself, and give thy rewards to another; yet I will read the writing unto the king, and make known to him the interpretation.

17. Tunc respondit Daniel, et dixit coram rege, Dona tua tibi sint,[1] et munera tua alteri da: tamen scripturam legam regi, et interpretationem *ejus* patefaciam ei.

First of all, Daniel here rejects the proffered gifts. We do not read of his doing so before; he rather seemed to delight in the honours conferred by King Nebuchadnezzar. We may inquire into the reason for this difference. It is not probable that the intention, feeling, or sentiments of the Prophet were different. What then could be his intention in allowing himself to be previously ennobled by Nebuchadnezzar, and by now rejecting the offered dignity? Another question also arises. At the end of this chapter we shall see how he was clothed in purple, and a herald promulgated an edict, by which he became third in the kingdom. The Prophet seems either to have forgotten himself in receiving the purple which he had so magnanimously rejected, or we may ask the reason why he says so, when he did not refuse to be adorned in the royal apparel. With respect to the first question, I have no doubt of his desire to treat the impious

---

[1] That is, may they remain with thee.—*Calvin.*

and desperate Belshazzar with greater asperity, because in the case of King Nebuchadnezzar there still remained some feelings of honour, and hence he hoped well of him and treated him more mildly. But with regard to King Belshazzar, it was necessary to treat him more harshly, because he had now arrived at his last extremity. This, I have no doubt, was the cause of the difference, since the Prophet proceeded straight forward in his course, but his duty demanded of him to distinguish between different persons, and as there was greater pertinacity and obstinacy in King Belshazzar, he shews how much less he deferred to him than to his grandfather. Besides, the time of his subjection was soon to be finished, and with this end in view he had formerly honoured the Chaldean empire.

As to the contrast apparent between his reply and his actions, which we shall hereafter see, this ought not to seem absurd, if the Prophet had from the beginning borne his testimony against the king's gifts, and that he utterly rejected them. Yet he does not strive very vehemently, lest he should be thought to be acting cunningly, for the purpose of escaping danger. In each case he wished to display unconquered greatness of mind; at the beginning he asserted the king's gifts to be valueless to him, for he knew the end of the kingdom to be at hand, and afterwards he received the purple with other apparel. If he had entirely refused them, it would have been treated as a fault and as a sign of timidity, and would have incurred the suspicion of treason. The Prophet therefore shews how magnificently he despised all the dignities offered him by King Belshazzar, who was already half dead. At the same time he shews himself intrepid against all dangers; for the king's death was at hand and the city was taken in a few hours—nay, in the very same hour! Daniel therefore did not reject this purple, shewing his resolution not to avoid death if necessary. He would have been safer in his obscurity, had he dwelt among the citizens at large, instead of in the palace; and if he had resided among the captives, he might have been free from all danger. As he did not hesitate to receive the purple, he displays his perfect freedom from all fear. Meanwhile he, doubtless, wished to lay prostrate the king's foolish arrogance, by which he was puffed up, when he says, *Let thy gifts remain with thee, and give thy presents to another!* I care not for them. Because he so nobly despises the king's liberality, there is no doubt of his desire to correct the pride by which he was puffed up, or at least to wound and arouse his mind to feel God's judgment, of which Daniel will soon become both the herald and the witness. It now follows,—

18. O thou king, the most high God gave Nebuchadnezzar thy father a kingdom, and majesty, and glory, and honour:
19. And for the majesty that he gave him, all people, nations, and languages, trembled and feared before him: whom he would he slew, and whom he would he kept alive, and whom he would he set up, and whom he would he put down.
20. But when his heart was lifted up, and his mind hardened in pride, he was deposed from his kingly throne, and they took his glory from him.

18. O rex,[1] Deus excelsus imperium, et magnitudinem, et præstantiam, et splendorem dedit Nebuchadnezer patri tuo.
19. Et ob magnitudinem quam dederat ei, omnes populi, gentes et linguæ tremuerunt, et formidarunt a conspectu ejus: quem volebat, occidebat:[2] et quem volebat *percutere*, percutiebat: et quem volebat *attollere*, attollebat: et quem volebat *dejicere*, dejiciebat.
20. Quando autem elevatum fuit cor ejus, et spiritus ejus roboratus est[3] ad superbiam, dejectus fuit e solio regni, et gloriam abstulerunt ab eo.

Before Daniel recites the writing, and adds its interpretation, he explains to King Belshazzar the origin of this prodigy. He did not begin the reading at once, as he might conveniently have done, saying *Mene, Mene!* as we shall see at the end of the chapter, since the king could not have profited by his abrupt speech. But here Daniel shews it to be by no means surprising, if God put forth his hand and shewed the figure of a hand describing the king's destruction, since the king had too obstinately provoked his anger. We see then why Daniel begins by this narrative, since King Nebuchadnezzar was a most powerful monarch, subduing the whole world to himself and causing all men to tremble at his word, and was afterwards hurled from the throne of his kingdom. Hence it more clearly appears that Belshazzar did not live in ignorance, for he had so signal

[1] Verbally, " Thou, O king," as he addresses him.—*Calvin.*
[2] That is, " whom he wished to slay was slain."—*Calvin.*
[3] Or, " he was hardened."—*Calvin.*

and remarkable an example that he ought to have conducted himself with moderation. Since then that domestic admonition did not profit him, Daniel shews the time to be ripe for the denunciation of God's wrath by a formidable and portentous sign. This is the sense of the passage. Passing on to the words themselves, he first says, *To King Nebuchadnezzar God gave an empire, and magnificence, and loftiness, and splendour ;* as if he had said, he was magnificently adorned, as the greatest monarch in the world. We have stated elsewhere, and Daniel repeats it often, that empires are bestowed on men by divine power and not by chance, as Paul announces, There is no power but of God. (Rom. xiii. 1.) God wishes his power to be specially visible in kingdoms. Although, therefore, he takes care of the whole world, and, in the government of the human family even the most miserable things are regulated by his hand, yet his singular providence shines forth in the empire of the world. But since we have often discussed this point at length, and shall have many opportunities of recurring to it, it is now sufficient just briefly to notice the principle of the exaltation of earthly kings by the hand of God, and not by the chances of fortune.

When Daniel confirms this doctrine, he adds, *On account of the magnificence which God conferred upon him, all mortals trembled at the sight of him !* By these words he shews how God's glory is inscribed on kings, although he allows them to reign supreme. This indeed cannot be pointed out with the finger, but the fact is sufficiently clear ; kings are divinely armed with authority, and thus retain under their hand and sway a great multitude of subjects. Every one desires the chief power over his fellow-creatures. Whence happens it, since ambition is natural to all men, that many thousands are subject to one, and suffer themselves to be ruled over and endure many oppressions? How could this be, unless God entrusted the sword of power to those whom he wishes to excel? This reason, then, must be diligently noticed, when the Prophet says, *All men trembled at the sight of King Nebuchadnezzar,* because God conferred upon him that majesty, and wished him to excel all the monarchs of the world. God has many reasons, and often hidden ones, why he raises one man and humbles another; yet this point ought to be uncontroverted by us. No kings can possess any authority unless God extends his hand to them and props them up. When he wishes to remove them from power, they fall of their own accord; not because there is any chance in the changes of the world, but because God, as it is said in the Book of Job, (xii. 18,) deprives those of the sword whom he had formerly entrusted with it.

It now follows, *Whom he wished to slay he slew, and whom he wished to strike he struck.* Some think the abuse of kingly power is here described; but I had rather take it simply, for Nebuchadnezzar being able to cast down some, and to raise others at his will, since it was in his power to give life to some and to slay others. I, therefore, do not refer these words to tyrannical lust, as if Nebuchadnezzar had put many innocent persons to death, and poured forth human blood without any reason; or as if he had despoiled many of their fortunes, and enriched others and adorned them with honour and wealth. I do not take it so. I think it refers to his arbitrary power over life and death, and over the rise of some and the ruin of others. On the whole, Daniel seems to me to describe the greatness of that royal power which they may freely exercise over their subjects, not through its being lawful, but through the tacit consent of all men. Whatsoever pleases the king, all are compelled to approve of it, or at least no one dares to murmur at it. Since, therefore, the regal license is so great, Daniel here shews how King Nebuchadnezzar was not carried away by his own plans, or purposes, or good fortune, but was entrusted with supreme power and rendered formidable to all men, because God had designed him for his own glory. Meanwhile, kings usually despise what they are permitted to enjoy, and what God allows them. For powerful as they are, they must hereafter render an account to the Supreme King. We are not to gather from this, that kings are appointed by God without any law, or any self-restraint; but the Prophet, as I have said, speaks of the royal power in itself. Since kings, therefore, have power over their subjects for life and death, he says, the life of all men was in the hand of King Nebuchadnezzar. He now adds, *When his heart was exalted, then he was cast down* (or ejected) *from the throne of his kingdom, and they deprived him of his majesty.* He follows up his own narrative. He wishes to shew King Belshazzar how God bears with the insolence of those who forget him, when they have obtained the summit of power. Desiring to make this known, he says, King Nebuchadnezzar, thy grandfather, was a mighty monarch. He did not obtain this mightiness by himself, nor could he have retained it, except he had been supported by God's hand. Now his change of circumstances was a remarkable proof that the pride of those who are ungrateful to God can never be endured unto the end, as they never acknowledge their sway to proceed from his benevolence. *When,* therefore, says he, *his heart was raised up and his spirit strengthened in pride,* a sudden change occurred. Hence you and all his posterity ought to be taught, lest pride still further deceive you, and ye profit not by the example of your father; as we shall afterwards relate. Hence this writing has been set before thee, for the purpose of making known the destruction of thy life and kingdom.

PRAYER.

Grant, Almighty God, since our own station in life has been assigned to us, that we may be content with our lot, and when thou dost humble us, may we willingly be subject to thee, and suffer ourselves to be ruled by thee and not desire any exaltation, which may lead us down to destruction. Grant us also, to conduct ourselves so modestly in our various callings, that thou mayest always shine forth in us. May nothing else be set before us than to assist our brethren to whom we are attached, as in thy sight; and thus glorify thy name among all men, through Jesus Christ our Lord.— Amen.

Lecture Twenty-sixth.

IN the sentence which we began to explain yesterday, the clause must be noticed where Daniel says, *The heart of King*

Nebuchadnezzar was strengthened by pride, signifying that he was not suddenly elated by folly, as vain men often swell with pride without a cause; nor does any interior affection of the mind precede; but he wishes to express in addition, the length of time during which this pride had been conceived; as if he had said, he was not seized by any sudden vanity, but his pride was studied, and obstinacy and obduracy were added to it. The change of number which afterwards occurs from singular to plural, some refer to the angels, as if they deprived him by God's command; but I rather think these words are taken indefinitely, implying merely his being deprived of his glory, as we have formerly observed similar forms of speech. It now follows—

21. And he was driven from the sons of men; and his heart was made like the beasts, and his dwelling *was* with the wild asses: they fed him with grass like oxen, and his body was wet with the dew of heaven; till he knew that the most high God ruled in the kingdom of men, and *that* he appointeth over it whomsoever he will.	21. Et a filiis hominum exterminatus fuit: et cor ejus cum bestiis positum est: et cum onagris habitatio ejus: herba sicut tauros cibaverunt eum: et rore cœli corpus ejus irrigatum fuit, donec cognosceret quod dominetur Deus excelsus in regno hominum, et quem velit imponat in illo.

First, with respect to the text; verbally, it is "he put," and thus some translate, "he placed his own heart among the brutes," which makes a tolerable sense; but others rather refer this to God, who placed his heart among beasts, and we know how often the noun substantive is defective in Hebrew and Chaldee; hence we may translate it verbally, Nebuchadnezzar himself placed his own heart, that is, assimilated his own senses to the brutes, so as to differ in no respect from them. It may also mean, God placed his heart among the brutes, that is, infatuated him so, as to render him like them. Others take the word שוי, *shevi*, absolutely; but it ought rather to be explained actively. Again, some translate the next clause, "Made him taste the grass, like a brute;" and others, that the grass supported him. The number is changed, but there is no doubt about the sense; for if we read, "The herb of the field supported him," the expression will be indefinite, similar to many others previously noticed; but if any one prefers using the plural number, the sense will be equally suitable; for "the herbs of the field gave him nourishment."

This verse does not need any long explanation, since Daniel only repeats what he had formerly written: His grandfather, Nebuchadnezzar, although not changed into a wild beast, was driven from the common society of men, and his whole body was deformed, whilst he abhorred the habits of men and preferred to dwell with the brutes. This was a horrible prodigy, especially in so great a monarch; and it was an example worthy of being handed down by posterity even to a thousand generations, had the monarchy endured so long. But his grandson quickly forgot this event, and thus he is deservedly convicted of the basest slothfulness. This is the reason why Daniel repeats the history again, *He was driven*, says he, *from the children of men; his heart was placed among the beasts*, meaning he was deprived of reason and judgment. We know this to be the principal difference between men and brutes—men understand and reason, but brutes are carried away by their senses. God, therefore, set forth a memorable example in despoiling this king of his reason and intelligence. *His dwelling*, says he, *was with the wild asses:* formerly he had dwelt in a palace, conspicuous throughout the world at large, from whom all the people of the East sought their laws. Since he was habitually worshipped as a god, this was a horrible judgment, since he afterwards dwelt among wild beasts, and *like a bull received his sustenance from the grass of the field*, when he had previously revelled in every delicacy, and was accustomed to luxurious habits, and to the whole wealth of a kingdom; especially, when we know how luxuriously the Orientals indulged themselves. Babylon was the mother of all indulgences, and when the king's condition was thus changed, no one could be ignorant of its cause— not mere chance or accident, but the rare and singular judgment of God!

He afterwards adds what he had formerly said, *His body was moistened by the dews of heaven, until he acknowledged God to reign supreme in the kingdom of men.* Here again the end of the punishment is expressed—that Nebuchadnezzar might feel himself to have been created king by divine power, and to shew how earthly kings could not stand unless God propped them up by his hand and influence. They think themselves placed beyond the changes of fortune, and although they verbally boast of reigning by the grace of God, yet they despise every deity and transfer the glory of the divinity to themselves! We gather from these words that this is the folly of all kings. For if Nebuchadnezzar had been persuaded of God's appointment of kings, of their dependence upon his will, and of their fall or stability according to his decree, he had not needed this punishment, as these words clearly imply. He excluded God, then, from the government of the world; but this is common with all earthly kings, as I have lately stated. All indeed will profess something, but the Holy Spirit does not regard those false protestations, as they are called. Hence in the character of King Nebuchadnezzar we have set before us, as in a glass, the drunken confidence of all kings, in supposing themselves to stand by their own power, and to free themselves from the authority of God, as if he were not seated as a judge in heaven. Nebuchadnezzar, therefore, ought to be humbled, until he acknowledged God's reign upon earth, since the common opinion fixed him up in heaven, as if contented with his own ease, and careless of the affairs of the human race. At length it is added, *and whom he wills, he exalts,* or sets up. What has been said obscurely is better expressed, since Nebuchadnezzar acknowledged, by being severely punished and subdued, the reign of God on the earth. For when earthly kings see themselves surrounded by guards, powerful in riches, and able to collect mighty armies by their nod; when they see they inspire universal terror, they think God deprived of his rights, and are unable to conceive any change; as it is said in the Psalms of all the proud, (Ps. x. 4,) and as Isaiah says to the same purport, Even should a blast pass by, or a deluge overwhelm the whole earth, yet evil shall not touch us. (Is. xxviii. 15.) As if they had said, although God should thunder from heaven, yet we shall be safe from all disaster and disturbance. Kings persuade themselves of this. Hence they begin to acknowledge God as king of the earth, when they feel themselves in his hand and at his disposal, to cast down those whom he has raised up, and to exalt the lowly and abject, as we have already seen. This clause of the verse, then, is an explanation of the former sentence. It now follows :

22. And thou his son, O Belshazzar, hast not humbled thine heart, though thou knewest all this.

22. Et tu filius ejus Beltsazar, non humiliasti cor tuum: qua propter[1] totum hoc cognoveras.

Daniel here shews why he related what we have hitherto heard concerning King Nebuchadnezzar's punishment; for Belshazzar ought to have been so affected by that domestic example, as to submit himself to God. We may believe, indeed, that his father Evil-Merodach had forgotten his punishments, since he would not have conducted himself so petulantly against God, nor trampled on true and sincere piety; for God spared the wretched tyrant who restrained himself within the bounds of moderation. But as to his grandfather Belshazzar, he was altogether intolerable; hence God stretched forth his hand. The Prophet now teaches this. *Thou art his son,* says he. This circumstance urges upon him with greater force the duty of not seeking an example in foreign nations, since he acknowledged himself to have sufficient at home of what was both necessary and useful. He enlarges upon his crime in another way, by saying, *Yet thou didst know this.* Men are accustomed to shield themselves under their ignorance with the view of extenuating the guilt of their crimes, but those who sin knowingly and wilfully are without the slightest excuse. The Prophet therefore convinces the king of manifest obstinacy; as if he had said, You have provoked God's anger on purpose; since he ought to have been aware of the horrible judgment awaiting all the proud, when he had such a remarkable and singular proof of it in his grandfather, which he ought to have kept constantly before his eyes. It follows,—

23. But hast lifted up thyself against the Lord of heaven; and they have brought the vessels of his

23. Et contra Dominum cœli te extulisti, et vasa domus ejus,[2] protulerunt in conspectum tuum: et tu,

---

[1] Verbally—but it means, " since."—*Calvin.*
[2] That is, of his temple.—*Calvin.*

house before thee, and thou and thy lords, thy wives and thy concubines, have drunk wine in them; and thou hast praised the gods of silver, and gold, of brass, iron, wood, and stone, which see not, nor hear, nor know: and the God in whose hand thy breath *is*, and whose *are* all thy ways, hast thou not glorified.

et proceres tui, uxores tuæ,[1] et concubinæ tuæ vinum bibistis in illis: et deos argenti, *hoc est, argenteos*, et aureos, æneos, ferreos, ligneos, et lapideos, qui non·vident, et non audiunt, et non intelligunt, laudasti: et Deum, cui *est* in manu ejus anima tua,[2] et cujus[3] omnia tua, non honorasti.

The Prophet continues his own sentence, and confirms what I have said, namely, King Belshazzar was intractable and wilfully blind to God's judgment. *For thou hast raised thyself,* says he, *against the Lord of heaven.* If he had raised himself thus insolently against men, his sin would be worthy of punishment; but when he had provoked God on purpose, this arrogance neither could nor ought to be borne. Again, therefore, the Prophet increases the guilt of the king's pride by saying, *he raised himself against the King of heaven.* He also expresses the manner of his doing so, *by commanding the vessels of the temple to be brought to sight; he drank from them!* This profanation was an indecent sacrilege, but Belshazzar was not content with that indignity; he used these vessels for luxury and foul debauchery, abusing them in the company of concubines and abandoned women; and added a yet greater reproach against God, *in praising his gods of silver and gold, brass and iron, wood and stone, which cannot feel.* This had not been said previously; but since Daniel here sustains the character of a teacher, he does not relate the events so shortly as at first. When he said at the beginning of this chapter, Belshazzar celebrated that impure banquet, he spoke historically; but he now executes, as I have said, the office of a teacher. *Thou,* says he, *hast praised the gods made of corruptible material, who neither see, nor hear, nor understand; but thou hast defrauded the living God of his honour, in whose hand is thy life,* on which thou dependest, and whence all in which thou boastest proceeds. Because thou hast so despised the living God, who had been so gracious unto thee, this ingratitude was both base and shameful. We see, therefore, how severely the Prophet

---

[1] Or, thy wife.—*Calvin.*
[2] That is, in whose hand is thy life.—*Calvin.*
[3] In whose power are all things.—*Calvin.*

reproves the impious tyrant of sacrilege, and mad rashness, and foul ingratitude towards God. I pass over these things lightly, since they have been treated elsewhere. It now follows,—

24. Then was the part of the hand sent from him; and this writing was written.

24. Tunc a conspectu ejus missa est particula manus,[1] et scriptura hæc notata fuit.

Some stress must be laid upon the adverb באדין, *badin*, "at that time," because God's wrath, or at least its denunciation, was now ripe. Daniel, therefore, shews how very patiently God had borne with King Belshazzar in not instantly taking up arms and inflicting punishment; but he now begins to come forth as a judge, and to ascend his judgment seat; for the haughtiness was now desperate, and the impiety no longer tolerable. We observe with what emphasis the word *then* is used; as if he had said, Thou canst not complain of the swiftness of the penalty, as if God had exacted it before the time. Thou canst not here complain of God's swiftness in punishing thee for think and consider in how many ways, and for how long a time, thou hast provoked his anger. And with regard to thy last crime, thou certainly hadst arrived at the height of impiety, when that hand appeared to thee. God, therefore, now drags thee to punishment in proper time, since he has hitherto borne with thee and thy sins. After this forbearance, what remains to prevent his destroying thee, because thou hast so proudly insulted him, and art utterly hardened, without the slightest hope of amendment.

He says also, *from himself;* for Belshazzar need not inquire whence the hand proceeded, it came *from the presence of God;* that is. This hand is a witness to the wrath of heaven; do not consider it as a spectre which will vanish away, but see in this appearance a proof of God's displeasure at thy wickedness; and because thou hast arrived at thy last extremity, thy punishment is also ready for thee. *And this writing,* says he, *has been marked;* as if he had said, The eyes of King Belshazzar were not deceived, since this

[1] Some translate, "the palm," but they understand a hand separate from the body—that portion of a hand, that is, a hand as if cut off from the body, was sent from God's presence, says he.—*Calvin.*

was really God's hand, being sent from his sight as a certain testimony of his wrath. He afterwards adds,—

25. And this *is* the writing that was written, MENE, MENE, TEKEL, UPHARSIN.	25. Et hæc *est* scriptura quæ notata *est*,[1] MENE, MENE, numeratum est, numeratum est, TEKEL, appensum est,[2] UPHARSIN, et dividentes.
26. This *is* the interpretation of the thing : MENE ; God hath numbered thy kingdom, and finished it.	26. Hæc interpretatio est sermonis : MENE, numeravit Deus regnum tuum et complevit.[3]
27. TEKEL ; Thou art weighed in the balances, and art found wanting.	27. TEKEL, appende, *vel, appensum est,* appensus es in trutina,[4] et inventus es deficiens.
28. PERES; Thy kingdom is divided, and given to the Medes and Persians.	28. Peres *pro upharsin,* divisum est regnum tuum, et datum Medis et Persis.

Daniel here explains these four verses which were written upon the wall. The king could not read them, either through stupor, or because God blunted all his senses, and blinded his eyes, as was formerly said. The same thing must be said of the magi and the soothsayers, for they could have read, had they not been rendered blind. First of all, Daniel recites the four words, MENE, MENE, TEKEL, UPHARSIN, and then adds their interpretation. He repeats the word MENE twice. Some conjecture this to apply to the numbering of the years of the king's life, and also to the time of his reign ; but the guess seems to be without any foundation. I think the word is used twice for the sake of confirmation ; as if the Prophet meant the number to be completed, since men usually allow calculations to be liable to error. To impress upon Belshazzar that his life and kingdom were at stake, God affirms the number to be complete, meaning, not a moment of time can be added to the boundary already determined. So also Daniel himself interprets it : *God,* says he, *has numbered thy kingdom ;* implying, God has appointed and prescribed a fixed end to thy kingdom ; hence it must necessarily come to an end, since its period is fulfilled.

Although God here addresses but one king by the writing set before his eyes, we may still gather this general instruc-

[1] Or, engraved.—*Calvin.*
[2] Some translate, number, number, weigh.—*Calvin.*
[3] Or, finished.—*Calvin.*   [4] Or, in a balance.—*Calvin.*

tion—God has prescribed a certain time for all kingdoms. (Job xiv. 5.) The Scripture bears the same witness concerning the life of each of us. If God has prescribed to each of us the length of his life, surely this applies more forcibly to public empires, of so much greater importance. Hence we may know how not only kings live and die according to God's pleasure, but even empires are changed, as we have formerly said. He fixes alike their origin and their destiny. Hence we may seek consolation, when we see tyrants rushing on so impetuously, and indulging their lust and cruelty without moderation. When, therefore, they rush on, as if they would mingle heaven and earth, let us remember this instruction, Their years are numbered! God knows how long they are to rage; He is not deceived; He knows whether it is useful to the Church and his elect, for tyrants to prevail for a time. By and bye he will surely restrain them, but since he determined the number of their days from the beginning, the time of his vengeance is not yet quite at hand, while he allows them a little longer to abuse without restraint the power and the sway which he had divinely granted them.

The exposition of the word TEKEL, *to weigh*, now follows :— *Since thou hast been weighed in the balance*, or scale, *and found wanting*. Here Daniel shews God so moderating his judgments, as if he was carrying a balance in his hand. The emblem is taken from the custom of mankind; for men know the use of the balance for accurate measurement. So also God is said to treat all things by weight and measure, since he does nothing with confusion, but uses moderation; and, according to ordinary language, nothing is more or less than it should be. (Wisdom xi. 21.) For this reason, Daniel says God *weighed Belshazzar in a balance*, since he did not make haste to inflict punishment, but exacted it with justice according to his own uniform rule of government. *Since he was found deficient*, that is, was found light and without weight. As if he had said, Thou thinkest thy dignity must be spared, since all men revere thee; thou thinkest thyself worthy of honour; thou art deceived says he, for God judges otherwise; God does not use a common scale, but holds his own, *and there thou art found deficient;* that is, thou art found a man of no consequence, in any way. From these words there is no doubt that the tyrant was greatly exasperated, but as his last end was approaching, he ought to hear the voice of the herald. And God, without doubt, restrained his fierceness, that he should not rise up against Daniel.

The word פְּרֵס, PHERES, is added, for the word PHERSIN, meaning *his kingdom was divided* among the Medes and Persians. I have no doubt that by this word God signified the dispersion of the Monarchy which was at hand. When, therefore, he says UPHARSIN, *and they shall divide*, it signifies the instability of the Monarchy, since he wished to destroy or utterly abolish it. But the Prophet alludes very appositely to the division made between the Medes and Persians; and thus his disgrace was increased by the Babylonians being compelled to serve many masters. This is indeed a grave and serious disgrace, when a people has obtained a wide and extensive empire, to be afterwards conquered and subjected to the yoke of a single master; but when it suffers under two masters, then the indignity is greatly increased. So Daniel here shews how God's wrath was complicated in the destruction of the monarch of Babylon, since it added to the severity of their punishment, to be subdued by both Medes and Persians. The city, indeed, was truly taken by the valour and industry of Cyrus; but since Cyrus admitted his father-in-law to the great honour of allowing him to partake of the royal authority, hence the Medes and Persians are said to have divided the kingdom, although there was properly no division of the kingdom. Cyrus afterwards engaged in other expeditions, as he was led away by his insatiable avarice and ambition. But Darius, as we shall afterwards see, died at the age of sixty years, dwelt quietly at home, and it is very well known that he was a Mede; and if we may believe the majority of historians, his sister, the mother of Cyrus, had been banished to Persia, in consequence of the oracle concerning the fortune and greatness of Cyrus. Since his grandfather had exposed him, he afterwards avenged the injury, yet not so cruelly as to take his life, for he desired him to retain some dignity, and hence appointed him a satrap. But his son afterwards reigned over the Medes, with the full permission of Cyrus, who next married his daughter; and thus, on account of this relationship, and through the influence of this new alliance, he wished to have him as a partner in the empire. In this sense, then, Daniel narrates the division of the Monarchy to be at hand, since the Medes and the Persians should divide it among them. It follows,—

29. Then commanded Belshazzar, and they clothed Daniel with scarlet, and *put* a chain of gold about his neck, and made a proclamation concerning him, that he should be the third ruler in the kingdom.

29. Tunc jussit Beltsazar, et vestierunt Danielem purpura, et torques aureus super collum ejus:[1] et clamabant coram ipso quod dominaretur tertius in regno.

This order of the king may excite surprise, since he had been so sharply reproved by the Prophet. He next seemed to have lost all spirit, for he had grown pale a hundred times, and would have devoted the holy Prophet of God to a thousand deaths! How happens it, then, that he ordered him to be adorned with royal apparel, and next to be proclaimed by his own herald the third person in the kingdom? Some think this was done because the laws of kings were sacred among the Babylonians; nay, their very words were held as binding, and whatever they proclaimed, they desired it to be esteemed firm and inviolable. They suppose King Belshazzar to have acted thus through ambition, that he might keep his promises. My opinion is, that he was at first utterly astonished, and through listening to the Prophet he became like a stock or a stone! I think he did so to consult his own ease and safety; otherwise he would have been contemptible to his nobles. To shew himself unmoved, he commands Daniel to be clothed in these robes, as if his threat had been perfectly harmless. He did not despise what the Prophet had said, but he wished to persuade his nobles and all his guests of his perfect indifference to God's threats, as if he did not utter them for the purpose of executing them, but only of terrifying them all. Thus kings, when greatly terrified, are always exceedingly careful not to shew any sign of their timidity, since they think their authority would

[1] Was placed.—*Calvin*.

become materially weakened. To continue, therefore, his reverence among his subjects, he is desirous of appearing exceedingly careless and undisturbed ; and I do not hesitate to pronounce this to have been the tyrant's intention in ordering Daniel to be clad in purple and in royal magnificence.

PRAYER.

Grant, Almighty God, that as thou didst once send forth a proof of thy wrath against all the proud, so it may be useful to us in these days. May we be admonished by the punishment inflicted on this man, and thus learn to conduct ourselves with moderation and humility. May we not desire any greatness which can be displeasing to thee ; and may we so remain in our station of life as to serve thee, and to extol and glorify thy sacred name, without being even separated from thee. Grant us also so to bear thy yoke in this world, and to suffer ourselves to be ruled by thee, that we may at length arrive at that happy rest and portion in thy heavenly kingdom, which thou hast prepared and procured for us, through the blood of thine only-begotten Son.—Amen.

Lecture Twenty-seventh.

30. In that night was Belshazzar the king of the Chaldeans slain.
31. And Darius the Median took the kingdom, *being* about threescore and two years old.

30. In illa nocte occisus *fuit* Beltsazar rex Chaldæorum.
31. Et Darius Medus accepit regnum, cum natus *esset* annos sexaginta et duos.

HERE Daniel shortly relates how his prophecy was fulfilled that very night. As we have before explained it, a customary feast-day had occurred which the Babylonians celebrated annually, and on this occasion the city was betrayed by two satraps, whom Xenophon calls Gobryas and Gadatas. On this passage the Rabbis display both their impudence and ignorance ; as, according to their usual habit, they babble with audacity about what they do not understand. They say the king was stabbed, because one of his guards heard the Prophet's voice, and wished to execute that heavenly judgment ; as if the sentence of God depended upon the will of a single heathen ! We must pass by these puerile trifles and cling to the truth of history ; for Belshazzar was seized in his own banqueting-room, when he was grossly intoxicated, with his nobles and concubines. Meanwhile, we must observe God's wonderful kindness towards the Prophet. He was not in the slightest danger, as the rest were. He was clad in purple, and scarcely an hour had passed when the Medes and Persians entered the city. He could scarcely have escaped in the tumult, unless God had covered him with the shadow of his hand. We see, then, how God takes care of his own, and snatches us from the greatest dangers, as if he were bringing us from the tomb. There is no doubt that the holy Prophet was much agitated amidst the tumult, for he was not without sensibility.[1] But he ought to be thus exercised to cause him to acknowledge God as the faithful guardian of his life, and to apply himself more diligently to his worship, since he saw nothing preferable to casting all his cares upon him!

Daniel adds, *the kingdom was transferred to the king of the Medes,* whom he calls Darius, but Xenophon terms him Cyaxares. It is clear enough that Babylon was taken by the skill and under the auspices of Cyrus; since he was a persevering warrior possessed of great authority, though he is not mentioned here. But since Xenophon relates that Cyaxares, here called Darius, was Cyrus's father-in-law, and thus held in the highest honour and estimation, it is not surprising to find Daniel bringing that king before us. Cyrus was content with his own power and with the praise and fame of his victory, and readily conceded this title to his father-in-law, whom he perceived to be now growing aged and infirm. It is uncertain whether he was the son of Astyages, and thus the uncle of Cyrus. Many historians concur in stating that Astyages was the grandfather of Cyrus who married his daughter to Cambyses; because the astrologers had informed him how an offspring should be born of her who should possess the sovereignty over all Asia! Many add the story of his ordering the infant Cyrus to be slain, but since these matters are uncertain, I leave them undecided. I rather think Darius was the uncle of Cyrus, and

---

[1] The Latin is "stipes:" the French, "une souche de bois;" literally, a log or block of wood.—*Ed.*

also his father-in-law; though, if we believe Xenophon, he was unmarried at the capture of Babylon; for his uncle, and perhaps his father-in-law, had sent him to bring supplies when he was inferior in numbers to the Babylonians and Assyrians. However this may be, the Prophet's narrative suits the circumstances well enough, for Darius, as king of the Medes, obtained the royal authority. Cyrus was, indeed, higher than he in both rank and majesty, but he granted him the title of King of Babylon, and under this name he reigned over the Chaldeans. It now follows,—

CHAPTER SIXTH.

1. It pleased Darius to set over the kingdom an hundred and twenty princes, which should be over the whole kingdom;
2. And over these three presidents, of whom Daniel *was* first; that the princes might give accounts unto them, and the king should have no damage.

1. Placuit coram Dario, et præfecit super regnum præsides provinciarum centum et viginti, qui essent in toto regno.
2. Et super illos *essent, atque ut essent super eos*, satrapæ tres, quorum Daniel unus *esset:* et ut præsides provinciarum illis redderent rationem: et rex non pateretur damnum.

As to the translation, some translate the last clause of the second verse, "That the king should not have any trouble;" but since נזק, *nezek*, signifies "to suffer loss," I willingly adopt this sense; because the king did not escape trouble, through a desire for ease, as he might have done, being an old man, but he willingly managed his own affairs, and committed the care of them to three men, lest anything should be lost through passing through too many hands. For experience shews us how confusion is caused by a multitude. If there had been only there an hundred and twenty governors of provinces, many inconveniences must have happened, and much loss would have occurred; hence the king placed three prefects over these hundred and twenty.

Here again we may perceive how God cared for his Prophet, not so much for any private reason or through private respect, as by his aid the wretched captives and exiles should be benefited. God wished to stretch forth his hand to the Jews by means of Daniel. And we may deservedly call him

God's hand in sustaining the Jews. The Persians, being barbarians, were not naturally more merciful than others; hence God interposed his servant Daniel to succour them. We must notice, in the context of this history, how Daniel alone was chosen by Darius one of these three superior officers. He was the third in rank under king Belshazzar, although for a moment, yet it might occasion envy under the new king that so great an honour was conferred upon him. Very probably Darius was informed of the previous predictions of Daniel; how the hand appeared upon the wall, how he interpreted the writing, and became a heaven-sent messenger to denounce destruction on king Belshazzar. For unless this rumour had reached Darius, Daniel would never have obtained so much authority under him. His own army abounded in numbers, and we know how every conqueror is surrounded in war by many dependents, all of whom wish to share in the spoil. Darius, therefore, would never have noticed a stranger and a captive, and admitted him to such great honour and power, unless he had understood him to be a known Prophet of God, and also a herald in denouncing destruction against the Babylonish monarchy. Thus we gather how providential it was for him to be among the first satraps, and even third in the kingdom, as this brought him more quickly under the notice of Darius. For if Daniel had been cast down by king Belshazzar he would have remained at home in concealment; but when he appeared clothed in royal apparel, the king inquired who he was? He heard the means of his arriving at so high an honour; hence he acknowledged him as God's Prophet, and appointed him one of the three prefects. Here also God's providence is again set before us, not only in preserving his servant in safety, but in providing for the safety of the whole Church, lest the Jews should be still more oppressed by the change of masters. But a temptation is afterwards inflicted, by which the holy Prophet and the whole people were severely tried; for the Prophet says:

3. Then this Daniel was preferred   3. Tunc Daniel ipse fuit superior,[1]

[1] The word נצח, *netzech,* means to surpass; hence he was superior or more excellent.—*Calvin.*

above the presidents and princes, because an excellent spirit *was* in him; and the king thought to set him over the whole realm.	supra satrapas et præsides provinciarum: propterea quod spiritus amplior, *vel, præstantior*, in ipso *erat:* et rex cogitabat eum erigere super totum regnum.
4. Then the presidents and princes sought to find occasion against Daniel concerning the kingdom; but they could find none occasion nor fault; forasmuch as he *was* faithful, neither was there any error or fault found in him.	4. Tunc satrapæ, et præsides provinciarum quæsierunt occasionem invenire contra Danielem a parte regni,[1] et omnem occasionem,[2] et nullum crimen potuerunt invenire: quia verax[3] ipse: et nulla culpa, et nullum crimen,[4] inveniebatur in ipso.
5. Then said these men, We shall not find any occasion against this Daniel, except we find *it* against him concerning the law of his God.	5. Tunc viri illi dixerunt, non inveniemus in hoc Daniele ullam occasionem, nisi inveniamus in ipso ob legem Dei sui.

The Prophet now relates, as I have said, the origin of a temptation which might naturally cast down the spirits of the elect people as well as his own. For although Daniel alone was cast into the lion's-den, as we shall afterwards see, yet, unless he had been liberated, the condition of the people would have been more grievous and severe. For we know the wicked petulantly insult the wretched and the innocent, when they see them suffering any adversity. If Daniel had been torn by the lions, all men would have risen up in a body against the Jews. God, therefore, here exercised the faith and patience of his servant, and also proved all the Jews by the same test, since they saw themselves liable to the most extreme sufferings in the person of a single individual, unless God had speedily afforded the assistance which he rendered. Daniel, first of all, says, *he excelled all others, since a more excellent or superior spirit was in him*. It does not always happen that those who are remarkable for prudence or other endowments obtain greater authority and rank. In the palaces of kings we often see men of brutal dispositions holding high rank, and we need not go back to history for this. In these days kings are often gross and infatuated, and more like horses and asses than men! Hence audacity and recklessness obtain the highest honours of the palace. When Daniel says *he excelled,* he brings to our notice

---

[1] That is, in his administration.—*Calvin.*
[2] That is, no occasion.—*Calvin.*
[3] Since he was faithful and thoroughly trusty.—*Calvin.*
[4] He repeats the noun for "crime" twice, שחיתה, *shechitheh.*—*Calvin.*

God's two-fold benefit: *first*, a greater portion of his Spirit was bestowed upon him; and *secondly*, Darius acknowledged this, and raised him to honour when he saw him endued with no ordinary industry and wisdom. We now understand the Prophet's teaching here, as first divinely adorned with prudence and other endowments; and then, Darius was a competent judge of this, in estimating his prudence and other virtues, and holding them in great repute. Since, therefore, *a noble spirit was in him,* hence *he overcame all others,* says he; therefore *the king determined to set him above the whole kingdom,* that is, to place him first among the three satraps. Although it was a singular privilege with which God once blessed his people and his Prophet, yet we ought to weep over the heartlessness of kings in these days, who proudly despise God's gifts in all good men who surpass the multitude in usefulness; and at the same time enjoy the society of the ignorant like themselves, while they are slaves to avarice and rapine, and manifest the greatest cruelty and licentiousness. Since, then, we see how very unworthy kings usually are of their empire and their power, we must weep over the state of the world, because it reflects like a glass the wrath of heaven, and kings are thus destitute of counsel. At the last day, King Darius alone will be sufficient to condemn them, for he had discretion enough not to hesitate to set a captive and a foreigner over all his satraps; for this was a royal, nay, a heroic virtue in Darius to prefer this man to all his own friends. But now kings think of nothing else than preferring their own panders, buffoons, and flatterers; while they praise none but men of low character, whom God has branded with ignominy. Although they are unworthy of being reckoned among mankind, yet they esteem themselves the masters of their sovereigns, and treat the kings of these days as their slaves. This happens through their mere slothfulness, and their discarding every possible anxiety. Hence they are compelled to deliver up their command to others, and retain nothing but the title. This, as I said, is a sure proof of the wrath of heaven, since the world is at this day unworthy of the government which God exercises over it by his hand.

With respect to the envy felt by the nobles, we see this vice rampant in all ages, since the aspirants to any greatness can never bear the presence of virtue. For, being guilty of evil themselves, they are necessarily bitter against the virtue of others. Nor ought it to seem surprising that the Persians who sustained the greatest labours, and passed through numerous changes of fortune, should be unable to bear with an obscure and unknown person, not only associated with them, but appointed as their superior. Their envy, then, seems to have had some pretext, either real or imaginary. But it will always be deserving of condemnation, when we find men selfishly pursuing their own advantage without any regard for the public good. Whoever aspires to power and self-advancement, without regarding the welfare of others, must necessarily be avaricious and rapacious, cruel and perfidious, as well as forgetful of his duties. Since, then, the nobles of the realm envied Daniel, they betrayed their malice, for they had no regard for the public good, but desired to seize upon all things for their own interests. In this example we observe the natural consequence of envy. And we should diligently notice this, since nothing is more tempting than gliding down from one vice to a worse. The envious man loses all sense of justice while attempting every scheme for injuring his adversary. These nobles report Daniel to have been preferred to themselves unworthily. If they had been content with this abuse, it would have been, as I said, a vice and a sign of a perverse nature. But they go far beyond this, for they seek for an occasion of crime in Daniel. We see, then, how envy excites them to the commission of crime. Thus all the envious are perpetually on the watch, while they become spies of the fortunes of those whom they envy, to oppress them by every possible means. This is one point; but when they find no crime, they trample upon justice, without modesty and without humanity, and with cruelty and perfidy lay themselves out to crush an adversary. Daniel relates this of his rivals. He says, *They immediately sought occasion against him, and did not find it.* Then he adds how unjustly and perfidiously they sought occasion against him. There is no doubt they knew Daniel to be a pious man and approved by God ; hence, when they plot against his holy Prophet, they purposely wage war with God himself, while they are blinded with the perverse passion of envy. Whence, then, does it spring? Surely from ambition. Thus we see how pestilential a plague ambition is, from which envy springs up, and afterwards perfidy and cruelty!

Besides this, Daniel admonishes us by his own example to study to strive after integrity, and thus to deprive the malevolent and the wicked of all occasion against us, which they seek. We shall find no better defence against the envious and the slanderous than to conduct ourselves righteously and innocently. Whatever snares they may lay for us, they will never succeed, for our innocence will repel their malice like a shield. Meanwhile we see how Daniel escaped utter ruin, since they sought a pretext against him in something else, namely, his worship of God. Hence let us learn how we ought to esteem piety and an earnest desire for it of more value than life itself. Daniel was faithful and upright in his administration: he discharged his duty so as to close the mouth of his enemies and detractors. Thus, as I have said, integrity is the best of all protectors. Again, Daniel was in danger because he would not leave off the sincere worship of God and its outward profession. Hence we must bravely undergo all dangers whenever the worship of God is at stake. This temporary life ought not to be more precious to us than that most sacred of all things—the preservation of God's honour unstained. We therefore see how we, by these means, are urged to the cultivation of integrity, since we cannot be more secure than when fortified by a good conscience, as Peter in his first epistle exhorts us to the same purpose, (iii. 16.) Now, whatever we may fear, and whatever events await us, even if we become subject to a hundred deaths, we ought never to decline from the pure worship of God, since Daniel did not hesitate to submit to death and enter the lion's den, because he openly professed the worship of Israel's God. As these nobles entered into this barbarous and cruel counsel for oppressing Daniel under the pretence of religion, here, again, we gather the blindness and rashness of mankind when ambition and envy seize upon their minds. For it is a matter of no moment with them to come into collision with the Almighty,[1] for they do not approach Daniel as a fellow-creature, but they leap into an insane and sacrilegious contest when they wish to extinguish the worship of God and give way to their own indulgence. Thus, as I have said, we are admonished by this example how ambition is to be guarded against and avoided, and also the envy which arises from it. The nature of this charge—the worship of God—afterwards follows:—

6. Then these presidents and princes assembled together to the king, and said thus unto him, King Darius, live for ever.

7. All the presidents of the kingdom, the governors, and the princes, the counsellors, and the captains, have consulted together to establish a royal statute, and to make a firm decree, that whosoever shall ask a petition of any god or man for thirty days, save of thee, O king, he shall be cast into the den of lions.

6. Tunc satrapæ et provinciarum præsides illi sociati sunt[2] apud regem,[3] et sic locuti sunt ei: Dari rex, in æternum vive.

7. Consilium ceperunt omnes satrapæ regni, proceres et præsides provinciarum, consiliarii, et duces, ut statuatur statutum regis,[4] et sanciatur edictum, ut quisquis petierit petitionem ab ullo deo et homine usque ad dies triginta *hos*, præterquam a te, rex, projiciatur in speluncam leonum.

The nobles of the kingdom purposely endeavoured to ruin the holy Prophet, either by casting him into the lion's den to perish, or else by causing him to desist from the outward profession of worshipping God. They knew him to be so really in earnest that he would not redeem his life by so great an act of impiety, and hence they thought him doomed to death. We perceive in them great cunning; but God met them on the other hand and aided his servant, as we shall see. Meanwhile their malice was the more detestable, since they desired to destroy Daniel by this very pretence. Although they did not worship Israel's God, they knew the Prophet's mind to be pious and straightforward, and then they experienced the power of that God who was unknown to them.

[1] The French editions of 1562 and 1569, *a Geneva*, translate the idiomatic phrase, *susque deque illis est*, by *ce leur est tout un ;* "it is all one to them."—*Ed.*

[2] For רגש, *reges*, properly signifies to "join and associate with."—*Calvin.*

[3] That is, they made a conspiracy, and approached the king.—*Calvin.*

[4] That is, royal, or from the king.—*Calvin.*

They did not condemn Daniel, nor blame the religion which he practised; for, as I have said, their hatred of this man urged them to such cruelty that they rushed against the Almighty. They could not disguise from themselves the duty of worshipping God: they worshipped and adored unknown deities, and did not dare to condemn the worship of Israel's God. We see how the devil fascinated them when they dared to impute this as a crime to the holy Prophet; while we are ignorant of the manner in which their opinion was changed.

Some suppose this was done because Darius could not bear with composure the glory of his son-in-law. For since he was an old man, and his relative in the flower of his age, he thought himself despised. Others think Darius to have been touched by secret emulation, and that he allowed his nobles to approach him for the purpose of deceiving the miserable and doting old man, and thus to throw dust in his eyes. But this conjecture does not seem to me sufficiently valid. Nor need I give myself much trouble in this matter, because it might happen that at the beginning of a new reign they wished to congratulate the king, and they fixed upon something new and unaccustomed, as we see often done by flatterers of royalty. Hence the old man might be deceived in this matter, since the monarchy was newly established. The king had hitherto ruled over none but Medes; now Chaldeans, Assyrians, and many other nations were added to his sway. Such an addition might intoxicate him with vain-glory, and his nobles might think this a plausible reason for offering to him divine honours. This single reason seems to me sufficient; I do not inquire further, but embrace what is probable and obvious at first sight. I defer the remainder till to-morrow.

PRAYER.

Grant, Almighty God, as thou didst govern thy servant Daniel when honours were flowing around on all sides, and he was raised to the highest dignity, and preserve him safe in his integrity and innocency amidst the universal licentiousness,—Grant, I pray thee, that we may learn to restrain ourselves within that moderation to which thou restrictest us. May we be content with our humble station and strive to prove ourselves innocent before thee and before those with whom we have to deal; so that thy name may be glorified in us, and we may proceed under thy shelter against the malice of mankind. Whenever Satan besieges us on every side, and the wicked lay snares for us, and we are attacked by the fierceness of wild beasts, may we remain safe under thy protection, and even if we have to undergo a hundred deaths, may we learn to live and die to thee, and may thy name be glorified in us, through Christ our Lord.—Amen.

Lecture Twenty-eighth.

WE said, yesterday, that the nobles who laid snares against Daniel were inspired with great fury when they dared to dictate to the king the edict recorded by Daniel. It was an intolerable sacrilege thus to deprive all the deities of their honour; yet he subscribed the edict, as we shall afterwards see, and thus put to the test the obedience of his people whom he had lately reduced under the yoke by the help of his son-in-law. There is no doubt of his wish to subdue the Chaldees, who up to that time had been masters; and we know how ferocity springs from the possession of authority. Since then the Chaldees had formerly reigned so far and wide, it was difficult to tame them and render them submissive, especially when they found themselves the slaves of those who had previously been their rivals. We know how many contests there were between them and the Medes; and although they were subdued in war, their spirits were not yet in subjection; hence Darius desired to prove their obedience, and this reason induced him to give his consent. He does not purposely provoke the anger of the gods; but through respect for the men, he forgets the deities, and substitutes himself in the place of the gods, as if it was in his power to attract the authority of heaven to himself! This, as I have said, was a grievous sacrilege. If any one could enter into the hearts of kings, he would find scarcely one in a hundred who does not despise everything divine. Although they confess themselves to enjoy their thrones by the grace of God, as we have previously remarked, yet they wish to be adored in his stead. We now see how easily flatterers persuade kings to do whatever appears likely to extol their magnificence. It follows:

8. Now, O king, establish the decree, and sign the writing, that it be not changed, according to the law of the Medes and Persians, which altereth not.

9. Wherefore king Darius signed the writing and the decree.

8. Nunc, rex, statue edictum, et obsigna scripturam, quæ non ad mutandum,[1] secundum legem Medorum et Persarum, quæ non transit.

9. Itaque *ipse* rex Darius obsignavit scripturam et edictum.

Here, as I have said, it is sufficiently apparent how inclined to fallacies are the minds of kings when they think they can benefit themselves and increase their own dignity. For the king did not dispute long with his nobles but subscribed the edict; for he thought it might prove useful to himself and his successors, if he found the Chaldeans obedient to himself and rather prepared to deny the existence of every god than to refuse whatever he commanded! As to the use of the word, some translate אסרא, *asra*, by "writing," deriving it from "*to cut in*," as we know that all laws were formerly graven on tablets of brass; but I interpret it more simply of their seeking from the king a signature of the writing, that is, he was to sign the edict after it was written. *Which cannot be changed*, they say—meaning, the edict is unchangeable and inviolable. *according to the law of the Medes and Persians, which does not pass away*—that is, which does not vanish, as also Christ says, Heaven and earth shall pass away, but my words shall not pass away, or shall never become vain. (Matt. xxiv. 35; Mark xiii. 31.) As to his joining the Medes with the Persians, this arises from what we said before, since Cyrus and Darius reigned in common as colleagues. Greater dignity was granted to Darius, while the power was in the hands of Cyrus; besides, without controversy, his sons were heirs of either kingdom and of the Monarchy of the East, unless when they began to make war on each other. When they say, the law of the Medes and Persians *is immutable*, this is worthy of praise in laws, and sanctions their authority; thus they are strong and obtain their full effect. When laws are variable, many are

---

[1] That is, which is immutable.— *Calvin*.

necessarily injured, and no private interest is stable unless the law be without variation; besides, when there is a liberty of changing laws, license succeeds in place of justice. For those who possess the supreme power, if corrupted by gifts, promulgate first one edict and then another. Thus justice cannot flourish where change in the laws allows of so much license. But, at the same time, kings ought prudently to consider lest they promulgate any edict or law without grave and mature deliberation; and secondly, kings ought to be careful lest they be counteracted by cunning and artful plots, to which they are often liable. Hence, constancy is praiseworthy in kings and their edicts, if only they are preceded by prudence and equity. But we shall immediately see how foolishly kings affect the fame of consistency, and how their obstinacy utterly perverts justice. But we shall see this directly in its own place. It follows:

10. Now when Daniel knew that the writing was signed, he went into his house; and, his windows being open in his chamber toward Jerusalem, he kneeled upon his knees three times a day, and prayed, and gave thanks before his God, as he did aforetime.

10. Daniel autem ubi cognovit quod obsignata *esset* scriptura, venit, *vel, ingressus est,* in domum suam (fenestræ autem apertæ *erant* ei in cœnaculo suo versus Jerusalem) et temporibus tribus in die,[1] inclinabat se super genua sua,[2] et precabatur, et confitebatur coram Deo suo, quemadmodum fecerat a pristino illo tempore.[3]

Daniel now relates how he was clothed in the boldness of the Spirit of God to offer his life as a sacrifice to God, because he knew he had no hope of pardon left, if his violation of the king's edict had been discovered; he knew the king himself to be completely in shackles even if he wished to pardon him—as the event proved. If death had been before the Prophet's eyes, he preferred meeting it fearlessly rather than ceasing from the duty of piety. We must remark that the internal worship of God is not treated here, but only the external profession of it. If Daniel had been forbidden to pray, this fortitude with which he was endued might seem necessary; but many think he ran great risks without sufficient reason, since he increased the chance of death when

[1] That is, three times every day.—*Calvin.*
[2] The verb and the noun are from the same root; "he bent upon his knees or inclined himself."—*Calvin.*
[3] That is, as he was accustomed to do.—*Calvin.*

only outward profession was prohibited. But as Daniel here is not the herald of his own virtue, but the Spirit speaks through his mouth, we must suppose that this magnanimity in the holy Prophet was pleasing to God. And his liberation shewed how greatly his piety was approved, because he had rather lose his life than change any of his habits respecting the worship of God. We know the principal sacrifice which God requires, is to call upon his name. For we hereby testify him to be the author of all good things; next we shew forth a specimen of our faith; then we fly to him, and cast all our cares into his bosom, and offer him our prayers. Since, therefore, prayer constitutes the chief part of our adoration and worship of God, it was certainly a matter of no slight moment when the king forbade any one to pray to God; it was a gross and manifest denial of piety.

And here, again, we collect how blind was the king's pride when he could sign so impious and foul an edict! Then how mad were the nobles who, to ruin Daniel as far as they possibly could, endeavoured to abolish all piety, and draw down God from heaven! For what remains, when men think they can free themselves from the help of God, and pass him over with security? Unless he prop us up by his special aid, we know how entirely we should be reduced to nothing. Hence the king forbade any one to offer up any prayer during a whole month—that is, as I have said, he exacts from every one a denial of God! But Daniel could not obey the edict without committing an atrocious insult against God and declining from piety; because, as I have said, God exacts this as a principal sacrifice. Hence it is not surprising if Daniel cordially opposed the sacrilegious edict. Now, with respect to the profession of piety, it was necessary to testify before men his perseverance in the worship of God. For if he had altered his habits at all, it would have been a partial abjuration; he would not have said that he openly despised God to please Darius; but that very difference in his conduct would have been a proof of perfidious defection. We know that God requires not only faith in the heart and the inward affections, but also the witness and confession of our piety.

Daniel, therefore, was obliged to persevere in the holy practice to which he was accustomed, unless he wished to be the very foulest apostate! He was in the habit of praying with his windows open: hence he continued in his usual course, lest any one should object that he gratified his earthly king for a moment by omitting the worship of God. I wish this doctrine was now engraven on the hearts of all men as it ought to be; but this example of the Prophet is derided by many, not perhaps openly and glaringly, but still clearly enough, the Prophet seems to them too inconsiderate and simple, since he incurs great danger, rashly, and without any necessity. For they so separate faith from its outward confession as to suppose it can remain entire even if completely buried, and for the sake of avoiding the cross they depart a hundred times from its pure and sincere profession. We must maintain, therefore, not only the duty of offering to God the sacrifice of prayer in our hearts, but that our open profession is also required, and thus the reality of our worship of God may clearly appear.

I do not say that our hasty thoughts are to be instantly spread abroad, rendering us subject to death by the enemies of God and his gospel; but I say these things ought to be united and never to be separated, namely, faith and its profession. For confession is of two kinds: first, the open and ingenuous testimony to our inward feelings; and secondly, the necessary maintenance of the worship of God, lest we shew any sign of a perverse and perfidious hypocrisy, and thus reject the pursuit of piety. With regard to the first kind, it is neither always nor everywhere necessary to profess our faith; but the second kind ought to be perpetually practised, for it can never be necessary for us to pretend either disaffection or apostasy. For although Daniel did not send for the Chaldeans by the sound of a trumpet whenever he wished to pray, yet he framed his prayers and his vows in his couch as usual, and did not pretend to be forgetful of piety when he saw his faith put to the test, and the experiments made whether or not he would persevere in his constancy. Hence he distinctly says, *he went home*, after being made acquainted with the signing of the decree. Had he been admitted to the council, he would doubtless have spoken out, but the rest of the nobles cunningly excluded him, lest he should interfere with them, and they thought the remedy would be too late, and utterly in vain as soon as he perceived the certainty of his own death. Hence, had he been admitted to the king's council, he would there have discharged his duty, and heartily interposed; but after the signing of the edict, and the loss of all opportunity for advising the king, he retired to his house.

We must here notice the impossibility of finding an excuse for the king's advisers, who purposely escape when they see that unanimity of opinion cannot be obtained, and think God will be satisfied in this way, if they only maintain perfect silence. But no excuse can be admitted for such weakness of mind. And, doubtless, Daniel is unable to defend them by his example, since, as we have already said, he was excluded by the cunning and malice of the nobles from taking his place among them as usual, and thus admonishing the king in time. He now says, *His windows were open towards Jerusalem.* The question arises, Whether it was necessary for Daniel thus to open his windows? For some one may object—he did this under a mistaken opinion; for if God fills heaven and earth, what signified his windows being open towards Jerusalem? There is no doubt that the Prophet used this device as a stimulus to his fervour in prayer. For when praying for the liberation of his people, he directed his eyes towards Jerusalem, and that sight became a stimulus to enflame his mind to greater devotion. Hence the opening of the Prophet's windows has no reference to God, as if he should be listened to more readily by having the open heaven between his dwelling and Judea; but he rather considered himself and his natural infirmity. Now, if the holy Prophet, so careful in his prayers, needed this help, we must see whether or not our sloth in these days has need of more stimulants! Let us learn, therefore, when we feel ourselves to be too sluggish and cold in prayer, to collect all the aids which can arouse our feelings and correct the torpor of which we are conscious. This, then, was the Prophet's intention *in opening his windows towards Jerusa-*

lem. Besides, he wished by this symbol to shew his domestics his perseverance, in the hope and expectation of the promised redemption. When, therefore, he prayed to God, he kept Jerusalem in sight, not that his eyes could penetrate to so distant a region, but he directed his gaze towards Jerusalem to shew himself a stranger among the Chaldeans, although he enjoyed great power among them, and was adorned with great authority, and excelled in superior dignity. Thus he wished all men to perceive how he longed for the promised inheritance, although for a time he was in exile. This was his second reason for opening his windows.

He says, *He prayed three times a-day.* This is worthy of observation, because, unless we fix certain hours in the day for prayer, it easily slips from our memory. Although, therefore, Daniel was constant in pouring forth prayers, yet he enjoined upon himself the customary rite of prostrating himself before God three times a-day. When we rise in the morning, unless we commence the day by praying to God, we shew a brutish stupidity, so also when we retire to rest, and when we take our food and at other times, as every one finds most advantageous to himself. For here God allows us liberty, but we ought all to feel our infirmities, and to apply the proper remedies. Therefore, for this reason, Daniel was in the habit of praying thrice. A proof of his fervour is also added, when he says, *He prostrated himself on his knees;* not that bending the knee is necessary in prayer, but while we need aids to devotion, as we have said, that posture is of importance. First of all, it reminds us of our inability to stand before God, unless with humility and reverence; then, our minds are better prepared for serious entreaty, and this symbol of worship is pleasing to God. Hence Daniel's expression is by no means superfluous: *He fell upon his knees whenever he wished to pray to God.* He now says, *he uttered prayers and confessions before God,* or he praised God, for we must diligently notice how many in their prayers mutter to God. For although they demand either one thing or another, yet they are carried along by an immoderate impulse, and, as I have said, they are violent in their requests unless God instantly grants their petitions.

This is the reason why Daniel joins praises or the giving of thanks with prayers; as, also, Paul exhorts us respecting both. Offer up, says he, your prayers to God, with thanksgiving, (Phil. iv. 6,) as if he had said, We cannot rightly offer vows and prayers to God unless when we bless his holy name, although he does not immediately grant our petitions. In Daniel's case we must remark another circumstance: he had been an exile for a long time, and tossed about in many troubles and changes; still he celebrates God's praises. Which of us is endued with such patience as to praise God, if afflicted with many trials through three or four years? Nay, scarcely a day passes without our passions growing warm and instigating us to rebel against God! Since Daniel, then, could persevere in praising God, when oppressed by so many sorrows, anxieties, and troubles—this was a remarkable proof of invincible patience. And, doubtless, he signifies a continuous act, by using the demonstrative pronoun דנה, *deneh*, which refers to his ordinary habit—*as he had done before, and from former times.* By noticing the time, he marks, as I have said before, a perseverance, since he was not only accustomed to pray once or twice, but by a regular constancy he exercised himself in this duty of piety every day. It afterwards follows:—

| 11. Then these men assembled, and found Daniel praying and making supplication before his God. | 11. Tunc viri illi sociati sunt,[1] et invenerunt Danielem orantem et precantem coram Deo suo. |

Here the nobles of Darius display their fraud when they observe Daniel, and unite in a conspiracy against him: for no other object but the death of Daniel could have induced them to dictate this edict. Hence they agree together, and find *Daniel uttering prayers and supplications to his God.* If Daniel had prayed with the slightest secrecy, he would not have been a victim to their snares; but he did not refuse the prospect of death. He knew the object of the edict, and expected the arrival of the nobles. We see, then, how willingly he submitted to instant death, and for no other purpose than to retain the pure worship of God, together with its outward profession. Go to, now, ye who desire to shield

---

[1] Or, "collected," as others translate.—*Calvin.*

your perfidy, pretending that you ought not to incur danger rashly, and when the wicked surround you on all sides! You become cautious lest you should rashly throw away your lives! For Daniel, in their opinion, was to be blamed for too great simplicity and folly, since he willingly and knowingly encountered certain danger. But we have already said, he could not escape from their snare without indirectly revolting from God, for he might have been immediately reproached—Why do you desist from your accustomed habit? Why do you close your windows? Why do you not dare to pray to your God? It appears, then, you regard the king of more importance than the reverence and fear of God. Because God's honour would have been thus sullied, Daniel, as we have already seen, spontaneously offered himself to death as a sacrifice. We are taught, also, by this example, how snares are prepared for the sons of God, however circumspectly they act, and however soberly they conduct themselves. But they ought to conduct themselves so prudently as neither to be too cunning nor too anxious, that is, they should not regard their own security so as in the meantime to forget God's requirements, and the preciousness of his name, and the necessity of a confession of faith in the proper place and time. It now follows:

12. Then they came near, and spake before the king concerning the king's decree; Hast thou not signed a decree, that every man that shall ask *a petition* of any god or man within thirty days, save of thee, O king, shall be cast into the den of lions? The king answered and said, The thing *is* true, according to the law of the Medes and Persians, which altereth not.

12. Tunc accesserunt et dixerunt[1] coram rege super edicto regio, An non edictum obsignasti, ne quisquam homo peteret ab ullo deo vel homine, usque ad triginta dies *hos*, præterquam abs te, rex,[2] projiceretur in speluncam leonum? Respondit rex et dixit, Firmus est sermo secundum legem Medorum et Persarum, quæ non transit.

Now the king's nobles approach the king as conquerors, but they do so cunningly; for they do not openly say anything about Daniel, whom they knew to be a favourite with the king; but they repeat their previous assertion concerning the impossibility of changing the edict, since the

[1] And they have said.—*Calvin.*
[2] It is preferable to translate it "that any man should ask from any god or man, for thirty days, except of thee, O king."—*Calvin.*

law of the Medes and Persians is inviolable and cannot be rendered void. Again, therefore, as far as they possibly can, they sanction that edict, lest the king should afterwards be free, or dare to retract what he had once commanded. We must mark the cunning with which they indirectly circumvent the king, and entangle him, by preventing the change of a single word; *They come*, therefore, *and discourse concerning the royal edict.* They do not mention the name of Daniel, but dwell upon the royal decree, so as to bind the king more firmly. It follows—*The king answered, The discourse is true.* We here see how kings desire praise for consistency, but they do not perceive the difference between consistency and obstinacy. For kings ought to reflect upon their own decrees, to avoid the disgrace of retracting what they have hastily promulgated. If anything has escaped them without consideration, both prudence and equity require them to correct their errors; but when they have trampled upon all regard for justice, they desire every inconsiderate command to be strictly obeyed! This is the height of folly, and we ought not to sanction a perseverance in such obstinacy, as we have already said. But the rest to-morrow.

PRAYER.

Grant, Almighty God, since thou hast reconciled us to thyself by the precious blood of thy Son, that we may not be our own, but devoted to thee in perfect obedience, and may consecrate ourselves entirely to thee : May we offer our bodies and souls in sacrifice, and be rather prepared to suffer a hundred deaths than to decline from thy true and sincere worship. Grant us, especially, to exercise ourselves in prayer, to fly to thee every moment, and to commit ourselves to thy Fatherly care, that thy Spirit may govern us to the end. Do thou defend and sustain us, until we are collected into that heavenly kingdom which thy only-begotten Son has prepared for us by his blood.— Amen.

Lecture Twenty-ninth.

WE began yesterday to explain Daniel's narrative of the calumny invented against him before King Darius. The nobles of the kingdom, as we have said, used cunning in their interview with the king; because if they had begun with Daniel, the king might have broken his word. But they dwell upon the royal decree; they shew the imminence of the danger, unless the authority of all the king's decrees was upheld. By this artifice we see how they obtained their object; for the king confirms their assertion respecting the wickedness of rendering abortive what had been promulgated in the king's name. For kings are pleased with their own greatness, and wish their own pleasure to be treated as an oracle. That edict was detestable and impious by which Darius forbade entreaties to be offered to any deity; yet he wished it to remain in force, lest his majesty should be despised by his subjects. Meanwhile, he does not perceive the consequences which must ensue. Hence we are taught by this example, that no virtue is so rare in kings as moderation, and yet none is more necessary; for the more they have in their power, the more it becomes them to be cautious lest they indulge their lusts, while they think it lawful to desire whatever pleases them. It now follows:

13. Then answered they, and said before the king, That Daniel, which *is* of the children of the captivity of Judah, regardeth not thee, O king, nor the decree that thou hast signed, but maketh his petition three times a-day.

13. Tunc loquuti sunt, et dixerunt coram rege: Daniel, qui *est* ex filiis captivitatis Jehudah, non posuit super te, rex, sensum,[1] neque ad edictum quod obsignasti: et vicibus tribus in die precatur petitionem suam.[2]

Now, when Daniel's calumniators see that King Darius had no wish to defend his cause, they open up more freely what they had previously conceded; for, as we have said, if they had openly accused Daniel, their accusation could have been instantly and completely refuted; but after this sentiment had been expressed to the king, their statement is final,

[1] Or, has not added his own sense, or given his mind to thee.—*Calvin.*
[2] That is, prays according to his custom, or as usual.—*Calvin.*

since by the laws of the Medes and Persians a king's decree ought to be self-acting; hence, after this is accomplished, they then come to the person. *Daniel*, say they, *one of the captives of Judah, has not obeyed thy will, O king, nor the decree which thou hast signed.* By saying, " Daniel, one of the Jewish captives," they doubtless intended to magnify his crime and to render him odious. For if any Chaldean had dared to despise the king's edict, his rashness would not have been excused. But now when Daniel, who was lately a slave and a Chaldean captive, dares to despise the king's command, who reigned over Chaldea by the right of conquest, this seemed less tolerable still. The effect is the same as if they had said, "He was lately a captive among thy slaves; thou art supreme lord, and his masters to whom he was subject are under thy yoke, because thou art their conqueror; he is but a captive and a stranger, a mere slave, and yet he rebels against thee!" We see then how they desired to poison the king's mind against him by this allusion, *He is one of the captives!* The words are very harmless in themselves, but they endeavour to sting their monarch in every way, and to stir up his wrath against Daniel. *He does not direct his mind to thee, O king;* that is, he does not reflect upon who you are, and thus he despises thy majesty and *the edict which thou hast signed.* This is another enlargement: *Daniel*, therefore, *did not direct his mind either to thee or to thy edict;* and wilt thou bear this? Next, they recite the deed itself—*he prays three times a-day.* This would have been the simple narrative, Daniel has not obeyed thy command in praying to his own God; but, as I have said, they exaggerate his crime by accusing him of pride, contempt, and insolence. We see, therefore, by what artifices Daniel was oppressed by these malicious men. It now follows:

14. Then the king, when he heard *these* words, was sore displeased with himself, and set *his* heart on Daniel to deliver him; and

14. Tunc rex, postquam sermonem audivit, valde tristatus est,[1] in se : et ad Danielem apposuit cor,[2] ad ipsum servandum : et usque ad

---

[1] Others translate "disturbed;" others again, "was very much displeased" or grieved, for באש, *bash*, signifies to grieve.—*Calvin.*

[2] There is a change in the letters here ; for בל, *bel*, is put for לב, *leb;* here it means, " he applied his heart."—*Calvin.*

he laboured till the going down of the sun to deliver him.

15. Then these men assembled unto the king, and said unto the king, Know, O king, that the law of the Medes and Persians *is*, That no decree nor statute which the king establisheth may be changed.

occasum solis fuit solicitus ad ipsum eruendum.[1]

15. Tunc conglobati sunt viri illi[2] ad regem, et dixerunt, Scias, rex, quod lex Medis et Persis *est*, ut omne edictum et statutum quod rex statuerit, non mutetur.

In the first place, Daniel recites that the king was disturbed, when he perceived the malice of his nobles which had formerly escaped him; for their intention and their object had never occurred to him; he perceives himself deceived and entrapped, and hence he is disturbed. Here again we are taught how cautiously kings ought to avoid depraved counsels, since they are besieged on every side by perfidious men, whose only object is to gain by their false representations, and to oppress their enemies, and those from whom they hope for booty or who may favour their evil courses. Because so many snares surround kings, they ought to be the more cautious in providing against cunning. They are too late in acknowledging themselves to have been overreached, when no remedy is left, partly through fear, and partly through wishing to consult their own credit; and they prefer offending God to suffering any outward disrespect from men. Since, therefore, kings consider their own honour so sacred, they persevere in their evil undertakings, even when their conscience accuses them; and even if justice itself were to appear visibly before them, yet this restraint would not be sufficient to withhold them, when ambition urges them in the opposite direction, and they are unwilling to lose the slightest portion of their reputation among men. The case of Darius supplies us with an example of this kind.

First of all, it is said, *He was sorrowful when he heard these words, and was anxious till the setting of the sun about the way of snatching Daniel from death.* He wished this to be done, if his own honour were sound and safe, and his nobles

[1] Or, to deliver him; that is, he desired to snatch him away.—*Calvin.*
[2] That is, conspired together, as if they approached the king in a body, to inspire the greater terror; "they assembled themselves therefore."—*Calvin.*

were satisfied. But on the one side, he fears disunion if his nobles should conspire to produce disturbance; and on the other side, he is moved by a foolish fear, because he does not wish to incur the charge of levity which awaited him, and hence he is vanquished and obeys the lusts of the wicked. Although, therefore, he laboured till the setting of the sun to free Daniel, yet that perverse shame prevailed of which I have spoken, and then the fear of dissension. For when we do not lean upon God's help, we are always compelled to vacillate, although anxious to be honestly affected. Thus Pilate wished to liberate Christ, but was terrified by the threats of the people, when they denounced against him the displeasure of Cæsar. (John xix. 12.) And no wonder, since faith is alone a certain and fixed prop on which we may lean while fearlessly discharging our duty, and thus overcome all fears. But when we want confidence, we are, as I have said, sure to be changeable. Hence Darius, through fear of a conspiracy of his nobles against himself, permitted Daniel to be an innocent sufferer from their cruelty. Then that false shame is added which I have mentioned, because he was unwilling to appear without consideration, by suddenly revoking his own edict, as it was a law with the Medes and Persians that whatever proceeded from kings was inviolable! Daniel now states this. He says, *those men assembled together;* when they saw the king hesitate and doubt, they became fierce and contentious with him. When it is said they meet together, this relates to their inspiring him with fear. They say, *Know, O king!* He knew it well enough, and they need not instruct him in any unknown matter, but they treat him in a threatening manner. "What? dost thou not see how utterly the royal name will be hereafter deprived of its authority if he violates thine edict with impunity? Will you thus permit yourself to become a laughingstock? Finally, they intimate, that he would not be king unless he revenged the insult offered him by Daniel in neglecting his commandment. *Know,* therefore, O king, *that the Persians and Medes*—he was himself king of the Medes, but it is just as if they said, What kind of rumour will be spread through all thy subject provinces; for thou knowest how far this prevails among the Medes and Persians—the king must not change his edict. If, therefore, thou shouldst set such an example, will not all thy subjects instantly rise against thee? and wilt thou not be contemptible to them?" We see, then, how the satraps rage against their king, and frighten him from any change of counsel. And they also join the edict with the statute, which the king had resolved upon, with the view of impressing upon him the necessity of not changing a single decree which he had often and repeatedly sanctioned. It follows:

16. Then the king commanded, and they brought Daniel, and cast *him* into the den of lions. *Now* the king spake, and said unto Daniel, Thy God, whom thou servest continually, he will deliver thee.

16. Tunc rex loquutus est,[1] et adduxerunt Danielem, et projecerunt *eum* in foveam leonum. Respondit rex, et dixit Danieli, Deus tuus quem tu colis ipsum jugiter,[2] ipse liberabit te.[3]

The king, as we have said, frightened by the denunciation of the nobles, condemns Daniel to death. And hence we gather the reward which kings deserve in reference to their pride, when they are compelled to submit with servility to their flatterers. How was Darius deceived by the cunning of his nobles! For he thought his authority would be strengthened, by putting the obedience of all men to this test of refusing all prayer to any god or man for a whole month. He thought he should become superior to both gods and men, if all his subjects really manifested obedience of this kind. We now see how obstinately the nobles rise against him, and denounce ultimate revolt, unless he obey them. We see that when kings take too much upon themselves, how they are exposed to infamy, and become the veriest slaves of their own servants! This is common enough with earthly princes; those who possess their influence and favour applaud them in all things and even adore them; they offer every kind of flattery which can propitiate their favour; but, meanwhile, what freedom do their idols enjoy? They do not allow them any authority, nor any intercourse with the best and most faithful friends, while they are

[1] That is, he decreed or commanded.—*Calvin.*
[2] The pronoun is superfluous.—*Calvin.*
[3] Or, if we receive it in the manner of a prayer—"may he deliver thee."—*Calvin.*

watched by their own guards. Lastly, if they are compared with the wretches who are confined in the closest dungeon, not one who is thrust down into the deepest pit, and watched by three or four guards, is not freer than kings themselves! But, as I have said, this is God's most just vengeance; since, when they cannot contain themselves in the ordinary rank and station of men, but wish to penetrate the clouds and become on a level with God, they necessarily become a laughingstock. Hence they become slaves of all their attendants, and dare not utter anything with freedom, and are without friends, and are afraid to summon their subjects to their presence, and to intrust either one or another with their wishes. Thus slaves rule the kingdoms of the world, because kings assume superiority to mortals. King Darius is an instance of this when he sent for Daniel, and commanded him to be thrown into the den of lions; his nobles force this from him, and he unwillingly obeys them. But we should notice the reason. He had lately forgotten his own mortality, he had desired to deprive the Almighty of his sway, and as it were to drag him down from heaven! For if God remains in heaven, men must pray to him; but Darius forbade any one from even daring to utter a prayer; hence as far as he could he deprived the Almighty of his power. Now he is compelled to obey his own subjects, although they exercise an almost disgraceful tyranny over him.

Daniel now adds—*the king said this to him, Thy God, whom thou servest,* or worshippest, *faithfully, he will deliver thee!* This word may be read in the optative mood, as we have said. There is no doubt that Darius really wished this; but it may mean, Thy God whom thou worshippest will deliver thee—as if he had said, "Already I am not my own master, I am here tossed about by the blast of a tempest; my nobles compel me to this deed against my will; I, therefore, now resign thee and thy life to God, because it is not in my power to deliver thee;" as if this excuse lightened his own crime by transferring to God the power of preserving Daniel. This reason causes some to praise the piety of King Darius; but as I confess his clemency and humanity to be manifest in this speech, so it is clear that he had not a grain of piety when he thus wished to adorn himself in the spoils of deity! For although the superstitious do not seriously fear God, yet they are restrained by some dread of him; but he here wished to reduce the whole divinity to nothing. What sort of piety was this? The clemency of Darius may therefore be praised, but his sacrilegious pride can by no means be excused. Then why did he act so humanely towards Daniel? Because he had found him a faithful servant, and the regard which rendered him merciful arose from this peculiarity. He would not have manifested the same disposition towards others. If a hundred or a thousand Jews had been dragged before his tribunal, he would carelessly have condemned them all because they had disobeyed the edict! Hence he was obstinately impious and cruel. He spared Daniel for his own private advantage, and thus embraced him with his favour; but in praising his humanity, we do not perceive any sign of piety in him. But he says, *the God whom thou worshippest, he will deliver thee,* because he had formerly known Daniel's prophecy concerning the destruction of the Chaldean monarchy; hence he is convinced, how Israel's God is conscious of all things, and rules everything by his will; yet, in the meantime, he neither worships him nor suffers others to do so; for as far as he could he had excluded God from his own rights. In thus attributing to God the power of delivering him, he does not act cordially; and hence his impiety is the more detestable, when he deprives God of his rights while he confesses him to be the true and only one endued with supreme power; and though he is but dust and ashes, yet he substitutes himself in his place! It now follows,—

17. And a stone was brought, and laid upon the mouth of the den; and the king sealed it with his own signet, and with the signet of his lords; that the purpose might not be changed concerning Daniel.	17. Ed adductus fuit lapis unus et positus super os speluncæ: et obsignavit eum rex annulo suo et annulo procerum suorum, ne mutaretur placitum in Daniele.[1]

[1] That is, "concerning Daniel." Those who render it "against," as if the king had purposely wished to oppose their violence, pervert the whole sense, since it was doubtless done at their instigation, lest the king should secretly provide for his liberation.—*Calvin.*

There is no doubt that God's counsel provided that the nobles should seal the stone with their own rings, and thus close the mouth of the cave, and render the miracle more illustrious. For when the king approached on the morrow, the rings were all entire, and the seals all unbroken. Thus the preservation of this servant of God was manifestly by the aid of heaven and not by the art of men. Hence we see how boldly the king's nobles had compelled him to perform their pleasure. For he might seem deprived of all royal power when he delivered up to them a subject dear and faithful to himself, and ordered him to be thrown into the lions' den. They are not content with this compliance of the king; they extort another point from him—the closing up of the mouth of the cave; and then they all seal the stone, lest any one should release Daniel. We see, then, when once liberty has been snatched away, all is over, especially when any one has become a slave by his own faults, and has attached himself to the counsels of the ungodly. For, at first, such slavery will not prevail as to induce a man to do everything which he is ordered, since he seems to be free; but when he has given himself up to such slavery as I have described, he is compelled to transgress not once or twice, but constantly and without ceasing. For example, if any one swerves from his duty through either the fear of man or flattery, or any other depraved affection, he will grant various things, not only when asked, but when urgently compelled. But when he has once submitted to the loss of freedom, he will be compelled, as I have already said, to consent to the most shameful deeds at the nod of any one. If any teacher or pastor of the Church should turn from the right path through the influence of ambition, the author of his declension will come to him again and say, What! do you dare to refuse me? Did I not obtain from you, yesterday or the day before, whatever I wished? Thus he will be compelled to transgress a second time in favour of the person to whom he has joined himself, and will also be forced to repeat the transgression continually. Thus princes also, who are not free agents through being under the tyranny of others, if they permit themselves to be overcome contrary to their conscience, lay aside all their authority, and are drawn aside in all directions by the will of their subjects. This example, then, is proposed to us in the case of King Darius, who after inflicting unjust punishment upon Daniel, adds this, *He must be enclosed in the cave*, and then, *the stone must be sealed*,—and for what object ?—*lest the doom should be changed ;* meaning, he did not dare to attempt anything in Daniel's favour. We see, then, how the king submitted to the greatest disgrace, because his nobles had no confidence in him; they refused to trust him when he ordered Daniel to be thrown into the lions' den, but they exacted a guarantee against his liberation, and would not suffer him to attempt anything. We thus see how disgracefully they withdrew their confidence from their king; next they use their authority against him, lest he should dare to remove the stone which had been sealed, unless he would incur the charge of falsehood by corrupting the public signatures, and of deception by falsifying the public documents. Hence this passage admonishes us against prostituting ourselves in slavery to the lust of men. Let every one serve his nearest neighbours as far as charity will allow and as custom demands. Meanwhile, no one ought to permit himself to be turned aside in different directions contrary to his conscience, because when he loses his free agency, he will be compelled to endure many affronts and to obey the foulest commands. This we see exemplified in the case of the panders to the avarice, or ambition, or cruelty of princes; for when once they are under the power of such men, they are most miserable victims; they cannot avoid the most extreme necessities, they become wretched slaves, and call down against themselves, a hundred times over, the anger of both God and man. It now follows,—

18. Then the king went to his palace, and passed the night fasting: neither were instruments of musick brought before him; and his sleep went from him.

18. Tunc profectus est rex in palatium suum, et pernoctavit in jejunio, *jejunus*, et instrumenta musica[1] non fuerint allata coram ipso,[2] et somnus *etiam* discessit ab eo.

[1] Others translate "banquet" or "supper;" but this does not agree, because he first said the king passed the night fasting, therefore a different interpretation is more suitable, namely, "musical instruments."—*Calvin.*

[2] And thus all joys and delights ceased.—*Calvin.*

Here Daniel relates the tardy repentance of the king, because although he was in the greatest grief, yet he did not correct his fault. And this occurs to many who are not hardened by contempt of God and their own depravity; they are drawn aside by others, and are dissatisfied with their own vices, while they still indulge in them. Would that the examples of this evil were rare in the world! but they occur everywhere before our eyes. Darius therefore is here proposed to us as intermediate between the ungodly and the wicked—the righteous and the holy. The wicked do not hesitate to stir up the Almighty against them, and after they have dismissed all fears and all shame, they revel in their own licentiousness. Those who are ruled by the fear of God, although they sustain hard contests with the flesh, yet impose a check upon themselves, and bridle their perverse affections. Others are between the two, as I have said, not yet obstinate in their malice, and not quite satisfied with their corruptions, and still they follow them as if bound to them by ropes. Such was Darius; for he ought constantly to have repelled the calumny of his nobles; but when he saw himself so entangled by them, he ought to have opposed them manfully, and to have reproved them for so abusing their influence over him; yet he did not act thus, but rather bent before their fury. Meanwhile he bewails in his palace, and abstains from all food and delicacies. He thus shews his displeasure at the evil conduct at which he connived. We see then how ineffectual it is for our own conscience to smite us when we sin, and to cause us sorrow for our faults; we must go beyond this, so that sorrow may lead us on to repentance, as also Paul teaches us. (2 Cor. vii. 10.) Darius, then, had reduced himself to difficulties; while he bewails his fault, he does not attempt to correct it. This was, indeed, the beginning of repentance, but nothing more; and when he feels any compunction, this stirs him up and allows him neither peace nor comfort. This lesson, then, we are to learn from Daniel's narrative of King Darius passing the whole of that night in wailing. It follows afterwards,—

19. Then the king arose very early   19. Tunc rex in aurora,[1] surrexit

[1] That is, "in the morning."—*Calvin.*

in the morning, and went in haste unto the den of lions. 20. And when he came to the den, he cried with a lamentable voice unto Daniel: *and* the king spake and said to Daniel, O Daniel, servant of the living God, is thy God, whom thou servest continually, able to deliver thee from the lions?	cum illucesceret, et in festinatione,[1] ad speluncam leonum venit. 20. Et cum appropinquasset ad foveam, ad Danielem in voce tristi, *aut, lugubri,* clamavit, loquutus est rex, et dixit Danieli, Daniel serve Dei viventis, Deus tuus quem tu colis ipsum jugiter, an potuit ad servandum te a leonibus ?[2]

Here the king begins to act with a little more consistency, when he approaches the pit. He was formerly struck down by fear as to yield to his nobles, and to forget his royal dignity by delivering himself up to them as a captive. But now he neither dreads their envy nor the perverseness of their discourse. *He approaches the lions' den early in the morning,* says he,—that is, at dawn, before it was light, coming during the twilight, *and in haste.* Thus we see him suffering under the most bitter grief, which overcomes all his former fears; for he might still have suffered from fear, through remembrance of that formidable denunciation,— Thou wilt no longer enjoy thy supreme command, unless thou dost vindicate thine edict from contempt! But, as I have said, grief overcomes all fear. And yet we are unable to praise either his piety or his humanity; because, though he approaches the cave and calls out, "Daniel!" with a lamentable voice, still he is not yet angry with his nobles till he sees the servant of God perfectly safe. Then his spirits revive, as we shall see; but as yet he persists in his weakness, and is in a middle place between the perverse despisers and the hearty worshippers of God, who follow with an upright intention what they know to be just.

PRAYER.

Grant, Almighty Father, since thou shewest us, by the example of thy servant Daniel, how we ought to persevere with consistency in the sincere worship of thee, and thus proceed towards true greatness of mind, that we may truly devote ourselves to thee. May we not be turned aside in any direction through the lust of men, but may we persist in our holy calling, and so conquer all dangers, and arrive at length at the fruit of victory—that happy immortality which is laid up for us in heaven, through Christ our Lord.—Amen.

[1] That is, "hastily."—*Calvin.* [2] That is, could he preserve thee?—*Calvin.*

Lecture Thirtieth.

WANT of time compelled me to break off our last Lecture at the point where Daniel relates how *the king approached the cave*. Now he reports his words,—*O Daniel, servant of the living God! thy God whom thou worshippest constantly, has he been able to deliver thee?* says he. Darius declares the God of Israel to be the living One. But if there is a living God, he excludes all those imaginary deities whom men fancy for themselves by their own ingenuity. For it is necessary that deity should be one, and this principle is acknowledged by even the profane. However men may be deluded by their dreams, yet they all confess the impossibility of having more gods than one. They distort, indeed, God's character, but they cannot deny his unity. When Darius uttered this praise of the God of Israel, he confesses all other deities to be mere fictions, but he shews how, as I have said, the profane hold the first principle, but afterwards allow it to escape entirely from their thoughts. This passage does not prove, as some allege, the real conversion of King Darius, and his sincere adoption of true piety; for he always worshipped his own idols, but thought it sufficient if he raised the God of Israel to the highest rank. But, as we know, God cannot admit a companion, for he is jealous of his own glory. (Isaiah xlii. 8.) It was too cold, then, for Darius simply to acknowledge the God whom Daniel worshipped to be superior to all others; because where God reigns, all idols must of necessity be reduced to nothing; as also it is said in the Psalms, Let God reign, and let the gods of all nations fall before him. Darius then proceeded so far as to devote himself to the true and only God, but was compelled to pay the greatest respect to Israel's God. Meanwhile he always remained sunk in his own superstitions to which he had been accustomed.

He afterwards adds, *Thy God, whom thou worshippest continually, could he free thee from the lions?* He here speaks doubtfully, as unbelievers do, who seem to have some ground for hope, but no firm or sure persuasion in their own minds.

I suppose this invocation to be natural, since a certain secret instinct naturally impels men to fly to God; for although scarcely one in twenty leans upon God's word, yet all men call upon God occasionally. They wish to discover whether God desires to assist them and to aid them in their necessities; meanwhile, as I have said, there is no firm persuasion in their hearts, which was the state of the mind of King Darius: *Could God deliver thee?* says he; as if God's power could possibly be doubted! If he had said, Has God delivered thee? this would have been tolerable. For God was not bound by any law to be always snatching his people from death, since, we very well know, this rests entirely with his good pleasure. When, therefore, he permits his people to suffer under the lusts of the impious, his power is by no means diminished, since their liberation depends upon his mere will and pleasure. His power, therefore, ought by no means to be called in question. We observe, that Darius was never truly converted, and never distinctly acknowledged the true and only God, but was seized with a blind fear, which, whether he would or not, compelled him to attribute the supreme honour to Israel's God. And this was not an ingenuous confession, but was rather extorted from him. It now follows:—

21. Then said Daniel unto the king, O king, live for ever.
22. My God hath sent his angel, and hath shut the lions' mouths, that they have not hurt me: forasmuch as before him innocency was found in me; and also before thee, O king, have I done no hurt.

21. Tunc Daniel cum rege loquutus est, rex, in eternum vive.
22. Deus meus misit angelum suum, et conclusit os leonum, et non nocuerunt mihi: quoniam coram ipso innocentia,[1] inventa est in me: atque atiam coram te, rex, pravitatem non commisi.

Here Daniel answers the king moderately and softly, although he had been cast into the cave by his command. He might have deservedly been angry and expostulated with him, because he had been so impiously deserted by him, for King Darius had found him a faithful servant, and had used his services for his own advantage. When he saw himself oppressed by unjust calumnies, the king did not take his part so heartily as he ought; and at length, being overcome by the threats of his nobles, he ordered Daniel to be cast

[1] Or, integrity.—*Calvin.*

into the pit. Daniel might, as I have said, have complained of the king's cruelty and perfidy. He does not do this, but is silent concerning this injury, because his deliverance would sufficiently magnify the glory of God. The holy Prophet desired nothing else, except the king's welfare, which he prays for. Although he uses the ordinary phrase, yet he speaks from his heart, when he says, *O king, live for ever!* that is, may God protect thy life and bless thee perpetually. Many salute their kings and even their friends in this way through mere form; but there is no doubt that Daniel heartily wished the king the enjoyment of long life and happiness. He afterwards adds, *My God*, says he, *sent his angel, and shut the lions' mouths!* Thus we see that Daniel openly assigns to angels the duty of rendering assistance, while the whole power remains in the hands of God himself. He says, therefore, that he was freed by the hand and assistance of an angel, but shews how the angel was the agent and not the author of his safety. *God*, therefore, says he, *sent his angel*. We have often seen how indistinctly the Chaldeans spoke when mentioning the Deity; they called their deities holy, but Daniel here ascribes the entire glory to God alone. He does not bring forward a multitude of deities according to the prevalent opinion among the profane. He puts prominently forward the unity of God, and then he adds the presence of angels as assisting God's servants, shewing how they perform whatever is enjoined upon them. Thus the whole praise of their salvation remains with the one God, since angels do not assist whomsoever they please, and are not moved by their own will, but solely in obedience to God's commands.

We must now notice what follows: *God had shut the lions' mouths.* For by these words the Prophet shews how lions and the most cruel beasts are in the hands of God, and are restrained by his secret curb, so that they can neither rage nor commit any injury unless by God's permission. We may thus learn that savage beasts are only so far injurious to us as God may permit them to humble our pride. Meanwhile, we may perceive that no beast is so cruel as to injure us by either his claws or his teeth, unless God give him the reins.

And this instruction is worthy of especial notice, since we tremble at the least danger, even at the noise of a falling leaf. As we are necessarily exposed to many dangers on all sides, and surrounded by various forms of death, hence we should be harassed by wretched anxiety unless this principle supported us; not only is our life under God's protection, but nothing can injure us while he directs everything by his will and pleasure. And this principle ought to be extended to the devils themselves, and to impious and wicked men, for we know the devil to be always anxious to destroy us, like a roaring lion, for he prowls about seeking whom he may devour, as Peter says in his First Epistle, (v. 8.) For we see how all the impious plot for our destruction continually, and how madly they are inflamed against us. But God, who can close the lion's mouth, will also both restrain the devil and all the wicked from hurting any one without his permission. Experience also shews us how the devil and all the impious are controlled by him, for we should perish every moment unless he warded off by his opposing influence the numberless evils which ever hang over us. We ought to perceive how the singular protection of God preserves us in daily safety amidst the ferocity and madness of our foes. Daniel says he suffered no loss of any kind, *because before God his righteousness was found in him.* These words signify that his preservation arose from God wishing to vindicate his own glory and worship which he had commanded in his law. The Prophet does not here boast in his own righteousness, but rather shews how his deliverance arose from God's wishing to testify by a certain and clear proof his approval of that worship for which Daniel had contended even to death. We see, then, how Daniel refers all things to the approval of the worship of God. The conclusion is, he was the advocate of a pious and holy cause, and prepared to undergo death, not for any foolish imagination, nor by any rash impulse, nor any blind zeal, but because he was assured of his being a worshipper of the one God. His being the defender of the cause of piety and holiness was, as he asserts, the reason of his preservation. This is the correct conclusion.

Hence we readily gather the folly of the Papists who, from

this and similar passages, endeavour to establish the merit and righteousness of good works. Oh! Daniel was preserved because righteousness was found in him before God; hence God repays every man according to the merits of his works! But we must first consider Daniel's intention in the narrative before us; for, as I have said, he does not boast in his own merits, but wishes his preservation to be ascribed to the Deity as a testimony to his true and pure worship, so as to shame King Darius, and to shew all his superstitions to be impious, and especially to admonish him concerning that sacrilegious edict by which he arrogated to himself the supreme command, and, as far as he could, abolished the very existence of God. With the view, then, of admonishing Darius, the Prophet says his cause was just. And to render the solution of the difficulty more easy, we must remark the difference between eternal salvation and special deliverances. God frees us from eternal death, and adopts us into the hope of eternal life, not because he finds any righteousness in us but through his own gratuitous choice, and he perfects in us his own work without any respect to our works. With reference to our eternal salvation, our righteousness is by no means regarded, because whenever God examines us, he only finds materials for condemnation. But when we consider particular deliverances, he may then notice our righteousness, not as if it were naturally ours, but he stretches forth his hand to those whom he governs by his Spirit and urges to obey his call; and if they incur any danger in their efforts to obey his will, he delivers them. The meaning then is exactly the same as if any one should assert that God favours righteous causes, but it has nothing to do with merits. Hence the Papists trifle, like children, when they use this passage to elicit from it human merits; for Daniel wished to assert nothing but the pure worship of God, as if he had said, not only his reason proceeded from God, but there was another cause for his deliverance, namely, the wish of the Almighty to shew the world experimentally the justice of his cause.

He adds, *And even before thee, O king, I have committed nothing wrong.* It is clear that the Prophet had violated the king's edict. Why, then, does he not ingenuously confess this? Nay, why does he contend that he has not transgressed against the king? Because he conducted himself with fidelity in all his duties, he could free himself from every calumny by which he knew himself oppressed, as if he had despised the king's sovereignty. But Daniel was not so bound to the king of the Persians when he claimed for himself as a god what ought not to be offered to him. We know how earthly empires are constituted by God, only on the condition that he deprives himself of nothing, but shines forth alone, and all magistrates must be set in regular order, and every authority in existence must be subject to his glory. Since, therefore, Daniel could not obey the king's edict without denying God, as we have previously seen, he did not transgress against the king by constantly persevering in that exercise of piety to which he had been accustomed, and by calling on his God three times a-day. To make this the more evident, we must remember that passage of Peter, "Fear God, honour the king." (1 Pet. ii. 17.) The two commands are connected together, and cannot be separated from one another. The fear of God ought to precede, that kings may obtain their authority. For if any one begins his reverence of an earthly prince by rejecting that of God, he will act preposterously, since this is a complete perversion of the order of nature. Then let God be feared in the first place, and earthly princes will obtain their authority, if only God shines forth, as I have already said. Daniel, therefore, here defends himself with justice, since *he had not committed any crime against the king;* for he was compelled to obey the command of God, and he neglected what the king had ordered in opposition to it. For earthly princes lay aside all their power when they rise up against God, and are unworthy of being reckoned in the number of mankind. We ought rather utterly to defy than to obey them whenever they are so restive and wish to spoil God of his rights, and, as it were, to seize upon his throne and draw him down from heaven. Now, therefore, we understand the sense of this passage. It follows,—

23. Then was the king exceeding glad for him, and commanded that

23. Tunc rex valde exhilaratus in se, *vel, super eo,* Danielem jussit educi

they should take Daniel up out of the den. So Daniel was taken up out of the den, and no manner of hurt was found upon him, because he believed in his God.

ex spelunca: et eductus fuit Daniel ex spelunca: et nulla corruptio, *vel, læsio,* inventa fuit in eo: quia credidit, *vel, confsus est,* Deo suo.

Daniel confirms what he had formerly narrated concerning the feelings of King Darius. As he had departed in anxiety to his palace, had abstained from food and drink, and had laid aside all pleasures and delights, so also he rejoiced in hearing of the wonderful deliverance from death of God's holy servant. He afterwards adds, *And by the king's command Daniel was drawn out of the cave, and no corruption was found in him.* This cannot be ascribed to good fortune. Hence God made his power conspicuous in providing for Daniel's safety from the grasp of the lions. He would have been torn to pieces had not God closed their mouths; and this contributes in no slight degree to magnify the miracle, since no scratch or touch was found upon his body. As the lions then spared him, it arose from God's secret counsel; and he marked this more clearly, when his calumniators were thrown into the cave, and were immediately torn by the lions, as he will soon add. But we must notice the reason which is given: *He was preserved, since he trusted in his God!* It will often happen, that a person may have a good cause, and yet succeed badly and unhappily; because he adds to what is otherwise worthy of praise, too great a confidence in his own counsels, prudence, and industry. Hence it is not surprising if those who undertake good causes often fail of success, as we often see among the profane. For the history of all ages bears witness, to the perishing of those who cherish a just cause; but this arises through their perverse confidence, since they never contemplated the service of God, but rather considered their own praise and the applause of the world. Hence, as ambition seized them, they became pleased with their own plans. Thus arose that saying of Brutus, "Virtue is a frivolous thing!" because he thought himself unworthily treated in fighting for the liberty of Rome, while the gods were adverse instead of propitious. As if God ought to have conferred upon him that aid which he had never hoped and never sought. For we know the pride of that hero's disposition. I bring forward but one example; but if we diligently weigh the motives which impel the profane when they fight strenuously for good objects, we shall find ambition to be the prevailing motive. No wonder then if God deserted them in this particular, since they were unworthy of experiencing his help. For this reason Daniel states, that he was safely preserved, *because he trusted in his God.* The Apostle refers to this in the eleventh chapter of the Epistle to the Hebrews, (verse 33,) where he says some were snatched away or preserved from the mouths of lions through faith. Hence he assigns the cause of Daniel's escaping in safety, and recalls us to faith. But we must here consider the meaning and force of the word "believing." For the Prophet does not simply speak of his deliverance as springing from believing Israel's God to be the true and only God, the Maker of heaven and earth, but from his committing his life to him, from his reposing on his grace, from his fixed determination that his end must be happy, if he worshipped him. Since, therefore, Daniel was certainly persuaded that his life was in God's hand, and that his hope in him was not in vain, he boldly incurred danger, and intrepidly suffered for the sincere worship of God; hence he says, *he believed in God.* We see then that the word "belief" is not taken coldly, as the Papists dream, since their notion implies an unfolded or dead and shapeless faith, for they think faith nothing else but a confused apprehension of the Deity. Whenever men have any conception of God at all, the Papists think this to be faith; but the Holy Spirit teaches us far otherwise. For we must consider the language of the Apostle,—We do not properly believe in God, unless we determine him to be a rewarder of all who diligently seek him. (Heb. xi. 6.) God is not sought by foolish arrogance, as if by our merits we could confer an obligation upon him; but he is sought by faith, by humility, and by invocation. But when we are persuaded that God is the rewarder of all who seek him, and we know how he ought to be sought, this is true faith. So Daniel did not doubt that God would deliver him, because he did not distrust that teaching of piety which he had learnt from a boy, and through reliance on which he had always called upon God. This, therefore, was the cause of his deliverance. Meanwhile, it is clear that Daniel's trust in God did not spring from any previous instruction concerning the result; for he rather committed his life to God, since he was prepared for death. Therefore Daniel could not acknowledge this before he was cast into the cave, and exposed to the lions, being ignorant whether God would deliver him, as we previously saw in the case of his companions, " God, if he pleases, will deliver us; but if not, we are prepared to worship Him, and to disobey thy edict." If Daniel had been taught the issue beforehand, his constancy would not have deserved much praise; but since he was willing to meet death fearlessly for the worship of God, and could deny himself and renounce the world, this is a true and serious proof of his faith and constancy. *He believed therefore in God*, not because he hoped for such a miracle, but because he knew his own happiness to consist in persisting in the true worship of God. So Paul says, Christ is gain to me, both in life and in death. (Phil. i. 21.) Daniel therefore rested in the help of God, but he closed his eyes to the event, and was not remarkably anxious concerning his life, but since his mind was erected towards the hope of a better life, even if he had to die a hundred times, yet he never would have failed in his confidence, because our faith is extended beyond the boundaries of this frail and corruptible life, as all the pious know well enough. What I have already touched upon afterwards follows,—

| 24. And the king commanded, and they brought those men which had accused Daniel, and they cast *them* into the den of lions, them, their children, and their wives: and the lions had the mastery of them, and brake all their bones in pieces or ever they came at the bottom of the den. | 24. Et jussit rex, et adduxerunt viros illos qui instruxerant[1] accusationem adversus eum, nempe Danielem; et in foveam, *speluncam*, leonum projecti sunt ipsi, liberi ipsorum, et uxores eorum, et nondum pervenerant ad fundum,[2] speluncæ, quando domirati sunt,[3] in eos leones, et omnia ossa eorum fregerunt. |

By this circumstance God's virtue shone forth more clearly

---

[1] " Had enacted," " had cried out ;" *qui avoyent dressè ceste calomnie.*—Calvin's own translation into French.

[2] Or, pavement.—*Calvin.*   [3] Or, prevailed.—*Calvin.*

in preserving Daniel, because those who had accused him were immediately destroyed by the lions. For if any one should say that the lions were satisfied, or there was any other reason why Daniel was not destroyed, why, when he was withdrawn, did such great madness immediately impel those beasts to tear and devour, not one man only, but a great multitude? Not one of the nobles was preserved; next their wives and children were added. Lions scarcely ever proceed to such a pitch of savageness, and yet they all perished to a man; then how did Daniel escape? We surely see how God by this comparison wished to bear witness to his own virtue, lest any one should object that Daniel was left by the lions because they were already gorged, and desired no other prey, for they would have been content with either three or four men; but they devoured men, women, and children. Hence the mouths of the lions were clearly restrained by the divine power, since Daniel was safe during a whole night, but they perished immediately, as soon as they were cast into the cave; because we again see how these beasts were impelled by sudden madness, so that they did not wait till their prey arrived at the bottom, but devoured them as they fell. We shall leave the rest till to-morrow.

PRAYER.

Grant, Almighty God, since we were created and placed in this world by thee, and are also nourished by thy bounty, for the very purpose of consecrating our life to thee,—Grant, I pray, that we may be prepared to live and die to thee. May we seek only to maintain the pure and sincere worship of thyself. May we so acquiesce in thy help as not to hesitate about breaking through all difficulties, and to offer ourselves to instant death, whenever thou requirest it. May we rely not only on thy promise, which remains for ever, but upon the many proofs which thou hast granted us of the present vitality of thy mighty power. Mayest thou be our deliverer in every sense, whether we live or die; and may we be blessed in persevering in our confidence in thy name, and thy true confession, until at length we are gathered into thy heavenly kingdom, which thou hast prepared for us by the blood of thine only-begotten Son.—Amen.

Lecture Thirty-first.

At the end of yesterday's Lecture, the enemies of Daniel who had malignantly, enviously, and cruelly slandered him, were cast into the lions' den, and were torn to pieces with their wives and children; and thus the miracle was more clearly conspicuous, as we have previously said. Here, again, we may learn how lions are governed by God's hand, and are restrained from shewing their ferocity everywhere and against every one, except when God permits them. As it is said in the ninety-first Psalm, Thou shalt walk upon the lion and the basilisk, and tread upon the lion and the dragon; (verse 13.) So also, on the other hand God denounces against the unbelievers by the Prophet Amos, (chap. v. 19,) The lions shall come to meet them, if they go forth from their houses. We see, then, how God restrains the cruelty of lions as often as he pleases, and how he excites them to madness when he wishes to punish mankind. With regard to their wives and children being also cast into the den, we need not dispute with any anxiety, whether or not this punishment was just. For it seems to be a sure rule of equity, that punishment should not pass on to the innocent, especially when it involves their life. In all ages, it has been the custom of well-ordered States, for many punishments to be inflicted on children as well as their parents, as in a public sale of goods, or any charge of violence or treason; in criminal cases also, the infamy of parents extends to the children, (but this is far more severe, to slay children with their parents,) though they cannot possibly be guilty of the same crime. Yet, although this is not one of the customary cases, we must not hastily condemn it as unjust. We see how God orders whole families to be exterminated from the world as a mark of his hatred; but, as a just Judge, he always is moderate in his severity. This example, then, cannot be precisely condemned, but we had better leave it in doubt. We are aware of the cruel and barbarous manner in which the kings of the East exercise their sway, or rather their tyranny, on their subjects. Hence there is no reason why any one should fatigue himself with the question, since King Darius was so much grieved at his being deceived. Hence he not only exacted punishment from these wicked slanderers for oppressing Daniel, but because he was himself affected by their injustice. He wished rather to avenge himself than Daniel; he was not content with retaliation, but condemned their children also to destruction. It follows,—

25. Then king Darius wrote unto all people, nations, and languages, that dwell in all the earth; Peace be multiplied unto you.
26. I make a decree, that in every dominion of my kingdom men tremble and fear before the God of Daniel; for he *is* the living God, and stedfast for ever, and his kingdom *that* which shall not be destroyed, and his dominion *shall be even* unto the end.
27. He delivereth and rescueth, and he worketh signs and wonders in heaven and in earth, who hath delivered Daniel from the power of the lions.

25. Tunc Darius rex, scripsit omnibus populis, et gentibus, et linguis qui habitabant in tota terra, Pax vestra multiplicetur.
26. A me positum est decretum in omni dominatione,[1] regni mei, ut sint metuentes et paventes,[2] a conspectu Dei Danielis;[3] quia ipse *est* Deus vivus, et permanens in seculum : et regnum ejus non corrumpetur, et dominatio ejus[4] usque in finem.
27. Eripiens et liberans, et edens signa et miracula[5] in cœlo et in terra : qui eripuit Danielem e manu leonum.

Here Daniel adds the king's edict, which he wished to be promulgated. And by this edict he bore witness that he was so moved by the deliverance of Daniel, as to attribute the supreme glory to the God of Israel. Meanwhile, I do not think this a proof of the king's real piety, as some interpreters here extol King Darius without moderation, as if he had really repented and embraced the pure worship prescribed by the law of Moses. Nothing of this kind can be collected from the words of the edict—and this circumstance shews it—for his empire was never purged from its superstitions. King Darius still allowed his subjects to worship idols; and he did not refrain from polluting himself with such defilements; but he wished to place the God of Israel on the highest elevation, thus attempting to mingle fire and water! We have previously discussed this point. For the

[1] Or, throughout the whole of the dominions.—*Calvin.*
[2] That is, that they should fear and be afraid.—*Calvin.*
[3] That is, before the God of Daniel.—*Calvin.*
[4] Or, power.—*Calvin.*
[5] "Wonders," as some translate it.—*Calvin.*

profane think they discharge their duty to the true God, if they do not openly despise him, but assign him some place or other; and, especially, if they prefer him to all idols, they think they have satisfied God. But this is all futile; for unless they abolish all superstitions, God by no means obtains his right, since he allows of no equals. Hence this passage by no means proves any true and serious piety in King Darius; but it implies simply his being deeply moved by the miracle, and his celebrating through all the regions subject to him the name and glory of the God of Israel. Finally, as this was a special impulse on King Darius, so it did not proceed beyond a particular effect; he acknowledged God's power and goodness on all sides; but he seized upon that specimen which was placed directly before his eyes. Hence he did not continue to acknowledge the God of Israel by devoting himself to true and sincere piety; but, as I have said, he wished him to be conspicuously superior to other gods, but not to be the only God. But God rejects this modified worship; and thus there is no reason for praising King Darius. Meanwhile his example will condemn all those who profess themselves to be catholic or Christian kings, or defenders of the faith, since they not only bury true piety, but, as far as they possibly can, weaken the whole worship of God, and would willingly extinguish his name from the world, and thus tyrannize over the pious, and establish impious superstitions by their own cruelty. Darius will be a fit judge for them and the edict here recited by Daniel will be sufficient for the condemnation of them all.

He now says, *The edict was written for all people, nations, and tongues, who dwell in the whole earth.* We see how Darius wished to make known God's power not only to the neighbouring people, but studied to promulgate it far and wide. He wrote not only for Asia and Chaldea, but also for the Medes and Persians. He had never been the ruler of Persia, yet since his father-in-law had received him into alliance in the empire, his authority extended thither. This is the sense of the phrase, *the whole earth.* This does not refer to the whole habitable world, but to that monarchy which extended through almost the entire East, since the Medes and Persians then held the sway from the sea as far as Egypt. When we consider the magnitude of this empire, Daniel may well say, the edict was promulgated *through the whole earth. Peace be multiplied unto you!* We know how kings in this way soothe their subjects, and use soft persuasions for more easily accomplishing their wishes, and thus obtain the implicit obedience of their subjects. And it is gratuitous on their part to implore peace on their subjects. Meanwhile, as I have already said, they court their favour by these enticements, and thus prepare their subjects to submit to the yoke. By the term "peace," a state of prosperity is implied; meaning, may you be prosperous and happy. He afterwards adds, *the decree is placed in their sight*, that is, they display their command before all their subjects. This, then, is the force of the phrase, *my edict has been placed;* that is, if my authority and power prevail with you, you must thus far·obey me; *that all may fear*, or, that all may be afraid and *tremble before the God of Daniel!* By fear and terror he means simply reverence, but he speaks as the profane are accustomed to do, who abhor God's name. He seems desirous of expressing how conspicuous was the power of the God of Israel, which ought properly to impress every one, and induce all to worship with reverence, and fear, and trembling. And this method of speaking is derived from a correct principle; since lawful worship is never offered to God but when we are humbled before him. Hence God often calls himself terrible, not because he wishes his worshippers to approach him with fear, but, as we have said, because the souls of men will never be drawn forth to reverence unless they seriously comprehend his power, and thus become afraid of his judgment. But if fear alone flourishes in men's minds, they cannot form themselves to piety, since we must consider that passage of the Psalm, "With thee is propitiation that thou mayest be feared." (Psalm cxxx. 4.) God, therefore, cannot be properly worshipped and feared, unless we are persuaded that he may be entreated; nay, are quite sure that he is propitious to us. Yet it is necessary for fear and dread to precede the humiliation of the pride of the flesh.

This, then, is the meaning of the phrase, *that all should fear or be afraid of the God of Daniel*. The king calls him so, not because Daniel had fabricated a God for himself, but because he was his only worshipper. We very properly speak of Jupiter as the god of the Greeks, since he was deified by their folly, and hence obtained a name and a celebrity throughout the rest of the world. Meanwhile, Jupiter, and Minerva, and the crowd of false deities received their names from the same origin. There is another reason why King Darius calls the God whom Daniel worshipped *Daniel's God*, as he is called the God of Abraham, not through deriving any precarious authority from Abraham, but through his manifesting himself to Abraham. To explain this more clearly—Why is he called the God of Daniel rather than of the Babylonians? because Daniel had learnt from the law of Moses the pure worship of God, and the covenant which he had made with Abraham and the holy fathers, and the adoption of Israel as his peculiar people. He complied with the worship prescribed in the Law, and that worship depended on the covenant. Hence this name is not given as if Daniel had been free to fashion or imagine any god for himself; but because he had worshipped that God who had revealed himself by his word. Lastly, this phrase ought to be so understood as to induce all to fear that God who had made a covenant with Abraham and his posterity, and had chosen for himself a peculiar people. He taught the method of true and lawful worship, and unfolded it in his law, so that Daniel worshipped him. We now understand the meaning of the clause. Thus we may learn to distinguish the true God from all the idols and fictions of men, if we desire to worship him acceptably. For many think they worship God when they wander through whatever errors they please, and never remain attached to one true God. But this is perverse, nay, it is nothing but a profanation of true piety to worship God so confusedly. Hence, we must contemplate the distinction which I have pointed out, that our minds may be always included within the bounds of the word, and not wander from the true God, if indeed we desire to retain him and to follow the religion which pleases him. We must continue, I say, within the limits of the word, and not turn away on either one side or the other; since numberless fallacies of the devil will meet us immediately, unless the word holds us in strict obedience. As far as concerns Darius, he acknowledged the one true God, but as we have already said, he did not reject that fictitious and perverse worship in which he was brought up;—such a mixture is intolerable before God!

He adds, *Because he is alive, and remains for ever!* This seems to reduce all false gods to nothing; but it has been previously said, and the circumstances prove it true, that when the profane turn their attention to the supreme God, they begin to wander directly. If they constantly acknowledged the true God, they would instantly exclude all fictitious ones; but they think it sufficient if God obtains the first rank; meanwhile they add minor deities, so that he lies hid in a crowd, although he enjoys a slight pre-eminence. Such, then, was the reasoning and the plan of Darius, because he held nothing clearly or sincerely concerning the essence of the one true God; but he thought the supreme power resident in the God of Israel, just as other nations worship their own deities! We see, then, that he did not depart from the superstitions which he had imbibed in his boyhood; and hence, we have no reason for praising his piety, unless in this particular case. But, meanwhile, God extorted a confession from him, in which he describes his nature to us. He calls him "the living God," not only because he has life in himself, but out of himself, and is also the origin and fountain of life. This epithet ought to be taken actively, for God not only lives but has life in himself; and he is also the source of life, since there is no life independent of him. He afterwards adds, *He remains for ever*, and thus distinguishes him from all creatures, in which there is no firmness nor stability. We know also how everything in heaven, as well as heaven itself, is subject to various changes. In this, therefore, God differs from everything created, since he is unchangeable and invariable. He adds, *His kingdom is not corrupted, and his dominion remains for ever.* Here he clearly expresses what he had formerly stated respecting the firmness of God's estate, since he not only remains essentially the same, but exercises his power throughout the whole world, and governs the world by his own virtue, and sustains all things. For if he had only said, " God remains for ever," we are so perverse and narrow-minded as to interpret it merely as follows :—God, indeed, is not changeable in his own essence, but our minds could not comprehend his power as universally diffused. This explanation, then, is worthy of notice, since Darius clearly expresses that God's kingdom is incorruptible and his dominion everlasting.

Secondly, he calls God his deliverer. Those who consider this edict as an illustrious example of piety, will say Darius spoke evangelically as a herald of the mercy of God. But, as we have previously said, Darius never generally embraced what Scripture teaches concerning God's cherishing his people with clemency, his helping them through his being merciful to them, and nourishing them with a father's kindness. King Darius knew nothing of this reason. Daniel's deliverance was well known ; this was a particular proof of God's favour. If Darius had only partially perceived God's lovingkindness towards his servants, then he would have acknowledged his readiness to preserve and deliver them. This would be too frigid unless the cause was added,—*God is a deliverer!* since he has deigned to choose his servants, and bears witness to his being their Father, and listens to their prayers, and pardons their transgressions. Unless, therefore, the hope of deliverance is founded on God's gratuitous adoption and pity, any acknowledgment of him will be but partial and inefficient. Darius, then, does not speak here as if truly and purely instructed in the mercy of God ; but he speaks of him only as the deliverer of his own people. He correctly asserts in general, " God is a deliverer," *since he snatched Daniel from the mouth of lions,* that is, from their power and fierceness. Darius, I say, reasons correctly, when he derives from one example the more extensive doctrine concerning the power of God to preserve and snatch away his people whenever he pleases ; meanwhile, he acknowledges God's visible power in a single act, but he does not understand the principal cause and fountain of God's affection to Daniel to be, his belonging to the sons of Abraham, and his paternal favour in preserving him. Hence this instruction should profit us and touch our minds effectually, since God is our deliverer; and, in the first place, we must confess ourselves to be admitted to favour on the condition of his pardoning us, and not treating us according to our deserts, but indulging us as sons through his amazing liberality. This then is the true sense.

He afterwards says, *he performs signs and wonders in heaven and earth!* This ought to be referred to power and dominion, as previously mentioned; but Darius always considers the events before his eyes. He had seen Daniel dwelling safely with lions, and all the rest destroyed by them; these were manifest proofs of God's power; hence he properly asserts, *he performs signs and wonders.* But there is no doubt, that Darius was admonished by the other signs which had taken place before he possessed the monarchy; he had doubtless heard what had happened to King Nebuchadnezzar, and then to King Belshazzar, whom Darius had slain when he seized his kingdom. He collects, therefore, more testimonies to God's power, for the purpose of illustrating his glory in the preservation of Daniel. In short, if Darius had renounced his superstitions, the confession of his piety would have been pure, and full, and ingenuous; but because he did not forsake the worship of his false gods, and continued his attachment to their pollution, his piety cannot deserve our praise, and his true and serious conversion cannot be collected from his edict. This is the complete sense. It now follows:

28. So this Daniel prospered in the reign of Darius, and in the reign of Cyrus the Persian.

28. Daniel autem ipse prospere egit[1] in regno Darii et in regno Cyri Persæ.

The word צלח, *tzelech,* properly signifies to "pass over," and the signification is here metaphorical, in the sense of being prosperous. There is no doubt, however, of there being a silent contrast between the kingdom of the Persians and the Chaldean monarchy, that is, to speak more concisely

---

[1] Or, passed.—*Calvin.*

and clearly, between the twofold condition of Daniel. For, as we have said, he was for some time in obscurity under Nebuchadnezzar; when this monarchy was about to perish he became conspicuous; and throughout the whole period of the reign of the Chaldeans he was obscure and contemptible. All indeed had heard of him as a remarkable and illustrious Prophet, but he was rejected from the palace. At one time he was seated at the king's gate, in great honour and respect, and then again he was cast out. During the continuance of the Chaldee monarchy, Daniel was not held in any esteem; but under that of the Medes and Persians he prospered, and was uniformly treated with marked respect, for Cyrus and Darius were not so negligent as instantly to forget the wonderful works of God performed by his hand. Hence the word "passing through," pleases me, since, as I have said, it is a mark of the continual possession of honour; for not only King Darius, but also Cyrus exalted him and raised him into the number of his nobles, when he heard of his favour. It is clear that he left Babylon and went elsewhere. Very probably he was not long among the Medes, for Darius or Cyaxares died without any heirs, and then his whole power passed to Cyrus alone, who was his nephew, through his sister, and his son-in-law being his daughter's husband. No doubt Daniel here commends God's favour and kindness towards himself, because this was not the usual solace of exile, to obtain the highest favour among foreign and barbarous nations, or attain the largest share of their honour and reverence. God, therefore, alleviated his sorrow by this consolation in his exile. Hence Daniel here not only regards himself in his private capacity, but also the object of his dignity. For God wished his name to be spread abroad and celebrated over all those regions through which Daniel was known, since no one could behold without remembering the power and glory of Israel's God. Daniel, therefore, wished to mark this. On the other hand also, no doubt, it was a matter of grief to him to be deprived of his country, not like the rest of mankind, but because the land of Canaan was the peculiar inheritance of God's people. When Daniel was snatched away and led off to a distance, as far as Media and Persia, without the slightest hope of return, there is no doubt that he suffered continual distress. Nor was the splendour of his station among the profane of such importance as to induce him to prefer it to that pledge of God's favour and paternal adoption in the land of Canaan. He had doubtless inscribed on his heart that passage of David's, I had rather be in the court of the Lord, than in the midst of the greatest riches of the ungodly : then, I had rather be a despised one in the house of God, than to dwell in the tents of the unrighteous." (Ps. lxxxiv. 10.) Thus Daniel had been taught. Ezekiel, too, properly includes him among the three most holy men who have lived since the beginning of the world. (xiv. 14.)[1] This was of the greatest moment ; for when he was a youth, or at least but middle aged, he was joined with Job and Noah, and was the third in rare and almost incredible sanctity ! Since this was his character, he was no doubt affected with the greatest sorrow when he perceived himself subject to perpetual exile, without the slightest hope of return, and of being able to worship God in his temple and to offer sacrifice with the rest. But lest he should be ungrateful to God, he desires to express his sense of the uncommon benevolence with which, though an exile and a stranger, and subject to reproach among other captives, he was treated and even honoured among the Medes and Persians. This, therefore, is the simple meaning of the passage. It is quite clear, as I have lately said, that Cyrus, after the death of Darius, succeeded to the whole monarchy ; and we shall afterwards see in its proper place how Daniel dwelt with Cyrus, who reigned almost thirty years longer. Thus, a long time intervened between his death and that of Darius. This, therefore, did not occur without the remarkable counsel of God, since the change in the kingdom did not influence the position of Daniel, as it usually does. For new empires we know to be like turning the world upside down. But Daniel always retained his rank, and thus God's goodness was displayed in him, and wherever he went he carried with him this testimony of God's favour. I shall not proceed further, as we shall discuss a new prophecy to-morrow.

[1] See DISSERTATION, No. xxv., at the close of this Volume.

PRAYER.

Grant, Almighty God, since by means of a man entangled in many errors, thou wishest to testify to us the extent of thy power, that we may not at this day grope about in darkness, while thou offerest us light, through the Sun of righteousness, Jesus Christ, thy Son. Meanwhile, may we not be ashamed to profit by the words of a heathen, who was not instructed in thy law, but who celebrated thy name so magnificently when admonished by a single miracle: hence may we learn by his example to acknowledge thee, not only the Supreme but the Only God. As thou hast bound us to thyself by entering into a covenant with us in the blood of thine only-begotten Son, may we ever cleave to thee with true faith; may we renounce all the clouds of error, and be always intent upon that light to which thou invitest us, and towards which thou drawest us; until we arrive at the sight of thy glory and majesty, and being conformed to thee, may we at length enjoy in reality that glory which we now but partially behold.— Amen.

DISSERTATIONS.

Dissertation First.

THE THIRD YEAR OF KING JEHOIAKIM.
Chap. i. 1.

A CORRECT idea of the scope and interpretation of these prophecies cannot be obtained without a due attention to the chronology of the events recorded. Hence, throughout these Dissertations it will be necessary to discuss some apparently unimportant points, and to combat some seemingly harmless opinions. We are thus compelled to enter into details which some may pronounce devoid of interest, but which will prove worth the labour bestowed upon them.

The necessity for comment on this first verse arises from the difficulty of reconciling its statement with the twenty-fifth chapter of Jeremiah. The relation of the reign of Nebuchadnezzar must be harmonized with those of the three last kings of Judah, to enable us to reconcile Daniel and Jeremiah. We must first ascertain the historical events which concern Jehoiakim, and fix their dates by comparing the Books of Kings and Chronicles, and the various allusions to him in Ezekiel and other prophets. Next, we must accurately define the events of Nebuchadnezzar's reign; and afterwards so compare them as to draw a correct inference from the whole, notwithstanding much apparent discrepancy. This has been done by some commentators, the results of whose labours will here be placed before the reader. WIL-LET's remark on Calvin is worthy of notice: "Calvin thinketh to dissolve this knot by the distinction of Nebuchadnezzar the father, and Nebuchadnezzar the son; that in one place the one is spoken of, and the other in the other, but the question is not concerning the year of Nebuchadnezzar's reign, but the year of Jehoiakim's reign wherein Jerusalem should be besieged; so that the doubt remaineth still."[1] He also answers Calvin's solution, by referring Nebuchadnezzar's second year not to the period of his reign, but "rather to the time of Daniel's ministry and employment with the king, that in the second year of his service he expounded the king's dream." Many learned Jews are of opinion that the last year of Jehoiakim's reign is intended, meaning the last of his independent sovereignty, since they treat him in former years as simply a tributary king to either the Egyptians or Babylonians. Josephus in his *Antiq.*, (Book x. 6,) is supposed to favour this theory; for he places Nebuchadnezzar's attack in the eighth year of Jehoiakim's reign, and does not allude to any previous one. WINTLE, however, does not consider that the words of Josephus justify this inference,[2] and suggests that the difference in the methods used by the Jews and Babylonians in computing their years, may tend to obviate the inconsistency. WINTLE suggests some reasons for dating the commencement of the seventy years' captivity from the completion of the siege in the fourth year of Jehoiakim, when Daniel and his associates were among the first captives. *Prideaux* supposes this event to have occurred six hundred and six years A. C., or the one hundred and forty-second year of Nabonassar's era; *Vignoles* and *Blair* fix the year following. *Wintle* agrees with the latter date, supposing the captivity not to continue during seventy solar years, and fixing their termination about 536 A. C.

Another commentator, who has paid great attention to chronology, deserves special notice, since he advocates a new theory respecting Cyrus and Nebuchadnezzar, which is worthy of remark, though it has been severely criticised. THE DUKE OF MANCHESTER has an elaborate chapter on this date, from which we shall extract the conclusions at which he has

---

[1] *Willet's* "*Hexapla in Dan.*" Edit. 1610, p. 13.
[2] See his "*Daniel.*" Edit. Tegg, 1836, p. 2.

arrived. He understands "Daniel to speak of Jehoiakim's independent reign, reckoning from the time that he rebelled against Nebuchadnezzar."[1] Jehoiakim was taken captive in the seventh of Nebuchadnezzar.

The oldest expositors felt the difficulty of the passage. *Rabbi Solomon Jarchi* asks, "How can this be said?" and then replies as follows :—This was the eighth year of Nebuchadnezzar and the third of Jehoiakim's rebellion against him.

HENGSTENBERG has not been forgetful to defend our Prophet from the charge of historical inaccuracy, to which this verse has given rise. He treats the assumption, that Nebuchadnezzar took Jerusalem before his accession to the throne, as inadmissible. "The assertion of his being associated by his father in the co-regency at that time is not adequately sustained."[2] CH. B. MICHAELIS and BERTHOLDT have made various attempts to reconcile the discrepancy. "The assumption," says Hengstenberg, "that Nebuchadnezzar undertook his first expedition in the eighth year of Jehoiakim, is an hypothesis grounded merely on one passage." Still, this passage, far from containing an error, affords a striking proof of the writer's historical knowledge. *Berosus*, as quoted by *Josephus*, (*Arch.* x. 11, 1,) narrates the victory of Nebuchadnezzar at Carchemish, which occurred about the close of Jehoiakim's third year. Carchemish was a city on the banks of the Euphrates, taken by Pharaoh-Necho about three years previously. Immediately after this victory, the conqueror marched against Jerusalem and took it. The process by which Hengstenberg arrives at this result, the various authors whom he quotes, and the complete refutation which he supplies of all the conjectures of his Neologian opponents, will be found amply detailed in the valuable work already quoted. ROSENMULLER also discusses the point, but leans too much to those writers whom Hengstenberg refutes.

[1] "The Times of Daniel," p. 29, chap. iii., where other dates of interest are clearly exhibited.
[2] *Dissertations on the Genuineness of Daniel.* Edinburgh, 1848, p. 43.

Dissertation Second.

NEBUCHADNEZZAR—ONE KING OR TWO?
Chap. i. 1.

The difficulty of reconciling the various statements of Scripture with themselves and with profane history, has raised the question whether there were two Nebuchadnezzars or only one. The Duke of Manchester is a strenuous advocate for the former hypothesis, and his view of the case is worthy of perusal. The first king he supposes to have overthrown Necho's army in the fourth year of Jehoiakim, as we have already stated. He came from the north into Judea, and took the people captive after the overthrow of Assyria. His eleventh year corresponds with the fourth of Zedekiah, while he reigned on the whole about twenty-nine years. He is to be identified with Cyrus, the father of Cambyses, well known in Persian history, so that the second Nebuchadnezzar was Cambyses himself. Although the astronomical Canon of Ptolemy is a formidable adversary, this writer shews much ingenuity in bending it to his purpose. The first king of this name began his reign A. C. 511, while Paulus Orosius determines the taking of Babylon " by Cyrus" about the time of the expulsion of the kings from Rome (A. C. 510.) Thus sixty-nine years elapsed between the overthrow of Necho and the conquest of Egypt by Nebuchadnezzar the second; and in the eighteenth year of the reign of this latter king the golden image was set up.

Having identified the second king with Cambyses, this writer brings forward many testimonies in favour of his being a Persian, and shews that the Chaldeans were not Babylonians but Persians. He treats him as identical with the

Persian Jemsheed, the contemporary of Pythagoras and Thales, and the founder of Pasargadæ and Persepolis, and justifies his positions by the authorities of Diocles, Hecatæus, Cedrenus, the Maccabees, Abydenus, and Alexander Polyhistor. "The evidence is deduced from direct testimony, from geographical position, from similarity in language and religion, in manners and customs, in personal character and alliances; from Babylonian bricks and cylinders; as also from historical synchronisms and identity of actions."[1] The statements of Herodotus are fully discussed and compared with the Egyptian sculptures, with the view of shewing that the second Nebuchadnezzar was the Cambyses of Herodotus, the son-in-law of Astyages and the conqueror of Egypt. The story of his madness, after profaning the temple of Apis, is said to apply accurately to this second monarch.

It could not be expected that a theory of this kind could be introduced into the world without severe and searching examination. Accordingly, BIRKS, in his preface to "*The two later Visions of Daniel*," writes as follows: "I have examined closely the two difficulties which alone give a seeming strength to his Grace's theory,—the succession of names in the Persian history, and the two covenants under Zerubbabel and Nehemiah,—and feel confident I can meet them both with a full and complete answer It seems to me surprising that a paradox of two Scripture Nebuchadnezzars, and a Scripture Cyrus, totally unknown to profane history, in the reign of Longimanus, contemporary with Cimon and Pericles, can ever be received by any mind accustomed to pay the least regard to the laws of evidence. Every fresh inquiry has only increased my confidence in the usual chronology derived from the Canon of Ptolemy, and its truth, I believe, may be almost entirely established even by Scripture evidence alone." VAUX, the learned author of "*Nineveh and Persepolis*," furnishes a clear sketch of Nebuchadnezzar's career, by combining the accounts of Herodotus and the Scriptures. In the thirty-first year of Josiah's reign, Necho fought the battle of Megiddo, in which Josiah was mortally wounded. He then took Cadytis, "the holy city"

[1] *Times of Daniel*, p. 141.

of the Jews, and at length returned to Egypt with abundance of spoil. After a lapse of three years he invaded the territory of the king of Babylon. The reigning monarch—Nabopolassar—was aged and infirm ; he gave the command of his army to his son Nebuchadnezzar, who defeated the Egyptians at Carcesium or Carchemish, and drove them out of Asia. He marched to Jerusalem, and reinstated Jehoiakim as its king, in subjection to himself; he spoiled the temple of the chief ornaments and vessels of value, and among the prisoners transmitted to Babylon were Daniel and his three friends. He next carried on war against the Egyptians, till the news of his father's death caused his return. The revolt of Jehoiakim caused a second attack upon the city, and the carrying off of many prisoners, among whom was Ezekiel, to the banks of the distant Chebar. Zedekiah, the brother of Jehoiakim, having been placed on the throne, and having made an alliance with Pharaoh Hophra, the Apries of Herodotus, he is deposed by the King of Babylon, and carried captive in blindness and chains. Thus for the third and last time this conqueror invaded Judea and profaned the temple. After a lapse of four years he besieged Tyre ; for thirteen years it resisted his arms, but was at length razed to the ground. He next succeeded in an expedition against Egypt, dethroned Apries, and leaving Amasis as his viceroy, returned to his imperial city. In the language of Jeremiah, "he arrayed himself with the land of Egypt, as a shepherd putteth on his garment." He next occupies himself in beautifying the city, and erecting a palace of extraordinary magnificence, and in constructing those hanging gardens mentioned by Diodorus, Megasthenes, and Arrian. The remainder of his history is easily gathered from the Prophet's narrative. "A careful consideration of the authorities seems to shew that CLINTON is right in his supposition that the reign of this prince was about forty-four years in duration, and that he was succeeded after a short interval by Belshazzar."[1] *Willet* arrives at the same conclusion as to the length of his reign by a different process of reasoning. The following dates are extracted from

---

[1] *Nineveh and Persep.*, p. 71, second edition.

Prideaux, whose caution and accuracy are most commendable:—

A.C.
586. Tyre besieged.
570. The death of Apries, coincident with the dream of the tree, (chap. iv.,) after his last return from Egypt.
569. Chap. iv. 30. Driven out into the fields.
563. Restored after seven years.
562. Death, after about forty-four years' reign.

Another series of dates has been displayed by the author of "*The Times of Daniel*," founded on a different chronological basis; we can only extract a few of them from pp. 282, *et seq.*:—

B.C.
510. Babylon taken by Cyrus, and kings expelled from Rome.
507. Commencement of Jehoiakim's independent reign. Dan. i. 1.
500. Nebuchadnezzar II. appointed; his dream. Dan. ii.
494. Golden Image set up. Dan. iii.
483. Nebuchadnezzar I. died.
441. Nebuchadnezzar II. died.

Dr. Wells has the following chronological arrangement of the chief events of Nebuchadnezzar's reign:—

A.C.
607. He is this year taken by his father "as partner" in the kingdom, falling in with the latter part of the third year of Jehoiakim, (Chap. i. 1.)
606. Jehoiakim carried to Babylon with Daniel and others. The first of the seventy years' captivity.
605. His father died. Nabopolassar in Ptolemy's Canon, the son's name being Nabocolassor. The Canon allows him forty-three years from this period.
603. Daniel interprets his dream. Chap ii.
588. He re-takes Jerusalem and Zedekiah.
569. Returned to Babylon, is afflicted with insanity. Ch. iv.
562. He dies "a few days" after being restored to reason.

Dissertation Third.

THE ANCESTORS AND SUCCESSORS OF NEBUCHADNEZZAR.

Chap. i. 1.

To understand aright the history of these times, we must take a cursory glance at the period both preceding and following that of the great Chaldean chieftain. His ancestors were largely concerned in the overthrow of the Assyrian empire. The origin of this monarchy is involved in great obscurity, and we are at this moment in a transition state with respect to our knowledge of its history. The deciphering of those inscriptions which have lately been brought home is rapidly proceeding, and will lead to a more complete knowledge of the events of this obscure epoch. Early in the Book of Genesis we read of Nimrod, the grandson of Ham, as the founder of an extensive monarchy in the land of Shinar. Out of this land he went forth into Ashur, or perhaps it is Ashur who went forth and built Nineveh and other cities. The records of succeeding ages are too few to enable us to follow the stream of history: we have nothing to guide us but myths, and legends, and traditionary sovereigns, whose names are but the fictions of imagination. It must never be forgotten that many centuries elapsed between Noah and Solomon, and that the most ancient profane history is comparatively modern. The late discoveries in Egypt, and the high state of civilisation attained by these "swarthy barbarians," have led the learned to the conclusion that we have hitherto lost many centuries between the flood and Abraham; and since the long list of Egyptian dynasties, as given by Manetho, has been proved accurate, it may fairly be supposed that the Assyrian sculptures will rather add to the credit of Ctesias than detract from it. At all events, Nineveh was "no mean city" when Athens was a marsh, and Sardis a rock. Whether Ninus is a fabulous creation or not, monarchs as mighty as the eagle-headed worshipper of Nisroch his god, swayed the sceptre for ages over a flourishing and highly civilized people. Herodotus gives us a hint of the antiquity and pre-eminence of Assyria when he says, "The Medes were the first who began to revolt from the Assyrians, who had possessed the supreme command over Upper Asia for five hundred and twenty years." Whether we adopt the view of Bishop Lowth or not, that Ninus lived in the time of the Judges,[1] we may correctly assume that some successful conqueror enlarged and beautified Babylon, five hundred years before the Chaldean era of Nabonassar, 747 A. C. Whatever the source of this wealth, whether derived from the spoils of conquered nations, according to Montesquieu, or from intercourse with India through Egypt, according to Bruce,[2] the lately discovered remains imply a very high style of art at a very remote period in the history of Assyria. The "Pul" of 2 Kings xv. 19, was by no means the founder of the monarchy, as Sir Isaac Newton and others have supposed; he was but one amidst those "servants of Bar," whose names are now legible on the Nimroud obelisk in the British Museum. The next king mentioned in Scriptures is Tiglath-Pileser, whose name we have lately connected with Pul and Ashur; and after him follow Shalmaneser, Sennacherib, and Esarhaddon, the three kings who are thought to have built the palace at Khorsabad, founded Mespila, and constructed the lions in the south-west palace of Nimroud. As the Medes revolted first, so the Chaldeans rebelled afterwards, according to the usual law of separation from the parent stock, when the tribe or race grows strong enough to establish its indepen-

[1] See his Notes on Isaiah, chap. xxiii. p. 132; and *Herod. Clio.* Edit. Gronov., p. 40.
[2] *Travels*, Book ii. chap. 1. See *Prideaux's* authorities, and his arrangement of the Assyrian kings, which differs slightly from that here adopted.

dence. The first prince who is known to have lived after this revolt is Nabonassar, the founder of the era called by his name. In process of time, other kings arose and passed away, till in the thirty-first year of Manasseh, Esarhaddon died, after reigning thirteen years over Assyria and Babylon united. He was succeeded by his son Laosduchius, the Nabuchodonosor of the Book of Judith, whose successor commenced his reign in the fifty-first year of Manasseh, being the hundred and first of the above mentioned era. From this effeminate king his Chaldean general Nabopolassar wrested Babylon, and reigned over his native country twenty-one years. This revolt is said to have taken place in the eighteenth year of King Josiah, when the powers of Media uniting with the power of Babylonia, took and destroyed the great city of Nineveh, and reduced the people under the sway of the rising monarchy. His son Nebuchadnezzar is said to have married the daughter of Astyages, the king of the Medes, and thus brings down the history to the times of our Prophet.

Among the ancient cities of the world, Nineveh is conspicuous for its grandeur. The phrase of Jonah, "that great city," is amply confirmed by the historian, Diodorus Siculus, (lib. ii. sec. 23,) who uses precisely the same expression, recording its circumference as four hundred and eighty stadia, with high and broad walls. The inference from the statement of the Book of Jonah is, that it was populous, civilized, and extensive. The language of both Jonah and Nahum imply exactly what the buried sculptures have exhibited to us, a state of society highly organized, with various ranks, from the sovereign to the soldier and the workman, yet effeminated by luxury and self-indulgence. The expressions of Scripture give us exalted ideas of its size and splendour, while they assign its wickedness as a reason for the complete destruction by which it was annihilated. Prophet after prophet recognises its surpassing opulence, its commercial greatness, and its deep criminality. The voice of Zephaniah is soon followed by the sword of Arbaces, and Sennacherib and Sardanapalus are eclipsed by the rising greatness of Nabopolassar and Cyaxares. Its temples and its palaces had become so encrusted in the soil during eight centuries of men, that Strabo knows it only as a waste, and Tacitus treats it as a *Castellum;* and in the thirteenth century of our era, Abulfaragius confirms the prophecy of Nahum and the narrative of Tacitus, by recording nothing but the existence of a small fortification on the eastern bank of the Tigris.[1]

The dates assigned to these events vary considerably; the following may be trusted as the result of careful comparison. In the year A. C. 650, Nebuchodonosor is found on the throne of Assyria, "a date," says Vaux, "which is determined by the coincidence with the forty-eighth year of Manasseh, and by the fact that his seventeenth year was the last of Phraortes, king of Media, A. C. 634. The Book of Judith informs us of an important engagement at Ragau between this Assyrian king and Arphaxad the king of the Medes. This victory at Ragau, or Rhages, occurred A. C. 634, just "fifty-seven years after the loss of Sennacherib's army."[2] After returning from Ecbatana, the capital of Media, the conqueror celebrated a banquet at Nineveh which lasted one hundred and twenty days. Cyaxares, the son of Phraortes, at length avenged his father's death at Rhages, and by the aid of Nabopolassar, threw off the yoke of Assyria, attacked and took Nineveh about 606 A. C., and thus, by fixing the seat of empire at Babylon, blotted out the name of Nineveh from the page of the world's history.

This renowned general is usually held to be the father of Nebuchadnezzar, on the authority of Berosus, as quoted by Josephus, and of the *Astronomical Canon* of *Ptolemy.* But the author of "The Times of Daniel" endeavours to identify him with either Sardanapalus or Esarhaddon; the arguments by which this supposition is supported will be found in detail in the work itself, while the original passages in Josephus and Eusebius are found at length in the notes to Grotius on "*The truth of the Christian religion.*"[3] He died A. C. 695.

[1] *Strabo,* lib. xvi. p. 737. *Tacit. An.,* lib. xii. sec. 13. *Hist. Dyn.*, p. 604.
[2] *Nineveh* and *Persepolis,* p. 37.
[3] Bk. iii. sec. 16, and *Euseb. Præpar.*, lib. ix. c. 40 and 41, also *Strabo,* lib. xv. p. 687.

His Successors.—According to the Canon of Ptolemy, Evil-Merodach succeeded Nebuchadnezzar, reigned two years, and was slain by his brother-in-law Neri-Glissar, who reigned four years; his son, Laboroso-archod, reigned nine months, though quite a child, and was slain by Nabonadius, supposed to be Belshazzar, a grandson of Nebuchadnezzar, who reigned seventeen years. Evil-Merodach is mentioned in 2 Kings xxv. 27, and Jeremiah lii. 31, but not by Daniel, and this gives some countenance to the supposition, that Belshazzar was the son and not the grandson of Nebuchadnezzar. It is not easy to assign with certainty the correct dates to each of these kings, the reckoning of Josephus is here followed, which he derives from Berosus. The testimony of profane antiquity to the truth and historical accuracy of Daniel may be found in a convenient form in *Kitto's Bibli. Cyclop.*, Art. *Nebuchadnezzar*, p. 406. The authorities are quoted at length, and the whole subject is ably elucidated. The limited space necessarily allowed for illustrating these Lectures, must be our apology for merely indicating where valuable information is to be obtained.

In the *New Monthly Magazine* for August and September 1845, there are two articles very full of illustration of our subject, by *W. F. Ainsworth*, entitled, *The Rivers and Cities of Babylonia.*

Dissertation Fourth.

THE CHALDEANS.

Chap. i. 5.

To determine the question which was raised in our last DISSERTATION, we must investigate the origin of the Chaldeans, as it was the tribe whence Nebuchadnezzar sprung. "The question," says Heeren, "what the Chaldeans really were, and whether they ever properly existed as a nation, is one of the most difficult which history presents."[1] They are first mentioned in Genesis (xi. 28,) as *Casdim*, (*Lec.* v. p. 122;) they were situated north of Judea, and are identical with the people who should, according to Jeremiah, destroy the temple from the north. (Jer. i. 13, 14, &c.) They are not mentioned by name again in the books of Scripture till many centuries afterwards they had become a mighty nation. The word *Chasdim* in the Hebrew and *Chasdaim* in the Chaldee dialects, is clearly the same as the Greek $Χαλδαῖοι$; and Gesenius supposing the root to have been originally *card*, refers them to the race inhabiting the mountains called by Xenophon *Carduchi*. Forster, indeed, has argued at considerable length in favour of their Arabian origin, and supposes them the well known Beni Khaled, a horde of Bedouin Arabs.[2] From this opinion we entirely dissent. The view of Gesenius in his Lectures at Halle in 1839, quoted in "The Times of Daniel," appears preferable,—"The Chaldeans had their original seat on the east of the Tigris, south of Armenia, which we now call Koordistan; and, like the Koords in our day, they were warlike mountaineers,

[1] Vol. ii., ch. i., *Babylon*, p. 147, Eng. Trans.
[2] *Geog. of Arabia*, vol. i. p. 54, and vol. ii. p. 210.

without agriculture, shepherds and robbers, and also mercenaries in the Assyrian army ; so Xenophon found them."[1] Vaux quotes Dicæarchus, a Greek historian of the time of Alexander the Great, as alluding to a certain Chaldean, a king of Assyria, who is supposed to have built Babylon ; and in later times, Chaldea implied the whole of Mesopotamia around Babylon, which had also the name of Shiner.[2]

Their religion and their language are also of importance. The former consisted in the worship of the heavenly bodies. They are supposed to have brought with them to Babylon a knowledge of astronomy superior to any then known, since they reduced their observations on the sun, moon, five planets, signs of the zodiac, and the rising and setting of the sun, to a regular system ; and the Greeks are said by Herodotus to have derived from them the division of the day into twelve equal parts.[3] The lunar year was in common use, but the solar year, with its division of months similar to the Egyptian, was employed for astronomical purposes. The learned class gradually acquired the reputation and position of "priests," and thus became astrologers and soothsayers, and "wise men" in their day and generation. Michaelis and Schlozer consider their origin to be Sclavonic, and, consequently, distinct from the Babylonians, who were descendants of Shem.

THEIR LANGUAGE.—The original *language* of this people is a point of great interest to the biblical critic. If the people were of old northern mountaineers, they spoke a language connected with the Indo-Persic and Indo-Germanic stem rather than the Semitic. In treating this question, we should always allow for the length of time which elapsed between the original outbreak of those hordes from their native hills and their conquest of Babylon under Nebuchadnezzar. Gesenius, in his *Lectures on Biblical Archæology*,

---

[1] *Anab.* iv. § 3, v. § 6, vii. § 8. See also *Strabo*, lib. x., and *Freret Rech. Hist. sur les anc. Peuple de l'Asie*, vol. iii., and other authorities quoted by the *Duke of Manchester*, pp. 104, 105.
[2] See *Dicæarch. ap. Stephan. de Urb.* voce Χαλδαῖος, and other authorities quoted by *Vaux*, p. 41, &c., also *Cicero de Divin.*
[3] *Herod.* ii. § 109.

reminds us of their being first tributary to the Assyrians, of their subsequent occupation of the plains of Mesopotamia for some centuries previously to their becoming the conquerors of Asia under successful leaders.[1]

From the fourth verse of chap. ii. we learn that they spoke the Aramaic dialect, which the Alexandrine Version, as well as Theodotion's, denominates the Syriac. From the Cyropædia (Book vii. 24) we ascertain that the Syriac was the ordinary language of Babylon. Strabo also informs us that the same language was used throughout all the regions on the banks of the Euphrates.[2] Diodorus Siculus calls the Chaldeans the most ancient inhabitants of Babylonia, and assigns to their astrologers a similar position to that of the Egyptian priests. Their devotion to philosophy and their practice of astronomy gained them great credit with the powerful, which they turned to account by professing to predict the future and to interpret the visions of the imaginative and the distressed.[3] The testimony of Cicero is precisely similar.[4] Hengstenberg has tested the historical truthfulness of the author of this book, by comparing his account of the Chaldean priest-caste with those of profane history. According to chap. ii. 48. the president of this caste was also a prince of the province of Babylon. Thus, according to Diodorus Siculus, Belesys was the chief president of the priests, "whom the Babylonians call Chaldeans,"[5] and governor of Babylon. In Jeremiah, (xxxix. 3-13,) the president of the priests belonged to the highest class in the kingdom, and is called רבמג, *rab-mag*, a word of Persian origin, and clearly applicable to the office as described by Daniel. The views of Hengstenberg are usually so correct, that the student may generally adopt them at once as his own.

[1] See *Eichhorn's Report*. vol. viii., and *Winer's Chaldee Gr.*, *Introd.*, also *Adelung's Mithridat*, th. i. p. 314. ff.
[2] Lib. ii. t. i. p. 225, ed. *Sieb.*, also lib. xvi.   [3] Lib. ii. ch. 20.
[4] *De Divinat.*, lib. i. cap. 1, also *Pliny's N. H.*, lib. vi. ch. 26.
[5] Lib. ii. § 24, *ap Heng.*, p. 275, *Edit. Ed.*, 1848.

Dissertation Fifth.

I. ASHPENAZ, A CHIEF OF THE EUNUCHS.

Chap. i. 7.

This proper name is interpreted by *Saadias* to mean "the man of a sorrowful countenance;" but *Rosenmüller* assigns the meaning of the Syriac and Arabic corresponding words as more probable, viz., "helping" and "alert." The Alexandrine Greek substitutes Abiezer for Aspenaz, being a Hebrew patronymic, signifying "father of help." "The chief of the eunuchs" seems the correct definition of his office. סרים, *saris*, is equivalent to the Greek *eunouchos*, and the office is similar to that at present exercised at the courts of Turkey and Persia as the *kislar agha*, "high-chamberlain of the palace." So much confidence was necessarily reposed in these domestic officers, that many affairs of the utmost importance and delicacy were intrusted to their care. Thus the children of the royal and noble families of Judea were committed to the care of Aspenaz. The word ספר, *sepher*, "book," in which he was to instruct them, must be extended to all the literature of the Chaldees. Œcolampadius treats it as including rhetoric, eloquence, and all those elevating pursuits which cultivate the mind and refine the manners. He then proceeds to treat the narrative as an allegory; the "prince of Babel, or, of the world," represents Satan; Daniel and his companions, the elect members of Christ. The family of David is supposed to imply this spiritual household of God, and the word פרתמים, *pharth-mim*, nobles, is pressed into this service by a preference for the rendering of Saadias, "perfect fruit." The eunuch is said to typify those spiritual flatterers who entice the children of God by flatteries and allurements to sin, and by substituting worldly sophistry for true wisdom, draw souls from Christ. Although such reflections are very profitable, yet CALVIN has shewn his matured judgment by excluding all fanciful allegory from his comments. ŒCOLAMPADIUS supposes the king to be liberal and benevolent in ordering the captives to be fed from his table, and prudent in proposing this indulgence as a reward for their diligence in study. Here also the king's character is allegorized; he becomes a model of Satan enticing God's elect, and offering them to partake of his own dainties, that he may win them more blandly to himself.

In commenting, too, on the change of names, *Œcolampadius* gives the usual meaning to the Hebrew words, but observes, how the name of God was omitted from them all, and the worthiness attributed to the creature. This, he thinks, to have been the eunuch's intention, while he points to the change as an instance of the contrast between human and divine wisdom. The conduct of Daniel may be illustrated by the practice of the early Christians, against whom it was objected by Cæcilius, that they abhorred meats offered to idols when commanded to partake of them.[1] *Willet* has discussed the questions—"Whether Daniel and the rest learned the curious arts of the Chaldeans?" and, "Whether it be lawful to use the arts and inventions of the heathen?" by collecting various opinions and summing them up with practical wisdom.[2]

II. THE NAMES OF THE THREE CHILDREN.

IT is the well-known custom of the East to change the names of persons on their admission to public office or to families of distinction. The change here recorded most probably arose from a desire to draw these young Jews away from all the associations of home, and to naturalize them as much as possible among their new associates. Hananiah is supposed to come from חן, *chanan*, to be gracious, and יה, *yah*, Jehovah, meaning "favoured of God." Mishael from ש, *ish*, he is, and אל, *el*, God, meaning "the powerful one

---

[1] Apud *Minuc. Fel.*, lib. viii. *Arnob.*
[2] *Quæst.* 38, 39, p. 28. *Edit. Cam.*, 1610.

of God." Azariah from עזר, *gnezer*, help, and יה, *yah*, Jehovah: "the help of Jehovah." A variety of conjectures have been hazarded concerning the Chaldee equivalents. Shadrach is probably from שדא, *sheda*, to inspire, and רך, *rak*, king, being a Babylonian name for the sun; others connect it with an evil deity. Meshach retains a portion of its Hebrew form, and substitutes שך, *shak*, for אל, *el*, that is, the female deity *Schaca*, which answers to the Venus of the Greeks. עבד־נגו, *gnebed-nego*, is the Chaldaic phrase for "servant of Nebo," one of their deities, or perhaps, servant of burning fire. The deity Nebo furnished names to many chiefs and sovereigns among the Assyrians and Chaldees, and modern researches and discoveries have enabled us to trace similar derivations with great accuracy. Compounds of Pul were used in a similar way: thus Tiglath-Pileser is Tiglath Pul-Asser; and Nabo-Pul-Asser is interpreted as Nabo, son of Pul, lord of Assyria.

The name of Daniel was also changed. The word is derived from דון, *dun*, to judge, and אל, *el*, God, meaning "a divine judge;" while his new name relates to the idol Bel, meaning "keeper of the treasures of Bel."

III. THE PULSE.

Chap. i. 12.

CALVIN's view of this verse is rather peculiar, and especially his comment on Deut. viii. 3; on verse 14, p. 106. The word "pulse," הזרעים, *hazerognim*, signifies the same as the Latin *legumen*, and may perhaps be extended to the *cerealia* as well. Vegetable diet generally is intended. The food provided from the royal table was probably too stimulating, and the habitual temperance of Daniel and his companions is here pointed out as conducing remarkably to their bodily health and appearance. Thus, while conscience refused to be "polluted," obedience to the laws of our physical nature produces a corresponding physical benefit. Wintle very appositely quotes *Virgil, Georg.* i. 73, 74, to illustrate the kind of food intended.

Dissertation Sixth.

CORESH—WAS HE CYRUS THE GREAT?
Chap. i. 21.

THE last verse of this chapter is connected with an interesting inquiry, viz., Was the CORESH here mentioned CYRUS THE GREAT, or any other Cyrus? The noble author of "*The Times of Daniel*" has thrown much "life" into the subject by his elaborate defence of a theory which we now proceed to state and discuss. Cyrus the Great he thinks identical with Nebuchadnezzar the First, and Cambyses with his son Nebuchadnezzar the Second; the exploits of the hero of Herodotus and Xenophon are attributed to the former, while Coresh becomes but a minor character, contemporary with Darius the Mede, after whom he is said to reign, and before Darius the son of Ahasuerus. This view also brings the story of Esther within the period of the captivity of Babylon. It has always been a subject of great difficulty with commentators on Daniel, to reconcile the scriptural narrative with those of both Herodotus and Xenophon. The majority finding this impossible, have decided in favour of one or the other of these historians; and the best modern writers usually prefer Herodotus. *Lowth*, in his Notes on *Isaiah*, says, "the Cyrus of Herodotus was a very different character from that of the Cyrus of the Scriptures and Xenophon;" and *Archbishop Secker* has taken great pains to compare all the profane historians with Scripture, and shews that the weight of the argument lies against the truth of the Cyropædia. Whether Cyrus was the grandson of Astyages or not, many believe with Ctesias that he overcame him in battle, and founded the Persian empire upon the ruins of the Me-

dian dynasty. It is scarcely possible that it should be left
for this nineteenth century to discover the identity between
a first Nebuchadnezzar and this conqueror of the East ; and
while the clearing up of every historical discrepancy is impossible, yet it is desirable to reconcile the occurrences which
are related by both Herodotus and Xenophon. The son of
Cambyses the Persian, and of Mandane the daughter of
Astyages king of the Medes, is said to have conquered
Cræsus king of Lydia, enlarged the Persian empire, subdued
Babylon and the remnant of the Assyrian power, and placed
his uncle Cyaxares over the united territories of Media and
Babylon. After the death of this relative, he reigned over
Asia, from India to Ethiopia, a territory consisting of 127
provinces. The manner of his death is uncertain, all the
historians differ in their accounts, but the place of his burial
is allowed to be Pasargadæ, as Pliny has recorded in his
Natural History. This tomb was visited by Alexander the
Great, and has lately been noticed and described by European
travellers. The plains of Murghab are watered by a river
which bears the name of Kur, and is thought to be identical
with the Greek Cyrus. A structure in a ruinous state has
been found there, apparently of the same date as the remains at Persepolis, bearing cuneiform inscriptions which
are now legible. The legend upon one of the pilasters has
been interpreted, " I am Cyrus the Achæmenian;" and no
doubt is entertained by the learned that this monument
once contained the remains of the founder of the Persian
monarchy. A single block of marble was discovered by Sir
R. K. Porter, on which he discovered a beautiful sculpture
in bas-relief, consisting of the figure of a man, from whose
shoulders issue four large wings, rising above the head and
extending to the feet.[1] The whole value of such an inscription to the reader of Daniel is the legend above the figure,
in the arrow-headed character, determining the spot as the
tomb of Cyrus the Great. It shews, at the least, that he
cannot be identified with Nebuchadnezzar.

The manner in which the author of "*The Times of*

[1] An engraving of this statue is given in *Vaux's Nineveh and Persepolis*,
p. 322.

Daniel" has commented on the prophecies relating to the overthrow of Babylon, is worthy of notice here. Isaiah xlv. 14, is referred by *Dr. Keith* to Cyrus, and objection is made to the supposed fulfilment in the person of Cyrus, (p. 293.) Keith is said to apply to Cyrus the primary historical fulfilment of all the prophecies relating to the overthrow of Babylon, and the justness of this inference is doubted. Isaiah xiii.-xiv. 27, is one of the passages where the asserted allusion to Cyrus is questioned, since it relates to a period in which the power of Assyria was in existence. The Assyrian is supposed to be Sennacherib, to whose predecessor both Babylon and Media were subject. "The Chaldeans, mentioned in Isaiah xiii. 19, I have already explained to have been a colony of astronomers, planted in Babylon by the Assyrian kings to carry on their astronomical observations, in which science they excelled." (P. 299, note.) Again, Isaiah xxi. 2, "Go up, O Elam ; besiege, O Media," is applied by *Dr. Keith* to Cyrus, to which the noble author objects, as well as to the supposition "that the overthrow of Belshazzar during his drunken revelry was predicted in Scripture, and that the minute fulfilment by Cyrus is recorded by Xenophon." "The feast of Belshazzar," it is added, "does not appear to correspond with the festival described by Xenophon, which was apparently periodical, and which, not a portion of the nobles, but all the Babylonians, observed by drunkenness and revelry during the whole night." "It also agrees with the mode in which Zopyrus got possession of Babylon." *Calvin* seems to give it this turn, "A treacherous one shall find treachery," &c. (P. 301.) Further comments are then made upon Isaiah xliv. and xlv., and on Jeremiah l. and li., evading the force of their application to Cyrus, and combating with some degree of success the assertions of *Keith ;* for the noble author, who is earnest in pulling down, is ingenious in building up. "From this short examination, it appears that the prophecy of Jeremiah (l. and li.) corresponds with the capture of Babylon by Darius the Mede of Scripture, and by Darius Hystaspes, according to Herodotus." (P. 306.) Some writers have supposed Cyrus to be identical with this Darius the Mede ; and *Archbishop Secker* acknowledges some ground for such a conjecture. " The first year of Darius the Mede is by the LXX. translated the first year of Cyrus,"[1] and the Canon of Ptolemy favours the identity. " Now all agree, as far as I have seen," says *Wintle*, " that the year of the expiration of the captivity, or the year that Cyrus issued his decree in favour of the Jews, was the year 212 of the era of Nabonassar, or 536 A. C. ; and there is no doubt but Darius the Mede, whoever he was, reigned, according to Daniel, from the capture of Babylon, till this same first year of Cyrus, or till the commencement of the reign alloted by Scripture to Cyrus the Persian." " The Canon certainly allots nine years' reign to Cyrus over Babylon, of which space the two former years are usually allowed to coincide with the reign of Cyaxares or Darius the Mede, by the advocates of Xenophon." (Prelim. Diss., p. xxvii.) Herodotus, Xenophon, and Ctesias all agree in the original superiority of the Medes, till the victories of Cyrus turned the scale, and gave rise to the Persian dynasty. At the fall of Babylon, and during the life of Darius, the Medes are mentioned by Daniel as superior, but at the accession of Cyrus this order is reversed, and Ezra, Nehemiah, and Esther, all assign the foremost place to the Persians.

The life of Daniel, *Rosenmüller* reminds us, was prolonged beyond the first year of king כרוש, *Coresh*, for the tenth chapter informs us of his vision in the third year of that monarch's reign. He explains the apparent contradiction, by saying that it was enough for Daniel to live, or to the liberation of the Jews in the first year of the reign of Coresh; that was the crowning event of his prolonged existence. The conjectures of *Bertholdt* and *Aben-Ezra* are mentioned, only to be disposed of by a few words of censure. An ingenious conjecture of a French critic is found in the *Encycl. Theol.*, Liv. xxvii. The objection of Bleek, Ewald, Winer, and De Wette, are ably treated at length by *Hengstenberg*, and really meet with more serious attention than they deserve. It is a useless waste of precious time to enter minutely into every "phantasy" of the restless neology of Germany, while the chronology of Daniel's life will form the subject of

[1] *Wintle's Transl., prelim. Diss.*, p. xxviii.

a subsequent Dissertation. As some Neologians dwell much on the historian CTESIAS, and lest the unlearned reader should be misled by their confident assertions, we may here state that we have only an epitome of his work preserved by the patriarch Photius. Bahr states that he lived about 400 B. C., in the reign of Darius Nothus, being a Greek physician who remained seventeen years at the Persian court. Diodorus informs us that he obtained his information from the royal archives, but there are so many anachronisms and errors of various kinds, that his statements cannot be safely followed as if historically correct. Ctesias, for instance, denies all relationship between Cyrus and Astyages. According to him, he defeated Astyages, invested his daughter Amytis with the honours of a queen, and afterwards married her. F. W. NEWMAN, indeed, prefers this narrative to that of both Herodotus and Xenophon, and thereby renders their testimony to the scriptural record uncertain and valueless. He also treats " the few facts " in regard to the Persian wars, "which the epitomator has extracted as differing from Herodotus," as carrying with them "high probability." The closing scene of his career, as depicted in the narrative of Ctesias, is pronounced " beyond comparison more credible" than that of Herodotus. This great conqueror died the third day after his wound in a battle with " the Derbices," and was buried in that monument at Pasargadæ, which the Macedonians broke open two centuries afterwards, (*Strabo*, lib. xv. § 3 ; *Arrian*, lib. vi. § 29,) and which has lately been explored and described by Morier and Sir R. K. Porter.[1]

Notwithstanding the hypothesis which has lately found favour with the modern writers whose works we have quoted, we feel that the views of the older critics are preferable ; and, on the whole, CALVIN'S exposition can only be improved upon in minor details. The authorities enumerated by *Archbishop Secker*, as given by *Wintle* in his preface, p. xviii. and following, are worthy of attentive perusal ; and we must refer again to *Hengstenberg's* able replies to a variety of objections which we are unable to notice. See chap. vi. p. 102 and following, *Edit. Ed.*

[1] See *Kitto's Bibl. Cyc.*, art *Cyr.*, and *Vaux's Nineveh*, p. 316.

Dissertation Seventh.

THE KING'S DREAM.

CHAP. ii. 1.

ITS DATE.—The assertion of the first verse has created some difficulty, in consequence of its not allowing time enough for the Jewish youth to become a man. Jerome attempts to solve it by supposing the point of departure to be not his reign over Judea, but of his dominion over other nations, as the Assyrians and Egyptians. He seems justified in this view by the words of Josephus, (*Antiq.*, lib. x. ch. 10. § 3,) who distinctly refers the dream to the second year "after the laying waste of Egypt." *Rosenmüller* objects to this explanation, and to that of *C. B. Michaelis*, and adopts that of *Saadias*, who supposes the dream to have happened in the second year, but not to be interpreted till the conclusion of the third.

ITS ORIGIN.—Nothing is more difficult to reduce to philosophic laws than the theory of dreams and their interpretation. The researches of physical science have thrown more light on the subject than all the guesses of ancient or modern divines. Jerome, for instance, thought that in this case, "the shadow of the dream remained," a sort of breath (*aura*) and trace remaining in the mind of the king. It is of no use whatever to seek for much light on these subjects in the works of the ancients, whether Fathers or Reformers; they are constantly displaying their ignorance whenever they treat of subjects within the domain of psychological science.

The physician has now become a far safer guide than the divine. Although Nebuchadnezzar's dream was supernatural in its origin, yet it seems like ordinary ones in its departing from the sleeper while he is completely unconscious of its subject.

Physical researches have proved the truth of Calvin's assertion on verse third, that "*Scientia est generalis et perpetua.*" Explanations have happily passed away from the theologian and the metaphysician to the physician and the chemist. The brain is now admitted to be the organ through which the mind acts during both the activity and the repose of the body, and dreams are now known to depend upon *physical causes* acting through the nerves upon the brain. The late researches of the celebrated chemist Baron Reichenbach seem to have led us one step nearer to the true explanation of these singular phenomena; the discovery of *odyle*, a new imponderable agent, like caloric and electricity, has enabled the modern philosopher to trace some of the laws of natural and artificial sleep. The existence of odyle in magnets, crystals, and the animal frame, and its intimate connection with lucidity, and impressions conveyed to the sensorium during magnetic sleep, seems now to be received by the best psychologists; their experiments will, doubtless, lead to our ascertaining the laws which regulate dreaming; and if the results said to be obtained by Mr. Lewis, Major Buckley, and Dr. William Gregory of Edinburgh, are ultimately admitted as facts by the scientific world, a new method of explaining the operations of the mind in sleep will be completely established.—See the "Letters" published by the Professor of Chemistry in the University of Edinburgh, 1 vol. 12mo. 1851.

This contrast between the ancient and modern methods of explanation is strikingly exemplified by Calvin's reference to the *Daimones* on page 119, which requires some elucidation to render it intelligible to the general reader.

The philosophers of Greece held various theories concerning them, among which that recorded by Plato in the Phædrus is the most singular. He commences by asserting the immortality of the soul, and its essential existence from all eternity. The explanation of this idea, as it really is, he treats as divine, but its similitude as human and readily comprehended. The simile is remarkable. The deities have all a chariot and horses, which are perfect, but ours have two horses, each of contrary dispositions. A whole armament of these winged spirits are led on under the concave of heaven, Jupiter himself leading the armament of gods and daimones. In attempting to ascend, the perfect horses of the deities succeed in reaching the convex surface, which no poet ever has described or will describe worthily; but some charioteers fail in their efforts, because one of their horses is depraved, and ever tends downwards towards the earth. In consequence of this depravity, the utmost confusion occurs—the daimones loose their wings and fall to earth, and become human souls. But the various ranks which arise from them deserve especial notice. Those who have beheld most of the glories beyond the heavenly concave become philosophers, and the next to them kings and warriors. Seven other classes of men spring up in the following order:—politicians, physicians, prophets, poets, farmers, sophists, and tyrants. After ten thousand years, the soul may recover its wings, and be judged—some in heaven and others in courts of justice under the earth, while some pass into beasts and then return again to bodies of men. This notion of the origin of the soul from the daimones is a very singular one, and helps us to understand the double sense of the word, like that of angels among us, both good and bad. Though it is not difficult to perceive its connection with dreaming, as the medium of intercourse between the souls of men and the disembodied spirits, yet such conjectures throw no light whatever upon the king's dream before us.

The passages alluded to by Calvin from Cicero are found in the First and Second Books *De Divinatione.* They consist of extracts from Ennius, and relate the fabled dreams of Priam, Tarquinius Superbus, and the mother of Phalaris, as well as that remarkable one which the magi are said to have interpreted for Cyrus. In the Second Book, Cicero argues wisely and strenuously against the divine origin of dreams. To pay the slightest attention to them he deems the mark of a weak, superstitious, and drivelling mind. He inveighs strongly against the pretence to interpret them, which had become a complete traffic, and displayed the imposture which always flourishes wherever there are dupes to feed it. He combats the views of Aristotle, which Calvin quotes, and supplies much material for discussion though but little illustration of our subject. The passages above referred to will be found quoted and explained in *Colquhoun's History of Magic*, vol. i. p. 203, while some useful observations on *sleep and dreams* occur in p. 60 and following.

Dissertation Eighth.

THE IMAGE AND ITS INTERPRETATION.
Chap. ii. 38.

"Thou art this head of gold." A question has arisen whether this expression relates to Nebuchadnezzar personally, or to his empire and dynasty continued to his grandson. The principle is an important one, although history has already removed all difficulty as to the facts. *C. B. Michaelis, Willet, Wells,* and others, consider the monarch as the representative of his empire, not only during his life but until its overthrow. In the quaint language of *Willet,* " In this short sentence, *thou art the head of gold,* there are as many figures as words." *Thou,* that is, thy kingdom ; *art,* meaning signifiest or representest ; *head,* means "the antiquity and priority of that kingdom, and the knowledge and wisdom of that nation ;" *gold,* " betokeneth their riches, prosperity, and flourishing estate." Compare also Is. xiv. 4, and Jer. li. 7, where the epithet golden alludes to the majesty and wealth of the city. *Wintle* interprets the golden head as representing the duration of the empire of Babylon from Ninus to Belshazzar, a period of 700 years ; but this is objectionable, since the father of Nebuchadnezzar was of a different race from the early sovereigns of Babylon, and the vision becomes far more emphatic, by being limited to Nebuchadnezzar and his immediate successors. *Œcolampadius* limits the period to his own times, and gives an ingenious reason for the head being of gold. He quotes the authorities for the extensive dominion of this king, viz.,

Berosus known to us through Josephus, and *Megasthenes* through Eusebius, as well as *Orosius*, who extend his sway over Syria, Armenia, Phœnicia, Arabia, Lybia, and even Spain; but this commentator is not satisfied with this allusion. He explains it of the justness of his administration. His earlier years were more righteous than his later, and though many faults may be detected in him, yet he was less open to the charge of injustice than the Persians and Greeks who succeeded him.

Ver. 39. The SECOND KINGDOM is the Medo-Persian, denoted according to Josephus by the two arms. Wintle very appositely quotes Claudian—

Medus ademit
Assyric, Medoque tulit moderamina Perses.[1]

The Vulgate here introduces the adjective "silver," adopting it from ver. 32, not as a translation, but, according to *Rosenmüller*, as a *modus interpretamenti.*

The THIRD KINGDOM is that of the Greeks, but the FOURTH is variously interpreted. It relates to either the successors of Alexander or to the Romans. The majority of the older commentators agreed with CALVIN in thinking it to mean the Roman empire, viz., Œcolampadius, Bullinger, Melancthon and Osiander, while Grotius and Rosenmüller, and Cosmas, the Indian traveller whom we have previously referred to as known to us through Montfaucon, advocate its reference to the Seleucidæ and Lagidæ. *Poole's Synopsis* will furnish the reader with long lists of varying opinions, each fortified by its own reasons, and *Willet* has carefully collected and arranged the arguments on both sides. The divines of Germany have added their conjectures to those which have preceded them. Kuinoel in his theological commentaries has preserved the view of *Velthusen*[2] and others; while the absurdities which some of them propose may be understood from the opinion of *Harenberg*, who thinks the stone which

[1] *II. Consul., Lib. de Stil.*, 163, 164.
[2] *Animad. in Dan.*, ii. 27-45. *Helmstad.*, 1785, preserved by *Kuinoel*, vol. v. p. 361, and following.

destroyed the image to be the sons and grandsons of Nebuchadnezzar, and *Doederlein* in his notes to *Grotius*, and *Scharfenberg* in his "*Observations on Daniel,*" approve the foolish conjecture.

A third view, very different from those which preceded it, has been ably stated and laboriously defended. DR. TODD of Dublin, in his valuable "*Lectures on Antichrist,*" considers the fourth empire as yet to come. The kingdoms of Nebuchadnezzar, Darius, and Cyrus, are said to be signified by the golden head, that of Alexander by the silver breast and arms, the Roman by the brass, while the iron prefigures the cruel and resistless sway of Antichrist, which shall not be overthrown till the second advent of Messiah. We shall have future opportunities for discussing this theory more at length; it has necessarily enlisted him in the ranks of the Futurists, whom *Birks* has confuted at length in his "*First Elements of Sacred Prophecy.*" We refer the student to these two works, each excellent of its kind, while we defer the discussion of this most interesting question till we treat the chapters contained in our second volume.

In descending to details, the arms of the image have been treated as symbols of the Medo-Persian empire; *Theodoret* considering the right arm to represent one, and the left the other. Various reasons have been given for the implied inferiority. *Willet* adopts one the direct contrary of *Calvin's*. While one author treats the inferiority as moral, in consequence of a general corruption of manners, *Willet* thinks the "government more tolerable and equal toward the people of God." Some have thought the silver to refer to remarkable wealth, and others to superior wisdom and eloquence. The belly and thighs being of brass, are thought to prefigure the intemperance, and yet the firmness of the Grecian powers. Alexander's personal debauchery and extravagance is said to be hinted at. The brass is said to imply his warlike disposition and his invincible spirit. The iron is thought to be peculiarly characteristic of the conquests of Rome; the mingling with clay signifies "the division and dissension of the kingdom," says Willet; while others refer it to the marriages between the Roman generals and the barbarians, or generally to the intermingling of the conquerors of the world with the tribes whom they subdued. The two legs are said to be the two great divisions of the Roman empire after the time of Constantine, though those who treat them as belonging to the successors of Alexander, think they mean Egypt and Syria. The mingling with the seed of men (ver. 43) is interpreted of the admission of the subject allies to the freedom of the state (*donati civitate*), and also of the fusion between the barbarians and the Romans, in the late periods of the declining empire. Whether the toes represent individual kings or distinct kingdoms, has been discussed by *Birks* in his "*Elements of Prophecy,*" pp. 124 and 130.

Dissertation Ninth.

THE STONE CUT WITHOUT HANDS.

Chap. ii. 45.

The stone "cut out of the mountain" is generally interpreted of the kingdom of Messiah, some writers applying it to his first Advent, and others to his second. If the fourth kingdom be the Roman, then the stone was cut "without hands," either at the birth of Christ, or, as Calvin when answering Abarbanel prefers, at the first spread of the Gospel. The reason why a "stone" here symbolizes "the kingdom of the heavens," is because Christ is spoken of in Scripture as a chief corner-stone. The passages in the Psalms, Isaiah, and Matthew, and others, are too familiar to the reader to require quotation. The mountain is supposed to be, either the Virgin Mary, or the Jewish people; without hands, may allude to our Saviour's marvellous birth, or to his spiritual independence of all human agency. The ancient fathers, as well as the modern reformers, agree in this allusion to Christ. See *Justin Martyr Dial. cum Tryph.*, sec. 32; *Irenæus adv. Hær.*, ver. 21; *Tertullian, De Resur.*, p. 61; *Apolog.*, p. 869; *Cyprian adv. Jud.*, lib. ii. sec. 17; *Augustine* in Psalm xcviii.

The question of the greatest interest is, whether this prophecy has been fulfilled at the first Advent, or is yet to be accomplished at the second. Willet has taken Calvin to task for his "insufficient" answers to the "Rabbine Barbanel," but as they vary only on minor points, it is not necessary to quote the corrections of his thoughtful monitor.

The theory of Joseph Mede, the great advocate of the year-day system, may be noticed here. He supposes the stone cut out at the first Advent, but not to smite the image till the second. This involves the existence of the Roman empire, throughout the whole Christian dispensation—an admission that Calvin would not make, and should not be hastily allowed. DR. TODD correctly remarks, " it assumes the Roman empire to be still in existence," and it further assumes that the prophecies revealed to Daniel advance beyond the first Advent of Messiah. CALVIN and the older commentators treat them as terminating with the establishment of the Gospel dispensation. TERTULLIAN, indeed, applies this passage to the second Advent, but MALDONATUS considers that expositor as "insanus," who thinks the Roman empire to be still existing. Yet both BELLARMINE and BIRKS argue for its present continuance, and each founds upon it his own views of Scripture prophecy.

As we shall have other opportunities for discussing these questions in our second volume, we simply state that CALVIN and our chief Reformers considered all Daniel's prophecies summed up and satisfied by the first Advent of Christ. As they did not adopt the year-day system, they treated these predictions as pointing the Jews to the coming of their Messiah, and as depicting the various kingdoms and sovereigns which should arise, and affect by their progress and dissensions the Holy Land. It never once occurred to them that the Book of Daniel relates in any way to the details of the history of modern Europe, and of either the Court or the Church of Rome.

Another view hinted at, but disapproved by BISHOP NEWTON, is that the third empire relates solely to Alexander, the fourth to his successors in Syria and Egypt, and the stone cut without hands to the Roman dominion. But with this popular writer as well as with Joseph Mede—the received view of the iron portion of the image is "little less than an article of faith."[1] The stone he reminds us was quite different from the image, so the kingdom of Christ was utterly distinct from the principalities of this world. He asserts that its smiting power was displayed at the first Advent, and is continued throughout the subsequent history of the world. But as BISHOP NEWTON is an advocate of the historical system of interpreting days for years, which CALVIN did not uphold, it is unnecessary to quote him further. The

[1] *Mede's Works*, Book iv., Ep. vi. p. 736.

reader will, however, derive benefit from consulting the authorities which he has brought forward in rich abundance.[1] As he is a valuable and a popular expounder of prophecy, it is necessary to make this passing allusion to so valuable an author; while the reader of these Lectures must be cautioned against adopting any views of prophecy which are inconsistent with the great principle upon which the Almighty deals with us, in our new covenant through Christ our Lord.

ŒCOLAMPADIUS in his comment upon verse 44, treats the kingdom of Christ as spiritual and eternal; like other earnest writers, he considers the troubles of his own days as peculiarly the marks of Antichrist. The blasphemy of the Mahometans, and the arrogance of the "Cata-baptists," seem to him intolerable. He is especially vehement against those who urge the necessity of a second baptism, and deny the value of outward ordinances, as the ministry and the sacraments; and argues for the permanence of external ceremonies till the second Advent of Christ.

He considers verse forty-five to relate to the second coming of Christ and the resurrection of mankind to judgment, but does not condemn the opinion of Jerome and other "fathers," who refer it to the incarnation of our Lord. The mountain, says he, is Zion, and the people the Jews, and by his crucifixion, Christ is said to grow into a mountain and fill the earth. He quotes Hippolytus as sanctioning its reference to the second Advent; and objects to the views of Irenæus, Tertullian, and Lactantius, who as Chiliasts turned this passage to their purpose. The gross ideas of some Jews and Christians, respecting a thousand years of carnal enjoyment upon earth, are wisely reprobated, and some very profitable remarks are made upon the spiritual reign of Christ in the hearts and souls of his people. Œcolampadius is on this occasion remarkably practical and searching in his comment; he is not so critical and literal as CALVIN, but he develops more of the deep feelings of the mature Christian than any other Reformer does on the OLD TESTAMENT.

---

[1] See DISSERTATION XIII. Edit. Lond. 1832.

Dissertation Tenth.

THE COLOSSUS AT DURA.

Chap. iii. 1.

Many points of interest are connected with the narrative of this chapter.

a. The *time* of its erection. This is unknown; various conjectures have been offered, but not the slightest historical foundation proved for any of them. *Theodoret* and *Chrysostom* fix upon the eighteenth year of the king's reign.

β. The *object* of its erection. It was probably intended to entrap the Jews and all conscientious worshippers of Jehovah. Calvin's view is adopted by the best writers.

γ. In whose honour was it erected? Willet agrees with Calvin in thinking it was consecrated to some deity, as Bel, the chief object of his worship.

δ. The *place* of its erection was the plain called by *Ptolemy*, Deira, between Chaltopis and Cissia, in the region of Susan.[1] The editor of the Chisian Codex derives it from the Persian word *dooran*, meaning an enclosure, thus strengthening the view of *Jerome*, that it was erected in an enclosure within the city.

A singular feature in the earliest commentators is the mystical application of such subjects. *Chrysostom*, for instance, takes it to denote covetousness;[2] and *Jerome*, (*in loc.*,) false doctrine and heresy; and *Irenæus*, the pomp and pride of the world, under the mastery of Satan.[3]

---

[1] Ptol., Geog., lib. vi. cap. 3.
[2] Hom., xviii., in Ep. ii. ad Cor.
[3] Adv. Hær., lib. v.

The disproportion of its form has occasioned some difference among expositors. *Bertholdt,* as usual, is full of fault-finding. "How was it possible for it to stand of itself?" But there is no proof that the statue had throughout a human form. Columns with a human head on the top were often erected by the Asiatics in honour of their deities. *Münter* in his *Religion of the Babylonians,* (p. 59,) treats it as similar to the Amyclæan Apollo, a simple column, to which a head and feet were added. *Gesenius,* too, has observed that the ruins of the tower of Belus are imposing only from their colossal size, and not from their proportions ; the Babylonians preferred everything huge, irregular, and grotesque. Idol-pillars were commonly erected by the Assyrians in honour of their deities. If, however, we strictly limit the word צלם, *tzelem,* to a human figure complete in all its parts, we may still vindicate the truth of Daniel by allowing for a pedestal which would be necessary. The proportion of six to one is correct for a human figure ; hence with a pedestal, ten to one by no means violates the principles of art. Of the difficulty of raising it we are no judges. The able remarks of *Heeren* are exactly suited to the occasion,— "The circle of our experience is too limited for us to assign at once the scale of what is possible in other lands, in a different clime, and under other circumstances. Do not the Egyptian pyramids, the Chinese wall, and the rock temple at Elephanta, stand, as it were, in mockery of our criticism, which presumes to define the limits of the united power of whole nations ?"[1]

The material of the Colossus is worthy of notice. It is scarcely possible that it could be all of gold. Some have thought it to have been hollow like the Colossus of Rhodes, which exceeded it in height by ten cubits. (*Pliny His. Nat.,* xxxiv. § 18.) *Chrysostom* thought it made of wood, and only covered with gold plating, and certainly we have authority for such a view from Exod. xxxix. 38, where an altar made of acacia wood, and covered with gold, is termed

---

[1] See *Selden de Diis Syr.,* c. iii. p. 49; *Jablonski, Panth. Æg.,* p. lxxx; *Gesenius* in *Encyc., Art.* Babylon, th. vii. p. 24; *Münter,* p. 59 ; and *Heeren, Ideen,* l. 2, p. 170, *ap. Heng.*

golden; and that in verse 39, merely covered with brass, is termed brazen. The immense treasures heaped together at Babylon favour the possibility of sufficient gold being at hand to cover so large a statue; while the weight of the golden statue of Bel, with its steps and seat, as recorded both by Herodotus and Diodorus, is far from sufficient to allow of their being massive gold throughout. Thus profane history becomes exceedingly valuable in enabling us to interpret correctly the language of the Old Testament. Many minds are inclined at once to discredit the erection of any such colossus all of gold; the mechanical and artistic difficulties are far too great; but when we find such historians giving us accounts of similar erections made of plated wood, or consisting of a mere hollow case, plated over, the whole of the difficulties vanish everything is reduced at once within the bounds of credibility, the historical accuracy of Daniel is vindicated, the captious insinuations of disbelievers are repelled, and the mind of the earnest inquirer is at rest on the firm rock which patient investigation has provided for it.

Hengstenberg's attention is occupied throughout this chapter with noticing the objections of his Neologian predecessors. *De Wette, Bertholdt, and Bleek,* have each attempted to discredit the historical veracity of Daniel. The period of the erection of the image—if ever erected at all—was that of Antiochus Epiphanes, say they, and his character is the supposed original of the fabulous Nebuchadnezzar, and the writer " merely invented these tales in order to inspire the Jews with fortitude under the religious persecutions of Antiochus."[1] *Bertholdt* also considers the address of the three Jews to the king as an instance of "revolting insolence and levity;" while *Theodoret* is quoted as "being amazed at the courage of these youths, their wisdom, their piety," in language exactly in the spirit of Calvin himself.[2] The preparation of the furnace has created some difficulty, especially when *Chardin* relates that a whole month has been taken up with feeding two ovens with fire, for the pur-

[1] *Reply to Objections,* p. 70.
[2] *Opp.,* vol. ii. p. 1110, *ap. Heng.,* p. 73; *Voy. en Perse,* iv. p. 276.

pose of destroying criminals; but this objection is removed by the natural supposition that the king anticipated refusal, and had prepared beforehand to execute summary vengeance on all who disobeyed. "What result is gained by the miracle?" ask the disbelievers. "How disproportionate was the colossus," he exclaims, "no such statue ever existed, no such miracle was ever performed." But history puts to flight a whole host of conjectures, for Herodotus mentions a statue in the temple of Belus, and Diodorus Siculus confirms his account.[1] *Hengstenberg* has collected a long list of authorities in proof of the erection of such statues by the ancient monarchs of the East, and we refer to his valuable labours for a reply to objections, which are happily unknown to the majority of our readers.

[1] Lib. i. sec. 183, and lib. ii. sec. 9.

Dissertation Eleventh.

THE NAMES OF THE MAGISTRATES.

Chap. iii. 2.

CALVIN has very judiciously declined to enter into the signification of each of these officers, as there is great difficulty in ascertaining the exact duties to be assigned to each. The best method of determining this point is to follow up the meaning of the corresponding words in the cognate languages of the East, and to bear in mind the officers of state at present in use. We will here state a few results of our researches, referring the reader for fuller information to *Castell's* valuable Lexicon, and *Rosenmüller's* and *Wintle's* comments, and punctuating the words after the best foreign scholars.

אֲחַשְׁדַּרְפְּנַיָּא, *achas-dar-penaja*, is derived from the Persian by both Castell and Rosenmüller; its meaning is *majestatis janitores*. *Wintle* translates correctly *satraps*.

סִגְנַיָּא, *signaja*, is also Persian; *Rosenmüller* renders it *supremus præfectus*, and *Wintle*, "senators," implying a viceroy of the first rank.

פַּחֲוָתָא, *pach-vatha*, is clearly equivalent to the Oriental "pasha."

אֲדַרְגָּזְרַיָּא, *adar-gaz-raja*, the Septuagint translates by "consuls," and *Theodotion* and *Jerome* by "leaders," and *Wintle* by "judges."

גְּדָבְרַיָּא, *gedab-raja*, is commonly rendered "treasurers."

דְּתָבְרַיָּא, *dethab-raja,* signifies the superior officers of the law.

תִּפְתָּיֵא, *tiph-taya,* is clearly connected with the Turkish word *mufti,* who is the chief religious officer of the Mohamedan faith.

שִׁלְטֹנֵי, *sil-tonei,* a general expression for "governors;" *Joseph Jacchiades* has explained it fully in his Chaldee paraphrase.

Poole's Synopsis may also be consulted with advantage. *Œcolampadius* departs here from his usual custom, by entering into the criticism of these words, and quoting *Rabbi Saadias,* the Septuagint, and the Chaldee paraphrasts.

Dissertation Twelfth.

THE MUSICAL INSTRUMENTS.

Chap. iii. 5.

It is not possible to define, as *Calvin* reminds us, what these instruments were. Researches have been made into the etymology of the Chaldee words, and a comparison instituted between the properties implied and those of modern use and construction. Travellers in the East have compared the music of the present day with that recorded in this verse. A similarity, too, has been pointed out between the instruments of the Syrians and Greeks. As no practical advantage can arise from quoting the conjectures of various writers, we simply refer to *Wintle* and *Rosenmüller in loc.*, where some interesting information is given *in extenso*. *Poole's Synopsis* also supplies much verbal criticism. Œcolampadius passes by altogether any explanation of these instruments, but makes some very appropriate practical comments. True religious worship, he justly observes, does not need this variety of external incentive; a pure conscience with trust in God and obedience to his laws is the best music in his eyes, while he applauds Plato's description of the best music which a soul can offer to its Creator. Antichrist, he asserts, delights in such outward and sensual gratifications, while the advanced Christian worships in spirit, calmly, quietly, and inwardly. True religion is thus the antagonist of all outward and idolatrous service; it is not prompted by fear nor promoted by a tyrant's command, but requiring no visible parade of instrumental minstrelsy, it worships with a cheerful heart and a free and buoyant spirit, inspired by the hope of everlasting life through the promises of God in Christ. This sentiment, although 300 years old, is worthy of the Reformer who uttered and maintained it.

Dissertation Thirteenth.

THE SON OF GOD.

Chap. iii. 25.

This translation of the Chaldee words לבר אלהין, *leber-alehin*, in our version is liable to mistake. *Wintle* has more correctly rendered them "a son of a god." It was far more likely that the heathen king would express his astonishment in this way than allude to what he could not comprehend, the appearance of the Logos in human form. *Calvin* correctly states it to be "one of the angels." Angels are called in Scripture, says *Wells*, sons of God, as in Job i. 6, and xxxviii. 7. "Some angelic appearance" is the correct comment of *Wintle*. *Jerome* takes it as a type of Christ descending into Hades, and *Münter* asserts it to be our Lord himself. *Wells* neither affirms nor denies this view, which has been held by a number of commentators who consider that the Logos appeared in human form on several occasions during patriarchal and Ante-Messianic times. *Justin Martyr* makes the same assertion when describing the pre-existence of the Logos to his philosophic persecutors. *Willet* leans to this view, after summing up a variety of opinions from able writers. Some of his reflections on the general narrative are edifying; but his discussion on the nature of angels is fancifully unprofitable, and his ignorance of natural science is singularly displayed in his treatment of the ordinary and extraordinary action of fire. *Rosenmüller* translates, "like a son of the gods," that is an angel, and the writers quoted by *Poole* come to the same conclusion; but *Œcolampadius* thinks the appearance to be that of Immanuel himself, and refers to other instances of his being visible to Abraham, Jacob, and Moses. He fortifies his view by quotations from *Chrysostom*, *Apollinarius*, and other ecclesiastical authorities.

Dissertation Fourteenth.

A WATCHER
Chap. iv. 13.

THIS is the correct rendering of the word עִיר, *gnir*, but it has been conjectured that its meaning is the same as צִיר, *tzir*, being the Chaldee word for "a messenger." *Jerome* ingeniously conjectures it to be the same as the Greek word *Iris*, the messenger of heaven. In Job xxxvi. 30, the Heb. is אִיר, *air*, where Origen reads *Irin* according to *Archbishop Secker*. *Willet* replies to the question "why the angels are called watchmen," and quotes *Calvin's* reason with approbation. *Rosenmüller* approves of *Jerome's* conjecture, and adduces Hom. Odys., lib. xviii. 5, in confirmation of it. He takes "the watcher and holy one" as a *hendia-dys*, reminding us that in Job xv. 15, angels are called "holy ones" by the figure *autonomasia*. The Scholia of the Alexandrine Codex interpret the word *eir*, as equivalent to angel, and *Isidorus Pelusiota*, according to *Rosenmüller*, (Ep. 177, lib. ii.,) considers the word to refer to the chief of angels. The Syrians in their hymns join watchers with angels as rejoicing over converted sinners, according to the learned editors of the Chisian Codex, p. 127, edit. Rom. See also *Critica Sacra*, vol. vii. p. 3246, edit. Frcof. The view of Œcolampadius is similar to those already expressed, but he takes the word "watcher" in the sense of an exciter or herald of divine punishment. *R. Saadias* supposes a terrible destroyer to be intended.

Dissertation Fifteenth.

THE MADNESS OF NEBUCHADNEZZAR.

Chap. iv. 25.

THE narrative of this chapter has met with much disbelief among the sceptical school of theology. The want of corresponding profane history is a subject of complaint. *Origen* found himself deserted by all ancient historians, and *Jerome* searched them in vain for any confirmation of the sacred text. We must remember, however, that the historians whom we reckon ancient, are very modern with reference to these early times. *Megasthenes*, for instance, wrote rather earlier than *Berosus*, about 280 A.C., at the court of Seleucus Nicator, king of Babylon, and we have only portions of their writings second hand. *Diocles*, the author of a Persian history, and *Abydenus*, of an Assyrian and Median, obtained their materials from Chaldee traditions, many ages after the events recorded. The Chaldee chroniclers, *Hengstenberg* assures us, were notorious for their national vanity and boasting,[1] and were not likely to record anything derogatory to their earliest hero. But even *Bertholdt* is compelled to confess that Abydenus has preserved a legend similar to the narrative of this chapter. "On ascending the roof of his palace, he became inspired by some god, and delivered himself as follows:—Babylonians! I Nebuchadnezzar foretell you a calamity that is to happen, which neither my ancestor Bel nor queen Beltis can persuade the Fates to avert. There shall come a Persian mule, (one having parents of different

---

[1] P. 86. See also as there quoted, *Niebuhr His. Gew.*, p. 189. *Schlosser, Geshichte*, &c., p. 172; and *Volney, Recherches*, &c., p. 150.

countries,) having your own gods in alliance with him, and shall impose servitude upon you, with the head of a Mede, the boast of the Assyrians."[1] Now madness and inspiration were usually connected by the ancients; the time and place too, correspond with Daniel's narrative; the extasis occurred after the completion of his conquests, and the phrase, "by some god," refers to a foreign deity, whom we know to be the Jehovah of the Hebrews. The narrative of the frenzy which rendered him unfit for government, is allowed to be credible by the chief sceptics of the continent. *Michaelis* allows " that this calamity more frequently attacks great and extraordinary minds than ordinary men." Our physicians can now explain the reason through their improved knowledge of the brain and its functions. Pathological and psychological science is here more useful than all the conjectures of disbelieving theologians. In the early days of the Church, the greatest difficulty was found in taking this narrative literally: hence expositors treated it as an allegory. The king was held to represent Satan falling from heaven, and the whole account of his dwelling with the beasts of the field was taken figuratively, and rejected historically. *Jerome*, however, while he records this view at great length, adheres to the literal account.[2]

The disbelief of the narrative above referred to may have arisen from an erroneous interpretation of the sacred text. For some writers have affirmed a complete metamorphosis of the man into the beast; a conclusion by no means warranted by the language of the passage. *Tertullian* has correctly explained the clause, "his hair became like eagle's feathers," by *capilli incuria horrorem aquilinum præferente*, since it was a natural consequence of his wild mode of life, and a usual mark of the sensualizing effect of prolonged insanity. And with reference to the time of this affliction, *Hengstenberg* quotes *Calvin* with approbation, for agreeing with the idea of an indefinite period implied by the word " seven." *Calvin*, however, inclines too much towards the

[1] *Euseb. Præp. Evan.*, l. ix. § 41, p. 456, *Edit Colon.*, and *Chron. Armen.*, p. 59.
[2] See *Rosenmüller's* extract from his Commentary on this chapter, Dan., p. 171, where the original Greek of *Abydenus* is also given at length.

theory of the indefinite use of definite numbers. There seems no good reason why the number "seven" should not be taken strictly and literally, nor why the word "times" עדנין, *gnidanin*, should not mean years. Even *Hengstenberg* gives way too much to the plausible conceits of his wily antagonists. *Rosenmüller* correctly limits the expression to seven years, a period by no means unnatural for the continuance of a highly excited state of the brain, producing mania, accompanied by all the symptoms mentioned in this chapter. *Œcolampadius* views it as a case of mental disease, and quotes many similar narratives from *Aben-Ezra*, *Pausanias*, and *Augustine*, bringing forward the fables of the heathen poets, as illustrating the passage. For the opinion of *Tertullian*, and various Jewish and continental writers, *Kitto's Bibl. Cyclop.* may be consulted, especially as the view there set forth by *Dr. Wright* is sound, judicious, and practical.

Dissertation Sixteenth.

THE EDICT OF PRAISE.

Chap. iv. 37.

This monarch probably lived but a single year after his recovery; and some writers have thought that his restoration produced a conversion to the worship of the one true God. But *Hengstenberg* agrees with our author: "Compare Calvin on the passages," says he, " who strikingly proves from them the incorrectness of the opinion of very many expositors as to the radical and entire conversion of Nebuchadnezzar." *Calvin* is clearly right, for it was customary with the Persians to blend the doctrines of Zoroaster with the Babylonian astrology.[1] The scriptural language of the king has been treated as an argument against the authenticity of the decree. *Eichhorn and Bertholdt* object to his speaking like an orthodox Jew in the phraseology of the Old Testament. But the affinity of certain phrases with other passages of Scripture, is no argument against its authenticity. The monarch had held much intercourse with Daniel; he had doubtless heard his method of expressing reverence and respect for the one true God, and he would repeat such expressions the more exactly in proportion to his want of personal experience of their meaning. In the case of the edict of Cyrus, brief as it is, several references are found to the prophecies of Isaiah.[2] As to the change of person from the third to the first, *Hengstenberg* approves of *Calvin's* suggestion. *Œcolampadius* considers the king really converted, and through knowing the angel to be the Christ, he supposes him not only a convert, but an apostle. This is far too favourable a view of his character; but it is instructive to ascertain the decisions of various eminent Reformers, and to observe which of them stands the scrutinizing test of an appeal to posterity.

---

[1] *Schlosser*, p. 279, *ap. Heng.*
[2] *Kleinert*, p. 142, and *V. Colln. ap. Heng.*, p. 96.

Dissertation Seventeenth.

BELSHAZZAR AND THE FEAST.
Chap. i. 1, 2.

This monarch is here said to be the son of Nebuchadnezzar. The Duke of Manchester takes this literally, while the usual opinion is that he was his grandson. "No king," says he, "in Berosus, Megasthenes, or Polyhistor, corresponds with him. The Scripture says that Nebuchadnezzar was his father, which most people say means grandfather, and it is not to be denied, that by son, grandson may be intended; but in this case it is contrary to all the evidence we have on the subject. The author of the Scholastical History reports that Belshazzar was son of the daughter of Darius. Nebuchadnezzar the Second did, as I conceive, marry the daughter of Darius, which would make Belshazzar his son. But admitting that Belshazzar was paternal grandson of Nebuchadnezzar, none of the successors of Nebuchadnezzar could have been in that relation to him." The Persian writer Merkhond is the next quoted, by whose help the duke identifies Ka'oos with Nebuchadnezzar the First, Afrasiab with Astyages, and Siyawesh, the son of Ka'oos, with Belshazzar. It is then conjectured that this king never reigned except during his father's lifetime : if he was "the king" during his father's madness, the omission of his name by profane historians is thus accounted for. An Oxford MS. is quoted to shew "that Nebuchadnezzar and Belshazzar were reigning at Babylon when Darius and Coresch were reigning over Persia."[1]

[1] "The Times of Daniel," pp. 256-258.

This hypothesis interferes so much with the ordinary deductions from ancient historians, that we must not pass it over without special notice.

The received hypothesis has been so clearly stated by *Wells*, that reference to it is all that is needed.[1] Jeremiah (chap. xxvii. 6) had predicted that Nebuchadnezzar's kingdom was to be prolonged through the life of his son and his son's son. Ptolemy's Astronomical Canon is the best known authority for the history of Nebuchadnezzar's successors, as we have detailed them in a former Dissertation, and they are also found in a readable form in *Stackhouse's* History of the Bible.[2] The last of these kings is Nabonadius, and he is supposed to be the same as the Nabonnedus of Berosus, the Labynetus of Herodotus, and the Belshazzar of Daniel.[3] During his reign, says Berosus, the walls of the city near the river were strengthened by brick-work and bitumen; and in its seventeenth year Cyrus advanced against Babylon, the king met him with a large army, but was defeated, and then enclosed himself within Borsippa. Cyrus then took Babylon, and having determined to pull down its outer fortifications, he returned to Borsippa and besieged it. Nabonnedus then gave himself up, and Cyrus permitted him to close his life peaceably in Carmania, where he remained till his death. The narrative of Herodotus is slightly at variance with this. Cyrus made war against Labynetus, the son of Nitocris, a very spirited and powerful queen, and succeeded to the kingdom of Assyria "from his fathers."[4] Having turned the stream of the river Euphrates, he entered the city through its bed, and when the centre was captured, those who dwelt at the extremities were ignorant of their disaster, for they "were celebrating a festival that day with dancing and all manner of rejoicing, till they received certain information of the general fate. And thus Babylon was the first time taken." Herodotus also records its second capture through the treachery of Zopyrus, in the reign of

---

[1] *Annotat.*, chap. v. p. 46.
[2] P. 984, *edit. fol.*, vol. ii., 1744.
[3] *Berosus ap. Joseph.* and *ap. Grotius de Veritat*, lib. iii., Note; *Hengstenberg's* remarks on this passage in Berosus are valuable, p. 264.
[4] Lib. i., sec. 188.

Darius Hystaspes, (lib. iii. sec. 159;) and with this second capture the noble duke supposes the scriptural narrative to be co-incident. The Cyropædia of Xenophon affords its testimony to a similar event, and as its historic value has been altogether denied, we cannot certainly pronounce the event *the same.* Vitringa has vindicated its historical truth, and *Gesenius* and *Bertholdt* have admitted it. *Hengstenberg* quotes lib. vii. sec. 5, combines it with Herod., lib. i. sec. 191, and remarks, "This testimony of Xenophon, too, is so much the more in our favour, as it confirms the particular circumstance that the nobles were at the feast assembled at the table of the king."[1] He adds, "The precise agreement of Daniel with Herodotus and Xenophon is acknowledged by *Münter*, l. c. p. 67, to be astonishing, and even *Gesenius, Z. Jes.* i., p. 655, cannot help calling it very astonishing." For a fuller discussion of all details, we refer at length to his conclusive work, merely giving our vote in his favour, and against the ingenious hypothesis which it has become necessary to state and explain.

THE GREAT FEAST.—The original word for feast is "bread," and this being united with "wine," becomes the usual mode of describing an eastern feast, where the people are all great eaters of bread. "To eat bread," and to "set on bread," is the scriptural method of indicating a feast. The number of the guests may not have amounted to a thousand, as this is an eastern expression for a large and surprising number, yet it is not incredible, since Harmer has informed us that "a quadrangular court, within the first or outer gate of the palace, was made use of for this purpose."[2] *Willet* reminds us of this eastern way of multiplying numbers by alluding to the 10,000 guests said to be present at Alexander's feast, and each of whom received a golden cup. Ptolemy, the father of Cleopatra, made a similar banquet for Pompey. It is supposed to have been an annual solemnity in honour of

---

[1] P. 261; see also *Vitringa Comment., Z. Jes.* i. 417; and Heeren, i. 2, p. 157, *ap. Heng.*
[2] As quoted by *Wintle,* p. 79, vol. i. p. 191.

some deity, and the art of "tasting of the wine" (verse 2) alludes to the custom of tasting the libation previous to the sacrifice. Wintle very appositely quotes *Virgil*, *Æn.*, lib. i. 741,—

"*Primaque libato summo tenus attigit ore.*"

This view is rendered highly probable by the Chaldean custom recorded by Athenæus,[1] of sacrificing to small images, of various metals, in human shape, an idolatry described in Baruch, chap. vi. 3. Willet quotes Junius as stating that this feast occurred on the 16th day of the month Loon, when it approached in character the Saturnalia and Bacchanalia of the Greeks. "Tasting the wine" is rendered by the Vulgate and the Alexandrine version as if its sense were "drunken," and thus the general idea of licentious revelry is carried out.

[1] *Deipnosophist*, ch. xiii. 2.

Dissertation Eighteenth.

THE QUEEN.

Chap. v. 10.

Calvin doubts whether this was the wife or grandmother of Belshazzar. But there is another possible solution. *Prideaux* supposes she was the mother of the king, following the narrative of Herodotus, though *Grotius* and *Josephus* represent her as the widow of Nebuchadnezzar. The author of "The Times of Daniel" differs from the received view of the times of Nitocris; she reigned, he concludes, "in the generation before Nebuchadnezzar's father."[1] Her name is not found in the Astronomical Canon, and consequently either Herodotus or the Canon must be mistaken. Nitocris, says Herodotus, lived five generations after Semiramis, but then, according to *Bryant*, eight different periods have been assigned for his reign, between A. C. 2177 and 713. Notwithstanding the celebrity which Herodotus has conferred upon his name, it is impossible now to ascertain whether she was the queen-mother alluded to in the text, but it is equally injudicious to pronounce positively that she was not. *Hengstenberg* has discussed this question with his usual sagacity. *Heeren* makes her the contemporary of Nebuchadnezzar, and probably his wife; but *Hengstenberg* inclines to the view of her being the queen-mother. "We may then justly compare what Herodotus says of Nitocris with that which occurs here of the queen, and it only need be quoted to shew a perfect agreement."[2] *Rosenmüller* agrees with Jerome in thinking her the widow of Nebuchadnezzar, and *Œcolampadius* adopts the same view, when commenting with great spirit and animation on this point.

[1] P. 183.
[2] See *Prideaux*, i. p. 227; *Eichhorn*, i. p. 79; *Jahn Archæol.*, ii. i. p. 217.

Dissertation Nineteenth.

THE HAND-WRITING ON THE WALL.
Chap. v. 25.

We are constantly reminded of the necessity of a knowledge of words, if we would interpret aright the Word of God. That record which is emphatically "The Word," is composed in detail of many words, and it is literally impossible so to understand Holy Scripture as to expound it fully, without a knowledge and use of single expressions. This remark is peculiarly applicable in the present instance. CALVIN takes each word separately in the perfect tense, while in the Arabic, the past participle is used, viz., *mensuratum, appensum, divisum*.

מנא, *mene*, is the participle *pihel* of the verb מנא, *mana*, *numeravit*, meaning to set bounds to the continuance of anything.

תקל, *tekel*, is the Chaldee word for the Hebrew שקל, *shekel*, to weigh—the shekel being a standard weight of silver money. The reference is to the Almighty weighing in the balances of Justice the conduct of the king.

ופרסין, *upharsin et dividentes*; *Calvin* thus literally, and *Rosenmüller* explains that the active participle plural is taken impersonally, and is thus equal to the part. pass. sing. The ending ן, *n*, it must be recollected, is the Chaldee equivalent for the Hebrew ם.

The allusion to the balance in relation to a kingdom is common among ancient classical writers. Homer, Iliad, lib. xxii. and Virgil, Æn., lib. xii., contain instances; as well as the Paradise Lost, Book vi.

Dissertation Twentieth.

THE MEDES AND PERSIANS.

Chap. v. 28.

It is highly interesting to the student of prophecy to trace the origin and progress of these empires which have gained repute in the history of our race. This interest is increased when we discover that the narratives of profane writers illustrate the sacred text. And as great efforts have been made to impugn the authenticity of this Book, we must again refer to some of the arguments which induce the best divines to rely on its historical accuracy.

The history of Media and its people frequently impinges upon the eccentric orbit of the Jewish tribes. It has been supposed that the name of the country was derived from כדי, *chadi*, the third son of Japhet, but this conjecture is rendered futile, when we remember that the first establishment of the kingdom dates only 150 years before Cyrus. It must never be forgotten, when treating of these early times, how very modern all writers are who lived after the times of Solomon. *To us* they appear ancient, and their authority for the truth of an event conclusive; but those historians of Asia, upon whom we are compelled to rely, lived many ages after the occurrences which they record. It seems now to be admitted, that we have lost many centuries between the flood and Abraham; hence the attempt to assign the origin of any empire to the immediate descendants of Noah is highly deceptive. We can only take the best testimony which we have, but with it we must correct the uncertainty of even the most positive assertions. The Medes, if we may trust Herodotus, were an offset from the Assyrians. They broke off from their sway, after the Assyrians had held the empire of Upper Asia for five hundred and twenty years. The interesting story of Deioces, and the foundation of Ecbatana is recorded, the account of that city corresponding precisely with that handed down to us in the Book of Judith.[1] In process of time the neighbouring tribes were subdued and united, till Phraortes, having reduced the Persians under his dominion, led the united nations against the Assyrians. Cyaxares his son succeeded him, and both extended and consolidated the Median sway. Astyages, the grandfather of Cyrus, was his son and successor; and during the whole period of these monarchs' reigns province after province was added to the growing empire. The constant testimony of history from Herodotus to Ctesias asserts the acquisition of Media by Cyrus to have been a forcible seizure. Here our chief object is to impress upon the reader the scantiness of our early materials, and the distance of time at which some of the historians who record them lived after the events. Ctesias, for instance, was a young physician at the Court of Artaxerxes, the brother of Cyrus the younger. Although he wrote twenty-three books of Persian history, we have but a few fragments collected by the diligence of Photion. Our attention is therefore turned with the greatest earnestness towards the deciphering of the monuments which abound on the banks of the rivers of Babylonia, and throughout the whole land of Shinar. These have become the best evidence in favour of the trustworthiness of Daniel, and against the ingenious and inconsistent guesses of neology.

M. M. J. Baillie Fraser and *W. Francis Ainsworth* have treated the geological and geographical portion of the subject with great success; the former in his work on "Mesopotamia and Assyria," and the latter in "Geological Researches." See also the two papers on "*The rivers and cities of Babylonia*" by the latter writer, in the *New Monthly Magazine*, August and September, 1845. *The Duke of Manchester* has collected much information from ancient historians, but has not availed himself of the antiquarian researches, which describe and identify the mounds and ruins at present in existence. *Vaux's* "Nineveh and Persepolis" also affords much material illustrative of this portion of Daniel.

[1] Chap. i. 1, and following.

Dissertation Twenty-first.

DARIUS THE MEDE.

Chap. v. 31.

The received views respecting this celebrated monarch have lately been impugned by the noble author of "The Times of Daniel." He gives five reasons for believing him to be Darius Hystaspes instead of the Cyaxares of Xenophon, the uncle and father-in-law of Cyrus. This assertion will therefore require some notice in detail, and compel us to repeat some statements with which the student of ancient history is familiar.

The views of the author already alluded to are thus expressed,—" Three kings," it is said, " of the name of Darius occur in Scripture; must we not presume that the first Darius there corresponds with Darius the first in profane history? that the second in each equally agree; and that the third Darius, with whom the list terminates in Scripture, is the third Darius with whom the line of Persian kings closes?" There are strong marks in corroboration of the Median of this verse being Hystaspes; some of these are as follows:—*First*, each is said to have taken Babylon. Both levied taxes, so that the second verse of chap. vi. is said to be parallel to Herodotus, Book iii., and Strabo,[1] Book xv. This levying taxes leads to a similar assertion respecting Ahasuerus in Esther, chap. x. 1, who reigned "from India even to Ethiopia." (Esther i. 1.) "Now, Ahashverosh, (meaning Ahasuerus,) who succeeded Darius the

---

[1] § 89. *Jahn* points out what he considers a mistake of *Strabo's*, *Arch. Bib.*, chap. ii. § 233.

Median, reigned over India," and, according to Herodotus, Darius Hystaspes conquered India; hence this Mede was Darius Hystaspes. Pliny's testimony is brought forward to shew that Susa was built by this Darius;[1] Ahasuerus resided at Shushan, which is identical with Susa, hence the conclusion is the same. Other reasons are given, and other collateral assertions made. Authorities are quoted by which it is laid down that Ahasuerus was Xerxes, the history of Esther occurred during the captivity, the son of Ahasuerus was Darius Nothus, the third Darius was Codomanus. " To complete the evidence, I will contrast the identification which I propose with that which is now most generally approved of."[2]

CANON OF PTOLEMY.	SCRIPTURE AS I PROPOSE.
Darius the First.	Darius the Median.
Xerxes.	Ahashverosh.
Artaxerxes the First.	Artaxerxes the First, (Coresch.)
Darius the Second.	Darius the Second.
Artaxerxes the Second.	Son of Ahashverosh.
Ochus.	Artaxerxes the Second.
Arostes.	. . . .
Darius the Third.	Darius the Third, (fourth from Coresch, Dan. xi.)

It is also suggested that chaps. l. and li. of Jeremiah apply to this Darius and not to Cyrus, as Dr. Keith asserts. Chap. li. verses 11 and 28, are said to apply to Zopyrus, and the language of the chapter is on the whole more suitable to the capture of Babylon by this Darius, according to Herodotus, Book iii., than to that by Cyrus.

The commonly received view is stated shortly by *Rosenmüller*,—that this Mede was the Cyaxares II. of Xenophon,[3] the son of Astyages, the uncle and father-in-law of Cyrus. Æschylus, in his tragedy of the *Persæ*,[4] introduces Darius the son of Hystaspes, reccunting his origin from Darius the Mede. *Josephus*, in the tenth Book of his Antiquities, says he was the son of Astyages; and *Theodoret*, in his Commentary, identifies him with Cyaxares. *Jerome*

[1] Lib. vi. ch. xxvii.   [2] P. 90.
[3] Cyrop., lib. i. chaps. 4, 5, and lib. iii. chap. 3. § 20.
[4] Line 762.

states that, in conjunction with his uncle Cyrus, he subverted the Chaldean empire.

"If Xenophon's account of Cyrus be in general admitted,"[1] says *Wintle,* "we cannot be at a loss to determine who was Darius the Mede; and if even the defeat of Astyages be received according to Herodotus, and it be placed in the tenth year of Cyrus's reign over Persia Proper, yet there seems no necessity to conclude but that the kingdom of Media might still, with the consent of Cyrus, be continued to Cyaxares, his mother's brother, who might retain it till his death, after the conquest of Babylon, which Herodotus attributes to Cyrus, after he had reduced the neighbouring powers." He next proceeds to obviate one or two chronological difficulties often considered as weighty objections to Xenophon's account. "The name of Darius is omitted in the Canon, although he is allowed to have reigned more than one year, if he reigned at all. How shall we then reconcile his history with the Canon? and where or in what part must this reign be placed? The same answer will serve for both inquiries. The Canon certainly allots nine years to Cyrus over Babylon, of which space the two former years are usually allowed to coincide with the reign of Cyaxares or Darius the Mede by the advocates of Xenophon." A MS. of *Archbishop Secker* is then quoted, in which he gives reasons why Berosus might have overlooked this reign as short-lived and nominal. *Prideaux* and *Usher,* and the *Ancient Universal History,* are referred to for additional information.[2] With reference to the period before us, it is concluded, from the close of this chap. v., "that Darius the Mede did not begin his reign till after the capture of Babylon; and this event I am inclined to place in the next year after the 17th of Nabonadius, in the 210th year of the Chaldean era, or 538 years before Christ, which was the first of Cyrus's nine years. Whether the defeat of Nabonadius and the taking of the city happened near the same time, I need not determine; but it seems clear from Daniel, (chap. v. 31,) as well as from Xenophon, that the

---

[1] *Preliminary Dissertation,* p. xxvi.
[2] *Con.,* part i. Books ii., iii.; *Annals,* pp. 80, 81; *History of the Medes and Persians,* vol. v.

king was slain on the same night that the city was taken; and this, I apprehend, must have happened about the real year of the captivity 67, supposing the fourth of Jehoiakim to agree with the year 605 before Christ, according to Blair."

Here again the researches of *Hengstenberg* afford us valuable aid in discussing and reconciling the various statements of historians. The silence of Herodotus and Ctesias concerning a Median king of Babylon is noticed, and even concealment on the part of the Persians is shewn to be highly probable.

Dissertation Twenty-second.

CAPTURE OF BABYLON.

Chap. v. 31.

If the period of the city's capture could be accurately determined, many difficulties would be cleared up. CALVIN supposes it to have occurred in the last and eighth year of Belshazzar's reign, but the majority of commentators place it in the seventeenth or eighteenth year. *Willet* makes his third year his last, as also *Bullinger* and *Œcolampadius*, and this is done by following the short Hebrew Chronicle, which places it at the fifty-second year of the desolation of Jerusalem, and the seventieth of the kingdom of Babylon. The Oriental Chronicle, according to the author of "*The Times of Daniel*," assigns twenty years, and the Alexandrian Chronicle only four to this monarch; and such being the conflicting testimony of the most ancient and authentic documents, it naturally happens that modern writers select their own dates and their own systems according, first, to their own acquaintance with the subject; and next, to their own judgment of the best selection of authorities which can be made. The only class of divines who appear disingenuous in such selections are those Germans who attempt to impugn the historical accuracy of this Prophet, by tacitly assuming that there is no real, and positive, and consistent knowledge to be obtained from profane writers, and then by asserting that a pseudo-Daniel has displayed either ignorance, carelessness, or deception. They appeal to the historians of Greece, as if they were contemporary with the events which they record, and prefer throwing doubt upon the sacred narrative, to sifting the evidence upon which they believe the profane.

Dissertation Twenty-third.

THE THREE PRESIDENTS.

Chap. vi. 2.

This division of the kingdom into 120 provinces is exactly in accordance with the assertion of Xenophon, who says that Cyrus appointed satraps over the conquered nations. *Usher*, in his *Annals*, p. 82, thinks that Darius followed the suggestion of Cyrus, who instituted this method of government. This verse is reconciled with the first of Esther, by remembering that after the conquest of Egypt by Cambyses, and of Thrace and India by Darius Hystaspes, seven provinces were added to the number. *Junius*, according to *Willet*, states, that after spending a year in settling the affairs of Babylon, he resigned all power to Darius. He approves of Calvin's phrase, "*regnare in commune*," implying the joint reign of both kings. *Josephus* is in error in multiplying the number by three. The reason for the appointment of these presidents may be understood variously. The Latin interpreter, says *Willet*, translates נזק, *nezek*, by *molestiam*, meaning "trouble," Darius is represented as sixty-two years of age, and naturally fatigued by the wear and tear of an active life. Daniel is elevated to an office equivalent to that of the Turkish grand Vizier, and the crime imputed to him seems similar to that of Rome—"*crimen læsæ majestatis*," a kind of high treason. The word עלה, *gnillah*, (verse 4,) is translated by *Wintle* very appropriately " action" in the forensic sense, equivalent to the Greek αἰτία. These presidents and princes came in concourse and tumultuously before the king. The Vulgate "*surripuerunt*," came by stealth, is disapproved by *Wintle*.

Ver. 7. THE DECREE by which Daniel was entrapped has occasioned the special cavil of *Bertholdt* and his adherents. They have treated it as an erroneous fiction, but have been appositely refuted by *Hengstenberg*. Oriental kings, he reminds us, were often treated as objects of exclusive worship. *Heeren* has stated " that the kings of the Medes and Persians were regarded and worshipped as representations and incarnations of Ormuzd."[1] In the sacred books of the Zend religion, " Iran, the Medo-Bactrian kingdom under Gustasp, is to him the image of the kingdom of Ormuzd; the king himself the image of Ormuzd; Turan, the northern nomad land, where Afrasiat rules, is the image of the kingdom of darkness, under the rule of Ahriman." The king was the visible manifestation of Ormuzd, like him, commanding, with unlimited power, the seven princes of the empire; next in rank to him were the representatives of the seven Amshaspands, who stood round the throne of Ormuzd. Similar testimony respecting the worship paid to the monarchs of the East, is given by Plutarch, Xenophon, Socrates, and Arrian. Curtius distinctly asserts, that the Persians worshipped their kings among their gods, so that the credibility of Daniel is fully vindicated by the records of profane antiquity. On the royal tombs at Persepolis, there are various sculptures representing the Persian kings as gods, and in De Sacy's Persian inscriptions, they are termed the offspring of gods.

Ver. 10. DANIEL'S CONDUCT AND PRAYER, as here recorded, have been questioned by some German critics, on the ground of practices and usages as yet unknown in Upper Asia. The custom of praying towards Jerusalem, it is said, did not arise among the Jews living abroad, till after the rebuilding of the temple. But it must not be forgotten that it prevailed among the Jews from early times. David prayed towards the sanctuary, and raised his hands towards it. The Dedication prayer of Solomon contains a distinct injunction to the same effect. The very place, says Stolberg, where the temple had stood and was again to stand, was holy to

[1] *Heeren. Ideen. Augs.*, 3te, i. l. p. 474, and *Heng.*, p. 103, *et seq*

Daniel.[1] The hours at which the Prophet offered up his prayer are said to belong to the fine-spun religiousness of the later Jews. But this assertion is made in forgetfulness of the ancient custom of all nations to have fixed and invariable periods for the worship of their deities. *Willet* approves of *Calvin's* comments on this passage, and *Œcolampadius* considers it a thanksgiving for the encouraging beginning, happy success, and prosperous end of our undertakings. *Willet* also discusses the propriety of Daniel's exposing himself thus openly to the malice of his enemies, after he knew of the king's decree. He agrees on the whole with the practical comment of *Calvin*, and adduces it as an example of perseverance in the line of duty, in full confidence of the protecting power of God, and in defiance of all the malice of the most inveterate foes.

Ver. 10. THE OPEN WINDOWS TOWARDS JERUSALEM.—Various writers have supposed this action of the Prophet's to be the result of ostentation. *Calvin* has treated this point ably, and *Weistein*, in his Notes on Acts i. 13, has explained the nature of "the upper chamber" in the Jewish houses, and their use either as oratories or for other solemn or festive purposes. *Shaw*, in his Travels, (p. 280,) alludes to their structure and use. The light was usually admitted into these upper rooms through large windows, and the Jews naturally turned towards Jerusalem in prayer, with earnest longing for speedy deliverance. The "three times a-day" has been used by *Bellarmine*[2] as an argument for the canonical hours of the Romish Church, and *Pintus* goes further to insist on seven, according to Psalm cxix. But all these arguments which enforce Christian duties by Jewish practices are erroneous. *Calvin's* principle is judiciously stated, but it is founded on enlightened and Christian common sense, and not in a blind adherence to Jewish traditions. Similar principles should guide us as to praying towards the east. *Œcolampadius* refers to the supposed Apostolic

---

[1] *Religionsg.*, iv. p. 48, ap. Heng., p. 116; also *Vitringa de Syn.*, p. 179. *Eisenmenger*, i. p. 584, eod. auct.
[2] Lib i. *De bon oper. in partic.*, c. xii.

tradition of worshipping towards the east, but he reprobates it as superstitious. *Nos patriam nostram in cœlis habemus, et a Deo originem.* Irenæus[1] ascribes this superstition as a heresy to the Ebionites. Daniel's open profession of his faith in God has been censured as too bold and ill judged for our imitation, but it has also been ably vindicated as an example of perseverance in religious duty when our conscience justifies us in maintaining God's truth before men. *Willet* approves of *Calvin's* distinction " of Confession, that it is of two sorts, *cum palam testamur, quod est in animo, et ne aliquod perversæ simulationis signum demus.*"

While this sheet is passing through the press, a very illustrative work, confirming the historical accuracy of Daniel, has been published, entitled "NINEVEH AND ITS PALACES: *the Discoveries of Botta and Layard applied to the elucidation of Holy Writ; by* JOSEPH BONOMI, F.R.S.L." It contains the latest and best interpretations of the cuneiform inscriptions, and is worthy of attentive perusal.

[1] *Adv. Hæres.*, lib. i. cap. xxvi.

Dissertation Twenty-fourth.

THE KING'S DECEASE.

Chap. vi. 28.

COULD we ascertain accurately when death closed "the reign of Darius," most of the controversies concerning the history of these times and personages would be set at rest. We have first to determine *who Darius was?* and secondly, to discover whether a portion of his reign is contemporaneous with that of Cyrus? With respect to the first point, it ought to be fully understood that there is no actual correspondence between this monarch and any well-attested ruler mentioned in profane history. The balance of probabilities is in favour of his being Cyaxares, but we have already stated how Xenophon, Ctesias, and Herodotus differ on the point; and we are careful to repeat this, because the futility of the Neologian arguments might otherwise entrap the unwary. For instance, *Dr. Wells* has the following Note:—" It is to be observed that in Ptolemy's Canon the two years of Darius the Mede's reign are reckoned to Cyrus, who accordingly has therein nine years assigned for his reign; whereas Xenophon assigns but seven years to it, reckoning the first year the same as Ezra doth, viz., from the death of Darius and Cambyses." *Wintle* again states, "there is no doubt but Darius the Mede, whoever he was, reigned, according to Daniel, from the capture of Babylon till this same first year of Cyrus, or till the commencement of the reign allotted by Scripture to Cyrus the Persian." (Preface, p xxix., where reference is made to a Memoir by *M. Freret* containing many just and accurate dates assigned to the life and transactions of Cyrus.) The reader cannot fail to perceive that this sentence leaves the two important questions in as much doubt as ever. DR. EADIE, of the American Presbyterian Church, states, too, positively, "The kingdom of Babylon was given by Cyrus to Darius the Mede, or Cyaxares II., as a reward for his services; and after his death, at the end of two years, this kingdom returned to Cyrus, and hence Cyrus is spoken of as if he were the successor of Darius at Babylon. Dan. vi. 28."—(Art., *Daniel*, in his *Bibl. Cycl.*) *Willet* informs us that *Tertullian* and *Cyril of Jerusalem* took Darius for Darius Hystaspes, (p. 175;) and the noble Duke, to whom we have already referred, agrees in this opinion, and argues very elaborately in its favour.

The German Neologians have not been slow to construct a charge of inaccuracy against Daniel, in consequence of these historic difficulties. Bertholdt, Bleek, and De Wette, treat it as an error to call Cyaxares II. by the name of Darius, and suppose it a confusion with the son of Hystaspes. But before the commentator on Scripture ventures to use the phrase, "historic inaccuracy," he must first clearly ascertain what historic accuracy really is. An unlearned reader might suppose from their reasonings that all the profane historians agreed in their accounts, and that the only element of confusion was that introduced by the narrative of Scripture. But the truth is far otherwise. No two authors agree in their statements throughout. Ancient history is, in fact, simply an ideal deduction from a variety of conflicting traditions. Of Cyaxares II., for instance, neither Herodotus nor Justin say anything. Neither of them mention any son of Astyages. Diodorus Siculus, Strabo, and Polyænus, agree with them in asserting that the Median empire closed with Astyages, and the Persian began at once with Cyrus; and yet there is evidence to shew that Darius the Mede was a real person. "Still farther," says Hengstenberg, "the author agrees in another special fact with profane history. Xenophon relates[1] that soon after the taking of Babylon, the conquered lands were divided into provinces, and governors set over them. All this is stated

---

[1] Cyropædia, lib. viii., chap. vi., &c.; Berth., ii. p. 848, ff.; Rosen. Alterthumsk, i. 1, p. 369; Jahn. Arch., ii. 1, p. 244.

in our book, too." Are we, indeed to infer, from a mere difference of names, that the author is chargeable with confounding them? The Cambyses of profane writers is called in the book of Ezra, Achaschverosh (Ahasuerus). Pseudo-smerdis bears in profane writers two different names—in Ctesias, Spendates; in Justin, Oropastes; and in Ezra he appears under a third name, Artachshasta (Artaxerxes). "Now, why is this appearance in all other cases unanimously explained on the ground that the names of kings were not *nomina propria*, but surnames, whilst, on the contrary, in this single instance, this explanation is not once proposed as possible? And yet in this very case this explanation is quite natural, since it is generally allowed that the name Darius in particular is an appellation. That it was a mere title appears from this, that several different kings bear it." Herbelot says the name Dara is Persian, and appellative, signifying "sovereign."[1]

When we descend to the historians of the Christian era, we find in the Armenian Chronicle of Eusebius a confirmation of the narrative under review. In a short appendix to a fragment of Abydenus, found also in the *Præparatio Evangelica*, Darius is distinctly mentioned as king; so that if it be impossible to be certain as to the identity of this king with Cyaxares, yet it must be remembered that profane history, *independently of Scripture*, is at variance with itself, and that no new element of discord is introduced by our Prophet. Let the objector first settle what the events connected with the overthrow of Babylon from uninspired authorities really were, and we shall then be prepared to shew that the writer of this book was free from inaccuracies, and that all the obscurity hovering over the subject arises from our very imperfect knowledge of the occurrences of this period. And the more fully the assertions of the Neologists are investigated, the more baseless will their charges against this Prophet of Jehovah appear.

[1] See *Hengstenberg's Authorities* on p. 41, where *Gesenius* and *Winer* are quoted as well as *Heeren Ideen*, i. 1, p. 163; and *Volney Rech. Nouv.*, t. i. p. 144. *Edit. Paris*, 1814.

THE PROLONGATION OF DANIEL'S LIFE.

Chap. vi. 28.

The prolongation of our Prophet's life till the era specified in this verse, is worthy of our notice, that we may, if possible, accurately ascertain his age at leading periods of his history. We cannot ascertain precisely the year of his entrance into public life. He was born shortly before King Josiah's death, probably about 620 B. C.; and thus he had many opportunities of cultivating that early piety for which he was conspicuous. He was about fourteen years old when taken captive to Babylon. Three years afterwards, the king of Israel threw off the Babylonian yoke, and thus he and his companions became hostages and forerunners of the capture of the whole nation. From *Jahn's Biblical Antiquities*, we learn how skilled he was in various sciences after three years' training, (pp. 99, 100;) and the high opinion which was entertained of his integrity, wisdom, and piety, is confirmed by the remarkable honour paid to him by the Prophet Ezekiel. He is connected, *while alive*, with Noah and Job. (See Ezek. xiv. 14, and Calvin's comment on the passage in our Edition, vol. ii. p. 68.)

The dream and its interpretation in chap. ii. occurred during Daniel's youth, and resulted in his promotion with his three friends to the highest offices of the kingdom. We now lose sight of him for thirty years, and it is impossible to determine whether he sat at the king's gate during the whole of this period. The erection of the image on the plains of Dura, and the subsequent punishment of his three companions, seem inconsistent with his residence at that time at Babylon as an adviser of his sovereign. The three " children," as they are termed in chap. i. 17, were now about fifty years of age; and it has become necessary to remark this, because some have spoken of them as still children when thus miraculously delivered from destruction.

We too often take for granted impressions of this kind, which we have imperceptibly imbibed in our earliest days; and besides this, the works of the great masters in painting have fostered the error. These splendid productions of European art are often glaringly untrue, yet while based upon fabulous anachronisms, they too often adhere to the imagination, and influence our thoughts in days of more mature advancement. At the period of the dream in chap. iv. Daniel was about fifty years of age; and thus we have another gap of about fifteen years. Belshazzar had now ascended his grandfather's throne. The mystic characters on the wall soon reveal a fearful reality. Darius the Mede still esteems the upright counsellor, and he had become a venerable "ancient of days" before he is thrust into the lion's den. During the first year of King Darius, he learned, from the Book of Jeremiah, the approaching period of Judah's deliverance. During the third year of Cyrus, he is favoured with a vision on the banks of the Tigris. (Chap. x. 1-4.) We cannot ascertain how long he lived after this period, but he was at least eighty years of age when he died. Various assertions and traditions exist among the Jews respecting both the time and place of his decease, and these have passed current, through the unsuspecting simplicity of some of our older expounders, who record as certain the hazardous statements of the authorities on which they rely. *Dr. Wells*, after comparing various dates, concludes, "that Daniel was about eighty-nine or ninety years old in the third year of Cyrus;" he pays no regard to the conjectures of some, who make him to have lived one hundred and thirty-eight, or one hundred and fifty years, and adds the possibility of his reaching one hundred years.

Our object in view in impressing this chronology is to disabuse the public mind of the Romish ideas connected with what they term, "The song of the three children." Their usual method of treating these three martyrs for truth and holiness is utterly erroneous, and like every other error of theirs, injurious and pernicious in proportion as it deviates from the WRITTEN AND INFALLIBLE WORD OF THE LIVING GOD.

Concluding Remarks.

HAVING brought our DISSERTATIONS on the HISTORICAL portion of this sacred book to a close, we have still another duty to discharge in editing these Commentaries. We have already defended our Reformer from the charges of the German Neologist, and from the censures of the fanciful expounders of prophecy; we have now merely to offer a few comments on the PRACTICAL INFERENCES which CALVIN so ably draws from the inspired narrative. While perusing this volume, the reader must often have felt the difference between the state of the world in the days of Nebuchadnezzar and his own. Those were emphatically days of visions, and marvels, and visibly divine interpositions. We, on he contrary, pass on along the even tenor of the walk of life, without expecting to behold a hand-writing on the wall, or to experience the all-devouring heat of a "burning fiery furnace." We see no vision in the night season foretelling the wonders of an unknown future, and expect neither magician nor prophet to expound with the authority of heaven the images of our sleeping hours. Yet, with our Reformer, we see the world agitated in all quarters with unexpected revolutions. Oppression, and intrigue, and tyranny, prevail among the rulers of Europe and of Christendom, and there seems no human means adequate to the task of stemming the tide of recklessness and infidelity as it overflows the nations. If these comments on scriptural prophecy are to be useful in our day and generation, they need some connecting links of interpretation which may apply the general principles enunciated to the practical problem to be worked out.

Otherwise, we either make no intelligent use of such a history as this volume contains, or else we apply it wrong. The latter error is a very common one; and as many are liable to its commission, we trust these CONCLUDING REMARKS will be found suitable and instructive. It may appear to many readers that CALVIN in his PRACTICAL EXHORTATIONS overlooks this difference between a miraculous dispensation and the ordinary condition of God's people under the New Covenant. If he be somewhat open to this charge, it is readily accounted for by the times in which he lived. CALVIN, like Daniel, was an exile from his fatherland. The house of Valois and their tyrant kings were to him the exact counterparts of the Babylonian monarchs. They were absolute sovereigns, and most ferocious persecutors of the people of the Lord. The Medici, the Guises, and the Lorraines of his day were to him the very antitypes of the nobles who fawned upon Nebuchadnezzar, and of the presidents who inveigled Darius. In his DEDICATORY EPISTLE prefixed to this volume, the pious in France are represented as in a position exactly similar to that of the Jews during their captivity. The parallel being in each case so striking and so different to what we see and experience in these days, we need not be surprised at CALVIN'S expectation of special interpositions, and at our own backwardness to appreciate the full suitability of his comments. Now there is clearly a sense in which such "special deliverances" are real, and a sense in which they are not. And as this is a point of some importance involving the idea of the Almighty which our Reformer has presented to us in the preceding pages, we shall comment at some length on a few passages of importance.

For instance, on chap. ii. 21, p. 144 and following, we have a full reply to unbelieving objections to God's providential government of the world. The profane are said to consider all things acted upon by a "blind impulse," and "others affirm the human race to be a kind of sport to God, since men are tossed about like balls." The chief cavils of the Reformation period were those which proceeded from complete scepticism. Philosophers having thrown off the

superstitions of Popery naturally doubted and disputed all
things. The reasoners of CALVIN's days were something like
those intelligent Hindoos who are now worshippers of neither Brahma nor Christ. They are in a transition state, and
having unlearned so much, they scarcely know where to lay
the foundation-stone of trustworthy belief. Throughout
these Lectures, our author is constantly answering the arguments of those contemporaries who felt the hollowness of
Rome, and had not yet tried the firmness of Geneva. Still
to us his replies may not be convincing. This remark applies to the following passage: " If the sun always rose and
set at the same period, or at least certain symmetrical
changes took place yearly, without any casual change ; if
the days of winter were not short, and those of summer not
long, we might then discover the same order of nature, and
in this way God would be rejected from his dominion." Here
we must remember that in Calvin's days most men were
ignorant of those general laws and all-pervading principles
by which the Author of nature governs and sustains the universe. In his day, there was scarcely any choice between
the system which represented the Almighty removed in a
kind of Epicurean repose far away from the works of his
hand, and a system which supposed him to interfere arbitrarily and suddenly in favour of one party, and to the discomfiture of another. Since this period, the researches of
modern science have discovered for us the numerous, the
simple, and seemingly self-acting principles, according to
which the days of winter are short, and those of summer
long. We can contemplate humbly " the same order of
nature" from year to year with undeviating regularity, and
yet never be tempted "to reject God from his dominion."
Yea, the marvel is this, the more we are trained to view
the comprehensive theories of physical astronomy, and chemistry, and magnetism, the more are we led to adore and to
magnify the Great and the All-powerful Original. Such
studies do not lead us to " erect nature into a deity," and to
reject the Creator from his own dominion. They rather lead
us to detect the fallacy in the expression " nature does this
or that ;" they prove to us that there is no such existence

as "nature," but that the word is but an expression for a complex and comprehensive idea of external objects, in the minds of men. The Almighty is seen by the true naturalist in all his works, not as interposing visibly and surprisingly at one time, and leaving all things to themselves at another; but rather as impressing on every created particle of matter its own condition of obedience to certain laws which we call either mechanical or chemical, vital or organic. And it is the merciful arrangement of providence that a persevering study of God's works prepares the mind for an intelligent perusal of his word. The habit of looking for such general principles as gravitation, attraction, organization, and development, of applying these theories to practice by the process of mathematical reasoning, or anatomical dexterity, and of arriving at results indisputably true,—this habit of mind is an excellent preparative for the equally discursive pursuit of revealed theology. Thus we readily detect the fallacy of ascribing the events of life to either fortune, or chance, or nature. CALVIN had to contend with them as if they were realities; we may profit by Locke's chapter on complex ideas, and treat them as expressions comprehending many separate existences, so related to each other that we form "a collective idea" of the whole.

By continuing this process of thought we are enabled to explain, although not to defend certain phrases of CALVIN's respecting the prerogatives of God. On chap. v. 11, men are said to "mingle God and angels in complete confusion," (p. 326,) and on ver. 21, God is said to be "excluded from the government of the world," (p. 338.) The moment our attention is turned to the point, we perceive that the ideas only of God and angels can be mingled, and in imagination only can men exclude the Almighty from his sway over the wills of mankind. Such phrases, we must remember, are the remnants of that *realism* which lingered in the minds of many of the Reformers, and still clings to the writings of some of their successors. Such expressions as we meet with on chap. vi. 10, " Draw down God from heaven," (p. 359,) and on ver. 16, " to deprive the Almighty of his sway," are better avoided. The same thought may be expressed in language more adapted to our enlarged views of the glory of our Creator. The Hebrew Prophets, it has been said, " dramatized the particulars of their mission," and their symbolical portraits of the Almighty were afterwards received as exact and literal descriptions of his character. The Jewish people, even in the time of Daniel, were but in the infancy of moral and intellectual growth ; and to them the well-known proverb most aptly applies, "*Omne ignotum pro magnifico.*" Everything marvellous was attributed at once to the direct agency of a deity, disturbing rather than controlling the occurrences of life. Thus the world, and its surprising tumults, successes, struggles, and reverses, appeared but a scene of fortuitous and capricious chance. But the more we advance from infancy to manhood, the more we gain power to methodize these moral phenomena under some fixed and intelligible arrangement.

It is possible to present from the word of God another reply to the Epicurean suppositions of CALVIN's day, on principles in advance of those which he adopts. While he represents kings as actually contending with the Almighty, and really attempting to hurl him from his throne in heaven, we must remember that such language can only be suggestive. The foundation of all true reverence for Deity is the idea of an infinite and invisible Being, of whose wisdom and might the material universe is the product, and of whose moral nature the conscience of man is the image. When asked for rigid proof of this assertion, we are constrained to refer it to that faith which is peculiarly his gift. The double postulate of that essential existence which is spiritual, and of something in ourselves, which is his image, is the necessary rock upon which we must be placed before we can understand our origin and our destiny—our position in the universe—our moral relation to that system of providence into which we find ourselves born. And this series of providential occurrences is in many respects exactly the opposite to that described in these six chapters of Daniel. Miraculous and supernatural agency is here variously employed to counteract what are known to us as the ordinary laws of nature. The simple will of the Almighty annihilates the effect of fire in the furnace, and the ferocity of lions in their den. A sweeping act of his power converts one despot into the appearance of a beast of prey, and affrights another by the ominous appearance of a hand writing vengeance on a wall. We cannot expect such special revelations, judgments, or deliverances. Our study of the character of Deity is contained in the revealed record of such wonders, and in the present and past history of man and of the physical world. Moral and natural philosophy, under the guidance of revealed religion, is for us the exponent of the idea of Deity. The omnipresence of mind in outward nature is now all but visible to every student. Vast as the universe is, we know it to be pervaded by a moral purpose, and this presents that view of Deity which provides for adoration, and love, and reverence, without limit, and satisfies the longings for worship which are implanted deeply in the human soul. Thus we clothe the idea of an infinite spirit with the attributes of a human conscience; we are not satisfied with " a dynamic centre of the universe," we desire to feel our souls overflow with that mingled wonder and love which constitutes the highest and noblest worship of him who is GOOD. The history of nations and of families impresses upon us the idea of a personal providential Divinity, having fellow-feeling with the wants and distresses, the joys and the sorrows of mankind. Now, we also believe that there are general, harmonious, ever-acting laws of his providential government as well as of his physical. And the study of ordinary sciences disciplines the mind, and qualifies it to perceive, and arrange, and reason upon analogous laws in the moral and religious government of our immortal spirits. A firm persuasion that there is no disorder or disturbance in God's moral sway—that he is not influenced by caprice, or swayed by favouritism, or turned aside by passionate entreaty, is necessary as the key-stone to the arch of Christian wisdom. Those very confusions of which our Reformer writes so vigorously in his DEDICATORY EPISTLE, ascribing them to the " red and sanguinary cohorts and horned beasts," (p. lxix.,) were all in accordance with those uniformities of action which we now designate *general laws*. So far from considering it possible for God to "sit at ease in heaven and desert and betray his own cause," our firm reliance on the permanence of those principles which underlie and encompass all others, is thereby tested and increased. The phenomena of political government, of religious persecution, and of social outbursts of fury and fanaticism, obey laws as orderly and as undeviating as those which regulate the motion of a planet or the passage of electricity along the wire. Through and by means of this "setting up and pulling down of kings," the Almighty speaks a language addressed alike to our reason, our conscience, and our faith. But the great guarantee of our spiritual improvement is the fundamental belief that there is harmony, and classification, and inflexible regularity throughout the whole moral government of God. The very possibility of accident, or favouritism, or isolated marvel, must be banished from our thoughts. We know, by long course of proof and experience, that they do not exist in the physical world, and we cannot allow them a single foot-print within the domain of our moral and spiritual nature. Nothing here can be an anomaly, nothing an exception. In the uncultivated mind, there is an avidity for the marvellous, and a morbid eagerness for a cheap and easy solution of the solemn mysteries concerning God and the soul; but our educated religious life is like "a star hovering on the horizon's verge between night and morning." Thus, by faith we stand at the parting of the two roads, imagined by Plato's great Parmenides, between the seeming and the true. As this star shines brighter over our path, mere external ceremonies and notional expressions become more and more objects of distrust; and the ideas of God and of the soul, of sin and of conscience, of heaven and of glory, become more and more vivid and real to us. And if any are afraid that the pursuit of either scientific, or moral, or religious truth, according to the principles here laid down, will injure true religion or saving faith, the single antidote to this fear is found in the exhortation, "Have faith in God." (Mark xi. 22.) Throughout these LECTURES our Reformer ever clings to this scriptural principle, and ever illustrates his subject ably, practically, and improvingly; while he all along labours under the difficult task of rendering a narrative interspersed with miracle available for the improvement of modern Christians who live under a totally different dispensation.

As another illustration of this difficulty, we may turn to chap. vi. 25-27, p. 392, where our commentator asserts of the profane, that they so unite minor deities with the true that "he lies hid in a crowd, although he enjoys a slight pre-eminence." Such simple and racy language is easily intelligible, but scarcely dignified enough. It justifies the assertion that in the infancy of great truths, language is an index of our ignorance rather than of our knowledge. Truly enough all men "wander confusedly" when they attempt to render palpable to others their contemplations of a Deity. This idea is the most vague and comprehensive of all—a universal solvent of all problems in the early stage of our religious existence. The Egyptians and the Greeks saw a god everywhere—in hill, in brook, in bird and beast. They manifested no lack of faith in the existence of beings far superior to themselves ; and when the priest set up the ugly idol in its gorgeous temple, he never imagined he was creating a god for either himself or the people. He only attempted, after his fashion, to give fixity and embodiment to the ideas of Deity which were floating about indefinitely in the minds of the multitude. But the interval was wide indeed between these metaphorical symbols and the simple abstract idea of one self-acting Being ruling the conscience and swaying the future destinies of all men. When the tree of knowledge was separated from the tree of life, a dark and forlorn interval succeeded, during which mankind underwent long struggles of disquietude in "feeling after" the Almighty One. And we have been permitted to find him. To believe in his permanent presence and providence, to cling to him with the trust of a child to a parent, to follow after him, with no voice but his word acting on conscience and cheering while it guides, to trust him even amid the darkest prospects, —this it is to have faith in God. And this trust is not the mere result of reason, or understanding, or sentiment, or speculation. It is woven into our deepest instincts and our noblest aspirations. It unites them all. It is completed in love. What the profane call Nature, all who sympathize in Darius's proclamation concerning Daniel's God, feel to be a legislation of love. A parent whose government is unerring and complete is ever setting before us the unalterable Law as an exhibition of unchanging love. The very severity and uncompromising character of this idea of Deity proves the crowning beneficence of his kingship over the powers of this world. Inflexible justice and unerring certainty become the highest proofs of all-pervading benevolence. Herein lies the perfection of constancy and truth. The conscience is thus felt to be the vicegerent of this Divinity within. Forms of thought and expression must change, and since CALVIN's time, in the course of three centuries, they have passed through many changes; and man's religious condition must always be modified by the extension of his knowledge, his experience, and his educated capacities. Many habitual modes of thought current in the days of *Œcolampadius* and *Willet* have been set aside; the disturbance of feeling which this occasioned has subsided, and our comprehension of God's moral sway over the affairs of men has been enlarged and purified by the change. His hand-writing is now legible to us on ten thousand walls where of old it was a blank. The wonder which has been removed from special facts has been transferred to general laws; and if "the dream and its interpretation" are not now sent as proofs of his providence, there has sprung up instead equally striking indications of it in every dewdrop and in every flower.

The PRACTICAL IMPROVEMENT which is so appositely made of every occurrence throughout this historical portion of the LECTURES, constitutes a large share of their value. They always plead fervently for justice; always and everywhere they place justice first. They shew us that the absolute will of the most unbending tyranny must ultimately yield to the Divine omnipotence of justice, and that all defences which human power may raise against human rights are utterly vain. He who would be god-like must first be just, and whatever else may be avoided, there is no escape from an avenging judge and a self-torturing conscience. These LEC-

TURES encourage us to harbour no distrust that permanent evil will arise to us from doing manfully our duty; they banish all fear that religion should suffer from the withdrawing of any supports which are proved to be unsound. They stir us up to do the work assigned to us while yet it is day with affectionate fidelity and all earnestness of zeal, and are specially instructive in an age like ours, more remarkable for the variety of its creeds than the intensity of its faith. Certainly the ancient spirit of righteousness, which flourished so vigorously under the crushing despotism of the House of Valois, is not strong within us. That spirit may be characterized as moral courage and religious earnestness combined with love to Christ and readiness to peril life for his name. And while it has almost died out in these days, the practical exhortations of these LECTURES may, by God's blessing, aid in its revival.

Connected with the practical exposition of our Prophet, we find a passage in chap. v. which demands our notice. In commenting on ver. 5, p. 315, and explaining that the hand which wrote upon the wall was not real, but only a figure, it is said, " Scripture often uses this form of speech, and especially when treating external symbols." "*Est ergo hæc etiam sacramentalis loquutio, ut ita loquar.*" It would surprise us to find the word " sacramental" introduced here, if we were unacquainted with the modes of thought and expression in which CALVIN was brought up. But when we remember the very strong hold which the phraseology of the schoolmen had upon the minds of all who were early imbued with it, we enter at once into the fulness of its meaning. We have already stated in our DISSERTATIONS ON EZEKIEL, that the theology of Europe was, during the middle ages, entirely moulded according to the teaching of either the Realists or the Nominalists. It was so then, and it is so now. These two classes of mental cultivation still govern the theological studies of mankind, and will probably do so till the end of our Christian dispensation. The theology of Rome is the growth of the scholastic philosophy built up by the Realists; the teaching of the Reformers springs entirely from that of the Nominalists. All leanings to Rome have in them the essence of Realism, made manifest by some Romanizing tendencies; and all Ultra-Protestantism verges towards a series of negatives based upon Nominalism. We have already alluded to the first nominalist, to whom Luther and Melancthon own their deep obligations. "The real originator of the Protestant principle," says the author of *The Vindication of Protestant Principles*, "the first man who truly emancipated himself from the trammels of Popish ecclesiolatry, the first, in fact, who referred everything to Scripture, and asserted the right of private judgment in its interpretation, was our own countryman, William of Ockham, in Surrey." He died at Munich in the year 1347, just 170 years before Luther fastened his ninety-five propositions to the church doors at Wittemberg. Leopold Ranke also asserts that the celebrated nominalist, Gabriel Biel, was chiefly an epitomizer of this favourite writer of Melancthon's. (See Vindic. Prot. Prin., p. 5, and note on p. 121.) The Zurich Letters (Ep. xxiii., Park. Soc.) inform us of the language of Bishop Jewel when writing to Peter Martyr, 5th November 1559,—" We have deserted the ranks of Scotus and Aquinas for those of the Occamists and Nominalists," (p. 53.) 1842. This sentence condenses under a short formula the very essence of the controversies which now agitate Christendom at large. We cannot dwell here on the proofs of this important statement; we can only remind the reader of these LECTURES that he will find some lingering traces of the realism which once pervaded the theology of Europe, and in which CALVIN was brought up. We all know how exceedingly difficult it is utterly to efface the earliest impressions made upon an earnest and deeply speculative mind. Whenever, for instance, some of the expressions with respect to the Almighty seem alien to our present modes of thinking, we are now able to trace them to their source, and to set them aside as remnants of a system which our Reformer energetically and vigorously opposed. He is always leading us to cultivate the idea of a moral mind pervading all that we know and read of now, and can know hereafter. This germinant truth shines like light within our souls; the images and visions, the trials and triumphs of Daniel and his companions, are no longer insulated atoms in chaos—a mighty maze, and all without a plan—but portions of one organic whole, in which we are personally bound up for both time and eternity. And the more we surrender ourselves to this trust in our Parent Spirit, the more shall we find our ignorance of the plans of Providence removed, and the cloud of mystery hanging over the prevalence of evil brightened and dispersed. Thus the discovery of the laws by which the universe is governed by no means excludes the Supreme Cause from our contemplation ; on the contrary, he becomes more manifest to us by his pervading and perpetual presence.

Throughout these LECTURES we are ever taught that we can see God only by being pure in heart. The preparation for spiritual insight into holy mysteries is purity of conscience and singleness of eye. But even these able comments do not clear up everything. Our lot on earth must be to walk more by faith than by sight. This is the chief exercise of the soul, which is essential to its vitality and growth. We must have at times our mountains of vision as well as our valleys of the shadow of death. Never let us doubt the essential permanence of justice, and righteousness, and truthfulness. By this we shall be borne up through regions of cloud into realms of light. Thus will our spirituality be strengthened and refined: thus we shall be permitted to obtain larger perceptions of God's character and maturer judgments of his purposes.

www.ingramcontent.com/pod-product-compliance
Lightning Source LLC
Chambersburg PA
CBHW071222290426
44108CB00013B/1260